Memoirs of the Prince De Talleyrand

THE PRINCE DE TALLEYRAND. 1838.

(*After* ARY SCHEFFER.)

MEMOIRS

PRINCE DE TALLEYRAND

MEMOIRS

OF THE

PRINCE DE TALLEYRAND

EDITED, WITH A PREFACE AND NOTES BY

THE DUC DE BROGLIE

Of the French Academy

TRANSLATED BY

MRS ANGUS HALL

VOLUME V (COMPLETING THE WORK)

WITH A PORTRAIT

LONDON

GRIFFITH FARRAN AND CO, LIMITED

NEWBERY HOUSE, CHARING CROSS ROAD, LONDON

1892

PREFACE BY THE EDITOR.

THE fifth and last volume of Prince de Talleyrand's Memoirs concludes the publication which his testamentary executors had bequeathed to their representatives The Editors have completed the task which they undertook, by depositing with the Director of the *Bibliothèque Nationale*, the MS volumes of which the text now printed is the exact reproduction It will thus be easy to ascertain, that the trust which they have received has not suffered any alteration or abridgment whatever

It is true, that the collection thus placed before the public, not being an autograph, but a copy, certified by the testamentary executors, such authentication can only serve to testify to the scrupulous good faith of the Editors, and would not of itself, in the absence of other testimony, be sufficient to put an end to the controversy which has been raised as to the character of the Memoirs themselves Happily the discussion to which this controversy has given rise, has already sufficed to dispel all doubts

The question of the authenticity of Talleyrand's Memoirs has been thrashed out by the Press, and their originality has been established beyond doubt, by eminent critics and judges, whose authority can hardly be disputed M Sorel in the *Temps*, M Chuquet in the *Revue Critique*, M Sustane Monod and M Farge in the *Revue Historique*, have pronounced for it with

the weight derived from their comparative study of all documents connected with contemporaneous history, and in support
of the same decision, M Pierre Bertrand has brought forward,
in the *Revue Encyclopédique*, curious details respecting the style
of Prince de Talleyrand's composition, which he has been able
to gather from many of the Prince's inedited letters, published
by him

If, therefore, I now revive a subject which may seem exhausted,
it is not with the view of adding anything to such conclusive
testimony, but simply to offer its reproduction and *résumé* to
those readers, who, not having followed the phases of the
controversy, desire to ascertain the true value of the entire work
now placed in their hands

A few words will suffice to recall the points on which the
dispute was maintained, and the exact limit to which it was
confined   No attempt has been made to compare Talleyrand's
Memoirs with those apocryphal compositions which abound in
our literature, veritable historic romances, compiled from all
kinds of documents by professional writers and then issued
under the name of such and such celebrated personage   The
undoubted origin of the documents, and the evidences of superior
ability visible in certain portions, do not permit such a supposition   It has only been sought to prove that the original
text has been revised and mutilated, and not made public
until it had undergone alterations which render it unrecognisable,
and in order to justify this, it is asserted, that there have been
found either omissions, which appear to be the effect of abridg-
ments made by a strange hand after the work was completed,
or a confusion of facts and names, which could not have
escaped the author's notice, as they would have been the introduction of errors with respect to events with which he was
personally connected, or with regard to contemporaries, friends,

or adversaries whom he had personally known The absence of an autograph manuscript would then account for the intention of those who transcribed it, to remove traces of the modifications which they did not hesitate to introduce

It must be remembered, that in the Memoirs all the events of the author's life, which have long ago appeared in his biography, do not, to say the least, present themselves with the same degree of detail and importance The narrative progresses rapidly, and without dwelling upon the commencement of Talleyrand's political career, the part he played in the Constituent Assembly, his relations with the illustrious personages of that period, and the missions and public offices which he filled during the early part of the Revolution Without even considering the extent of the narrative, there are but few chapters devoted to these early years, compared with the complete and detailed exposition of the great negotiations of 1814 and 1830. But so far from this difference being surprising, it is only what might be expected, and it presents nothing to us but what is natural

In the course of an almost secular existence, Talleyrand, associated as he was with all the vicissitudes of which Europe and France were the theatre during this turbulent period, had actually seen the whole aspect of the world around him change, and as the effect of such long experience, accompanied by repeated disappointment, he as well as most men of his generation, must have found that the same feelings and ideas which he had shared together with the wisest of his contemporaries, no longer existed.

When he took up his pen after the Restoration, to which he had so powerfully contributed, Prince de Talleyrand, representing as he did legitimate Monarchy at Vienna, in the presence of assembled Europe, must have retained but few ideas and traits in common with the Abbé de Périgord, sitting on the Left in the

Constituent Assembly, and he could scarcely have recognized this almost effaced likeness of himself after so distant a past. He had learnt much, and perhaps also forgotten a little. Many resolutions which he had taken during times of hope, of disappointment and of anxiety must have appeared to him, if not the result of influence, against which he was not proof, at least necessities to which he must submit. Would he not then have hastened to turn over this page of his history, in order to arrive rapidly at that on which were inscribed the eminent services he had just rendered to his country? How could he linger, to recapitulate with complacency for the benefit of posterity, impressions which he perhaps no longer retained, which did not even affect him, or in any case revive their memory?

A man who exercised an influence on the political affairs of his time, such as that ascribed to Talleyrand, would not set himself to write like an ordinary author, to soothe his old age by recalling the reminiscences of his youth. His constant thought was to obtain full appreciation of the efforts he had made to protect the interests that were confided to him, and the results which he took credit to himself for having obtained.

From this point of view, 1789 recalled nothing to M. de Talleyrand but wasted energy. Is it therefore a matter of astonishment that he should have preferred to concern himself most with the incontestible greatness and utility of the *rôle*, which he played in 1814 and 1830? No one moreover could have occupied so great a position in his time, without being subject to much accusation and censure.

The intention of the Memoirs therefore is not to reveal unknown facts, but to prepare matter for a case to be examined by history, and history itself ought to search therein, less for fresh information than for fitting elements to enlighten the judgment which it is called on to pronounce.

I am well aware that a general impression had been created respecting Talleyrand's Memoirs totally different to that which a full knowledge of them now conveys In consequence of the perhaps excessive precautions taken by the testamentary executors to prevent premature publication, people have been inclined to imagine that the secret would not have been kept so long had not the Memoirs contained facts of a delicate and mysterious nature, and that the veil once lifted, *piquante* revelations, satirical portraits, malicious anecdotes, who knows what all would be made public, perhaps even the facilities which a lax morality afforded to the worldly clergy of the *Ancien Régime*. The grave style of the narrative, quite in keeping with the nature of the subjects treated, has disappointed this frivolous curiosity, and from that, to the supposition that everything which would have satisfied it has been intentionally suppressed, is but a step.

But it was not necessary to have known M de Talleyrand ; it was enough to have lived with those who knew him, to prevent the conception of or a belief in any illusion of the kind It would even suffice to remember that among all the reproaches of every kind that have been laid to his charge, that of want of tact and good taste is perhaps the only one of which he is acquitted

If serious writers have looked for interest of this kind in these Memoirs, and are astonished at not finding it, they have displayed a want of judgment which does not permit them to call themselves historians

Moreover, it is difficult to understand how anyone in the least accustomed to write history from original documents, could attach any real importance to such errors in chronology or proper names as might be found in the *Memoirs de Talleyrand*. Instead of regarding them as evidence of forgeries, they ought to be recognized as being. what is plain to everyone, the

failure of memory inevitable at the close of a long life, passed
under such varied circumstances. I venture to assert that
there are no known Memoirs, not even those whose authenticity is beyond doubt, which do not contain errors more or less
grave, and if subjected to criticism would stand the test so
well.

For instance, I have had occasion, in the course of my
labours, to study the memoirs of men who during the sixteenth
century played an important part as ministers, generals, or
ambassadors, and I will cite amongst others, Marshal de Belle
Isle and the Marquis d'Argenson. After comparing their
narratives with the correspondence written by them during their
life-time, I have found not once, or by accident, but constantly,
differences and even contradictions apparently irreconcilable,
between the details of facts described by them in their retirement and after the events, and their letters written the next or
even the same day on which these events occurred. Most of
these differences no doubt have arisen from a desire to excuse
themselves from certain reproaches, or to enhance the merit of
certain services; but others are without explanation, except
that of forgetfulness or involuntary confusion of ideas.

Further, two politicians who have occupied an important
place in our contemporaneous history, and of whom one is dead,
having kindly placed at my disposal, either in whole or in part,
their unpublished recollections, I ventured to point out to them
in their narration of events, where they figured as principal
actors, inaccuracies, doubtless very harmless and very innocent,
but much more serious than those of which they accuse
Talleyrand's Memoirs, when merely on my observation they
expressed an eager desire to admit and correct them.

I must add, that having been called upon myself to publish
my father's memoirs, I can show from his own testimony, how

the most conscientious man, writing after the lapse of years, ought to mistrust his memory and take precautions to prevent its deceiving him

It is well known that the first and one of the most characteristic acts of my father's political life, was the determination he came to in 1815, to take his seat in the Chamber of Peers during Marshal Ney's trial, although he was not legally of age and would not attain his majority until the day the sentence was pronounced I have many times heard him relate the particulars of the first sitting in which he took part, and of which an ineffaceable impression ought to have remained engraven on his memory, from the novelty and gravity of the spectacle before him The subject of debate on that day, he told me, was the decision of perhaps the most important point in the trial, namely, whether Marshal Ney should be given the benefit of the amnesty promised to rebels by the capitulation of Paris Judge of my astonishment at finding in his Memoirs these same details but related with the following reservation

" I took my seat," he writes, " on the 4th December At 11 o'clock in the morning, I entered the Chamber , the members were already assembled in the Council Chamber, namely the picture gallery, in which they deliberated in private I still recollect the position of every member I knew, and the place where I was myself seated on the last bench, but, inconceivable as it may appear, were I called upon, I would take my oath, that the subject under deliberation was, to decide whether Marshal Ney could be permitted to plead the capitulation of Paris in extenuation It is well known that the error, the great error, I would almost say crime, committed by the Chamber, was, in having in this way closed the mouth of the accused I heard M Molé take one side and Lanjuinais and Porcher de Richebourg the other This sitting was an epoch in my life How then

could I have made a mistake ? Nevertheless it must be so, for
the official report places this sitting not on the first, but on the
last day of the proceedings or completion of the pleadings   But
while fully admitting my mistake, my common sense alone, gives
in   My memory remains unconvinced and I here repeat, that I
would take my oath against the official report "

Let us now suppose that the narrator had not been able to
consult the official reports of the Chamber of Peers, and had
written his recollections, such as he retained them, would this
error in date have been sufficient to invalidate either the veracity
of the writer or the authenticity of the text ?[1]

Finally, if an error in capacity on the part of a public individual is sufficient to question the veracity of a work, how is it
to be accounted for that among the small number of M de
Talleyrand's autograph letters which we possess, mistakes are to
be found in this respect more important than those which have
been pointed out in his Memoirs ?   For instance, how can it be
explained, that when speaking to the Emperor Alexander, he
gives the title of brother-in-law of King Frederick William to
the head of a house, certainly very illustrious, but who was not
connected with the Royal Family of Prussia except by a much
more distant relationship ?[2] and how is it to be accounted for, that
instead of correcting this mistake, he repeats it two days afterwards, when giving Louis XVIII an account of his interview ?

[1] An error in date of this description caused a momentary doubt as to the
authenticity of a letter from Louis XVIII to Talleyrand, relative to the design of the
Prussians to blow up the Bridge of Jena   In citing this letter in his Memoirs (vol iii
p 160), M de Talleyrand heads it, " *Paris, 15th July*, 1815   *Saturday*, 10 *o'clock* "
This date could not be correct, because the event to which the letter refers happened on
Saturday, the 15th, not Saturday 15th July   Fortunately the original letter exists
It has been photographed and is reproduced at the commencement of the first volume
of the Memoirs, and it bears no other date than this— " *Saturday* "   The error, therefore, is evidently the mistake of the author of the Memoirs, who, desiring to place a
certain date upon the letter as a reminder, has made the mistake of a week   This,
for an incident of little importance, is not to be wondered at

[2] See vol iii p 18

Assuredly for a courtier and a diplomatist, living and holding converse with Sovereigns. and knowing how much they dislike any mistakes concerning themselves, he thereby displayed an incorrectness or committed a blunder, much greater than that which consisted in giving the Director Carnot in 1796 the rank of general, which was not conferred upon him till 1813. It would therefore be useless to try and take advantage of inaccuracies inevitably certain in such minutiæ, as a means of questioning the authenticity of the Memoirs

It remains to be explained, why the manuscript left by the testamentary executors is a certified copy and not the autograph text. The answer is most simple, such a text—at least under the supposed conditions—had probably never been in their hands, and knowing M de Talleyrand's habits, they themselves were not surprised at it.

All those who were acquainted with M de Talleyrand, knew, in fact, that as heavy work fatigued him, he never himself wrote any but completely private letters, or those which out of respect for the persons addressed he considered ought not to be written by a secretary At all other times he dictated his correspondence. Having done so, he revised it, making such corrections as he deemed necessary, then the writing thus revised was re-copied and filed amongst his papers Sometimes when he had confidence in the ability and intelligence of his secretary, he contented himself with giving him the gist of his ideas, leaving to him the care of drafting them and reserving to himself the task of correcting their form and giving them more force and elegance It was the text thus prepared, but no portion of which probably was in the handwriting of the author, that M de Bacourt received in trust, and in transcribing it afresh, he did not dream of altering its character in the least, or, above all, of depriving it of any guarantee of exactitude and authenticity

What would in fact be gained by having before us these
original writings—(remember I have never said originals)?
They would only be copies like those we have received, except
that instead of being bound in volumes and in the same handwriting, they would be in loose sheets, perhaps in different
writing, all equally susceptible and open to the suspicion of suppression or interpolation, and, to believe in them, it would still be
necessary to have confidence in the loyalty of the testamentary
executors and particularly of M de Bacourt [1]

I am well aware that doubt has been cast, even on M de
Bacourt's good faith, notwithstanding the unanimous opinion to
the contrary of those who knew him   In support of this we are
reminded, that the mark of confidence with which Talleyrand had
honoured M de Bacourt, was not the first of the same nature,
which had been conferred upon him   His name figured at the
head of a publication some years ago containing very important
documents relative to Mirabeau's relations with the Court of
Louis XVI, of which the Comte de la Marck, afterwards
Prince d'Arenberg, had been the intermediary   M de la Marck
when dying had charged M de Bacourt to publish these

[1] M Bertrand, after explaining in detail the style of M de Talleyrand's com-
position, with which the letters and documents emanating from him, extant at the
Foreign Office, made him familiar, thus sums up his opinion on the subject of the
Memoirs themselves

The character of the private manuscripts and of his Memoirs, is very well
described by the following mention of the copy left by M de Bacourt, in the inventory
of his papers attached to his will

" Four volumes, bound in leather, which are the only authentic and complete copy
of the *Memoirs of Prince de Talleyrand*, compiled from the dictated manuscripts and
copies respecting which M le Prince de Talleyrand had given him instructions "

Here we see it is a question of dictated manuscripts and copies   The manuscripts
are evidently all writings emanating from different personages, of which the originals
possessed by Talleyrand, are now in the possession of M le Duc de Broglie, and of
which some have been inserted by M de Bacourt in the copy of the Memoirs   We
may, therefore, conclude that the copies spoken of in the inventory are copies made
for Talleyrand from documents amongst the State papers, or possessed by private individuals   There remain the dictated writings, but what can these dictated writings
be except the original manuscript of the Memoirs?

documents, in order to establish the character of these secret relations of Mirabeau, which, according to him, were not properly appreciated M. de Bacourt is accused of not having been sufficiently conscientious in the fulfilment of this request. In some of the documents, suppressions and evasions have been traced, and it has therefore been concluded that Talleyrand's Memoirs have in their publication suffered similar eliminations at the hands of M de Bacourt Were this fact true, as alleged, which I shall not discuss here, I do not see what conclusion could be justly come to from an assimilation of two situations which have nothing in common.

M de la Marck had collected a great mass of papers of different date and origin—letters and notes, some from Mirabeau himself, others addressed to him, others subsequent to his death From this rather confused collection of documents, M. de Bacourt undertook to justify the illustrious man whose friend and confident he had been But to attain this end, and produce the desired effect, or even to introduce a little order and clearness in the arrangement of the documents, and make their sense and intention plain to the reader, a classification and consequently a selection was necessary.

To this task M de la Marck had applied himself, but the decline of his health did not permit him to accomplish it, and he bequeathed to M de Bacourt the duty of finishing it in the spirit and intention known to him In whatever manner the proxy fulfilled his commission, he only exercised his right, and, above all, deceived no one ; for nowhere is it stated that he was enjoined by M. de la Marck, to publish without distinction all that had been handed over to him by the will, nor has he himself pretended that no portion of what was placed in his hands has been eliminated.

Finally, and this in the present case is most important, it is

not stated or even hinted at, that M de Bacourt has himself
fabricated any of the documents which he has published, with
the intention of issuing his own composition under the shelter
and the name of others [1]

Quite different and much more serious, would be the wrong
or rather injury done to the memory of M de Bacourt, were the
imputation admitted   Each manuscript volume of Talleyrand's
Memoirs bears, as is known, an attestation on the last page,
signed by M. de Bacourt himself, to the effect that the contents
are *authentic and complete*   Let us however admit that by a
subtilty of conscience, very difficult to conceive, a man of honour
could believe himself justified in attesting the integrity of a collection which he had himself altered and mutilated   But having
made the erasures and alterations, it would be necessary to use
a pen to fill up the gaps and re-establish the interrupted tran-
sitions in order to obliterate, in what follows, and in the plot of
the narrative, the solutions of continuity too plainly visible.   In
a word, the Editor would thus attribute to the author, speaking
in the first person, like a personage in a play, a language which
he had not held

M de Bacourt's critics have not retired in the face of this sup
position; they pretend that there are even entire chapters in which
Talleyrand's elegant and delicate touch cannot be recognised,
the composition of which they do not hesitate to attribute to
M de Bacourt, who, they declare, has sheltered himself behind
his name   Here there is no circumlocution possible.   The fact,
if it were true, would be pure and simple falsification, and that
without the least extenuating circumstance.

How then can we refuse to take into consideration the
almost unanimous testimony and indignant protestations of all

---

[1] See the explanations given by M   .   , relative to this publication by M de
Bacourt of documents respecting Mirabeau — *Vie de Mirabeau*, pp 258-267

those who knew M. de Bacourt, and of whom there is not one who does not bear witness, that the most salient trait in his character was a delicacy pushed to scrupulous fastidiousness Such besides was his profound and almost superstitious admiration for the master whom he worshipped, that the idea of taking his place and speaking in his name, was an excess of presumption which could never have entered his head.   He would never have supposed that the reader could be in doubt for a moment

The conclusion is therefore beyond question.   The *Memoirs of Talleyrand* can take a high place in that rich collection of historical souvenirs, which is one of the greatest ornaments of our literature, and they can be perused with as much confidence as the *Memoirs of Richelieu,* which no one now contests, although no manuscript is extant, or three-fourths of the *Letters of Madame de Sévigny,* of which no one possesses the original

Duc de Broglie.

CONTENTS.

PART XI

THE REVOLUTION OF 1830

1832—1833

PART XII

THE REVOLUTION OF 1830.

1833- 1834

MEMOIRS

OF THE

PRINCE DE TALLEYRAND

PART XI

REVOLUTION OF 1830

1832—1833

Talleyrand returns to London—He gives a brief *résumé* of the general position of affairs in Europe—Letters from the different members of the new French Cabinet under Marshal Soult—They ask to be allowed to drive the Dutch out of Antwerp and then place the citadel in the hands of the Belgians--Russia and Prussia object—The French Government suggests that Prussia should temporarily occupy Venloo and certain portions of Limburg and Luxemburg—Prussia refuses—The Countess de Flahaut intrigues against Talleyrand—Despite the obstinate resistance of the King of Holland and the delays of Russia and Prussia, the Convention empowering England and France to use coercive measures against Holland is signed—The French and English squadrons blockade the Dutch ports—The French army enters Belgium and marches on Antwerp—Arrest of the Duchess de Berry at Nantes—Another attempt on the life of Louis Philippe—Madame Adelaide gives Talleyrand an account of the siege of Antwerp and the Duc d'Orléans' bravery—Russia withdraws from the Conference—Arrival of the Marquis de Palmella in London on a mission from Dom Pedro—Draft of the treaty between Holland and Belgium—M de Marcuil's complaint at being put aside—Talleyrand interferes on his behalf—M de Mareuil is sent to Naples—Antwerp capitulates—The Dutch garrison is allowed to return to Holland unconditionally—Death of the Princess de Vaudémont—The Hague accepts the Convention of May 31st—General Pozzo's secret mission to the various Continental Courts—Austria and Prussia are asked to combine with Russia against France and England—M de Medem shows the Duc de Broglie the secret instructions sent to General Mouravieff respecting Egypt—M de Rayneval's account of the state of affairs in the Peninsula—Colonel Campbell is sent to Alexandria to inform

B 2

BEFORE resuming the history of the events in connection with my Embassy in London, whither I returned in the beginning of October, 1832, I should like to recall some incidents which had taken place during my absence

On arriving in Paris in June, I found the French Ministry much weakened by M Casimir Périer's death, and unable to settle down, or establish itself on any solid basis   Intrigues of all kinds were rife in the Government offices , the ambition of individuals caused less embarrassment than the presumption of all Hence arise revolutions which create such confusion

I hurried away to take the waters, having no desire to be mixed up in matters with which I had nothing to do However, they did not leave me long in peace, and insisted upon my immediate return to England

This urgency was in consequence of another intrigue They desired to prove that M Durant de Marcuil, who replaced me, was incapable, because I had given him the preference over M. de Flahaut, who was strongly supported by General Sebastiani. But I did not allow myself to be affected by all these machinations I replied, from Bourbon l'Archambaud, that there was nothing pressing which called for my presence in London, where matters were progressing in their legitimate course , that any undue haste would hinder rather than assist them , and that before putting on pressure it was, above all, desirable to be rational, and to take into consideration the advantages and the difficulties of one's position—one must not even seem to be hurried. Finally, that we had taken our stand as the ally of England, and as co-operating with her, and that to this end everything must be sacrificed, all else being quite secondary Notwithstanding this they returned to the charge, pretending alarm at the violent complaints uttered against the London Conference by the Belgian Chambers, which might, they declared, lead to a resumption of hostilities.

In order to appease this clamour and put an end to the intrigues, I announced my intention of cutting short my leave and returning to London in August, though fully determined not to do anything of the kind , I felt the need of complete rest after taking the waters of Bourbon This, however, sufficed to upset the Flahaut-Sebastiani intrigue, and I was left in peace At the same time, I expressed myself very strongly against the arrogant behaviour of the Belgians, who did not deserve that our Government should compromise itself for them. But my advice on this point was not followed , on the contrary, they hastened,

and most injudiciously according to my view, to conclude the
marriage of Madame la Princesse Louise d'Orléans with King
Leopold, which took place at Compiègne on the 9th of August

It was perfectly evident that the hurried accomplishment of
this marriage could only embarrass our affairs, by increasing the
demands of the Belgian and French revolutionary parties   Fortunately, the King of Holland took upon himself to assist us out
of the difficulty, by the bad faith he displayed in his negotiations
with the London Conference.   The latter, after endless verbal
and written discussions with the Dutch plenipotentiaries, being
unable to arrive at any result, found itself obliged to declare, in
a Protocol dated October 1st, 1832, that it had become necessary
to employ coercive measures against Holland, in order to compel
her to carry out the conditions of the treaty signed between the
five Powers and Belgium [1]   It is true, that after this declaration
there was some dissent among the members of the Conference
as to the nature of the coercive measures to be employed   The
plenipotentiaries of Austria, Prussia, and Russia only consented
to join in the pecuniary considerations , whilst those of France
and England reserved to themselves " to have recourse to more
efficacious measures for the purpose of carrying out a treaty
which had been ratified by their Courts for months past, and the
prolonged non-fulfilment of which, exposed the peace of Europe
to continual and increasing dangers '

The principle having thus been laid down, it was necessary
to develop its results, and in order to obtain this, I decided
to return to London in the beginning of October, 1832   Nevertheless, before starting on my journey, I wished to make
sure that they had succeeded in forming in Paris, a Ministry

---

[1] This declaration was made by the English plenipotentiary , the views of the
French plenipotentiary were even stronger   He would, he said, adhere to every
point of this declaration, and in addition "reserved to his Government full power to
enforce the execution of the treaty concluded with Belgium, according to the powers
therein contained, and as the tenor of her engagements and the interests of France
might require "

As to the pecuniary coercive measures, respecting which, as is mentioned
further on, the Conference had come to an agreement, they consisted in freeing
Belgium from the arrears due to Holland since the 1st of January, 1832, and in
deducting one million florins weekly from the total amount of the debt due by
Belgium to Holland, if at the end of a delay accorded for the cancelling of the
arrears, the effect hoped for was not produced

which would offer some prospect of solidity and continuance
This assurance I obtained from the lips of the King himself, the
evening before my departure for London, on the 9th of October,
1832 [1]

I think I cannot give a better idea of the position of the new
French Cabinet and how it affected me in London, than by
inserting here, the letters which the principal members of this
Cabinet wrote to me on the 11th of October, the day following
my departure.

THE DUC DE BROGLIE TO THE PRINCE DE TALLEYRAND

PARIS, *October* 11*th*, 1832

MON PRINCE,

I believe you were aware, on the eve of your departure,
that the aspect of affairs had again changed At five o'clock
last evening, the future Cabinet assembled—this morning it is
announced in the *Moniteur*.

I need not tell you, that this Cabinet is composed of all those
whom the party of good order, peace, and legally constituted
authority counts as the staunchest among its ranks I have
confided to you in full detail all my earnest desires and hopes
It depends upon Europe, and above all upon England, to consolidate this Cabinet, and thus put an end to the dangers which the
victory of the opposition would entail, and of which Europe
would assuredly incur a large share We intend to fight for the
cause of civilization, and civilization must assist us , it is for you,
mon Prince, to tell me what is needed to enable us to begin our
session with *éclat.* If the English Cabinet will listen to you, our
triumph is assured, even in the opinion of the most timid

About myself, I say nothing , I will not speak of my
feelings toward you , but I ask your advice and assistance,
feeling sure of obtaining it, and knowing in whose hands our
future now rests.

V BROGLIE.

P.S —I inclose, with these few hurried lines, a letter for
Lord Grey and another for Lord Palmerston You see I have
not forgotten your instructions, and have much pleasure in carrying them out You will probably receive a despatch from me on

---

[1] The following was the Ministry which was formed on the 11th of October
President of the Council and War Minister, Marshal Soult , Foreign Affairs, the
Duc de Broglie , Interior, M Thiers , Finance, M Humann , Public Instruction,
M Guizot , M Barthe, M d'Argout, and M de Rigny—Justice, Trade, and Marine

the same day, respecting the important matter of which you are
aware   Time is pressing , I commend it once again to your
friendship, and to your influence over those with whom you
come in contact

M GUIZOT TO THE PRINCE DE TALLEYRAND

PARIS, *October 11th*, 1832

MON PRINCE,

I regretted exceedingly not having had ten minutes longer
chat with you yesterday   I wished again to impress upon
you how much we need your active and determined co-
operation.   We are engaged in a great struggle   We accept the
honour and the burden of maintaining the cause of order, of
peace, of legally constituted interests, of true social principles—the cause of civilization, and the security of Europe   We
shall devote ourselves to it entirely, without intermission or reservation, and I have every reason to hope that France, equally
with ourselves, desires the triumph of this grand and noble cause.
But mon Prince, do your utmost to make our position clearly
understood , let them see that the confidence of honest, sensible
men, outside France as well as in France, strengthens our hands,
and that it cannot be too quickly or too clearly manifested
Invested with this confidence we can, I venture to affirm, do
much   If, on the other hand, it is wanting, lukewarm, or doubtful, if we cannot reap the fruits of it for our country, we shall
meet with enormous difficulties   For my part I am quite ready to
face them, but they might disappear, or at any rate be greatly
diminished, from the very commencement

In this you will aid us, mon Prince   Such a success merits
some sacrifices   You know how truly I am ever yours,

GUIZOT.

ADMIRAL COMTE DE RIGNY TO THE PRINCE DE TALLEYRAND

PARIS, *October 11th*, 1832

MON PRINCE,

I cannot let Madame de Dino depart without sending
you a line as to the composition of our new Ministry and its
future

Its future (I ought to say its duration) is of importance to
the whole of Europe , and Europe, up to a certain point, can
greatly influence its duration

Notwithstanding the violence which will be exhibited in our debates, we shall triumph, if we can announce a reasonable termination of the Belgian affair, they are all with us respecting the evacuation of Antwerp. We must be allowed to ask for this beneath its walls, and then retire next day.

For this, however, the approbation of the London Cabinet is necessary. Silence on the part of the others will be the result. But without it, the parliamentary struggle may sweep us away, and with us the last barrier.

Your great influence, mon Prince, can alone aid us. The work is worthy of you. Our alliance with England will become indestructible, and the civilisation of Europe will be saved.

Madame de Dino will tell you that the appointments were signed last night at half-past twelve.

I renew the homage of my respectful devotion.

C. DE RIGNY.

M. THIERS TO THE PRINCE DE TALLEYRAND

PARIS, *October* 11*th*, 1832.

MON PRINCE,

Before this reaches you, you will have heard by telegraph of the selections made by the King. We resisted for some time, and were compelled to do so, in order to be fully assured of the stability of the royal decisions. Now I believe we can count upon the King's firmness. He will uphold by every constitutional means the new administration he has just formed. He looks upon the men who compose it as the last supporters of M. Périer's policy, and he is convinced that this policy of moderation, at home as well as abroad, can alone insure peace to France and to Europe. But the King's decision will not suffice, we must receive assistance from all sides. You, mon Prince, can do this more than any one else, you can enlighten the English Cabinet as to its interests as well as ours—they are now identical.

This Antwerp business will decide everything. None of the Ministry wish to be exacting, but every one feels the necessity of putting an end to these prolonged uncertainties, and of calming men's minds. The countries which have the most to gain in common are England and France. It is necessary for both that the uncertainty which is involved in the Belgian question should cease, and that a positive result should end all doubts. We have reached a point in France when every one, especially those of the moderate party, demands that this Belgian business should be concluded. No matter what Ministry is formed, the same task will be imposed upon it—namely, *to show results*. This phrase has now become a proverb, and is on every one's lips   M Dupin,[1] M Odilon Barrot, and M Périer, if he had lived, would all have been obliged to do the same thing, for the premeditated resistance of Holland must be put an end to, no matter by what Ministry The question is   Is it better we should do it, or another ?   If, for example, we were to take the citadel of Antwerp, our word could be relied on , we should evacuate it three days after we had taken it   The entire Council will pledge itself to this   M de Broglie's word is, I should think, the most reassuring of all   For my part, I will pledge my word as a Minister, and my word of honour as a man , and you know that my principle is, that great undertakings can only be carried out by keeping good faith

I do not think any one will cast a doubt upon our given promise, but perhaps there might be a question as to our power of keeping it, and whether we might not soon be succeeded by others, who would rid themselves of the engagements undertaken by us To this I have an answer which I think is conclusive

We have an assured majority, if we can show the country any immediate results   We are told that we can hope for a majority if we can defend our position, but we are promised it with certainty if this Antwerp business is brought to an end This parliamentary exigency has become quite irresistible, and it is absolutely necessary to satisfy it   Moreover, it is a matter which the dignity of England, and that of France, equally demand   If it is done, we can answer for everything   It will be for us to see that the promise we have given is effectually carried out   If not we shall be exposed to all the chances of the tribune and the ballot   But after us there only remains Dupin, allied to Odilon Barrot , and the requirements of these gentlemen will assuredly not be less, and will not always be founded, like ours, on the thoroughly recognized interests of both countries   Therefore, mon Prince, second us with the whole strength of your genius and with all your influence   The question resolves itself in these words   "Every one wants Antwerp."   If we obtain it, we shall have an assured majority, and the other Powers will have the advantage of consolidating with us, the policy of moderation   *We only want it for three days*

Pardon me, mon Prince, for mentioning these matters, which

[1] André Marie Dupin, born 1783, advocate under the Restoration   Deputy in 1827, Procurator-General of the *Cours de Cassation* in 1830, President of the Chamber of Deputies 1832-40, re-elected in 1848   He was President of the Assembly in 1851   He gave in his resignation as Procurator-General, in consequence of the decree which confiscated the property of the Orleans family   But he resumed office in 1857, and became a Senator   He died in 1865

you know much better than I do, but it is necessary to speak of them to every one, and on every occasion

Accept, I pray you, the assurance of my most profound respect and devoted friendship

.\ THIERS

THE DUC DE BROGLIE TO THE PRINCE DE TALLEYRAND

PARIS, *October 12th*, 1832

MON PRINCE,

In sending you the accompanying despatch, allow me to recall our position, our needs, and our hopes to your recollection and your friendship

Half the present Ministry is composed of M Périer's colleagues, and half, of those of his political friends who were pledged even more than he was to uphold order and peace, and who had been kept in reserve by him until more propitious times

These times have now arrived You have seen for yourself that the state of France is thoroughly satisfactory Peace reigns in every portion of her territory, order has been restored everywhere, and men's minds have become reassured

All the bye-elections are rational and moderate, business both in town and country, has visibly recovered itself, the harvest has been excellent, one difficulty alone remains to be overcome That is, the maintenance of the majority gained last year with so much care and labour The political divisions, as you are aware, have broken up this majority, absurd prejudices, purely literary rivalries, and wretched cavillings, threaten to give our adversaries an advantage over us which will cost Europe torrents of blood and years of incalculable calamity

If the present Ministry had not taken upon themselves the burden of affairs, you know well, mon Prince, for you have seen it yourself, that power would have passed into the hands of those who, without being aware of or even desiring it, would inevitably have transmitted it to the party of anarchy and war

If the present Ministry were to succumb in the struggle, its defeat would even more effectually and more directly have the same result We are all fully convinced that there is a certain means of preventing this Let England (without taking alarm) allow us to take the citadel of Antwerp from the Dutch and hand it over to the Belgians If the coming session opens under such auspices, you can count on a brilliant triumph If, on the contrary, we have again to excuse from the Tribune all the political delays, postponements, and procrastinations, our position will be a very dangerous one, and the weight of prejudice against us will be greatly increased I doubt whether we shall be able to stand against it

When I mentioned these ideas to Lord Granville in your presence, he made various objections He said . " But if Europe does trust to your word, how can she be sure that you will remain long enough in power to redeem it ? " To this my answer was . " If England consents, we can enter Belgium between the 20th and 22nd Our troops are ready , we should be before Antwerp on the 26th or 27th , from the 8th to the 15th of November the citadel would be ours and between the 16th and 20th our troops would have again re-entered French territory The session does not commence till the 19th , the address will not take place before the 1st of December , therefore any danger from this quarter is impossible "

Lord Granville then said to me ' But suppose the Dutch attack you during the siege, what will you do then ? " My answer was equally simple ' If the Dutch attack us, we shall drive them back to the limits of the Belgian territory We will pledge ourselves not to advance one inch beyond It will be notified in the *Moniteur*, which would announce the entry of our troops into Belgium, that they will not even enter Antwerp , that the citadel will be given up to the Belgians from the moment of the capitulation , and that our withdrawal will commence on that very day "

Lord Granville seemed still uneasy, on account of the possible intervention of the Prussians , but, in the first place, an expedition conducted with such a degree of celerity would not leave them time to concentrate their troops, which are greatly scattered Again, we offer, as you know, to allow them to occupy Venloo and all that portion of Dutch territory which is at present in the hands of the Belgians The reply to this proposal cannot reach us for three weeks The orders for the assembly of Prussian troops would necessarily take about the same time to reach the generals Our expedition would be ended ere they were in a position to make a serious demonstration [1]

[1] The relations between France and Prussia passed through a very critical period during the expedition to Antwerp Frequent allusion to this is made in these memoirs (see pages 25, 45, and following) We also think it useful to give some explanations on this subject Prussia watched with great jealousy the French intervention in Belgium M Ancillon, personally hostile to France, made no secret of his keen irritation , and M Bresson, in his correspondence, transmitted its echoes to Paris Thus M Ancillon declared, that if the French army entered Belgium, Prussia would be obliged to take such precautionary measures as could not fail to encourage the Dutch in their resistance *despatch of M Bresson, 11th of October*, giving an account of M Ancillon's interview with Lord Minto On the 13th of October, M Bresson added, that in the event of French intervention Prussia would mass her troops on the Meuse, and that if a single French soldier entered Holland, Prussia would consider it a *casus belli*

If the English Government refuses this proposition, see what will be the result! First, it is doubtful whether we shall succeed in restraining the Belgians. King Leopold is at present without any Government whatever. No Minister will undertake the charge of affairs, unless the King is prepared to have recourse to energetic measures. General Goblet is the sole member of the Cabinet, and he wishes to retire in a few days[1]. King Leopold's hand will be forced; the Belgians will attack, the King of the Netherlands will attack in his turn; we shall be obliged to defend them; and there you have a regular war!

Supposing even that this does not happen, though I can see no possibility of preventing it, the position of the French Cabinet at the opening of the Chambers will become a very dangerous one; and if we succumb in the struggle, power will pass into the hands of the war party, and the expedition to Antwerp will only be one of the least of its enterprises. It therefore seems to me that this expedition to Antwerp is no longer a matter with regard to which Europe has any choice. It is not a question whether it is to be done, but who shall do it—whether the Belgians or the French, whether it is to be accomplished by the war or the peace party.

Looking at the question in this light, I do not see that there can be any doubt about it.

This expedition will not in any way prevent the blockade

M. Bresson was not however to be intimidated. He assured them in Paris that, no matter how much she might be displeased, Prussia would not dare to oppose the action of France (*despatches of 22nd and 24th of October*; see also in the Appendix, letter No 2, an able letter which M. Bresson wrote to the Duc de Broglie on the 24th of October). In order to allay the irritation of the Berlin Cabinet, the French Government bethought itself of proposing to Prussia that she should take possession, under a conditional guarantee, of the territories assigned to Holland by the treaty of November 15th, which Belgium was improperly occupying, i.e. Venloo and certain districts of Limburg and Luxemburg (*despatch of the Duc de Broglie to M Bresson, October 8th*; see this letter in Appendix, letter No 1). M. de Talleyrand, being consulted, approved of this idea (*letter of M de Talleyrand to the Duc de Broglie of 27th October*, Appendix, letter No 3). M. Bresson also approved, with the exception of Luxemburg, (*despatch, 17th of October*). The Prussian Cabinet was sorely perplexed. M. Ancillon appeared disposed to accept the proposal, but asked for Liège in addition, which was refused him (*despatch, 24th of October*). Finally he refused, fearing to become embroiled with Russia by seeming to accede to the proposed coercive measures against Holland, and requested that the disputed territories, instead of being handed over to him, should be given direct to the King of the Netherlands. The French Cabinet could not accept this proposal, although England appeared willing to consent to it. Lord Palmerston, in fact, wrote to Lord Minto that the five Powers ought to come to some arrangement offering the said territories to King William (*despatch of M Bresson, 19th of December*). Briefly, no resolution was arrived at, and this long negotiation had no further results than gaining some time, and enabling the French army to take possession of Antwerp without opposition on the part of Prussia, which had been the real object of the French Cabinet.

[1] General Goblet had been appointed Minister of Foreign Affairs on the 18th of September, and retired on the 27th of September following.

We shall not make the acceptance of the treaty, or the solution of the Scheldt question, a condition of our withdrawal, these are points which must be settled either by negotiation, or if necessary by means of maritime or pecuniary coercion   Our undertaking to quit Belgium immediately after the surrender of the citadel, would be absolute   If you gain this point, mon Prince, the Cabinet, of whose formation you are aware, and of which you have had the goodness to approve, is certain to be established, and if it is established, the peace of France and that of Europe are assured   In a contrary event, I can foresee nothing but misfortunes before us, the number and extent of which it is impossible to estimate

In conclusion I will add, that our army is now very concentrated, and in a position to act   If the expedition does not take place we must disperse it, we dread that any moment cholera might break out, and if we are reduced to scattering it, what a multitude of accusations will be raised against us!

Pardon this long letter, mon Prince   I have not had time to think it over, or even to read it through   I trust to your kindness and your indulgence to excuse whatever I may have written inconsiderately, and to supply whatever I may have omitted

Our fate is in your hands   Accept, with your accustomed kindness, the expressions of my most sincere and devoted attachment

V BROGLIE

I reached London on the 15th of October, after a very trying passage, and did not lose a moment in resuming the work that had been intrusted to me   The very day of my arrival, I had a long interview with Lord Palmerston, in which I took up the course of affairs since my departure, and dealt with the important question which at this moment pressed so heavily on the Cabinets of London and Paris—namely, the execution of the treaty of November the 15th   I at once saw that M   Durant de Mareuil had very thoroughly prepared the way

As I have already stated, the Conference had reassembled on the 1st of October, in order to determine whether coercive measures against Holland had become necessary, and what these measures should be   No one had called in question the necessity for coercive measures, but as these measures might be of two kinds, pecuniary or material, there had been some disagreement on this point between the plenipotentiaries, those of Austria, Prussia, and Russia declaring that they could not associate themselves with anything but the pecuniary measures, whereas the plenipotentiaries of France and Great Britain, considering these measures insufficient, announced the intention of their Courts to proceed to more efficacious ones A protocol was drawn up, establishing this position This may be considered as the last public act of the Conference, though for a long time it continued to exercise the great influence it had acquired It was necessary to develop the principle laid down by the plenipotentiaries of France and England in the protocol of October 1st, by a fresh negotiation between these two Powers What more efficacious measures could they adopt? The French Cabinet proposed to proceed with their troops to compel the evacuation of the citadel of Antwerp, while the combined squadrons of France and England blockaded the coasts of Holland The English Cabinet (for reasons which will be explained further on) would have preferred confining the measures to the blockade I had to begin by bringing Lord Palmerston and Lord Grey round to the views of the French Cabinet, and after lengthy and tedious efforts I succeeded It will be soon seen that the difficulties I met with in the English Cabinet were still further increased by intrigues which originated in Paris, and were directed against our Cabinet I will now proceed to give extracts from my despatches and letters, and from those which I received, which, I think, will plainly describe the progress of the negotiations

THE PRINCE DE TALLEYRAND TO THE DUC DE BROGLIE.

LONDON, *October 16th*, 1832

MONSIEUR LE DUC,

M de Marcuil received a letter yesterday from Berlin, in which M Bresson informed him of the account he had given you of a conversation which he and Lord Minto[1] had had with

[1] Gilbert Elliot, Earl of Minto, born in 1782, entered the House of Commons in 1806, and the House of Lords in 1814, on the death of his father He sided with the Whig party In 1832, he was sent as Ambassador to Berlin In 1835, he became Postmaster-General, then First Lord of the Admiralty He resigned in 1841, and became Lord Privy Seal in 1846 He retired from public life in 1852, and died in 1859

M Ancillon, after the arrival of Comte Douhoff,[1] the bearer of the protocol of October 1st

I requested M de Mareuil to go to Lord Palmerston, and ask him whether he had not received the same accounts from Lord Minto, and whether he did not see in them a fresh reason for accelerating the decisions of the French and English Cabinets

M de Mareuil has just given me an account of his interview Lord Palmerston appeared to him, as he did to me, to be fully impressed with the urgent necessity for full and prompt decision on the great question of the moment The Cabinet Council held yesterday morning, also went fully into details on this matter It would seem that some doubt was expressed as to the success of a hasty attack upon the citadel of Antwerp, for Lord Palmerston asked M de Mareuil, whether he had such positive information on this point as might inspire full confidence, and shortly after, Lord Durham came and expressed the same desire to me Without being more positive than was advisable, M de Mareuil replied, that in Paris, in Brussels, and even at the Hague, he had heard professional men, who knew the strength and the weakness of this citadel, state that it could not possibly hold out against a well-directed attack He added, however, that if it was defended, it would probably not be taken without considerable damage resulting to the town, which induced him to repeat that it would be necessary to acquaint Belgium, formally, that such damage would be compensated Lord Palmerston seemed quite to agree in these remarks, and he confirmed the hope he had given me, that I should receive a full communication of the resolutions come to by the Government either this evening, or at latest to-morrow morning

During the course of this interview, Lord Palmerston mentioned an incident which had caused some surprise in the Cabinet You are already aware, through a despatch from Vienna, which Lord Granville will have communicated to you, that some utterances by Marshal Maison appeared very premature to Sir Frederick Lamb, and had called forth serious remonstrances on the part of Prince Metternich

Still greater surprise was felt, on learning through a communication from Baron d'Ompteda,[2] the Hanoverian Minister,

---

[1] Councillor of the Prussian Legation

[2] Louis Charles George, Baron d'Ompteda, born in 1767 a Hanoverian statesman and diplomat He was Secretary to the Legation at Dresden in 1791, then *Chargé d'Affaires* at Berlin in 1795 Hanover having passed under the rule of Prussia, M d'Ompteda passed into the service of that Power, which he represented at Dresden He was several times charged with important missions, especially to

that the French Minister at Hanover had officially announced
the immediate joint action of the French and English Governments against Holland, and it certainly must have appeared
somewhat strange that a resolution of the King of England
should have been notified to the King of Hanover, whilst
deliberations as to the principle and the forms of this co-
operation were still being carried on under the Prince in whom
the two crowns were united   However, Lord Palmerston
displayed no bitterness whatever when he made this observation
to M. de Mareuil, and he only drew one conclusion from it,
similar to that which he had already expressed to me—namely,
that after the hints given in the newspapers respecting the resolutions of France and England, it was imperative to carry them
out with the least possible delay . .

THE PRINCE DE TALLEYRAND TO THE PRINCESS DE VAUDÉMONT.

LONDON, *October* 16th, 1832

I am regularly surrounded here by the intrigues of Madame
de Flahaut, who hardly ever quits Lady Grey, to whom she says
all she can against our present Government " It cannot possibly
last ; the Ministry cannot hold out , it will have no majority, no
one will have anything to say to it   " This is what she
repeats everywhere To-day she is sitting in judgment at Lord
Holland's.   To have to deal with difficult affairs, and to be
at the same time exposed to society scandals which are perpetually renewed, is really unbearable   The fact is, that her
husband in Paris, and she in London, really do harm to the new
Ministry : this is very wrong.   At first I could not believe all
I was told about it ; now I am forced to admit that I was a
fool, when I rejected as calumny, all I was told of that *ménage*
   I forgot to tell you that Madame de Flahaut sounds
Sebastiani's praises loudly, adding " The King will have to
recall him again.".

THE PRINCE DE TALLEYRAND TO THE DUC DE BROGLIE

LONDON, *October* 17th, 1832

MONSIEUR LE DUC,
         The plenipotentiaries of Russia, Prussia, and Austria
have several times during the last few days asked Lord Palmer-

Vienna. In 1815, having again become a Hanoverian subject, he was accredited to
Berlin In 1823, he became a Minister of State, and later on, Minister in attendance
on the King in London He retired in 1837, and died in 1854

ston to reassemble the Conference, in order to discuss the measures to be adopted against Holland They have also come to me with the same request , but I have asked Lord Palmerston to refuse this demand, pointing out to him the inconveniences of a discussion which just now could only have unpleasant results Lord Palmerston quite agreed with me as to this, and he will not call the Conference together, until he is in a position to communicate to it our resolutions, definitely drawn up

Evening of October 18th

. .   This morning I saw Lord Palmerston, who permitted me to hope, that at the close of the Cabinet Council I should receive a positive communication as to the resolutions of the Cabinet. Nevertheless, up to this hour, the Minister has been unable to give me the decision I so anxiously await True, the King, who was to have returned to London to-day, will not arrive till to-morrow, and his presence is necessary for a definite sanction But I have also reason to believe, after a very long conversation with Lord Palmerston, of which I will give you a detailed account, that the matter, having been brought before the whole Cabinet, has given rise there, not to any opposition as to the actual fact of the execution of the treaty (on this point every one is agreed), but to the necessity of carrying to the utmost limits the examination of the consequences which might result from coercive measures employed jointly by France and England , and moreover that discussions as to the position of home affairs (which I will explain in a letter to-morrow) might suggest the idea that more time should still be gained These are the views of severa¹ members of the Cabinet , I have combated them, will do so again, and hope to succeed , but it is only a hope To-morrow I shall see the King, and after the Cabinet Council, I shall have an explanation with Lord Palmerston, which I will at once report to you

I must tell you that I feel firmly convinced that this prolonged discussion need not disquiet you in any way, and that it will only result in giving greater weight to the decision that will be taken . . .

Morning of October 19th

I really am distressed to have to tell you each day, that what has been promised the evening before is again put off to the following day

The King came up from Windsor yesterday, and I had the honour of paying my respects to him I found all the members of the Cabinet at St. James's, and I was able to remind several of them, how very important it was to come to some decisive resolution respecting the co-operation of France and England in carrying out the treaty of November 15th. All admitted this necessity, but, nevertheless, the Cabinet Council held by the King, which sat from four in the afternoon till half-past seven, was solely occupied with the report in the *Recorder* on the criminal convictions, which have taken place during the last few months, and by the discussion which followed it. Lord Palmerston assured me last night that the political question of the moment was not even touched upon, and that it was put off till the meeting which is to take place to-day at Lord Grey's at East Sheen, where all the members of the Cabinet are to meet and dine.

But I owe you the explanation of these delays, at least as far as I have been able to ascertain them during the last conversations I have had with Lord Palmerston. Last night he added a few further details to what he had already told me.

On the one hand, it seems that after having apparently quite decided to adopt the principle of co-operation, and the successive and simultaneous employment of naval and military forces, the Council discovered that some of its members, though admitting that the new French Government inspired thorough confidence, expressed some anxiety as to its stability; that reports had come over from Paris, brought here by persons whom one credited with more discretion, which had roused the opposition, and even sensible people were now afraid that if joint coercive measures were brought to bear on Holland by France and England, they might lead to a general war; and that a change of Ministry in Paris would turn this into a propagandist war, with which England would not care to be associated.

On the other hand, this hesitation of the Cabinet is also due to home affairs, which require to be carefully dealt with.

The difficulties caused by the negro question in the West Indies and the Island of Mauritius, as well as the necessity of providing against them, have already occasioned lengthy deliberations[1]. This matter is evidently of far greater

---

[1] People's minds in England were greatly exercised on the question of negro slavery. It was decided to abolish it in 1834. From 1832, the Government gradually worked on towards this end, while discussing various measures in Parliament for regulating the fate of the slaves in the colonies (Order in Council of November 2nd). The feeling roused by these discussions stirred up serious troubles in the colonies. The insurrection in Jamaica in 1831, was very serious. In Trinidad and St. Lucia, the colonists refused to submit to the orders of the Home Government. In the Mauritius, the Governor-General having published a pamphlet in favour of the liberation of the blacks, the colonists rose in rebellion. All these were grave indications, which justly and rightly alarmed the English Cabinet.

importance than was at first supposed, for Lord Palmerston has
spoken to me about it at two different conferences Besides,
Lord Palmerston, while seeing the necessity of ending the matter,
and the need there is that France and Belgium should be able
to declare, at the opening of the Chambers, that a definite
resolution had been taken, and its execution begun, finds
himself obliged to confess that the English Government almost
felt a contrary necessity, and that, as far as he was concerned,
a delay of some weeks would be very advantageous This is
the explanation he gave me Parliament is prorogued till
the 11th of December It is the intention of Government to
dissolve it They think it would be inconvenient to assemble
it again, meanwhile if coercive measures were at once employed
against Holland, as such would not be a formal declaration
of war, convoking Parliament could be dispensed with But if
the King of Holland was himself to make an actual declaration
of war, it would be necessary, according to the Constitution,
either to assemble the present Parliament, or to dissolve it and
convoke a new one In the first case, a very strong opposition
might be expected, and there is reason to believe that it is
specially with this hope that the King of Holland will feel
disposed to make the declaration in question In the second
case, and if Parliament is dissolved, it is necessary to ascertain
that the registration of the electors, according to the new law,
is sufficiently completed, so that there may be no fear, in the
case of an immediate election, of the still more dangerous
choice that might be made by men whom the effect of the
Reform Bill would deprive of the right to vote, and who would
consequently exercise it for the last time

This singularity in the position of the English Cabinet
requires to be fully recognised It was easier for me to combat
the fears that had been expressed regarding the stability of
our Ministry, and I could make use of the consideration accorded
to it, to show how necessary it was for the policy of both
Cabinets to assist ours in its present position I therefore
eagerly urged that the proposals which had been made here,
and which Lord Granville had confirmed to you, should be
promptly and fully carried into effect I am very far from
losing all hope of this The last letters from the Hague, the
King of Holland's speech at the opening of the States-General,
the virulent language of the newspapers which are inspired
by the Dutch Cabinet, have been fully appreciated here as
evident symptoms of a still more obstinate resistance ; and
unless the intervention of the Berlin Cabinet, and the letters which
M de Donhoff is bringing, produce a complete change at the

Hague (which we shall know in the course of a couple of days,) I have grounds for believing that the English Government does not wish to go back from its original proposals, and I willingly accept as a proof of its steadfastness, the formal permission it has just given for our vessels to take up their station with its fleet at Spithead   . .

19th October, Eight o'clock in the Evening.

We received a summons from Lord Palmerston to attend a conference, late this afternoon   This meeting took place at the request of the Dutch plenipotentiary, who had addressed a sealed packet to the Conference   Lord Palmerston could not refuse it as we had arranged, since it was not instigated by one of the three plenipotentiaries, and besides it was necessary to hear the explanations which had come from Holland, and might be of great importance

When Baron de Zuylen's packet was opened, we heard a long statement read, in which it was attempted to refute protocols 69 and 70   I may remark that the latter had not been communicated to the Dutch plenipotentiary   Anyhow, this long polemic effusion is of no consequence ; it ought not and will not have any influence whatever on the Conference ; it is evidently a document intended to be read before the States-General of Holland   We looked upon it as such, and adjourned without any discussion on it . . .

THE DUC DE BROGLIE TO THE PRINCE DE TALLEYRAND

PARIS, *October* 18th, 1832

MON PRINCE,

Your letter confirmed the hopes with which M de Marcuil's despatch and Lord Granville's conversation had inspired me   We now await your courier of to-morrow with great impatience, and are preparing ourselves for all contingencies

The political position of the Ministry is much better than we at first dared to hope for   After a great amount of wrangling, people have ended by coming to their senses and asking themselves what all the fuss was about   They are generally disposed, if not to be friendly, to be at least attentive ; the most usual remark one now hears is "Let us see what this Ministry will do "   Our fate, therefore, depends more and more on our actions from the present until the commencement of the session, and of all our actions, the principal, the only one that occupies public attention—is this expedition to Antwerp   On this point, opinion grows stronger every day, it is not the turbulent minority, but the reasonable majority which importunes I am therefore all the more rejoiced at the part the English Cabinet has just taken, for even if it had decided against our expedition, I do not see how it would be possible to avoid it

If we carry it out, our success in the Chamber is assured We shall neglect nothing to prevent any unforeseen complications Our fleet is all ready, it is composed of officers, who for the most part have served with the English I will not conceal from you, that if it were possible for both fleets to be jointly engaged at the mouth of the Scheldt, and if some cannon shots were fired simultaneously at the English and French, it would have the best possible effect here. the alliance would become more and more popular, and we should be more at liberty to act in conformity with the wishes of the English Cabinet

I must conclude, mon Prince, by once again placing our interests in your hands all my hope, and all my peace, lies in the knowledge that you are in London

October 19th, Ten o'clock in the Morning.

. . . I have this moment received your despatch of the 16th, and I reply by courier without loss of time, in order to put you in a position to give all the explanations that may be asked of you

The French army assembled on the northern frontier is 48,000 strong About 18,000 are destined for the siege of Antwerp, and 30,000 will take up their position on the road to Bergen-op-Zoom and Breda, within the limits of the Belgian territory, so as to cover the siege

The French outposts will relieve the Belgian outposts over the entire front of the circle of military operations

We shall ask the King of the Belgians to assemble his army behind Turnhout, so as to threaten the flank of the Dutch army, if it advances against our army of observation, in the same way that our army of observation will threaten its flank, if it advances against the Belgian army within the limits of Belgian territory

As to the facility of taking the citadel, Marshal Gérard thinks it could not hold out more than ten days He has obtained all requisite information respecting this Everything is ready There need not be the slightest disquietude on this point

THE PRINCE DE TALLEYRAND TO THE DUC DE BROGLIE.

LONDON, *October* 22nd, 1832

MONSIEUR LE DUC,

I have received all the despatches you did me the honour to write, up to the 20th October inclusive, I quite understand the impatience of the King's Government at this critical moment, and you may have seen that I fully shared his wish to arrive at the end of these tedious uncertainties on the Belgian question Nevertheless, the hesitation of the English Ministry is entirely due to the gravity of the situation. Lord Grey and Lord Palmerston wished to get as many members of the Cabinet together as possible, so as to obtain that unanimity of decision which circumstances render highly important. I feel it is necessary to dwell on this point, as it is due to these two ministers to state, that it is impossible for anyone to be more favourably disposed towards us than they are in all my transactions with them You will find the proof of this, Monsieur le Duc, in the Convention I have just signed with Lord Palmerston, and which I have the honour to transmit to you. it will, I hope, fully satisfy the wishes of the King's Government

It is midnight, and I have not time to enter into the different articles of this Convention, I can only say that it was impossible to obtain more.

It is absolutely necessary, that the ratifications should leave Paris by Thursday evening, the 25th, so as to be in London on the 27th

I have no need to impress upon you the necessity for complete secrecy as to this Convention. We do not wish it to be known, until after it has been communicated to the plenipotentiaries of the three Powers at the Conference, which will take place the day after the exchange of the ratifications.

You will no doubt deem it advisable to inform the King's consuls, so that French interests should not be compromised . .

As this despatch announced, I had signed the Convention with England on the evening of October 22nd, which the French Government so earnestly desired By it, both Powers agree to proceed to carry into effect the treaty of November 15th in conformity to their engagements that the territorial evacuation would be the first step taken, that the Governments of

Holland and Belgium would be requested to carry out this evacuation reciprocally by the 12th of November, and force would
be employed against whichever of these governments had not
given its consent by the 2nd November   That in case of a refusal on the part of Holland, an embargo would be laid on al
Dutch vessels, and that on the 15th of November, a French army
would enter Belgium to lay siege to the fortress of Antwerp

The disquietude at Paris was immense, and all the letters I
received, showed how impatiently the result, which I at last succeeded in obtaining, was awaited   This impatience at times in-
commoded me greatly ; I therefore wrote a letter to the Princess
de Vaudémont at this period, from which I will cite a few
passages

THE PRINCE DE TALLEYRAND TO THE PRINCESS DE VAUDÉMONT.

LONDON, *October 25th*, 1832.

. . The Marquis of Lansdowne[1] leaves for Paris to-day, he
will inspire our Ministry, which is rather easily frightened, with
fresh courage   In all and in everything, they always appear too
hurried   This does not inspire confidence in those who look on.
I have been here eight days, and have obtained all that they
wished, which had been well prepared by Durant.   But though
it is hardly a week since I have returned to London, I have
already received an impatient letter from *Mademoiselle*   Do you
remember when it was thought the Belgians were going to enter
Holland, and that is now three months ago ?

I told them the Broglie Ministry would settle down all right ;
but they would not believe me.   Well ! now it has established
itself, and will last for some time, if it does not make such foolish
prosecutions as that of M Berryer[2]   Now they are fully armed to
face the Chamber, having received the authority to march on

---

[1] The Marquis of Lansdowne was President of the Council in the English
Cabinet   He went to Paris to negotiate the exchanges that were to take place in
the custom duties.

[2] The Ministry had ordered the arrest of Messrs Berryer Chateaubriand, Hyde
de Neuville, and Fitz James, accused of complicity with the Duchess de Berry
(7th June)   The three last were soon set at liberty, nothing having been proved
against them   M Berryer was brought before the Court of Assizes at Blois, on
October 16th   The charge was so badly drawn up, that the public prosecutor
had to dismiss the case, and the accused benefited by an acquittal, which resolved
itself into a triumph

Antwerp. What we now want is to be on better terms with Prussia at any price, for she is well disposed towards us. That done, the rest will run on wheels . . .

Immediately after the signature of the Convention of October 22nd, therefore, and while awaiting the ratifications which did not arrive from Paris until the 27th, I made all arrangements with Lord Palmerston for carrying it into effect. Accordingly, simultaneous with the exchange of the ratifications, the ratified Convention was transmitted to the three Courts, accompanied by a brief and simple Note, so as to avoid, as much as possible, any request for explanations from them. A steamboat was in readiness and started immediately for Rotterdam, carrying to the Hague the communication to be made by the *Chargés d'Affaires* of France and England to the Government of the Netherlands, which, by referring everything to the Convention, was short and peremptory. Lastly, a courier was also sent off to Brussels, who carried to the Belgian Government a Note precisely similar to that sent to the Dutch Government By this we wished to show our complete impartiality, and also to demand that the Belgians on their part should surrender Venloo and those portions of territory which they still held unfairly, and which were to be given back to the King of the Netherlands on the day that he accepted the treaty of November 15th We rather wished to make the most of this restitution demanded of the Belgians, in order to detach the Prussian Cabinet from those of Austria and Russia. With this object, we proposed that the Prussian troops should occupy Venloo and the territories of Limburg and Luxemburg, which the treaty of November 15th, handed over to Holland, or undertake to guard them until the king had agreed to the treaty, and not to give them up to him until after the execution of his share of its conditions This proposal gave rise to a private and rather complicated negotiation with the Berlin Cabinet, which seemed at first disposed to accept it, but finally refused,[1] not daring to join in the coercive measures taken by the two maritime Powers The

[1] See page 13

result was that the Belgians kept the territories which had been demanded of them, and were thus placed in a still more favourable position as regards Holland

We will now return to the despatches and letters

THE PRINCE DE TALLEYRAND TO THE DUC DE BROGLIE.

LONDON, *October 26th*, 1832

MONSIEUR LE DUC,

Lord Palmerston called the Conference together this morning, at the request of M de Bulow, who said he had a communication to make to us This communication was the draft of a treaty sent by the Cabinet of the Hague. Lord Palmerston and I at once declared, that in conformity with the strict rules we had hitherto followed, we could not entertain proposals from any other intermediary, excepting the plenipotentiary recognized by the Court who made them to us ; that if M de Zuylen had anything to communicate to us from his Court, we were quite ready to hear it, but that we could not entertain M de Bulow's request [1] The latter did not insist We thus avoided all explanations The draft treaty was not even read. The principal clause in it was the recognition of the free navigation of the Scheldt, with the reservation of imposing dues of three shillings per ton, instead of one shilling, as agreed to by King Leopold and by Prussia I trust our ratifications will have arrived before M de Zuylen himself submits to us this project of his Court, which just now would not be in much favour with the Conference We are all agreed, that the meeting this morning is not to be considered as a conference held at the Foreign Office

THE DUC DE BROGLIE TO THE PRINCE DE TALLEYRAND

PARIS, *October 25th*, 1832

MON PRINCE,

Your courier arrived here yesterday at five in the afternoon I at once took the Convention to the king , in the

---

[1] A last attempt had been made by Prussia to prevent a rupture. The Berlin Cabinet had transmitted to the Hague a statement of the concessions required by the Conference On the 23rd October, the Dutch Minister for Foreign Affairs, announced to the envoys of Russia, Prussia, and Austria, that the king would adhere to this scheme, with the exception of some modifications The treaty was then sent to London It has been seen how it was received by the Conference A few days later, on the 9th November, the Dutch Minister in London communicated it to Lord Grey, who replied that this treaty did not remove all the difficulties, and that besides it had come too late, and the evacuation of Antwerp would henceforth be the indispensable preliminary of all fresh negotiations

evening we held a Cabinet Council. The night was passed in preparing the ratifications, the courier is just about to start, and you will receive them early to-morrow

I need hardly tell you with what joy this piece of news has been received. Neither will I speak to you of our gratitude for so great a success You alone could have accomplished it ; you could not have rendered your country a greater service, and now allow me to ask you a few questions as to how this treaty is to be executed

The King of the Belgians is summoned, simultaneously with the King of the Netherlands, to evacute that portion of territory which does not belong to him, according to the terms of the twenty-four articles.

If the King of Holland refuses by the 2nd November, to evacuate, will the King of the Belgians be obliged to do so? and in that case, to whom would he hand over Venloo and the other portions of Limburg?

It is impossible to conceive that it should be to the King of Holland.

If the King of the Netherlands accepts the proposal, if he consents to evacuate the Belgian territory, ought the King of the Belgians to hand over to the King of Holland the territory now occupied by the Belgians, before the King of Holland has accepted the remainder of the twenty-four articles, and whilst still contesting arrangements concerning the Scheldt, the syndicate,[1] and the navigation of the intermediary waters? Would this be prudent?

I put these questions to you, in order that we may be quite sure as to what directions we have to give to the King of the Belgians Besides you know that his people are not the most reasonable, and as soon as they gain a little confidence, they will give us no end of trouble Kindly give me your idea as to the solution of these questions However I hope to receive a letter from you to-day, which will perhaps solve all our doubts.

Accept   .

[1] This question of the syndicate was a very difficult one, and requires some explanations.

A law of December 27th, 1822, had created a sinking fund syndicate, in place of the syndicate of the Netherlands and the sinking fund office This sinking fund syndicate had been endowed with 250 million of florins But in consequence of default or irregularity in the accounts, it was found impossible in 1832, to ascertain how this credit had been used, hence it was impossible to determine exactly the amount of the debt of the Netherlands, and on this subject, the Belgian and Dutch plenipotentiaries argued till they could not see The treaty of the twenty-four articles fixed the division of the debt, but the King of the Netherlands had refused to accept the figures of the Conference

THE PRINCE DE TALLEYRAND TO THE DUC DE BROGLIE.

LONDON, *October 27th*, 1832

MONSIEUR LE DUC,

I have this morning received the ratifications of the Convention of 22nd October, which you have done me the honour to send, together with your despatch No 77 I see with pleasure that this Convention has fulfilled the requirements of the King's Government, and I repeat again, that I feel convinced that its important results will be more appreciated each day

We have just effected the exchange of ratifications with Lord Palmerston, I will send you those of England in the next despatch

We have transmitted the ratified Convention to the plenipotentiaries of the three Courts of Austria, Prussia, and Russia, together with the Note, of which I send you herewith a copy

A steamboat will leave this in an hour for Rotterdam; it takes Note No 2 to the French and English *Chargés d'Affaires* at the Hague, and a courier who also starts this evening will carry Note No 3 to Brussels

As for the explanations you request, Monsieur le Duc, respecting the clause of the Convention relative to the giving up of Venloo by the Belgians, I can assure you, that we never had the slightest intention of handing over Venloo to the King of the Netherlands, before the complete execution of the treaty of November 15th The summons will be made to the Belgians, to show our impartiality, but we propose to deal with this town as follows To-morrow, Lord Palmerston and I intend to propose to Baron de Bulow, that the Belgians should hand Venloo over to H M the King of Prussia, under the condition, that that sovereign will undertake not to restore it to the King of the Netherlands, until the latter has fulfilled all the stipulations of the treaty of November 15th I will inform you of the result of this proposal, which I agreed to, knowing that it would completely meet the king's views . .

THE KING LOUIS PHILIPPE TO THE PRINCE DE TALLEYRAND

NEUILLY, *October 25th*, 1832.

MON CHER PRINCE,

In signing the important document you have just sent us, I must congratulate you on your success in having obtained it It is one of the greatest services you could have rendered me, and one of the greatest advantages that could have been assured to France, for it is the honourable pledge of a general peace.

I have only time to reiterate the expression of all those sentiments which you know I have so long felt for you

Louis Philippe

Madame Adelaide d'Orléans to the Prince de Talleyrand.

Neuilly, *Thursday, October* 25*th*, 1832

I have this moment received your admirable letter of the 23rd, and hasten, mon cher Prince, to thank you for it, all the more so as you have relieved me from a terrible anxiety, by telling me that this great business is finished, and that the Convention has been signed. It appears the need of secrecy was so strongly impressed upon him, that our beloved king thought himself obliged not to mention it, either to his wife or his sister, he also exacted this from M de Broglie, and I can certify that he has thoroughly kept it. When I went to him in triumph with your precious letter, he only laughed, saying: "I have not told you anything about it." I thank you for it with all my heart, and need hardly tell you that there will be no indiscretion on my part, though I must confess I cannot see why there should be all this secrecy. However any way, it is no business of mine, I only know that you have done me a very great kindness in sending me this grand and good piece of news, over which I rejoice with you with all my heart. You have cut the Gordian knot, as I asked you to do. It is a very great matter, which assures the prosperity of our beloved France, and of the reign of our dearly-loved king. Now I trust all will go well. Our beloved king desires me to tell you, how greatly he is satisfied with the great success of all your efforts, and that he hopes and counts upon your achieving equally happily the great work, which he says, you alone could complete. . . .

M Guizot to the Prince de Talleyrand

Paris, *October* 26*th*, 1832

I felt sure, mon Prince, that you would do the impossible, for that is your habit. I hope we may accomplish what you have done. Now that we possess a dowry our cause will be espoused. You are quite right, it is necessary to humour the prejudices of the country you are in, and not to place the British Cabinet in opposition to British instincts We are in exactly the same position, we have our prejudices which are very strong, and our ignorances which are infinite We ask that these also should be considered Let us know what it wants, and tell it what we want We shall succeed both here and in London, God and you helping us

Nothing is ever finished in this world, and after all that you have just done, we shall probably ask you to do much more still We must needs seek for common sense everywhere, for we have not sufficient at hand You will furnish us with some, will you not?

I have asked the king to restore the class of moral and political sciences at the Institute [1]

They have a very good effect here, and I was fortunate enough to find you were connected with them I regret exceedingly that you will not be here for the elections which are about to take place, but however important the Academies may be, what you are doing in London is far more so . . .

THE PRINCE DE TALLEYRAND TO THE DUC DE BROGLIE.

LONDON, *October 28th*, 1832

MONSIEUR LE DUC,

I have just received from the two plenipotentiaries of Russia, the letter and the Note of which I have the honour to send you copies It is only what we might have expected from them It has made no impression whatever on Lord Palmerston, nor on M de Wessenberg or M de Bulow It seemed to them a kind of precaution taken by the Russian plenipotentiaries, who acted according to some former instructions of their court, and who having been once blamed for taking too much upon themselves, wished this time to make a reservation [2]

[1] See M Guizot's report to the King (*Journal des Débats*, 28th October) The class of moral and political sciences had been established on the 3rd Brumaire, year IV, by a law of the Convention, and had been suppressed by a Consular decree of the 3rd Pluviôse, year XI

[2] The Russian plenipotentiaries addressed the following Note to M de Talleyrand and Lord Palmerston in reply to the communication made to them at the Conference of the 22nd October

"The undersigned, in compliance with a formal order from the emperor their master, make the following declaration That the adoption of coercive measures which France and Great Britain have resolved to take against Holland has brought about a position in which the Russian plenipotentiaries by virtue of the instructions with which they are furnished (the tenor of which is not unknown to the plenipotentiaries of the other Cabinets), find themselves under the necessity of withdrawing from the Conferences They will at once report to their court the grave circumstances, which by changing the character of the pacific mediation in which they have been called to take part, permit them no longer to associate themselves in the labours of their colleagues In suspend-

In reading the Note, you will no doubt notice the first words of the fourth paragraph M de Lieven and M Matusiewicz only mean to suspend their participation in the Conferences ; there is therefore no question of a rupture, or even a coolness towards the two courts · that, according to my view, is the essential point to which we must confine ourselves.

I hear that Comte Pozzo di Borgo, who must have arrived at Paris on his return from Russia, has spoken very favourably concerning our affairs at Berlin, Vienna and Munich. I should advise you to act towards him in the sense I have just had the honour to point out to you ; that is the way in which I mean to treat this question here I even think, that upon the whole, this temporary absence of the Russian plenipotentiaries from the Conference, which moreover will not reassemble for some time, will be rather useful to us while executing the measures we have in hand The Hollando-Belgian business must be finished in about twenty days, by the course of action which will be adopted That will be the length of time required to obtain an answer from St Petersburg to the communication of our Convention , the assembling of the Conference during this period would be useless, and might be inconvenient I believe that the position taken by Russia in this matter will have no other result than perhaps to encourage the King of the Netherlands somewhat longer in his obstinacy

Austria and Prussia will do nothing further, than simply acknowledge the communications we made to them when sending this Convention .

I have the honour to transmit herewith the ratifications of Great Britain, to the Convention of October 22nd .

October 30th, 1832

I have just been informed by Lord Palmerston, that orders will be sent down this evening to Admiral Malcolm at Portsmouth, directing him to send off three English frigates to-morrow, one to cruise off Texel, another at the mouth of the Meuse, and the third at the mouth of the Scheldt These frigates are to require all English merchant vessels that may wish to enter the Dutch ports, not to go thither They have orders not to commence hostilities, and not to impede Dutch commerce in any way, but to defend themselves if they are attacked by Dutch men-of-war

ing their participation in the Conferences, the Russian plenipotentiaries while awaiting the ultimate decision of their court are moved by the gravity of the circumstances to make this declaration

" LIEVEN
" MATUSIEWICZ "

When Lord Palmerston gave me this information, he asked me to take the same steps with the French admiral in command of our squadron at Spithead I did not hesitate to give the required instructions to M Ducrest de Villeneuve,[1] telling him I should at once report the steps I had taken to the king's government I have therefore asked him to despatch to-morrow in concert with Admiral Malcolm three French frigates, which will be entrusted with the same work and the same orders as the English frigates, and which will act towards the French merchant vessels, in the same manner as the former will towards the English merchantmen

I trust, Monsieur le Duc, that His Majesty will approve the step I have taken , as time did not permit of my waiting for instructions from Paris, I was compelled to act on my own responsibility

The Duc de Broglie to the Prince de Talleyrand.

PARIS, *October 29th*, 1832.

MON PRINCE,

You have done wonders , the treaty, as I told you, satisfied us completely We are now equally content with the steps you have taken to carry it out The only point to which we wish to draw your immediate attention to, is that the King of the Belgians should not be required to actually evacuate Venloo, until our troops have got to Antwerp It might create difficulties, cause disturbance in the Belgian Chambers, and complicate our operations It is only a matter of a day or two, and we must not for that run the risk of some gross act of folly on the part of the Belgians If the Prussians do not accept our proposal, there ought to be no difficulty in delaying for two or three days, not the undertaking to evacuate Venloo, but the *actual* evacuation of the fortress I am not sure whether in such a case, you would consider it advisable that the evacuation should take place, for to whom could the fortress be given up ? If the Prussians accept, arrangements must be made, that they should not arrive there before the 15th or 16th of November I, on my side, will use my best efforts with M de Werther

Ministerial matters here are going fairly well, at least as far as one can judge at present, when only a comparatively small number of Deputies have yet arrived If our undertaking

[1] Alexandre Louis Ducrest de Villeneuve, born in 1777, entered the navy at fourteen, and became captain in 1814 In 1830, he was made rear admiral of the fleet of Toulon He commanded the squadron sent to the Scheldt in 1832 In 1834, he was made marine prefet at Lorient He retired in 1838, and died in 1852

succeeds, as I have every hope of its doing, it will be entirely due to you. As for me, I place even a greater value on the sentiments you have expressed towards me, than on the advantages which will result therefrom to my country

ADMIRAL DE RIGNY TO THE PRINCE DE TALLEYRAND.

PARIS, *November 2nd,* 1832.

MON PRINCE,

When I sent our vessels from Cherbourg, I gave orders to Rear-Admiral Ducrest de Villeneuve, to inform you of his arrival, and also to carry out any instructions you might consider it necessary to give him

I deemed it quite in order, that such directions should come from London, without passing through Paris   Time is precious, and must not be wasted in useless circumlocution   You, mon Prince, who have in this instance utilized it so effectually, will fully agree with me.

Our dissentients are getting rather more reasonable ; nevertheless it would not be safe to say that matters will all be arranged   Dupin has arrived and saw the king yesterday   He says that he will not offer any opposition, and that he will sit neutral on the Presidential chair   Being one of the members of the commission for the address, he will have some weight   The Opposition propose to put in a word with reference to the *quasi-legitimacy* matter

We believe that we shall receive the answer from the Hague, probably *via* London, on the 4th or 5th , you might send it to us by the Calais telegraph

The *Melpomène* and the *Créole* have started for Spithead . .

THE PRINCE DE TALLEYRAND TO THE DUC DE BROGLIE

LONDON, *November 2nd,* 1832

MONSIEUR LE DUC,

I have this morning received a despatch from M le Comte de Latour Maubourg, who informs me of a difficulty in which he has been placed, by a request from General Goblet. The latter, on receiving the requisition made in consequence of the Convention of October 21st, for the surrender, by the Belgian Government, of Venloo and the territories of Limburg and Luxemburg, has demanded an official declaration, tending to guarantee, that in no case would the town of Venloo and those territories which are destined to be restored to Holland, be occupied by foreign troops before the citadel has been surrendered to the Belgians

You will have seen by the letter, a copy of which I had the honour to send you the day before yesterday, that I had authorised M de Latour Maubourg, to announce confidentially to General Goblet when sending him the requisition, that the surrender of those territories would in no case be made to the Dutch, and that we were occupied in arranging this matter here, in the way most tranquillising for Belgium.

It seems to me that this communication was more than sufficient to allay the anxieties of the Belgian Government, at a time when both France and England are so energetically supporting the interests of Belgium   I feared, and I think with reason, the indiscreet publications which the Belgian Ministry has never denied itself   The articles in the Belgian papers have already caused us too much trouble, not to put us on our guard

The official declaration demanded by General Goblet will, I feel sure, produce a very bad effect on the Cabinets   If, as M de Latour Maubourg writes me, Sir Robert Adair considered himself authorised to give this declaration, I cannot understand why the immediate publicity of all the Acts sent to the Brussels Cabinet, should not have been stopped at once

It is far more important for us just now, to reassure the Powers by our actions, than to satisfy the puerile susceptibilities of the Belgians   I think, therefore, that the declaration asked for by General Goblet, which under any circumstances would be fraught with difficulties, should be flatly refused by M de Latour Maubourg, it is in this sense that I discussed the matter with Lord Palmerston in my first interview with him, he has gone into the country until the day after to-morrow, but I shall see him as soon as he returns   .[1]

November 5th, 1832

AN hour ago I received the King of the Netherlands' reply to the communication made to him by the *Chargés d'Affaires*

---

[1] In sending this despatch, M de Talleyrand wrote to the Duc de Broglie the following private letter —I write to you to-day that you may be thoroughly aware, in your relations with General Goblet, with whom you have to deal   General Goblet is an Orangist   He does all he can to please the insurgents in Belgium by creating disturbance, in order to complicate matters so as to leave the door open to the Orangist party   I have had the opportunity of forming an opinion about him here, where his presumptuous objections never cease to cause us trouble   He plays at Brussels a similar *rôle* to that of those of our Carlists who have become republicans   In my correspondence with Sebastiani, I have many times warned him not to place any confidence in him

of France and England.[1]   I have the honour to send you a copy
herewith, although I suppose you will have received one direct
from the Hague   This answer is a refusal, but couched in
sufficiently mild terms . . .

Lord Palmerston to the Prince de Talleyrand.

Foreign Office, *November 6th*, 1832.

Mon cher Prince,

I send you *quite confidentially*, a copy of a letter I have
to-day sent to the Admiralty, as a guide to that department for
the instructions they are to give Admiral Malcolm , I have
sent a copy this evening to Granville, for communication
to your government, so that they may judge whether it
would be suitable to give similar instructions to Admiral Villeneuve.   It would, nevertheless, be as well that you should bring
these instructions confidentially to the knowledge of your
admiral, for he ought to be made aware of the orders that have
been given to his colleague

Ever yours,
PALMERSTON.

The Prince de Talleyrand to the Princess de Vaudémont

London, *November 7th*, 1832.

THE declaration of the Russians is of no consequence, except
for the chatter it occasions   The fact is, M de Lieven did not
wish to make it, and it was Matusiewicz who persuaded him
to do it.   We must not look upon this as anything   Pozzo is
made to say all sorts of things   Every one makes use of his
words to suit their own views   M de Lieven has gone so far as
to say that in the state matters are in at present, we could do
nothing more than make a convention containing final conditions,
and that the terms in which ours has been drawn up, appeared
most suitable to him   The date of my letter induces me to
hope that we shall arrive at the 15th, without striking a blow.
What will happen after that is beyond my guidance, it will be

---

[1] The Dutch Cabinet refused to submit to the injunctions of the Convention of
October 22nd   It declared that the evacuation of Belgium by its troops, before the
exchange of the ratifications of the treaty of November 15th, would be contrary to
the intention of the negotiations, and that moreover it was the absolute duty of
Holland, not to give up, by the surrender of Antwerp, the pledge which would aid
her to obtain equitable conditions of separation

D 2

for those men who conduct the war, to take all necessary precautions Politically, our affairs are on the right road ; that is all I was entrusted with, and what I have been entrusted with, I have carried out When I left Paris I was told "This is essential, else we shall not gain a majority" The thing is done , will they have a majority now ?

THE DUC DE BROGLIE TO THE PRINCE DE TALLEYRAND

PARIS, *November 8th*, 1832

MON PRINCE,

I send you two lines to say that I am not able to write to you more fully It is time for the courier to start, and I could not return sooner You will easily understand the reason, when I tell you that Madame la Duchesse de Berry was yesterday arrested at Nantes

We have spent the whole morning in concerting the necessary measures for her security This will assure us a large and certain majority Accept . .

MADAME ADELAIDE D'ORLEANS TO THE PRINCE DE TALLEYRAND

PARIS, *November 9th*, 1832

Certainly, mon cher Prince, i am *thoroughly satisfied with you*, with all you have done, and with your letter of the 1st of this month, for which I thank you with all my heart. I intended doing so yesterday, when the grand news of the arrest of the Duchesse de Berry arrived She was taken at Nantes , this is a most important matter, and I feel sure you will approve of the article in the *Moniteur* of to-day, and of the resolution taken by our Government with regard to this It seems to me that it will satisfy every one The whole thing passed off very quietly at Nantes From the previous day, periodical visits had been made to the house, warning having been given that she was there, but nothing was discovered , then the general and the prefet ordered a troop of the National Guard to surround all the entrances of a number of houses which formed a sort of island, in one of which it was thought, and with reason, that Madame de Berry was concealed Here the prefet had left a guard of gendarmes, who having lit a fire in the grate of a small room on the third floor to warm themselves, heated the slabs to such an extent, that Madame la Duchesse de Berry, who together

with M de Mesnard,[1] M de Guibourg and Mademoiselle de
Kersabiec, was hidden in a small chamber at the back, being
almost asphyxiated, could stand it no longer, and came forth and
gave herself up But for this extraordinary incident, it is probable
that she would not even now have been discovered She was at
once taken to the chateau at Nantes   That is all I know up to
now of this important event, which I hasten to communicate
to you.

Chartres and Nemours leave on Sunday for the army I hope,
and we have need of it just now, that their absence will not be for
long, and that they will soon come back to us with the grand and
good news of the surrender of Antwerp I think that the King
of Holland's reply, though it is a refusal, does not seem to me to
mean any great resistance All difficulties appear gradually to
disappear before our just, noble and grand cause, and I have
more and more the sweet and firm conviction, that our beloved
king will yet enjoy the recompense of all his troubles and
sacrifices, in seeing our beautiful France, peaceful, happy and
prosperous.

THE PRINCE DE TALLEYRAND TO THE DUC DE BROGLIE

LONDON, *November* 11th, 1832.

MONSIEUR LE DUC,

Monsieur le Baron de Zuylen, after having several times
vainly attempted to renew negotiations with Lord Palmerston,
has at last addressed himself to Lord Grey, in the hope, no
doubt, of obtaining some concessions which Lord Palmerston
had refused him He went to Lord Grey yesterday and gave
him the draft of the treaty proposed by the Berlin Cabinet,
about which I wrote to you, and the document of which I have
the honour to send you a copy [2] I also add a copy of the draft
of the treaty, which I could not procure till last night

After his conversation with M de Zuylen, Lord Grey invited
us to come to him, so that we might arrive at some understanding
with Lord Palmerston He then informed us of what I have just

[1] Louis Charles, Comte de Mesnard, born in 1769 was captain of the regiment o
Conti in 1789 He emigrated, served in Condé's army, and remained in England
until the Restoration He was afterwards made Colonel and aide-de-camp to the
Duc de Berry, then first equerry to the Duchess de Berry, and peer of France in
1823 After the Revolution of 1830, he accompanied the Duchess de Berry to
England, and Italy, and followed her to France where he was arrested, tried, and
acquitted He left France, and died in 1842

[2] See page 26, and note the reply which Lord Grey made to M de Zuylen on
the subject of this treaty The document here referred to is a Note which further
explained this reply

told you I was able at once to express my opinion on the new proposals from the Hague, and I felt obliged to say, that there was
no longer a possible basis for negotiations until after the surrender
of the citadel of Antwerp, and until the King of the Netherlands had given an undertaking to accept the treaty of November 15th, with such modifications as Belgium could agree to

Lord Grey, who is quite of my opinion, drew up a scheme
on these lines, but he said that he thought he was nevertheless
obliged to lay the matter before a Cabinet Council, and he fixed
a meeting for to-day at Lord Palmerston's after the Council   I
went there as agreed on, and he gave me the subjoined Note, which
has been approved by the Council and sent to M le Baron de
Zuylen, in reply to his communication of yesterday.

You will perceive, Monsieur le Duc, that by this Note we demand the evacuation of the citadel of Antwerp, as an indispensable
preliminary to any fresh negotiations   Lord Grey told me that
the Council did not think it advisable to adopt the second condition of the scheme arranged between us yesterday, as it allowed
no opening whatever for any future negotiations, by first imposing
the obligation on the Government of the Netherlands to accept
the treaty of November 15th, and then submitting any possible
modifications of this treaty to the wishes of Belgium alone

You will observe that Lord Grey's Note to the Baron de
Zuylen is not signed, which takes away its strictly official
character, nevertheless it appeared sufficiently important to M
de Zuylen, for he sent it at once by courier to the Hague

I have in this instance, as in all the others, found Lord Grey
and Lord Palmerston possessed of a sincerity and an uprightness
beyond all praise

THE PRINCE DE TALLEYRAND TO THE PRINCESS DE VAUDEMONT

LONDON, *November 13th*, 1832

I am looking forward to the 16th, with more pleasure than
anxiety, it will deliver us from the fatiguing uncertainty in which
we now are   M de Zuylen has injured himself greatly by his
trickery, his reservations, and I may say, by his bad faith, in a
matter which every one wished to clear up and finish   He did
not go straight, he allied himself with the Tories, in order that
the papers might say what would suit the enemies of the English
Ministry   With M Falck, everything would have been arranged
six months ago, and the King of Holland would have been in a
better position

14th November

We are approaching the moment when our troops will enter Belgium, in a few hours they will be on the march   I have done all that was necessary on my side, and trust that all has been prepared for action in Paris; no time must be lost   The shorter the expedition, the more brilliant it will be, and the less inconvenient to Europe   The English squadron is off the Dutch coast, under Admiral Malcolm   Any demonstration on the part of England is favourable to us, for it is only by our union with her that war will be avoided, no matter what the French papers may say   Our Convention with England is too much like an offensive and defensive treaty, not to cool the the most zealous partisans of war   Adieu, it is most necessary that I should be kept *au courant*, from day to day, of the march of our army and the movements of the Prussian troops, of which mention is made in the papers   [1]

THE PRINCE DE TALLEYRAND TO THE DUC DE BROGLIE

LONDON, *November 16th*, 1832

MONSIEUR LE DUC,

We are impatiently awaiting news of the French army, whose entry into Belgium, it was said, would take place this morning   It is in this direction that we must in future turn our attention, and I beg you to keep me most fully posted as to whatever of interest may occur, there is no doubt that many persons will endeavour to circulate all kinds of false reports here about our army, and it is very important that I should always be in a position to refute them; I should even wish, if it is possible, to be informed direct by the telegraph from Lille to Calais   Those who are best disposed towards us express great anxiety, they fear that we have not sufficient troops on our northern frontier, and that this will furnish the Prince of Orange with an opportunity to throw himself into the centre of Belgium.   I try to allay their fears, but it is necessary that I should be able to contradict the false reports which will serve as a foundation for them   . .

THE DUC DE BROGLIE TO THE PRINCE DE TALLEYRAND

PARIS, *November 19th*, 1832

MON PRINCE,

I have barely time to send you a few lines   The outrage of this morning adds to the anxieties of this day   The

---

[1] Upon the entry of the French troops into Belgium, the Prussians had concentrated an army of observation on the Meuse, but did not make any offensive movement

indignation in the Chambers and in the whole of Paris is very great Probably this may help the good cause ; I say probably, for we are terribly changeable here The king, as he always is on these occasions, was very calm, very self-possessed, and displayed great courage He did not wish that the news of the occurrence should reach the Chamber ere his arrival, and no one would have suspected it from the tranquillity of his voice and face. The effect of his speech was excellent , I hope you will approve of its general tone, its firmness, and its reticence I had added a final paragraph respecting the negotiations that are being carried on in England, with regard to postal arrangements, wines, books, &c, but at the last reading, this paragraph was eliminated as adding to the length of the speech and accentuating it , I will however take care to speak of it in the discussion

Adieu, mon Prince, the assassin has not yet been discovered. [1]

MADAME ADELAIDE D'ORLEANS TO THE PRINCE DE TALLEYRAND.

TUILERIES, *Monday, November 19th,* 1832

For what acts of mercy we have to thank Providence, mon cher Prince! A horrible outrage has just failed, thanks to Heaven! A monster fired a pistol at our dearly beloved king, as he was riding across the *Pont Royal* on his way to the Chamber He behaved splendidly and was perfectly calm, continuing his route as if nothing had happened ; he did not even wish it to be mentioned in the Chamber, and delivered his speech in a calm and unmoved voice It was admirably received Unfortunately the monster has not yet been arrested. As soon as the Chambers were informed of this horrible outrage, both the Peers and Deputies arrived here simultaneously , La Fayette and Dupont de l'Eure alone were missing, but perhaps they will still come I do not know whether you will be able to read this, mon cher Prince, but you will quite understand how my hand shakes , I wanted, however, to write to you at once by special messenger

THE DUC DE BROGLIE TO THE PRINCE DE TALLEYRAND.

PARIS, *November 22nd,* 1832

MON PRINCE,

Lord Granville has communicated to me Lord Palmerston's letter, respecting all the tittle-tattle of the Belgian Govern-

[1] The assassin was never discovered, which caused the Opposition to declare that the outrage had only been a trick of the police A man named Bergeron was finally arrested, but he was acquitted

ment   Lord Palmerston attaches more importance to it than I do.   As the Belgians made use of his name in their dispute with us respecting the indemnity in M Pescatore's [1] affair and various other points, I was very glad to know what truth there really was in their proposals   Otherwise all these little bickerings are not worth the trouble of noticing

To-day General Chassé will be summoned to surrender   Will he defend himself?   We shall know this very soon, but it is impossible to conjecture   You have no need to remind me of the resolution to evacuate Belgium after the taking of the citadel, and of keeping to the letter, the engagement entered into on the 22nd October.   I would not continue in office half an hour, if there could be any doubt about this

Lord Lansdowne will tell you that ministerial affairs are progressing favourably here, and that the majority seem quite of one mind   Our friends have no doubt as to our success   I am not so confident. . . .

THE PRINCE DE TALLEYRAND TO THE DUC DE BROGLIE.

LONDON, *November 26th,* 1832

MONSIEUR LE DUC,

I may tell you that our position here has greatly improved within the last few days   The despatches that have arrived from Vienna and Berlin show a decided modification in the feelings that were noticeable during the first state of excitement   The Austrian and Prussian Ministers in London have even gone so far as to evince the desire that the measures adopted by France and England to overcome the obstinacy of the King of the Netherlands may prove successful

The more one thinks over it, the more one feels convinced, that the various Continental Cabinets will try and break up the union between France and England , but one also feels, that they will have to resign themselves to this union and its results, as long as they have to recognize such evident symptoms of its duration . . .

November 29th, 1832

I am very grieved to see, by the information you have kindly sent me, that fresh delays have occurred in the siege operations against the citadel of Antwerp   The anxiety here

---

[1] M Pescatore was a member of the civil government of Luxemburg, who had been arrested in October 1831, by the Belgian gendarmerie in reprisal for the arrest of M Thorn   The two prisoners were exchanged in the end of 1832

increases each day, and the English Cabinet has even gone so far as to say, that they lay as much stress on the speedy reduction of that citadel as the new French Cabinet could have done on the conclusion of the Convention of October 22nd This language shows the importance of this question to the Government, it is by no means exaggerated, and I fully share this view

I am not at all surprised at the neglect and carelessness of the Belgians, of which you complain One must be prepared for all sorts of hindrances from them, and I think that our general method of dealing with them is not suitable to so new and so self-conceited a Government

The delays respecting the Antwerp expedition, show us more than ever, how necessary it is not to hurry anything in our negotiations with the Prussian Cabinet

Time is a great teacher and solves many difficulties for us You will no doubt think that it is necessary to allow oneself great latitude when one is committed to the chances of a siege, and I advise you not to settle anything with Berlin, before you are sure of the result at Antwerp You will perceive that if you had kept to the 5th December (the date last fixed by you for the surrender of Venloo to the Prussians) you would now be placed in a very difficult position As the negotiation is being carried on by M Bresson with Lord Minto's help, there ought to be no difficulty in retarding it, by expressing the need of joint instructions from the Paris and London Cabinets

I have just communicated to Lord Palmerston your despatch No 101, relative to the expenses of our expedition into Belgium which you consider you ought to demand from the Belgian Government I read him the whole of it. After listening to it with great attention, Lord Palmerston replied that it did not alter his opinion in any way, because all the reasons given by the King's Council remained in their entirety I tried in vain to give a fresh turn to the arguments with which your despatch had furnished me, but I must tell you candidly, that I was unable to modify this opinion, which appeared to me to be irrevocably fixed

I, thereupon, at once spoke to Lord Palmerston respecting the mission which England is said to have entrusted to an agent of the Ottoman Porte He replied, that he had certainly been informed by a letter from Constantinople of the 26th October, of the Sultan's resolution to send Namick Pasha, Colonel of the Guards, to England; that this resolution had not received the assent of the Divan, which had however consented to Namick Pasha's proceeding *via* Paris; that moreover, although it was well known that Namick's mission related to the war which was going on between the Porte and the Pasha of Egypt, the exact nature of the communications he was bringing to the English Government was not known,[1] but it was supposed that the Porte only intended thereby to give sufficient *éclat* to this mission in order to disquiet the Pasha of Egypt, who could not fail to hear of it Lord Palmerston also assured me, that Sir Stratford Canning[2] had never made any suggestion that might be interpreted as an offer of actual assistance on the part of England, and that you were quite right in thinking, that he had only confined himself to such expressions' of goodwill as it is customary to make use of on such occasions . . .

THE DUC DE BROGLIE TO THE PRINCE DE TALLEYRAND.

PARIS, *November 27th*, 1832

MON PRINCE,

The answer which I send you is an official one. I fancy that Lord Palmerston has adopted this course so as to be able to answer any questions in Parliament It is for this same cause that I am so importunate

You know that the reason which induced us to ask for re-imbursement from Belgium for our extraordinary expenditure, was due to the positive refusal of the Chamber of Deputies last year, to grant us the expenses of our Belgian expedition in 1831. We should, therefore, be without an answer, if we could not show publicly that we had used every effort to protect the interests of the Treasury However, we have but little hope of being enriched by what we shall get for it

Nevertheless, the fact is, our position is not the same as that of England She furnishes a squadron for the common cause , we do the same She wants nothing from Belgium , nor do we for that matter. But, in addition, we undertake an expedition on land, infinitely more costly, which we carry out at our expense alone.

Lord Palmerston thinks that it is solely in European interest that we are acting. I do not think so The best proof that it is at the same time in purely Belgian interest is, that we have only sent our troops at the express request of Belgium If we did not take Antwerp, the Belgian army would have to take it , and what we now ask of her is much less than it would have cost

---

[1] The mission of Namick Pasha See pages 67 and 75

[2] Sir Stratford Canning, at one time English Ambassador at the Porte, had been sent to Constantinople in November 1831, on a special mission He was to ask for an extension of frontier, in favour of Greece

her to do this   It is true Belgium does not pay for a single
soldier less, but she does not pay for all the actual expenses of
the siege, which we conduct at our expense

Lord Palmerston adds, that we ourselves desired, in the interests of the formation or continuance of the Ministry, that
this expedition should take place   This however is quite outside
the circle of general discussion   It is a discussion on what takes
place in the lobbies   It is a reason that we cannot urge publicly
If we desire thus to take into consideration the secret causes of
things, we might then say, that the dread of Belgian absurdities,
the fear of seeing them organise an expedition against Holland, the
necessity of extricating them from their present position, are
among the various reasons which have made us wish to undertake
the expedition against Antwerp   Without doubt, the provocations
of the Belgians and their effect on public opinion in France,
have more than half contributed towards rendering this expedition inevitable

Besides, I say again, one must not take things for more than
they are worth   the object of our request is to cover our
responsibility   I believe that Lord Palmerston's despatch is
precisely of the same nature, and I beg you to assure him that I
have not the slightest wish to see anything else in it

Our expedition does not progress as quickly as I could have
wished   The whole army arrived at the date fixed, but the
transport of the siege artillery and ammunition has been and
is still greatly delayed   Marshal Gérard does not wish to issue
his summons, until he is in a position to answer a refusal with a
fierce fire   I am assured that the summons will be made to-day,
but I still fear delays .   .

THE PRINCE DE TALLEYRAND TO THE DUC DE BROGLIE

LONDON, *November* 30th, 1832

MONSIEUR LE DUC,

M le Marquis de Palmella arrived in London yesterday, charged with a mission from Dom Pedro to the English
Government, he left Oporto on the 22nd of this month   It
appears that this city is beginning to feel the necessity of putting
an end to the state of affairs which is now laying Portugal waste,
the Marquis de Palmella is therefore to ask the English Cabinet [1]
for an armistice   He spoke to me on this subject.   Such

[1] It will be remembered that Dom Pedro had landed on the island of Terceira on
the 3rd March, 1832   On the 8th July, he entered Oporto, which became the centre
of the Constitutional Government, while Dom Miguel maintained an absolute
government at Lisbon   A fierce struggle was carried on between the two brothers

an armistice as he asks for would have no weight unless it is made jointly with France and England

Having obtained this armistice, they would then try to effect a mediation in which the Powers most interested, *i e* Spain, England, and France, should take part, and it is more than probable that if these three Powers agree as to what is required to re-establish order in Portugal, the country would insist on the two princes of the House of Braganza adopting the proposals made to them

I will keep you posted as regards M. de Palmella's actions with respect to the English Government, and as to the resolutions which that Government may be disposed to adopt   Have the goodness to inform me what I should say, if M. de Palmella's proposals are accepted here. . .

December 1st

MON CHER DUC,

We have got no further   this state of affairs becomes more and more unpleasant for the English Cabinet, and more awkward for me   I fear that this embarrassment will be still further increased by Berlin, we carried the negotiation about Venloo thither, hoping that the long distances and the hesitations of M Ancillon would have given us time to take Antwerp and thus sever the greatest difficulty of all   The time you gave me as being required for the movements of our army, has unfortunately not proved sufficient, and we are now on the eve of seeing a Convention signed at Berlin, before anything has been effected at Antwerp   The foolish bragging of the Belgians with their threat of not handing Venloo over to the Prussians until after Antwerp has been taken, may complicate everything in a manner truly fatal to the peace of Europe

What ought to be done now ?   Nothing—unless it be to obtain fresh delays, spin out all the details of the negotiations, hasten everything connected with the army, and above all, put down with a strong hand the meddlesome spirit and ridiculous pretensions of the Belgians   I have seen it proved here, where, so far from encouraging them, they are treated with a degree of haughtiness, which it would be well if they experienced from us

I therefore entreat you, mon cher Duc, only to send M Bresson very vague instructions, and give him to understand that what we desire least is a speedy conclusion   Moreover, I also think, what I neither could or would point out in my despatch, that the *dénoûment* between Belgium and Holland would be far more easily arranged, if we could feel assured of Prussia's friendly neutrality, without calling upon her to take a more active part I believe this is not impossible, if we can yet make ourselves masters of Antwerp without much delay, and if they will only keep on negotiating matters in Berlin without bringing them to a conclusion

I think I have found a combination on those grounds which will not be without value, but I must first mature it before submitting it to you I therefore confine myself for the present to begging you to leave all negotiations open, and not to conclude any

We must not forget that England evinced some regret that the negotiations with Prussia had been carried on in Berlin All the greater reason that M Bresson should do nothing without Lord Minto's most complete co-operation But, as I said before, what is most required is, that he should do *nothing* there just now, and that he must be most cautious in what he says ..

MADAME ADÉLAIDE D'ORLÉANS TO THE PRINCE DE TALLEYRAND

TUILERIES, *December 2nd*, 1832

MON CHER PRINCE,

I hasten to give you news of our army, which has just come to hand I send you a copy of what has been sent me, dated four o'clock in the afternoon, November 30th "We opened the first trench before the citadel yesterday, M le Duc d'Orléans was in command, and on this first occasion of his being under fire and in actual warfare, the Prince Royal displayed a great deal of coolness, foresight, and zeal in all his preparations, he constantly passed along the line of working parties, visited his main guards and looked after his reserves did in fact what an experienced soldier would have done Thanks to a very dark and wet night, we were enabled to hide this delicate operation from the enemy, and it was not till daylight that they found us covered by a parallel of two thousand seven hundred fathoms, and sheltered from his fire I think, therefore, that it was only in order to give pleasure to M le Duc d'Orléans, that he commenced about mid-day to send a few shells and some shot The siege has advanced so rapidly within these few hours, that it is hoped the king will very shortly receive the keys of the citadel "

This is what we earnestly desire for every one's sake, mon cher Prince, for you can well imagine how anxious we are Marshal Gérard, who was in the trench with Chartres, wrote to the king,

that no one could have shown more coolness or greater bravery
The marshal's aide-de-camp, who brought the despatches,
says that when the first bullet passed over Chartres' head he
leapt for joy, and all the soldiers began to dance

We still do not know whether the perpetrator of that
horrible outrage of the 19th November, has been discovered ,
the police hope they are on the track   One thing is certain,
however, this outrage has made it more universally and warmly
evident than ever, that France feels she possesses a rare treasure
in her king, and that she would be exposed to innumerable
dangers were he not there   Everything connects itself with
him and the Constitutional Monarchy ; it is this that gives us
so large a majority in the Chamber, which is turning out
excellently, and affords us every assurance of a happy session
What we now want is to finish this Antwerp business , then we
shall be all right. Truly, the Belgians ought to be very
grateful, happy, and satisfied , but they are not. I must candidly
tell you, that I am very angry at their folly and their in-
gratitude. Why, they are actually grumbling now at General
Schramm's[1] division, which, after the anxiety expressed by the
English Government, that we had not sufficient troops in
Belgium, the king sent thither   It really seems to me, that the
English Government ought to make them feel how foolish they
are, and what harm they do to themselves by it . . .

THE DUC DE BROGLIE TO THE PRINCE DE TALLEYRAND

PARIS, *December 6th,* 1832

MON PRINCE,

At last I am enabled to send you some news of the
siege, which may and ought to satisfy the English Ministry
The mistake has not been in failing to keep our promise, but in
not having allowed sufficient time for preparation during this
terrible season of the year   The army has made superhuman
efforts , the placing of the last battery, carried out in the open
under the very glacis of the citadel, is, they say, one of the
most daring enterprises that has ever been executed. It is
thought that in eight, or at the latest ten days, and probably
much sooner, the citadel will be taken   I hope the news will
arrive in the midst of the English elections

[1] Jean Paul Adam, Comte Schramm, born in 1789, entered the service in 1803,
and was made Brigadier General in 1813   He lived in retirement during the
Restoration, took part in the expedition to Antwerp, and became General of
Division, and a Peer of France in 1839   He was War Minister in 1850, and created
a Senator in 1852   He died in 1883

You will see by my despatch of to-day, that I have been, and had cause to be, greatly surprised to find the affair of Venloo suddenly terminated by an offer to give this place and Limburg back to Holland Anyhow, I cannot understand the course of this business It went to Berlin in a Note from you and Lord Palmerston Sent back to London, it was returned to Berlin, Lord Palmerston making it rather a grievance, as you yourself remarked to me, that it was done without his consent ; and now the matter is wound up by an offer, of which neither you nor I are cognizant, and of which I only know the conditions through letters from Lord Palmerston to Lord Granville [1] I greatly fear that this offer will plunge us into endless difficulties when it comes to the question of carrying it out, and place us, meanwhile, I feel sure, as regards Prussia, in an uncertain and changeable light which vexes me extremely

The king is greatly opposed to this offer, and I think, on more accounts than one, that he is right

I had a long talk this morning with M d'Offalia,[2] who is leaving his post as Spanish Ambassador here, to return to Madrid, where he will be Minister of the Interior The following is what he stated after touching on divers other matters.

If the English Government thinks it has cause of complaint on account of the shots that were fired at one of its vessels at the mouth of the Douro, the Spanish Government will be quite willing to give it satisfaction But if the English Government makes use of this to break up the neutrality and declare itself in favour of Dom Pedro, the Spanish Government will at once send an army into Portugal

I interrupted M d'Offalia, and asked him in what capacity he spoke to me, was it merely an ordinary conversation, or was it a proposal he was making me in the name of his Government He said he was not speaking to me as an ambassador, as he no longer considered himself as such, but that he was very glad to be able to tell me in the course of conversation, that such was the opinion of his Government, and that he would not become the King of Spain's Minister except under that condition

I then asked him what use he wished me to make of his conversation, and whether he wished me to communicate it to the

---

[1] See page 13
[2] D Narcisco de Heredia, Comte d'Offalia, a Spanish statesman, born in 1777, ... attached to Embassy in Washington in 1800 He retired into private life during ... In 1823 he was made Minister of Justice, then envoy ... to London in 1827, and ambassador at Paris in 1828 He was Minister of the Interior in the Zea Bermudez Cabinet, in 1832 In 1837, he became head of the Cabinet and Minister of Foreign Affairs He retired in 1838, and died in 1843

English Ambassador He informed me that such was his wish and entered at some length into this subject After having listened to him for some time, I told him, that as all this was a mere conversation and without any official character, I would carry it on in the same tone, and would ask him a question which had just struck me, disavowing any inference he might draw therefrom, beyond that of my own personal satisfaction to learn his views on an eventuality

"Supposing," I said to him, "that the cause of Dona Maria could be separated from that of the Constitution, and it chanced that there was a question of placing her on the throne, putting the Constitution on one side, would you then still be disposed to interfere by force of arms in Dom Miguel's favour?"

He plainly told me, "No," it was the Constitution on which Spain laid such great stress, and that the present Government could not be interfered with without collapsing

I did not push the conversation any further, and I have told Lord Granville about it I believe you will be equally glad to know of this conversation However, I foresee many obstacles and difficulties without number, to the project you mentioned to me[1] I will wait, if necessary, before speaking about it to his friends, until England makes us some definite proposals.

Adieu, mon Prince, get well quickly, I shall look forward to hearing from you with the utmost impatience . . .

The Prince de Talleyrand to the Duc de Broglie.

LONDON, *December* 10*th*, 1832.

MONSIEUR LE DUC,

I have received the despatch you did me the honour to write on the 6th of this month, and it was with some surprise that I read the information it contained I at once communicated it to Lord Palmerston

It would be very easy, in bringing forward all the contradictions which presented themselves with regard to the manner in which the affair of Venloo was conducted, to show many causes for explanation and recrimination But this would produce no result, and might even compromise the issue of the very serious questions with which we are now dealing and which must go before everything, I have therefore thought it better to cut short all these explanations

Moreover, we need hardly be surprised that a negotia-

---

[1] The project of mediation about which M de Talleyrand wrote to the Duc de Broglie in his letter of the 30th November (*See* page 44)

tion which has successively been carried on in Paris, London, and Berlin should have occasioned some misunderstandings, especially when the principal object was to obtain delays   The want of proper instructions, the necessity of the desire to do without them, words lightly spoken or wrongly interpreted, and a thousand other circumstances, have no doubt contributed to create the greater part of the difficulties with which we have just had to contend

You must not however imagine, M le Duc, that I have neglected to express my surprise to Lord Palmerston, with all the seriousness which your letter demanded   I was personally entitled to do so, since I had read the despatch, No 37, which I had the honour to send you on the 6th , he had thoroughly approved it, and I had even at his request slightly altered a phrase of no importance   He never said a word to me then, as to the instructions he deemed it necessary to send to Lord Minto

I recalled this circumstance to him with sufficient warmth for him to say, that if he had done wrong in acting thus, he had himself to blame for what had passed with regard to the summons made by Marshal Gérard, in the name of the French and English Governments , that his sovereign, on that occasion, had been made to say things without his having been previously consulted, and that the king had shown the greatest displeasure thereat

I repeat again, M le Duc, that I could no doubt have still further urged this matter on Lord Palmerston, without any real result accruing therefrom to the interests of the king's government   I therefore deemed it more prudent to end my interview without any bitterness   I hope you will share my opinion, and that you will consider it better to let all the wrong that may be deemed to have been done involuntarily, sink into oblivion   It will be a lesson for the future, by which we shall do well to profit, to confine ourselves always to official conduct and communications   I have therefore requested Lord Palmerston to inform you through Lord Granville, with regard to the new arrangement which we have discussed, an account of which I shall have the honour to send you   Before doing so, however, it is necessary I should answer another question contained in your despatch

You ask me to let you know, what reasons I had for believing in the possibility of reassembling the Conference after the taking of the citadel of Antwerp   I always thought, and so did Lord Palmerston, that this fact once accomplished, we should find the plenipotentiaries of the other three Powers favourably disposed to resume the negotiations which were interrupted by the use of coercive measures against Holland ; this would have been a grand calmative for the tranquilization of Europe Our hopes with regard to this seemed perfectly justified, until the arrival of a courier the day before yesterday, with despatches from St Petersburg for M de Lieven and M Matusiewicz In these despatches, the emperor expressed great satisfaction at their conduct when the Convention of October 22nd had been communicated to them, and they were furthur informed that the powers with which they had been entrusted to act at the Conference, and which they had declared to Lord Palmerston and me were only suspended, were withdrawn. This upset the design we had formed, of assembling the Conference immediately after the taking of the citadel of Antweip

Under these circumstances, it is a matter of the utmost importance, that England and France should arrange what course they would deem it most suitable to adopt, if they were called upon to put an end to the Hollando-Belgian question without the aid of the other three Powers This is the aim of the new project to which I wish now to draw all your attention :

France and England having united in order to overcome the obstinacy of the King of the Netherlands, believe that it is their duty, as the Conference no longer exists, to propose for the acceptance of the Cabinet of the Hague, a treaty agreed to by Belgium, containing the following conditions —

1 The surrender to the King of the Netherlands of those territories which are to be his ,

2 The surrender, on the part of that sovereign, of the Forts of Lillo and Liefkenshok, which are dependent on Antwerp ,

3 The recognition by Holland of the free navigation of the Scheldt, in consideration of the dues of one florin per ton ;

4 Determining the right of establishing buoys and pilotage in the intermediary waters ,

5 The opening of the Meuse ,

6 The opening of two routes for the commercial intercourse of Belgium with Germany ,

7. A general amnesty for all political offences ,

8 An act by which all the former subjects of the King of the Netherlands shall be released from their oath of allegiance

This treaty entered into between France and England shall be sent to the Hague by the French and English plenipotentiaries I pray you, Monsieur le Duc, to kindly transmit me your orders respecting this

The English Cabinet has just ordered Sir Stratford Canning to proceed to Madrid, there to carry out the mediation between the two princes of the House of Braganza, of which I have already informed you. He will pass through Paris, where he will remain several days, in order to come to some understanding with you. He is to give you full particulars as to the object of his mission. You will then be able to send M. de Rayneval whatever instructions you deem most suitable.

THE COMTE DE LATOUR MAUBOURG TO THE PRINCE DE TALLEYRAND

BRUSSELS, *December* 18th, 1832

PRINCE,

Just as the courier was about to start and my packet was already closed, I received news from Antwerp, stating that in consequence of various delays occasioned by the heavy rains of the last few days we shall not be able to commence making a breach until the day after to-morrow. I must therefore, in this respect, alter the information I had the honour to send you in my despatch of this morning.

Marshal Gérard is greatly hurt at certain articles in some of the English papers, in which it is said that our soldiers can only be got to work in the trenches by means of brandy and ill-treatment on the part of the officers. He hopes that these falsehoods will be contradicted by the Embassy in London. I all the more gladly hasten to inform you of his wishes with respect to this, as I know that Colonel Caradoc (the English military commissioner at the French headquarters) is writing in the same sense to Lord Palmerston.

THE BARON DURANT DE MAREUIL TO THE PRINCE DE TALLEYRAND

PARIS *December* 15th, 1832

I hardly know how to inform you, mon Prince, of what has just happened to me.

Ever since my return here from London, I have not ceased to ask the Ministry for my last instructions for Berlin. First I was told, that I had better await the opening of the Chambers, the discussion over the speeches, and the first acts of the two Assemblies. Everything going on satisfactorily, I at last asked officially for my credentials, my instructions, and my passports, when yesterday M. le Duc de Broglie informed me, that under present circumstances, M. Bresson is the man who is required at Berlin, and that he cannot consent to his being removed. There is however more than this, for I was made to understand, that despite my representations, despite the appeal I made to all the reasons which could render this proceeding especially painful to me, it is more than probable that M Bresson will ere long be definitely appointed to the mission at Berlin

It is true, some very fine speeches accompanied the blow thus dealt me, my services were fully recognized, ample justice was done to my ability, and the first vacant Embassy was promised me, though just at present they could only offer me Florence But I ask to remain where I am, and as I am, until they consider it proper to send me to Berlin It is very probable that I shall not obtain this I have experienced many a painful moment in my political career, but this is the worst The change of fortune which I owed to your influence, and which, in making me share your labours, was of such great value to me, did not prepare me for this disgrace .

I pray you to give me your interest and your advice Pardon me for intruding this personal matter upon the great questions that occupy you . . .

THE PRINCE DE TALLEYRAND TO THE PRINCESS DE VAUDÉMONT

LONDON, *December* 20th, 1832.

I shall write first to Durant and then to his minister It is quite out of the question not giving him something better than Florence If there is a change in the Embassies, and if Barante[1] is sent to a larger Embassy than Turin, it would only be natural, and according to the custom of the Tuileries, to appoint M de Rumigny to Turin, and give Switzerland to M. Durant, That is the best thing to do You and I *are* always sincere and loyal in all our relations I take care to see that we are not sometimes rather deceived

December 21st

I am writing to Durant to-day I say *to you*, that what they are doing is very unfair, it lowers the Government I shall insist on their giving him Turin, if it becomes vacant But what good will my insisting do? I have done all that was

[1] Amable Guillaume-Prosper Brugière, Baron Barante, born at Riom in 1782, Auditor to the State Council in 1806, Sub-Préfet, then Préfet He tendered his submission during the Hundred Days, became then State Councillor, then Deputy and a Peer of France (1819) After the July revolution, he was appointed Ambassador at Turin, and subsequently at St Petersburg, where he remained till 1848 He died in 1866

necessary, they do not require me any more, and men are only valued by the use they are

Marshal Gerard complains that the English papers find fault with the slowness of the siege, and it is said that this greatly discourages the soldiers. Surely, although some papers say this, others say the contrary, therefore it cannot greatly influence general opinion. The Tory papers speak ill of the expedition, the Whig and Radical papers speak well of it, one must put up with that. The king, the queen, and all the English ministers have to submit to it.

December 25th

Antwerp is taken!!!![1] The garrison have been made prisoners of war until the forts are reduced, as I am informed by telegraph. So our princes are out of all danger. I am delighted. It has been a real anxiety to me for the last month. I have lived almost entirely by myself, for when one is anxious and troubled, one is ill at ease with strangers.

You have not told me why Pozzo is coming here. I believe, it is (but this is for your ear alone) that, as senior of the *corps diplomatique*, he would have had to make the speech on New Year's day, and this would have embarrassed him. This is what I think, and I believe I am right. I always tell you all that comes into my head, no matter whether it be sense or folly.

My work is not ended yet, for we must endeavour to make the King of Holland do something, and you know whether that is easy or not. Meanwhile, I am going to dine to-morrow with Namick Pasha and some other Turks. The pasha has a fine face, and speaks French very well; he even writes it. His dress is somewhat European, though you can tell the Turk by his head.

THE PRINCE DE TALLEYRAND TO THE DUC DE BROGLIE.

LONDON, *December 26th*, 1832

MONSIEUR LE DUC,

The news of the reduction of the citadel of Antwerp has been received in London as a fresh pledge of the maintenance of peace, and one may say, that looking at it in that light, the satisfaction is general. Thanks to the kindness of M. le Préfet du Nord, I was the first to hear of the capitulation, and I made good use of this information by contradicting the erroneous statements of several papers.

---

[1] General Chassé capitulated on the 23rd December, twenty-five days from the opening of the trenches and after nineteen days of bombardment.

THE DUC DE BROGLIE TO THE PRINCE DE TALLEYRAND.

PARIS, *December 24th,* 1832

MON PRINCE,

The end has arrived   You will have heard of it at the same time as we did   We have not yet received any details   The telegraphic despatch was interrupted by bad weather   The future is now in your hands, and this makes me feel tranquil   I am impatiently waiting to hear your news.   Here matters are going on very well . . .

THE BARON DURANT DE MAREUIL TO THE PRINCE DE TALLEYRAND

PARIS, *December 25th,* 1832

I hope this letter, which I am sending by special courier, will arrive before my preceding one, as I wish to tell you that at last they have dealt fairly with me.   I am going as ambassador to Naples   I told you why I should have preferred being ambassador at Berlin , but there is more than one compensation in this appointment, and my gratitude is divided between the king, the minister, and you, as I am sure that you have powerfully contributed to gain me such prompt and full justice   I was all but forgetting to rejoice with you at the result of Antwerp   Here it has made a great and very good effect, and will no doubt have done the same in London. .

LORD GREY TO THE PRINCE DE TALLEYRAND

EAST SHEEN, *December 30th,* 1832

DEAR PRINCE TALLEYRAND,

A thousand thanks for your welcome letter.   The news it contained was nothing less than I expected from the wise policy and the good faith of the French Government. The decision to send back the Dutch garrison unconditionally, is even better than releasing them on parole

Believe me yours always

The citadel of Antwerp was taken   The whole of this business was satisfactorily ended, and every one was rejoicing at this happy termination, when a heavy blow fell upon me that caused me the deepest grief   The Princess de Vaudémont,

after an illness of only a few days, died on the night of the 31st
December, 1832. I thus lost a friend whom I had known for
fifty years. I met her first at her mother-in-law's, Madame
la Comtesse de Brionne, where I spent the happiest years of
my youth; our relations never varied, and I cannot even now
reconcile myself to the loss of so dear and faithful a friend.
She even rendered me a service after her death, for her heirs
sent me back the greater part of the letters I had written
to her; from these, as has been seen, I have been able to
extract many of the details which have served to connect my
memoirs, and which without this aid, would probably have
escaped my memory. I shall therefore be pardoned, if I here
insert a few of the many testimonies to her noble character by
those who, more fortunate than myself, were able to be with her
at the last.

BARON PASQUIER TO THE PRINCE DE TALLEYRAND

PARIS, *January 2nd,* 1833

MON PRINCE,

The misfortune that has just befallen us, makes me feel
the need of joining my sympathy with yours, being fully assured
that no one felt deeper or more profound affection than yourself.

You will, of course, have been informed of Madame de
Vaudémont's illness, the progress of which was so rapid, that
the news of her death reached us almost at the same time . . .

Those who had the good fortune to be numbered among
her friends, may well confess that they have suffered the greatest
possible loss they could experience. Her praise can be
summed up in a few words. She had a great many friends
but she never forsook one, and never lost one through any
fault of her own. I know how greatly you were attached to
her, and fully understand the terrible loss you have sustained.

MADAME ADELAIDE D'ORLÉANS TO THE PRINCE DE TALLEYRAND

THUILERIES, *January 6th,* 1833

The misfortune which I had foreseen only too well, and
which I dreaded for ourselves, and above all for you, mon cher

Prince, has very speedily followed the letter I wrote to you I am most anxious to hear from you after this cruel blow, and I again entreat you to write to me You are constantly in our thoughts, and we deeply and sorrowfully feel the loss of our beloved princess, from whom I received so many proofs of real friendship, and who so warmly identified herself with our cause and our interests I wish with all my heart that I could in any way soften the great grief you must experience, and which I share to the depths of my soul . .

I will now again take up my narrative, which was interrupted by this sorrowful incident

I have already given extracts from the letters which led up to the taking of Antwerp, not wishing to interrupt the recital of that event , but before arriving at this result, it may well be supposed that we had to think over the consequences which might result therefrom, and above all what measures the French and English Governments would have to adopt This will necessitate my going back a little

It will have been seen from my despatch of 10th December, 1832, that ever since that date, both Lord Palmerston and I, had thought over what steps it would be necessary for us to take when the citadel of Antwerp had surrendered

The Duc de Broglie, after the communications I had had with him on this subject, sent me an admirable memorandum containing a complete *résumé* of the question I will confine myself here to enumerating its conclusions

" As soon as the citadel of Antwerp is taken, the French army will retire ,
' The embargo will continue ,
" The fleets will remain united, and will not leave the Downs until they receive the order to do so from both Governments
" The French and English Cabinets will draw up the draft of a treaty on the following bases —

" 1 The surrender to the King of the Netherlands of those territories which are to belong to him
" 2 The surrender by this sovereign of the forts of Lille and of Liefkenshok, dependent upon Antwerp, if they have not already fallen into the hands of the French, together with the citadel ,

"3 The recognition by Holland of the free navigation of the Scheldt, in consideration of a due of one florin per ton ;

"4 The determination of the right to establish buoys and pilotage on the Scheldt and the intermediary waters ;

"5 The opening of the Meuse ;

"6 The opening of two routes for the commercial intercourse of Belgium with Germany ;

"7 A general amnesty for all political offences ;

"8 An act by which, all the former subjects of the King of the Netherlands shall be released from their oath of allegiance.

'This treaty will be arranged with Belgium, and will then be sent on to the Hague by the English and French *Chargés d'Affaires* at Brussels

'An understanding can be come to beforehand with the Vienna and Berlin Cabinets, so that they may second the offer made by France and England to the King of the Netherlands

"The treaty presented to the King of the Netherlands must be accepted by him, purely and simply, without any discussion

' If it is accepted, the coercive measures will cease at once and the *embargo* will be removed ;

" If it is refused, a provisional occupation by the Prussians of Venloo and Luxemburg will be arranged

' After these preliminaries have been settled, the Conference will assemble to modify the treaty of 15th November, in concert with Holland and Belgium (if Holland shows a conciliatory spirit), or to find a solution of the Belgian question independent of the wishes of the King of the Netherlands

" This solution would be —

' 1 To determine a *statu quo*, such as would quickly compel the King of the Netherlands to accept the treaty ;

"2 To place the territory of Belgium under the guarantee of Europe, and assure her sufficient aid, so that her disarmament could be insisted upon, and yet leave her under no fear of an invasion "

I could not communicate this project to Lord Palmerston at once, as he was out of town on account of his election, rendered necessary by the dissolution of Parliament. He had told me he would not be back before the 22nd of December. I saw him the next day, and the following letter gives an account of our interview

THE PRINCE DE TALLEYRAND TO THE DUC DE BROGLIE

LONDON, *December* 24th, 1832

MONSIEUR LE DUC,

  I only succeeded last night in seeing Lord Palmerston, and in speaking to him respecting the course which the king's government proposes to follow as soon as the citadel of Antwerp shall have fallen into our hands   Before giving him the statement of which I had the honour to send you a copy, I read it out to him, so as to be able to discuss successively in the course of conversation the different questions contained in it

  In reading this statement, M le Duc, you will see that I have reproduced, almost word for word, the various considerations which you have turned to such good account in the last letters which I have had the honour to receive from you

  Our proposal has been very well received by Lord Palmerston ; he recognizes the correctness of the facts contained in the statement, and he thinks the measures indicated are very suitable and might prove very useful   He thanked me for having shown him this document, and promised me that he would very shortly submit it to a Cabinet Council, at which he intended to support it   I cannot tell you exactly on what day this will take place, as several of the ministers have not yet returned to London   The Lord Chancellor, the Marquis of Lansdowne, and some others are still away

  I also spoke to Lord Palmerston about the anxiety that might be felt respecting the intention, announced by the King of the Netherlands, to obstruct the navigation of the Scheldt, and I begged him to let me know what line he thought the British Government would consider it ought to take, if this design was realized   He replied, that the question might resolve itself in two ways, according to the measures taken by the Dutch Government   " In fact," he said, " the King of the Netherlands must declare that he only closes the Scheldt to the flags of France, England, and Belgium, or that he closes it to all nations "

  " But in that case," I replied, " he would be declaring war against us "

  " Yes," he answered, " it would be war, but *he* would declare it against us , and he must be aware that the valuable merchandise which has fallen into our hands, in consequence of the blockade and the *embargo*, would then suffer the fate of prizes taken in time of war "

  " If," added Lord Palmerston, " King William thinks he ought to close the Scheldt to all the nations, we shall be entitled to demand the co-operation of those Cabinets which took part in the acts of the Congress of Vienna, and who are all more or less interested in the free navigation of the rivers, a principle solemnly recognized at Vienna

" In this latter case, nothing will prevent our proceeding also to condemn those Dutch vessels, which we at present only hold under sequestration "

It seems to me, M le Duc, that this line of action would only be fair and reasonable, and might possibly modify the resolutions of the Cabinet of the Hague, which is quite aware of the profound impression which the seizure of the Dutch vessels now held by France and England would produce in Holland, and as this would be one of the surest ways of separating the interests of Holland from those of the king, it must not be neglected

December 30th

It was with great satisfaction that I received this morning the despatch which you did me the honour to write on the 27th I at once communicated to Lord Palmerston and Lord Grey the orders which had been issued to Marshal Gérard, respecting the return of our army to France and the release, on parole, of the Dutch garrison   They both expressed their thanks to me in such a manner, as to make me feel the great value they attach to this noble and loyal conduct on the part of the king's government

We thought, M le Duc, that no time should be lost, as you yourself informed me in your despatch, in trying the measures which we deemed would be effective with the Hague, whether they prove successful or not , and we have, therefore, in conjunction with Lord Palmerston, drawn up a memorandum containing our proposals to the King of the Netherlands   it will be sent off this evening, and will be forwarded, as you wished, by the *Chargés d'affaires* of France and England at the Hague [1]

---

[1] Draft of Convention presented to the Dutch Government by the Marquis of Vérargues in the name of France and England

1   The King of the Netherlands undertakes to withdraw his troops from the forts of Lille and Lofflensholt

2   He pledges himself to open the Meuse and all its branches, immediately after the ratifications

3   The navigation of the Scheldt shall be free until the conclusion of a definite peace

4   The Belgians will evacuate and give back to the King of the Netherlands, Venloo, the Dutch part of Limburg, and the German part of Luxemburg

5   The Belgians will have free use of a route into Germany *via* Limburg, as well as of the routes of Maestricht and Sittard

6   The King of the Netherlands promises a full and complete amnesty

7   The Dutch army will be placed on a peace footing

8   The Belgian army the same

9   The embargo laid by France and England on Dutch vessels will be removed

I have the honour to send you a copy of this memorandum. You will notice that we have kept very closely to the proposals you sent me on the 22nd of this month,[1] and that we have carefully eliminated everything that might excite public opinion against us in Holland

The unison, which I think exists between our memorandum and the proposals you sent me, the advice contained in your despatch of to-day, and lastly, the news we have received from the Hague, which makes us feel the necessity of hastening our communications to the Dutch Government, have all decided me to sign and send off our memorandum to Holland at once, without awaiting fresh orders from you, I trust that you will not disapprove the step I have taken in this matter

I insisted that our memorandum and our proposals should be drawn up in the plainest terms, so as not to furnish any subjects for controversy to the Cabinet of the Hague, which is always so ready to seize on anything

The French and English *Charges d'Affaires* at the Hague handed our note of the 2nd January, 1833, to the Government of the Netherlands   The King of Holland, urged no doubt by the complaints of his people respecting the effects of the embargo and the blockade of the ports, felt that he could not well decline to enter into negotiations with the two Powers who offered to put an end to a state of affairs so injurious to the interests of his country   He therefore sent a counter-proposal[2] on the 9th January, 1833, by M de Zuylen, in reply to ours of 30th December, and thus negotiations were begun between France and England on the one part, and the Netherlands on the other[3]

It is not my intention to give the details here of this tedious negotiation, which lasted nearly five months, before arriving at

---

[1] See these proposals, p 57

[2] The Dutch counter-project approached somewhat closely to the Franco-English one   Nevertheless, Article II only spoke of the Meuse, not of its branches   For the Scheldt, the Dutch Government claimed the right of imposing tonnage dues An additional article laid down, that France and England should undertake to obtain from Belgium the payment of an annual sum of S,400,000 florins to Holland   No mention was made of disarmament   Finally, toll dues were to be established on the route *via* Limburg

[3] A letter will be found in the Appendix from King Louis Philippe to the Duc de Broglie (letter No 4), and also a private letter from the Duc de Broglie to M de Talleyrand, in which is explained the line of *conduct* which the French Government intended to adopt, during that period of the negotiations which followed the expedition to Antwerp

the results which I shall relate further on   It will suffice to say
in a few words, that the King of the Netherlands, faithful to his
system of procrastination and evasion, tried in every possible
way to escape the recognition of the treaty of November 15th,
and to maintain a provisional position, which might enable him
to commence the struggle again, if chance at all favoured him
Nevertheless, we did not allow ourselves to be diverted from
our aim, which was, either the full recognition of the treaty of
November 15th, or a provisional position so advantageous to
Belgium and so unfavourable to Holland, that it would oblige
the latter to come to some definite arrangement   M de Zuylen
exhausted all the quibbles of chicanery to draw us on to other
ground, but in vain, and tired of fighting, he quitted his post in
the middle of March, and the negotiation remained suspended
for some days   But the consequences of the blockade and the
embargo made themselves felt so strongly in Holland, that the
king was obliged to put an end to them   He therefore sent a
new plenipotentiary, M S Dedel, to London, who was much more
conciliatory than his predecessor, and whose pleasant demeanour
greatly assisted in smoothing our discussions   But the powers
he had received were so limited, that it took more than two
months before the Convention of May 21st, to which I shall
have to revert later on, was concluded   Until then, I will put
aside these tiresome Hollando-Belgian affairs, which had become
a matter of almost secondary importance [1]

[1] It is necessary to say a few words to complete this outline of the Hollando-
Belgian question   After the counter project of the 9th January, and the claim of
Holland to interdict the navigation of the Scheldt to French, English, and Belgian
vessels, a rupture had taken place between the parties   But when the Cabinet of
the Hague gave in, negotiations were again resumed   The Conference rejected the
counter project of January 9th, and proposed a second draft of Convention, somewhat
like the former one, adding that the plenipotentiaries were ready to sign a definite
treaty on the bases offered   M de Zuylen refused, and a second counter project
was submitted, February 5th   A very sharp reply followed, 14th February from
the members of the Conference, who absolutely refused to entertain it   Holland
appeared inclined to give in   M de Zuylen was recalled, replaced by M Dedel, and
the Dutch Minister announced from the Tribune, that this change should be looked
upon as being favourable to the measures of conciliation   Nevertheless, the first
project presented by M Dedel still contained some singular demands, such as
refusing to recognise the neutrality of Belgium (23rd March)   The Conference
replied, dated April 2nd   M Dedel answered, April 16th   Finally, on receipt of a
complete and threatening note from the Conference, dated April 22nd, the Cabinet
of the Hague gave in, and on the 16th May proposed conditions which were accepted, and formed the subject of the Convention of May 21st (see pages 106 and 114)

The attention of France and England had been directed to various other quarters at the same time   Eastern affairs,[1] as has already been seen, had become greatly complicated by the successes of Mehemet Ali, Pasha of Egypt, against the Ottoman Porte   The new Greek Government likewise experienced great difficulty in establishing itself [2]

In another quarter, the presence of M de Zea-Bermudez at the head of the Spanish Ministry, just at the time when Ferdinand VII was struggling with the malady which was to bring him to the grave, had revived difficulties[3] greatly aggravated

[1] The Eastern question became at this period a subject of much importance with M de Talleyrand in London   This question, which for nearly ten years had given endless trouble to European diplomacy, was the rivalry between Sultan Mahmoud and Mehemet Ali Pasha of Egypt   The latter, born in 1769, at one time a simple Albanian soldier, had become Viceroy of Egypt (1806), and had been recognized as such by the Ottoman Porte   By his energy and ability he had created in Egypt an army, a fleet, and a government   At the same time he subdued the whole of Upper Egypt, Nubia, and part of Arabia and did not conceal his intention of founding an Egyptian Empire, at the expense of that of Turkey

A rupture between the sovereign and the vassal became inevitable   In 1831, Mehemet found a pretext for it, in the refusal of the Sultan to give him Syria as the price of his co operation in the war of Grecian independence   His son Ibrahim immediately invaded this province (November 1831) and possessed himself of Gaza, Jaffa, and St Jean d'Acre, routing the Turkish forces at Homs and Beilan   From Syria, Ibrahim advanced into Anatolia, where he gained a great victory at Konieh (21st November, 1832)

Then Europe intervened   Russia offered aid to Turkey, and it was this step which, very justly awakening the distrust of France and England, turned the whole attention of diplomacy to the shores of the Bosphorus

[2] King Otto embarked at Brindisi on January 14th, 1833, for Nauplia   All sorts of difficulties assailed the new government   Not only were the Pallikares (the boldest and most turbulent part of the population), with the redoubtable Colocotroni at their head, hostile to it, but an entire administration had to be created in a country which was barely civilized and almost without financial resources

[3] The question of the Spanish succession occasioned great excitement throughout the Peninsula, and Europe did not view it with indifference

King Ferdinand had by his fourth marriage a daughter, the Infanta Isabella, born 10th October, 1830   Females had formerly reigned in Spain   but the law of succession established by the first Bourbon King, Philip V, in 1714, excluded them from the throne   According to the Salic law, therefore, the throne reverted on the death of Ferdinand to his brother Don Carlos   But Ferdinand had in 1830, revoked the law of 1714   After having reconsidered the revocation, he confirmed it afresh and then died (29th September, 1833), leaving the crown to his daughter Isabella, under the Regency of her mother Maria Christina

Then arose a desperate war between the partizans of Don Carlos and those of Queen Isabella, which lasted many years   Don Carlos represented absolute power   Maria Christina in order to resist him, had to lean on the Constitutional party   She therefore did not hesitate to dismiss her minister, Zea Bermudez, who was a thorough Absolutist   The crisis in Spain was closely allied to that which raged in Portugal, for the establishment of either an absolute or a constitutional government at Lisbon would necessarily recoil at Madrid   Therefore, as long as King Ferdinand lived he upheld Dom Miguel   The Queen Regent, on the contrary, was favourable to Dona Maria

by the prolonged civil war in Portugal, between the two brothers
Dom Miguel and Dom Pedro   Just at this period, also, General
Pozzo, the Russian Ambassador in France, thought it necessary to make a journey to London   M. Pozzo had recently
returned to his post in Paris, from a visit he had made to St.
Petersburg by order of his sovereign, who wished to confer with
him   On his return, he stopped at Munich and Stuttgard, having
been instructed, it was asserted, to confer with these different
Courts [1]   No sooner had he returned to Paris, than he at once
started for London, just at the time when his being senior of the
corps diplomatique would have placed him in the position of
having to offer congratulations to King Louis-Philippe on New
Year's day   These brief indications will suffice to explain the
correspondence, of which we will confine ourselves to giving
extracts   I wish again to recall the fact, that the English
Government had just nominated to represent it temporarily at
Madrid, Sir Stratford Canning, whom the Court of Russia, out
of rancour at his conduct at Constantinople,[2] had refused to
receive as ambassador at St Petersburg.

Sir Stratford Canning, who was going to Spain *via* Paris,
received orders to stop there to have an interview with the
Duc de Broglie, respecting the mission he had to carry out at
Madrid   M. de Broglie informed me of the result of this interview by the following letter —

Besides, if Dom Miguel was successful, Dom Carlos would find an asylum and every
description of aid in Portugal   it will therefore be easily understood, that, in the eyes
of European diplomacy, the Spanish succession and that of Portugal were only one
and the same question, and that France and England were especially interested in the
sovereignty of Queen Isabella and a Constitutional Cabinet

[1] It appears that Comte Pozzo, during his journey through Europe, had addressed a project of alliance from Russia to the Austrian and Prussian Cabinets
This project stated first that the Convention of October 21st, between France and
England, and the dangers that might result therefrom, imposed upon the other three
Courts the necessity of combining to maintain peace in Europe   It was consequently
stipulated, that as soon as a French army entered Belgium, a Prussian army would
advance to the front   and take possession of Venloo and those portions of Limburg
and Luxemburg which were destined for Holland   Prussia would guard these
territories   in the name, and under the authority of the three contracting parties, in
order to place them in the hands of the Dutch, after the taking of Antwerp   Russia
and Austria agreed to join in these operations with Prussia, accepting the joint
responsibility, and promising to support her with all their power.   (Extract from a
despatch of M. Bresson to the office, 14th February, 1833)

[2] Sir Stratford Canning's mission to Constantinople (see page 43 and note).

THE DUC DE BROGLIE TO THE PRINCE DE TALLEYRAND.

PARIS, *December* 20*th*, 1832

MON PRINCE,

. . Sir Stratford Canning has spent two days here, and has communicated his instructions to me His object is first to obtain an armistice, and then to conclude the Portuguese business by setting aside both the brothers, and establishing a regency in the name of Dona Maria, on condition of renouncing the Constitution of 1826 In the present state of the Spanish Government, I have but little hope that Sir Stratford Canning's arguments will be listened to. No mention is made as to the intervention of France in Sir Stratford Canning's instructions , nevertheless, at the close of our conversation, he expressed the wish that the French Government should be associated with his mission I referred the matter to the Council, and this is the reply the king has decided upon by my advice

1 If Sir Stratford Canning's mission should, sooner or later, tend towards the employment of force against Dom Miguel, and consequently against Spain, the French Government considers it only loyal to declare at once, that it could not be associated with it. Against Dom Miguel alone, England has no need of our support. If Spain intervenes, we cannot make war with her in the interest of Dom Pedro and his daughter, without such an enterprise at once assuming a revolutionary character on both sides of the Pyrenees. It would be the counterpart of our expedition of 1823 , a universal war would be the consequence It would be impossible to prevent the general impression that we had only entered Spain in order to re-establish the Cortes Government

2 Sir Stratford Canning proposes to bring forward the argument, that the situation and the rights of the young Dona Maria are analogous to those of the young Infanta of Spain To this line of reasoning we cannot agree either. It would give colour in advance to the question of the Spanish succession, and be quite opposed to the real interests of France It would be pledging ourselves against the maintenance of the Salic law, and for the benefit of a weak, vacillating party, which to all appearance will get the worst of the struggle, if it engages in it

With these two limitations, we should be ready and willing to give M de Rayneval instructions to second Sir Stratford Canning The demand for an armistice seems to us the most important point , there is no inconvenience attached to such a demand, it has the advantage, if it succeeds, of giving time for the formation of a third party in Portugal, which party would equally reject both brothers and declare itself in favour of Dona Maria without a Constitution. I do not know whether the elements of such a third party exist, but if they do not, there is evidently nothing to be done.

As for pacific measures subsequent to the armistice, we think that even to obtain a hearing, Sir Stratford Canning will do well not to express himself in too categorical terms, but show himself ready to try various measures—either Dona Maria alone, an amnesty with Dom Miguel, a marriage, or anything.

If he is too precise in his proposals at first, he will be refused point blank. Whereas if he keeps to generalities, until the state of Portugal furnishes him with a point of departure, it is possible that negotiations may be opened up.

I am sending instructions to Rayneval to this effect. He will second Sir Stratford Canning in his demand for an armistice, and in all measures which may tend towards the pacification of Portugal.

I trust, mon Prince, that you will consider that we have taken a just position with regard to this delicate proposition. Sir Stratford Canning seemed to me quite satisfied. . .

THE PRINCE DE TALLEYRAND TO THE DUC DE BROGLIE

LONDON, *January 6th*, 1833

Yesterday Lord Palmerston invited the members of the Conference to meet on the affairs of Greece, in order to communicate to them the last despatches received from the boundary commissioners of the three Powers in the Morea. The result of these despatches is, that difficulties have arisen in consequence of the inaccuracy of the map on which the commissioners had to base their work; this map, it is said, is full of errors, nevertheless they hope to arrive at a proper and exact demarcation, which will not cause any difficulties.

After the Conference, I spoke to Lord Palmerston, as you wished, about the negotiations being carried on here by Namick Pasha. He began by telling me the circumstances which had brought this envoy from the Porte to England. It seems, that the Court of St. Petersburg has lately proposed to the Grand Signior to assist him with an army of fifty thousand men against the Pasha of Egypt; this force would be taken from the Russian troops in the Caucasus, and would join the army in Syria under the command of the Grand Vizier. The Sultan declined the Emperor Nicholas's offer by saying, that what he needed just now was maritime help It is therefore for the purpose of obtaining such assistance from the English Government, that Namick Pasha has been sent to London Since his arrival, he has made a formal request for the support of a British maritime force in the Levant, in order to compel the Pasha to return to his allegiance

This request will be submitted at the first Cabinet Council, which will not take place before the end of this month, as the English ministers do not return to London till then

Lord Palmerston, even while saying that he had not formed his opinion on this matter, nevertheless, allowed me to understand that there was a very plausible reason for the request of the Grand Signior " Here," he said, " it is not a question of one of those interventions, to which England has always been opposed ; it would only be assistance given to an ancient ally against a rebellious subject, whose revolt, if it were crowned with success, must have most dangerous consequences for the future tranquillity of Europe For it is probable that Russia, who now makes a parade of vain-glorious generosity towards the Sultan, would not fail to secretly support the pasha in his rebellion. It is therefore to the interest of Europe to recognise that the Porte, placed as she is between the ambition of Russia and that of the Pasha, could not in her present state of depression sustain such a struggle If the necessity for the existence of the Ottoman Empire is admitted, the critical position in which it is now placed, must render it equally necessary to give it that support, which can alone save it from ruin "

Lord Palmerston's view of the matter has no doubt been strengthened by the remarks we have often made in our conversation on the encroaching policy of Russia, for I must admit, that I have never allowed an occasion to pass without bringing it to the notice of the English ministers.

However, as I had the honour of telling you, Lord Palmerston will submit the Sultan's request to the Council, and I will take care to acquaint you with the decision they arrive at. Meanwhile, I will see those members separately who are in London, and endeavour to learn the opinion which will probably prevail in the Cabinet

The happy influence exercised by the taking of the citadel at Antwerp, has made itself forcibly felt by the rise in all the public funds, this is a peaceful symptom, not always certain, but which must be noticed, especially when it is simultaneous in London and Paris, and even in Amsterdam. No one can deny that this event has given great strength to the present Governments of Belgium, France, and Great Britain. Belgium can, in fact, count her existence as an independent State from the time of the reduction of Antwerp. France feels the good effects of it, by the smoother progress of the discussions in the Chamber, and the English Ministry, upheld by the new elections, gains fresh strength every day.[1] It has just obtained a proof of the consolidation of its power in a circumstance which might otherwise be insignificant, but just now is of some importance.

H.M. the Queen of England had been obliged last year, on the reiterated insistance of the ministers, to dismiss her first Chamberlain, Lord Howe,[2] who voted against the Ministry on the Reform question. Up to the present, Her Majesty had refused to name a successor to Lord Howe, at last she gave in, and selected Lord Denbigh,[3] a very pronounced partizan of the Ministry. The latter looks upon this selection as the first step towards a reconciliation with the Court.

General Pozzo, accompanied by M. de Lieven, came to see me a few hours after his arrival in London. We had a fairly long talk, during which I must say he spoke very judiciously. Such conduct on his part is in no way remarkable, and I only mention it to you, because I think, that under the circumstances, we ought to put on one side, any doubts we may have as to Russia's intentions. General Pozzo expresses himself perhaps with some bitterness concerning the English Cabinet, and the line of policy it has adopted; the English ministers are certainly rather distrustful of Russia, nevertheless, they are excessively polite to General Pozzo. I should, I think, place myself in a false position, were I not to follow their example.

I need not say, that I shall be excessively cautious in my intercourse with this ambassador, but at the same time, I shall take as his real opinion, all the good he may consider it necessary to express to me, respecting France and the King's Government.

11th January, 1833

What you tell me respecting the language held by M. de Zea to M. de Rayneval, on the occasion of Sir Stratford

---

[1] The elections had been very favourable to the Ministry. The new House recruited in great measure from the Whig party, had only two weak groups in opposition—the Tories on one side and the Radicals on the other.

[2] Richard William Penn, Earl Howe, grandson of the admiral of that name, was born in 1806, entered the House of Lords in 1820, under the title of Viscount Curzon, and had been for fifteen years Grand Chamberlain to the Queen of England.

[3] William Basil Percy Fielding, Earl of Denbigh, born in 1796, succeeded his grandfather in the House of Lords. He was Grand Chamberlain to the Queen.

Canning's mission to Madrid, has not surprised me in the least This language seems to me to be quite in accordance with M de Zea's[1] known antecedents

I wish I was in a position, M le Duc, to furnish you with the information you ask of me, as to the real aim of the English Cabinet in sending Sir Stratford Canning to Spain, but I must draw your attention to the fact, that it is almost impossible to procure any other intelligence on this point than what has been given you by Sir Stratford Canning himself When I questioned Lord Palmerston on this subject, he replied that Sir Stratford Canning had received orders to communicate all his instructions to you, since then he has told me that this ambassador, in rendering an account of the observations you had made to him in his different interviews with you, seemed perfectly satisfied with them, and had added that he considered them quite in accordance with your position. This ambassador has not yet entered Spain, it would therefore be rather difficult to find any real reason for supposing that any alteration had taken place in the instructions given him

I am led to believe that Sir Stratford Canning has been allowed great latitude of action in his powers, it might therefore be possible that, in admitting M de Zea's invincible repugnance to adopt the proposals made to him, the English Cabinet had foreseen the eventuality, in which it would be necessary to try and remove this minister from office, the state of M de Zea's health, would, as it were, offer a very plausible pretext This would surprise me still less, as the influence the Russian Court exercises over M de Zea's mind, is well known in London He has been successively Spanish consul and minister at St Petersburg, and has been more than once nominated Minister of Foreign Affairs by King Ferdinand VII, at the instigation of Russia, and as it might naturally be supposed, that under present circumstances the influence of Russia would be exerted to oppose the views of the English ministers, the hidden aim attributed to Sir Stratford Canning's mission might be easy of explanation.

But whether or not there is anything in these suppositions, you have at Madrid, in M de Rayneval, a sufficiently able

[1] M de Rayneval, the French Ambassador at Madrid, wrote as follows on this matter, "that nothing could prevent M. de Zea from entering into explanations as to Sir Stratford Canning's mission, that M de Zea considered the proposal of an armistice made to a prince in possession of the throne by a Power which had thrust war upon him, quite chimerical, and that he expressed his firm determination, to oppose any violation of the neutrality by every means in his power" According to M de Rayneval, Sir Stratford Canning had no chance of succeeding in his mission, until he had upset M de Zea (*Extract from M de Rayneval's despatch to the Department*, 29 *h December*, 1832)

Minister to quickly discover the real intentions of the English Ambassador, and I have no doubt that he will constantly send you valuable information, which it would be impossible for me to procure here

Lord Palmerston informed me confidentially, that the Emperor Nicholas had stated that he would not receive Sir Stratford Canning as ambassador at the Court of St Petersburg, which post he was to have held on his return from Madrid   The English Cabinet does not conceal its dissatisfaction at this decision   I was not called upon to give my opinion on this matter, nevertheless, I did not fail to profit by it to make some remarks, which I have reason to believe will not be thrown away

BARON PASQUIER TO THE PRINCE DE TALLEYRAND

PARIS, *January 11th*, 1833

MON PRINCE,
                    I can quite understand your determination to *stop there*, when you have finished the great undertaking which you alone could have achieved, and which I like to think, has nearly reached its end, nevertheless, I cannot imagine what will happen to the policy of our France, when it is no longer under your guidance   In the general state of European affairs, it would be very difficult to prevent grave circumstances from cropping up at any moment, and I have not as yet seen among the new men who have arisen round us, anyone who would be in a position to direct them ably, I might almost say, even to understand them   All my hope, in truth, is in the *va da sé*

If I can be of any service to you here, I beg of you most urgently to make use of me   I knew you were always kept so carefully informed by our poor friend,[1] that I did not think there was anything for me to tell you   Now, if matters are different, let me know, I am quite at your orders

Our position at home has visibly improved, we cannot help seeing it, and the manner in which the order of the day, on the subject of the Duchess de Berry, was lately carried in the Chamber of Deputies, has relieved the Government from a most serious embarrassment with which it might have had to contend[2]   It is

---

[1] The Princess de Vaudémont, who had just died

[2] Sitting of January 5th   A discussion arose on M Sapey's report, respecting the various petitions that had been addressed to the Government relative to Mdle la Duchesse de Berry—some demanded that the princess should be set at liberty, others requested that a plébiscite should decide her fate —all contained protestations against the revolution of July   The Chamber, after a long and tumultuous sitting, voted the order of the day, pure and simple, as demanded by the Government, which reserved its liberty of action

therefore now quite certain that with ordinary ability, matters will go on right

Pozzo, as you represent him in London, is just what I expected The disposition he showed here only too plainly was, I have no doubt, caused by the terrible fear with which his Emperor had inspired him   He has come back positively terrified, to speak plainly   This is a matter about which there can be no doubt, and I do not think it would be easy to get him now to undertake a journey similar to the one he accomplished during the last six months of the year 1832

Kindly accept, mon Prince, together with the assurances of my great esteem, those of a devotion which I beg you to put to the proof, on every occasion when you may deem it can be of use . . .

THE PRINCE DE TALLEYRAND TO THE DUC DE BROGLIE

LONDON, *January* 17*th*, 1833

. . I must inform you of a rather important communication, which has just been made to the English Ministry by the Austrian Ambassador in London   It relates to the present state of Portugal, and to the means of putting an end to the civil war, which is desolating that country

The Austrian Minister has been instructed by his Court, to offer to the English Government the mediation of the Vienna Cabinet in the affairs of Portugal, and in mentioning it to Lord Palmerston, he added, that the first condition of this mediation would be the recognition of Dom Miguel as King of Portugal, he undertaking to issue a general amnesty and to remove all the sequestrations that had been laid on special properties.

In support of this proposal, the Cabinet of Vienna insisted, that for the last four years the Infant Dom Miguel had occupied the throne of Portugal , that while admitting all the evils attributed to his government, it was impossible not to recognize the fact that a large majority of the Portuguese nation were in his favour, and that the small success which had attended Dom Pedro's enterprise was a proof of this, if such were needed

The Austrian Minister, in concluding this communication, which he had been ordered to make, stated, that his sovereign had quite determined upon taking this step, no matter how greatly it was opposed to the interests of his granddaughter,[1] as he felt

---

[1] Dona Maria was in fact a granddaughter of the Austrian Emperor through the Archduchess Leopoldine who was Dom Pedro's first wife

convinced, that the pacification of Portugal had, by its connection with the tranquillity of the Peninsula, become a question of vital importance to the peace of Europe, and that this pacification could only be promptly effected by the recognition of the Infant Dom Miguel, but he intended that the amnesty, which would be insisted on with this prince, should be without any restriction, and given in such a manner as to reassure all parties

Lord Palmerston at once replied, that Baron de Neumann [1] did not fully explain the views of the Vienna Cabinet in this matter; that it appeared to him very strange, to say nothing more, to propose to Dom Pedro to quit Portugal, to give up the Azores, to completely abandon his daughter's cause, and to offer him nothing in exchange for all these concessions, but an amnesty, for which, besides, there would be no actual guarantee other than the word of a prince well known for not keeping faith in his engagements   Lord Palmerston ended by declining to accept Austria's mediation in the terms offered

Thus ended a discussion which had been carried on rather warmly, both by Lord Palmerston and M de Neumann

In one of the last despatches you did me the honour to write, you expressed a wish to know what foundation there was for the reports spread abroad in Madrid as to the real object of Sir Stratford Canning's mission   In my reply on the 11th of this month, I pointed out to you the difficulties which prevented my procuring precise information on this point, but I have nevertheless tried to verify some of the facts which you have stated to me   A member of the diplomatic body, in whom I place some confidence, gave me almost the identical information contained in M de Rayneval's despatch; but he supported his statement by a circumstance, which would tend to strengthen the opinion held in Madrid as to the disquietude exhibited by M de Zea   I refer to the solemn act by which the King of Spain, when renewing his first declaration relative to the right of the Infanta Isabella to succeed to the throne, annulled the dispositions, which he stated had been drawn from him during his illness [2]   He thought that this act was a measure taken by M de Zea to thwart the manœuvres of Sir Stratford Canning who was, as you informed me, to try and assimilate the interests of the Infanta Isabella to those of Dona Maria, by promising to the Queen of Spain the support of the English Government in obtaining the recognition of her daughter's rights, if she, on her

[1] Secretary of the Austrian Embassy in London   He acted as Chargé d'Affaires during the absence of Prince Esterhazy, the Ambassador

[2] See page 63

side, would protect the young Queen of Portugal M de Zea,
it is said, would have deprived the English Ambassador of one
of his most powerful arguments, had he pronounced himself
strongly in favour of the rights of the Infanta Isabella before
the arrival of that Ambassador

As the information given me may also have come from
Madrid, I only transmit it to you with the greatest diffidence
You will soon be in a position to verify its truth, and I repeat
again, that you may rely on M de Rayneval's ability to discover
all the intrigues which cannot fail ere long to be rife in the
Peninsula

Among the various explanations given for General Pozzo's
journey to London, there is one which does not seem to me
improbable It is said, that for some months past, St Petersburg has received rather contradictory despatches regarding
England from Prince de Lieven on the one hand, and
Count Matusiewicz on the other ; that uncertain as to what
opinion to form between the very different statements of his
ministers in England, the Emperor Nicholas wished to send
General Pozzo, (who had acquired his full confidence during the
sojourn he had just made at St Petersburg), to London, so as to
receive from him some positive information, according to which
he might regulate his political relations with Great Britian
This journey would then, therefore, be but the completion of
General Pozzo's mission to Berlin and the various German Courts
You will know best, whether this explanation is of any value
or not   . .

20th January

. . . .I have already had the honour to draw your attention
to a question, concerning which the members of the English
Cabinet often speak to me, and which is of great interest to them
It is with regard to the changes which it is much desired here
might be adopted in our custom-house tariffs

The petitions lately addressed to the Chamber of Deputies
on this subject, by the industries of Lyons, Bordeaux, Nantes,
and other commercial towns, have found a warm echo in England,
where it is asserted, that public opinion in France has undergone
a great change as regards prohibitive duties. It is thought that
it would be easy now for the French Government to adopt
a more liberal scale, and this is wished for very serious
reasons

The present English Cabinet regards this question in a
political, even more than in a commercial light , for under this

latter aspect, it has been found that Mr Huskisson's [1] system had already produced the happiest results, and that the diminution of the import duties on silk, gloves, and other articles, had been more than compensated for by the enormous increase in the consumption   Therefore, even if only taking into consideration the commercial interests of England, the ministers might perhaps dispense with reciprocal measures from other countries, and still derive great advantages from the liberal system which they advocated   But important political interests now make it their duty to endeavour to extend still further commercial relations with France

During the last elections, several speeches were made in the different manufacturing towns of England, which cannot have escaped your notice, and which you may have remarked, contained numerous allusions to the recent alliance between France and Great Britain , it is often referred to, as a matter which ought soon to place the relations between the two countries on a more equal footing   The newspapers, whose influence is so great in England, have warmly supported this new tendency on the part of the industrial classes

The Ministry feel, that as the House of Commons is now constituted, they could not count upon a substantial majority, nor on the support of public opinion, if they did not show some advantageous results from this alliance with the French Government   The privileges they ask for, are by no means detrimental to France , what they desire is a more equitably arranged exchange of the products of both countries   By these means the ties which unite both nations will be drawn closer from day to day, and their utility and importance become more fully realized

We must not lose sight of the fact that by strengthening the power of the present English Cabinet, we insure a certain continuance of the close alliance which has only subsisted for a few months between France and England , and that this alliance, by creating a fresh power in Europe, checks all the intrigues from the North, and forms a real *point d'appui* for all the interests of the world

I cannot help thinking, that considerations of such very great political significance will be appreciated by the King's Government, and I feel sure that you will do your utmost to point out their full value

As I have already had the honour to inform you, all the ministers requested me to express to you their earnest wishes

_____
[1] William Huskisson, 1770-1830, had been President of the Board of Trade in 1823, and in that capacity had been one of the most ardent advocates of Free Trade.

on the matter I have just indicated. I shall be extremely obliged, if you will always put me in a position to make known to them the influence which these earnest wishes exert on the decisions of the French Government   .

THE DUC DE BROGLIE TO THE PRINCE DE TALLEYRAND.

PARIS, *January 21st*, 1833

MON PRINCE,
          I have very little to add to the official despatch I sent you   I have spoken quite frankly to Lord Granville respecting the contents of this despatch   It is impossible to say what may happen in the East , but events have not found us unprepared, for very reasonable proposals (admitted to be such by every-one endowed with any degree of sense in the Council of the Divan) have been obtained by our Consul from Mehemet Ali, and transmitted to Constantinople by our *Chargé d'Affaires*, and it is on these proposals that the present negotiations are being conducted [1]   It is very important that Lord Palmerston should be informed that he must not trust Namick Pasha in anything , he is a very insignificant intriguer, sent, not by the Porte, but by the Seraglio, which never can carry out anything. We must now negotiate at Constantinople   I believe that the interests of the English Government on this point are identical with ours, and time is pressing   I have every reason to believe that if our Governments come to an understanding, Austria will end by joining us to counteract the possible aggrandisement of Russia   This is the object for which you strove at the Congress of Vienna, and which the Hundred Days upset   It is for you to accomplish it now . . .

MADAME ADELAIDE D'ORLÉANS TO THE PRINCE DE TALLEYRAND.

TUILERIES, *January 24th*, 1833

MON CHER PRINCE,
          I at once informed the King of what you told me respecting the customs   He desires me to say, that he is quite of your opinion on this point, and that he never ceases to speak in this sense, in order to bring about the result which you and

---

[1] Mehemet Ali had sent his proposals to the Sultan in the beginning of January He offered to enter into negotiations on the following bases

The Porte to cede the Pashaliks of Syria, and the district of Adana, subject to a tribute

The tie which united Egypt to the Porte was to be modified in such a way, as to place the Pasha of Egypt on the same footing as the ancient Beys of Algiers.

he with so much wisdom and reason both desire, for, in
truth, our alliance with England is now more fortunate and
more important than ever, both for us and for her

Ibrahim Pasha's victory is a great piece of news,[1] our
beloved King is very anxious to know your views respecting this
event   What will be its consequences ?   What do you think
ought to be done, and what arrangements made to prepare for
the results arising therefrom, and also for the future ? He thinks
rightly, that no one could be a better judge of this than you,
and having such great confidence in your judgment, he is most
anxious to have your opinion on this important question. . . .

THE PRINCE DE TALLEYRAND TO THE DUC DE BROGLIE

LONDON, *January 28th*, 1833

My despatch, No 56, will have informed you of the many
obstacles that intervened to prevent my communicating to Lord
Palmerston, as soon as I could have wished, the contents of the
despatch you did me the honour to send on the 21st of this
month.   I was only enabled to do so the day before yesterday,
and Lord Palmerston then promised me to submit the proposals
of the French Government to a Cabinet Council, which he
would summon for that purpose the next day   This Council
was held yesterday, Sunday, but before making known to you
the result of its deliberations, I must inform you of some circumstances that preceded it

If you will have the goodness to recall the despatch I had
the honour to send you on the 6th of this month, you will notice
that I was then already greatly occupied with the events that
were taking place in the East, I must confess, that the despatches
I received from you on the 10th and 14th, did not fully reassure
me and I was still of opinion that some species of action
on the part of France and England would soon become imperative   In my conversations with the members of the English
Cabinet, I had tried to draw their attention to the various consequences that might result from the struggle between the
Sultan and the Pasha of Egypt, if the continued successes of
the latter should compel the Ottoman Porte to seek the protection of Russia

In the midst of all this, I received your despatch, No 13,
which proved to me that my previsions had been unfortunately

---

[1] The battle of Konieh, December 21st, 1832, in which the Turkish army was
cut in pieces   It was in consequence of this battle that the negotiations were begun,
of which mention has already been made

realized This despatch contains an admirable account of the present state of the East, and the measures that will be needed to arrest the dangers that threaten the Ottoman Empire[1] This document struck me as so remarkable, that I thought I ought to read it to Lord Palmerston at the interview I had with him on Saturday evening He was struck quite as much as I had been by the considerations so ably dealt with in this despatch, and became convinced of the necessity for immediate action by England and France, and of commencing it by offering to Constantinople and Alexandria, an armed mediation, in which Austria would be asked to join

After I left Lord Palmerston, I still busied myself in devising such measures as might ensure the promptest success to our mediation; and yesterday morning I wrote him a letter, from which I herewith send you an extract

" If the English Cabinet approves the projected mediation, which I put before you last night, it will be necessary that the measures adopted should be carried out with as little delay as possible The following course, according to my opinion, might be adopted

" Instructions should be drawn up for Sir Frederick Lamb. They would be transmitted to Lord Granville, who would communicate them to the Duc de Broglie He would no doubt also deem it his duty to draw up for Marshal Maison, instructions similar to those of Lord Palmerston M le Duc de Broglie would probably at once communicate them to Lord Granville and arrange with him for the despatch of a courier by each to Vienna These couriers should start together

" The instructions to both ambassadors would contain an order to propose to M de Metternich to unite Austria's offer of mediation with those of France and England

" If the Cabinet of Vienna accepts the proposal thus made, the two ambassadors, guided by the instructions from which they would not be empowered to depart, would arrange with M de Metternich the terms of the mediation to be proposed to Constantinople, and the English, French, and Austrian couriers would then at once continue their journey to that capital There they would deliver the instructions from their respective Courts to the representatives of Austria, England, and France

" If the Cabinet of Vienna refuses the proposal, the English and French couriers would, notwithstanding, proceed direct to Constantinople It is of course understood, that in both cases

---

[1] In this despatch (despatch No 13, dated January 21st), the Duc de Broglie requested M de Talleyrand to propose to the English Cabinet a project of joint mediation with reference to the East See this despatch in the Appendix, letter No 6.

the couriers would be the bearers of powers and instructions direct from Lord Palmerston and the Duc de Broglie to the representatives of England and France at the Ottoman Porte"

This, M le Duc, was the plan I proposed to follow, it had the advantage, in my opinion, of hastening as much as possible the execution of those measures which you recommended to me in your despatch of the 21st, and at the same time of inducing Austria to come forward

The English Ministers, after discussing for some hours the projected mediation as I had sent it to Lord Palmerston, wound up by adopting the somewhat curious idea of extending the offer of joining in the mediation not only to Austria but also to Russia They resolved on this course in consequence of the great importance, under these circumstances, of uniting the policy of Russia to that of the other three Courts

This resolution was at once communicated to me by Lord Palmerston, and I have done my utmost to combat it in a conference which lasted more than five hours I will give you full details of this to-morrow, but you have no doubt already foreseen all the reasons which it was my duty to bring forward against the co-operation of Russia I had effected nothing yesterday when we separated On leaving Lord Palmerston, I begged him to think over the painful complications in which the resolution of the English Cabinet would involve us, and we appointed to meet again to-day I have just come from another conference, and after a very lengthy discussion, I have at last obtained, that the mediation shall be offered in the names of France and Great Britain only The conditions will not be arranged until to-morrow I have barely time to finish this despatch, and you will therefore quite understand how impossible it is for me to enter into more details to-day I will reserve these for to-morrow

I will only add, that Lord Ponsonby has received orders to start at once for Constantinople,[1] and that the English Consul at Alexandria, of whose conduct you complained, has been recalled Parliament meets to-morrow, and the speech from the throne will be read at 5 o'clock. . .

January 31st

You have no doubt been surprised at not hearing ere this, the result of the communication which you desired me to make to the English Government, and I must therefore give you some explanation on this subject

---

[1] Lord Ponsonby had just been appointed Ambassador to the Porte

It must never be lost sight of that here, home affairs always take precedence of all others, no matter what interest may attach to the latter. Just now Parliament is reassembling, the Cabinet has several measures of great importance to bring forward—the state of Ireland, the tithes of the clergy, the finances—all require its most serious attention, and I often find it very difficult to recall it from all these conflicting and pressing interests, to questions of foreign policy. For the last eight days, all my efforts have tended towards making it clear, that the Eastern question needs speedy action to prevent our intervention becoming ridiculous, everyone agrees with me, they promise to go into the matter at once, and every day the question is deferred till the morrow. You will understand better than anyone else, that all these delays are but the result of the position in which the Cabinet is placed.

I informed you in my despatch of the 28th, that I would send some further details of the conversation I had with Lord Palmerston on the subject of our mediation.

As I have already had the honour to acquaint you, the design of the English Ministers is based on their desire to arrest the encroaching policy of Russia, while preserving the appearance of a friendly understanding, they believe that this end would be attained by the inclusion of that Power in our mediation. In opposing this scheme, I was obliged to draw attention to all the dangers which it presented. I pointed out to Lord Palmerston, that rapidity of execution was the first condition to the success of our enterprise, that we would lose this by putting ourselves in the position of having to wait for an answer from Russia, and that the inevitable consequence would be that we should arrive too late both at Constantinople and Alexandria, that this question of time would, in addition, possess the great inconvenience of preventing France and England from taking any action, as they would be bound, from the very fact of their proposal to Russia, not to take any steps before receiving the reply from that power, whilst the Cabinet of St Petersburg, still free from all engagements, would not fail to profit by this circumstance, further, that in consequence of the mission of General Mouravieff [1] to the Sultan, the Court of Russia had

---

[1] General Mouravieff had been sent by the Czar to offer assistance to the Sultan against Mehemet Ali. The Sultan, suffering under the defeat of Konieh, at first eagerly accepted it, and also gave his assent to General Mouravieff, going on a mission to Alexandria, to summon Mehemet to surrender with his troops.

Nicholas Nicolaievitch, Prince Mouravieff-Karski, born in 1793, entered the army), took part in the campaign of 1812 and 1815, became Major General in 1829, Lieutenant-General after the Polish war (1831), and was sent in 1832 to Turkey and Egypt. Dismissed from 1838 to 1848, he became, in 1854, Commander-in-chief of the army of the Caucasus, then State Councillor (1855), and died in 1866.

taken up the position of ally to Turkey, and that the Pasha
of Egypt would therefore have the right to refuse to accept her
as a mediator

Finally, I succeeded in getting Lord Palmerston to admit
one consideration, which has always great weight with an
English minister, namely, the constitutional side of the question I was able on this subject to point out to him, that a
mediation carried on solely by two countries under the rule of
Constitutional Governments, would meet with more favour in
the English Parliament and in the French Chambers, than if
Russia took part therein This consideration sufficiently impressed Lord Palmerston, to make him deem it necessary that
the Cabinet Council should reconsider its decision, and as
here everything ends by resolving itself in parliamentary questions, it is probable that the English Cabinet has been induced
to alter its first decision, on the ground I have just pointed
out

But if the mediation itself has been decided upon, nothing
has yet been arranged, either as to its form or the course
that is to be pursued with regard to it For the last three
days, these questions have been put off till the next day,
and as I had the honour of telling you at the commencement of this despatch, all my efforts up to the present have
had no results. I am led to believe that the last news from
Constantinople, announcing that the Sultan had decided to
treat with the Pasha of Egypt, still further increases the hesitation of the ministers, and it is quite possible that they will end
by not coming to any decision

However this may be, M le Duc, I think the King's
Government is in a very good position, and has done every
thing that could be expected of it under the circumstances
Russia is already pledged, and Austria has refused to join in
the mediation . .

THE DUC DE BROGLIE TO THE PRINCE DE TALLEYRAND.

PARIS, *January 28th*, 1833

MON PRINCE,

The evening before last, in the midst of a state reception, M de Medem,[1] the Russian *Chargé d'Affaires*, came up to
me, and asked me whether I should like him to inform me confidentially of the instructions which had been given to General
Mouravieff

[1] The Comte de Medem, Councillor of the Russian Embassy in Paris, acted as
Chargé d'Affaires during the absence of the Ambassador, Comte Pozzo di Borgo

I thought I ought not to show too great eagerness, and therefore confined myself to saying that I should be very pleased to hear them

This morning he came personally to renew his offer, adding, that it was in the strictest confidence that he mentioned it, as he had received no instructions from his Court   He produced from his pocket, first a despatch containing a statement of the general reasons which decided the Emperor Nicholas to send General Mouravieff, and then a notification that the communication of the instructions given to that general had only been made to M de Medem himself, that he was not to acquaint the French Government with them, as relations with it were not *sufficiently intimate* for the Russian Ambassador to anticipate any explanations

Nevertheless, mon Prince, you will notice that it was the *Chargé d'Affaires* who made all the advances, that I only replied to his overtures with great indifference, and that he came back again to the charge

After the despatch had been read, there followed the instructions, the substance of which was somewhat as follows

The instructions open by a *résumé* of events in the East and Mehemet Ali's progress during the last six months

It is then stated that the continuation of this progress must necessarily lead to some catastrophe, that as the result of this would be to give Russia a neighbour, probably but little disposed to respect the treaty of Adrianople, Russia would be obliged to adopt a *threatening attitude*, which she is anxious to avoid

It is further added that the Emperor knows that Mehemet Ali has said, that if it had been possible to foresee the progress of the Egyptian army, Russia would have taken good care not to withdraw her consul from Alexandria

The object of General Mouravieff's mission is an answer to this idea

The general is first to go to Constantinople, and there deliver an official letter to the Sultan, containing the assurance of Russia's unalterable friendship, and the horror she experienced on hearing of Mehemet Ali's rebellion, concluding by soliciting the consent of the Porte, to the course the general is instructed to take with regard to the Pasha

Having obtained this assent, the general is to proceed to Alexandria, and use all possible solemnity in his intercourse with the Pasha, he is to place before him in the blackest colours, all the enormity of his attempt, he is to invite him to return to his duty, and, in case of refusal, he is to tell him that he will only have himself to blame for the consequence of his conduct Nothing more

If Mehemet Ali, touched by this remonstrance, asks the general to mediate between him and the Porte, the general is to refuse, because Russia does not wish to interfere in the affairs of others, any more than she will allow others to interfere in hers.

(N B This is probably the real object of the communication it is intended either as an indirect reproach or warning to France.)

If Mehemet Ali persists in his folly, the general is at once to return to St. Petersburg and report himself to his master.

It is added in a postscript, that if the general does not obtain the assent of the Porte to his mission, he is to return to St. Petersburg without going to Alexandria, but the Russian Minister would write to Mehemet Ali, informing him of what M. de Mouravieff was commissioned to tell him.

The Russian *Chargé d'Affaires* exhausted himself in protestations, as to the firm determination of his master only to use persuasive measures, he even stated that the Emperor Nicholas was more worried than enriched, by the provinces he had acquired from the Porte, and that he was much more inclined to give up his conquests than to extend them further.

My opinion respecting this communication is, that only one half of it is true, that what it says about the instructions given to General Mouravieff, in the event of the conflict between the Porte and the Pasha remaining doubtful, is really a fact, but that it also contains other contingent instructions, should it so happen that the Mussulman army is defeated, and that he has acted in conformity with these instructions, as I had the honour of informing you in my last despatch. The source whence I received the information I sent you in that despatch, is of such a nature as to leave me in no doubt on this point.

I confined myself to replying to this communication in very few words and very general terms, laying stress on our pacific intentions, and our desire to see this quarrel speedily brought to an amiable termination.

M. de Medem having advised the most profound secrecy with regard to this communication, I pray you, mon Prince, to keep this information to yourself, although I feel sure that M. de Medem has not run any risk in confiding it to me.

THE COMTE DE RAYNEVAL TO THE PRINCE DE TALLEYRAND

MADRID, *January 25th*, 1833

PRINCE,

I think that under the present circumstances, you might like to be informed directly and exactly, as to the position in which Sir Stratford Canning has found Spain   I therefore take advantage of the first courier he is sending, to give you some details on this subject, and I do so all the more readily, as it gives me an opportunity of bringing myself to your recollection, and begging you to continue your former kindness to me

It was only natural to suppose that the change in the home policy of Spain would equally affect her foreign policy.   It was thought that the party which the Queen and her adherents had to oppose (being that which by its ardent wishes and, probably, by its secret aid, supported the cause of Dom Miguel), the interest shown by the Spanish Cabinet in this Prince would disappear before one nearer and more pressing   But the Spanish Ministers reasoned differently   According to them, the Government cannot succeed in holding the apostolic[1] party in check, except by treating them with great circumspection They believe that this party would procure them all the Royalists in Spain, if they favoured Dom Pedro, who is looked upon as the head of all the liberals in the Peninsula, and if they failed in fulfilling the previous engagements entered into with Dom Miguel.

When it is suggested that it might be possible to eliminate Dom Pedro and the constitution, they reply that it would not be possible to eliminate his partizans, his ministers, and his councillors, some of whom are much more dangerous than himself This is the view taken by M de Zea and M d'Offalia   As long as they continue at the head of affairs, one need not expect Spain to adhere to a conciliatory project, and to cease from insisting on the maintenance of the neutrality of all the Powers   The various parties each work on their own account, and with equal ardour, against these ministers   Nevertheless, their fall cannot be looked upon as an immediate certainty   Just now, the course they are pursuing with regard to the succession assures to them the confidence and the favour of the King and Queen.

The events that are taking place in Portugal will really decide their fate, and possibly that of the Spanish monarchy We all feel this, and it is on this account, that there is great anxiety as to the consequences which may result from the differences that have arisen between our Government and that of Dom Miguel, respecting a French vessel sunk in the Douro, which will be further aggravated by a fresh insult to our flag at the mouth of the Tagus   The Spanish Cabinet maintains that the fault is on our side, and that consequently we are not in a position to demand reparation ; but it does not accuse us of any

---

[1] Name given to the absolutist party, that is to say the Carlists

mental reservations The public are more severe than ever since the departure of General Solignac [1] for Oporto, it is openly stated, that we wish to intervene, either directly or indirectly, in the struggle between the two brothers, and put an end to it by force of arms The Spanish Government thinks that our interference would prove more dangerous than that of England, to Dom Miguel and the peace of the Peninsula Therefore, just now, our quarrel with Portugal interests them far more even than Canning's mission.

Such, mon Prince, is the present state of affairs All this may lead to such complications, and so strongly excite men's passions, that no human power will be able to save the country from a catastrophe Under these circumstances, I feel the burden that has been laid upon me too heavy to support What would I not give to be able to avail myself of your advice ? But the great distance and the speed with which all these events happen, are unfortunately opposed to it Nevertheless, a few words (whereby I could learn your views as to the position of affairs in the Peninsula), would be very helpful to me, and I cannot refrain from expressing the pleasure and the gratitude with which they would be welcomed

I am writing at a time when you are experiencing a great sorrow In losing the Princess de Vaudémont, you have suffered one of those losses for which there is no reparation I do not think there has ever been a truer friendship than hers for you It was impossible to know her and not to love her I myself was sincerely attached to her, which I could hardly fail to be seeing that her kindness to me was unceasing

Please to accept, Prince

I am very pleased to be able to give here this letter of M de Rayneval's, which does as much honour to his heart, as to his good sense, and his judgment He draws a picture of the Peninsula, which enables one perfectly to seize the difficulties of the present, and to foresee the still greater ones of the future His previsions have come true with rare exactitude ; and even now as I am writing these memoirs, Spain and Portugal are a prey to a state of disorder, of which it is impossible to predict the end It will soon be seen what efforts the French and English Governments made, in order to prevent the disasters which threatened the unhappy Peninsula May these efforts some day

[1] The French General Solignac commanded one portion of Dom Pedro's troops at Oporto

bring about a happy result[1] I do not want to anticipate the
march of events , but it affords me pleasure to express in passing,
the high opinion I always had of the character and ability of M.
de Rayneval, who broke down under the burden, the weight of
which he had already found too heavy, when he wrote me the
admirable letter I have just quoted Is there any need for me
to say here, as I have already done on other similar occasions,
that I should like to eliminate from the letters I quote, all the
passages that flatter and praise me, did I not feel that the very
praise in such circumstances is but a reflex of the situation
itself, and that the more one is embarrassed and troubled, the
more one feels called upon to praise others ?

THE PRINCE DE TALLEYRAND TO THE DUC DE BROGLIE.

LONDON, *February* 3rd, 1833

MONSIEUR LE DUC,

　　The difficulties which I pointed out to you in my
despatch No 59,[1] with regard to Eastern affairs, have not
prevented my continuing to ask for assistance from the
English Government, in a question which has always appeared
to me of the highest interest to Europe I can at last inform
you that my efforts have not been absolutely without some
result The following action has been decided upon by England

Colonel Campbell has just been appointed Consul-General
at Alexandria , he starts to-morrow with all speed for his post
The instructions which he is to take with him will be sent this
evening to Lord Granville, who is to communicate them to you
I can tell you pretty nearly what these instructions contain.

It has been deemed necessary under present circumstances,
and at such a great distance, to allow for two possibilities
either, that peace has not yet, or that peace has already been
concluded between the Sultan and the Pasha, by the time that
Colonel Campbell reaches Alexandria

In the first case, he will, on his arrival, loudly proclaim the
interest that England takes in the Sultan, and give Mehemet
Ali to understand in plain language, the full extent of the protection which this interest will assure to the Porte on the part
of England.

If, as there is every reason to believe, peace has already been
signed between Turkey and Egypt, Colonel Campbell will con-

[1] See page 78 Despatch of January 31st

fine himself to the *rôle* of a spectator, while at the same time plainly indicating what the original object of his mission was

In both cases, Colonel Campbell is to preserve intimate relations with the French and Austrian Consuls, but only to be on friendly terms with the Russian Agent, and to listen to all he has to say, without displaying to him the same confidence as to the other two

You will no doubt see, with me, that these instructions, which moreover are very fully detailed, are quite in accordance with the course which you have adopted with regard to the Pasha of Egypt

The English Government has been informed of the Sultan's resolution to treat with Mehemet Ali at the instance of the Austrian internuncio, it is therefore of opinion that a direct appeal to the Porte has now become useless, and it will, for its part, confine itself to hastening the departure of Lord Ponsonby for Constantinople

8th February

I have received your despatch of the 4th of this month The news from Constantinople which it contains, and which you will no doubt have communicated to Lord Granville, has caused the greatest possible satisfaction here　The intervention of France which has stopped Ibrahim's onward march, and by the re-establishment of peace in the East, prevented a complication, which in various ways threatened to become dangerous,[1] is greatly approved here　It is very noticeable, that the idea, which just now is prevalent all over Europe, is to avoid anything approaching to an affair.　This disposition, in individuals as well as in cabinets is too favourable to us not to encourage it by our line of policy　The conduct of the French *Charge d'Affaires* at Constantinople during the late events, is therefore beyond all praise

The English papers, which you receive every day, keep you so fully *au courant* respecting the debates in Parliament, that I

[1] When the first moment of alarm caused by the battle of Konieh was over, the Sultan Mahomet quickly perceived the imprudence he had committed, in calling the Russians into Turkey　He therefore changed his mind, and deferring to the advice of M. de Varennes, the French *Charge d'Affaires*, decided to enter into negotiations with the Pasha　He sent the venerable Captain Halil Pasha to Egypt in January, whilst M. de Varennes wrote to Mehemet Ali to endeavour to persuade him to accept his overtures and to Ibrahim Pasha asking him to postpone his march　This latter waited it Kutaya　At the same time, the Turkish Plenipotentiary disembarked at Alexandria, on the 21st January, with a proposal to invest the Pasha with the governments of Acre, Tripoli Nauplia, and Jerusalem　Mehemet claimed the whole of Syria and Adana　These conditions were accepted by the Sultan on the 5th of May following.

do not think I need mention them to you   You will have
seen that the King's Government has been nobly defended by
Lord Grey, and well supported by the members who vote with
the Ministry

11*th February.*

The observations which you transmitted to me in your letter
of the 8th, with regard to the views of the Vienna and Berlin
Cabinets, are I believe thoroughly justified   You have, I think,
very clearly explained the object of the complaints which these two
Cabinets bring against the English Government; there is no
doubt that every effort is being made to separate France from
England. Last year, there were complaints that France exercised
undue influence over the English Cabinet; this year, England is
accused of preponderance   But as there is no more truth in this
accusation than there was in that of last year, we can only see in
all this, the real facts, namely, that they find at St Petersburg,
Vienna, and Berlin, that an alliance which places France and
England at the head of Europe becomes stronger every day, and
by insuring the maintenance of universal peace removes all hope
of forming any coalitions [1]

[1] The *entente* between France and England had strangely alarmed the Continental
Cabinets   M Ancillon especially did not conceal his irritation, and M Bresson, in his
correspondence, insisted on the dissatisfaction experienced at Berlin by the separate
negotiation of France and England with Holland   "Well-disposed persons here,"
he wrote, "like M de Bernstoff for example, are anxious that our negotiation with
the King of the Netherlands should end satisfactorily, but that would not suit M
Ancillon, who looks forward to fresh difficulties, which might enable him to regain
some little ascendency, or at least some importance   I am convinced that he is
deceiving us, when he says that he continues to urge the Cabinet of the Hague to
make fresh concessions "   (*Despatch of Feb* 10*th*)   "The offensive arrogance of the
English Cabinet," M Ancillon said to M Bresson, is no doubt due to the personal
character of Lord Palmerston; but an end must be put to this " (M Bresson's
despatch of January 17*th*)   Lord Minto, on his side, wrote to M Bresson, after having
had an interview with the Prussian Minister, "No species of dishonesty could surprise
me, but I must confess that I was not prepared for such criminal folly as I encountered
in him last night   He denied everything he had said to me on Belgian matters
ever since we had known each other " (*M Bresson's despatch of February* 10*th*)   In
Vienna, irritation and fears were no less rife   It was this which decided the two
German Courts to try and disturb the union of the two Western Powers, by sowing
seeds of distrust between them   Hence also arose the attempt, made at this period by
Austria and Prussia, of a nearer approach to friendliness with France   M d'Appony
and M de Werther made a proposal to the Duc de Broglie, to resume the negotiations
of the Conference relative to Belgian affairs, by giving up coercive measures   The
Duc de Broglie, in transmitting this information to M de Talleyrand, added   "In
comparing the conducts of the Cabinets of Vienna and Berlin in their present joint
attitude, and the greatly moderated language which the Court of Russia has lately adopted,
we are led to believe that these three Governments, fearing lest the Belgian question
should unravel itself without their aid, are impatient to escape from the passive *rôle*
to which they condemned themselves in a moment of thoughtless irritation   This
feeling specially predominates at Berlin, where M Ancillon's policy has met with
almost universal disapprobation   Possibly also these approaches towards friendship

The English Ministry has just displayed great prudence in its conduct towards the House of Commons; it has allowed the debates on the address in reply to the speech from the throne, to be prolonged for several days. Without taking any direct part in the discussion, the most advanced members of the Radical party showed no tact whatever in their speeches, and the violence of their language resulted in their losing a great number of their adherents, who either through distaste or conviction have sided with the Government, by voting against the amendments of the Opposition and in favour of the address . .

February 18th, 1833

The Austrian *Chargé d'Affaires* showed me a letter yesterday from M de Metternich, in which the views of Austria, respecting the present affairs of Switzerland, are fully set forth. M de Metternich seems greatly engrossed by the designs of the party, which now demands considerable modifications in the federal compact, and the success of such an attempt might, according to him, lead to complications fatal to the interests and the peace of that portion of Europe [1]

Without either sharing, or entirely rejecting this opinion, I must tell you, that even before receiving Baron de Neumann's communication, I am induced to think that we ought to oppose any alteration just now in the home and foreign policy of Switzerland You know how very quickly revolutionary parties go to great extremes, and if they went the length of assailing the neutrality of Switzerland, Austria, Piedmont, and France would at once find themselves placed respectively in very different positions from what they are in now

My views in this respect are not merely applicable to Switzer-

are intended to sow the germs of division, or at any rate doubt, between France and England, and on that hypothesis we can quite explain the constant complaints addressed to us by Austria and Prussia, as to the revolutionary tendencies and the assumption of superiority of the English Government " (*The Duc de Broglie to the Prince de Talleyrand, despatch, February 7th* Also in Appendix, letter No 7, a long letter from the Duc de Broglie, giving his conversation with these two ambassadors)

[1] Serious disturbances had agitated Switzerland for the past two years Following the revolution of July, insurrections had broken out in several cantons, new cantonal constitutions had been established, so much so, that it had become necessary to place the federal compact in harmony with the special reforms The Diet assembled on the 2nd July, 1832, and voted a revision of the Compact A scheme presented by M Rossi, was acceded to by the Diet, although with numerous modifications, and submitted for sanction by the Cantons This occasioned serious disturbances in several Cantons, degenerating into civil war The Diet therefore adjourned the matter *ad referendum* The revised Constitution was not put into force, and everything remained suspended

land, as to whose condition my notions are somewhat vague, but I think that in a general way, the French Government ought to avoid giving any encouragement to this spirit of innovation, which, under the guise of improving them, has taken possession of several countries bordering on France   I think it is better for the welfare of Europe, rather to postpone improvements than to provoke an upheaval

I have spoken to Lord Palmerston about Swiss affairs, very much in the sense I have indicated to you, and if you are of my opinion, I think it would be well to discuss the matter with Lord Granville

It might also be advisable to let it be known through the French Embassy in Switzerland, that France rejects in advance, any participation in the attempts of the agitators, which will no doubt become apparent in the Helvetian Diet, when it assembles at the beginning of next March   .

February 22nd.

. . . . I have only this morning received the despatch of the 18th of this month   The explanations you wished to give me respecting Russia's new views have just been confirmed by Prince de Lieven, whom I met at the King's levée, and who expressed himself very strongly as to the desire of his Government to be on good terms with France   Prince Lieven is to show me this evening, the last despatch he has received from St Petersburg, and which is probably couched in the same terms as that communicated to you by the Comte de Medem

I had the honour of a private audience with His Majesty before the levée, during which the King spoke for a long time of his attachment to the King of the French, how delighted he was at the great success of his Government, and the special confidence he placed in you, Monsieur le Duc   Altogether, I could not fail to be highly gratified at the reception and friendly language of His Majesty

March 4th

. . M le Comte Pozzo quits London the day after to-morrow to return to his post at Paris   I must say again, that I could find nothing in this ambassador's language during the whole of his sojourn here, except what was favourable to us   On the whole, Comte Pozzo's presence in London, will in my opinion have been rather useful to the affairs with which the French Government is dealing just now

THE DUC DE BROGLIE TO THE PRINCE DE TALLEYRAND

PARIS, *March 9th*, 1833

MON PRINCE,

I wish that my courier could bring you some news, but we are very dull here. The Ministry is going on fairly well, and there is every prospect of our reaching the end of the session without any hindrance. The majority still holds together, and only separates on questions of minor importance; our opponents are greatly divided and completely routed. Dupin, especially, has regularly collapsed. Of foreign matters I know very little; our policy seems to me to be stationary and expectant as regards Holland, Belgium, and the East.

We do not think we can release the Duchess de Berry before her *accouchement*. There is a sort of semi-Carlist plot trying to draw us on, and when once she is out of our hands, she can deny everything. It is only after the event has taken place that the party will lose all hope, and we must therefore put off all pardon until then.

It seems to me that the Ministry in England is doing very well.

THE PRINCE DE TALLEYRAND TO THE DUC DE BROGLIE

LONDON, *March 14th*, 1833

Yesterday, at the King's levée Lord Grey spoke to me about the sitting in the French Chamber of Deputies at which the occupation of Algiers was discussed. He expressed himself very strongly, as to the language which had been held on that occasion, assuring me that it would cause him great trouble in the House of Lords, where the question will be constantly brought forward. He would have liked that the King's Government should have avoided making such positive engagements, more especially as the promises made to England by the last French Government had been so hostilely revealed last year by Lord Aberdeen.

I had to tell Lord Grey that I should have the honour to make his remarks known to you and I added, that the speech made by M. le Président of the Council on this subject, contained several phrases sufficiently vague to prevent the intentions of the King's Government with respect to the occupation of Algiers from being prejudged, and that I also believed that there never had been any other idea, than to use this territory as a penal colony.

It would I think be well to verify the nature of the promises which, according to Lord Aberdeen, were given by the Prince de Polignac. Evidences of them must exist in the Foreign Office

You can understand, Monsieur le Duc, that from the very difficult position in which the English Cabinet is placed, it dreads the slightest shock that may come from abroad, and above all from our Government, which has shown itself opposed to their views on the question of the customs duties The Cabinet, as yet, hardly knows the feeling of the new House of Commons, and it dreads, probably not without reason, that a discussion started inopportunely might have a baneful influence on the deliberations of that Chamber, which is just now occupied with most complicated and important business

On the other hand, I am quite aware that the King's Government also has its parliamentary difficulties, and I have more than once regretted that our Chamber of Deputies does not better understand the real interests of France, and that questions have been imprudently raised, on which it would have been better to maintain silence In the English Parliament, even the Opposition would not seek to embarrass the Government by bringing forward indiscreet demands which might compromise the material interests of the country   .

March 18*th*

. It is with great satisfaction, that I have read the postscript of your despatch No 34, which contains the telegraphic despatch from the French *Chargé d'Affaires* in Vienna The news it gives about Constantinople, and which has been confirmed to me by the Austrian *Chargé d'Affaires*, seems to me of the utmost importance I must congratulate the King's Government, on the result obtained by Admiral Roussin , it is a great and splendid success for the honour of France and the tranquillity of Europe I am fully convinced that we shall speedily feel its good effect, and that the present policy of France will make a profound impression on all the various Cabinets [1]

[1] This is what had occurred at Constantinople

The French Ambassador, Admiral Roussin, had arrived at Constantinople on the 17th February, just as the Russians were entering the Bosphorus He at once declared that he would leave immediately, unless the Porte insisted on the departure of the Russian fleet The Sultan replied, that the Russian fleet was his only safeguard against the troops of Ibrahim Pasha The admiral answered, that he would undertake to impose peace on Mehemet Ali and make him accept the conditions that Halil was taking to him (see page 86 and note) The Divan, delighted to see France espousing its cause so warmly, at once required the Russians to depart, and they left in the course of a few days This retreat was at first looked upon as a victory for France , but the

Baron Neumann has told me of the despatch sent to him on this subject by Prince Metternich, you will have received the details by telegraphic despatch, but I can give you the assurance that M. de Metternich's letter is noticeable for the satisfaction it expresses at the failure of Russia's attempts[1]

It is quite evident that all the Powers, who are called on to reap the benefit of our efforts, must share the sentiments of the Vienna Cabinet. As for ourselves, we shall have thereby gained the enormous advantage of having exercised the noblest patronage, in the solution of a question which is both a French and a European one, and of having again linked our interests to those of the other Governments by a fresh tie. It is, I repeat again, a grand success, which places the King's Government in the high position which is its due.

THE DUC DE BROGLIE TO THE PRINCE DE TALLEYRAND

PARIS, *March 18th*, 1833

MON PRINCE,

I quite feel with you, all the annoyance and puerile folly of bringing the affairs of Algiers forward just now. But we have to do with people who are so unreasonable, that it is impossible to avoid all discussion on this wretched subject. Nevertheless, there is one point I should greatly like made clear between the English Government and ourselves, that is, as to the engagements made with England on the subject of Algiers. I have carefully gone through the whole correspondence before saying anything. Each page shows not only the absence of all engagements, but a most obstinate resistance to any engagement of this nature, a resistance which continued up to the taking of Algiers, and all but caused a rupture between France and England. I sent for M. de Bois-le-Comte,[2] who had

---

following month, Mehemet having distinctly refused Ibibil's conditions, the Sultan notwithstanding the remonstrances of the admiral recalled the Russians, and the position of our ambassador, who had thus imprudently pledged himself, became awkward.

[1] This also was the feeling in the English Cabinet if one is to believe what Lord Palmerston wrote to his brother, Sir William Temple "Roussin," he says in his letter of 21st March, "has admirably ended the dispute between the Turk and the Egyptian and has done well in sending back the Russian admiral with his tail between his legs." *Private correspondence of Lord Palmerston.*)

[2] Charles Joseph Edmund, Comte de Bois-le-Comte, born in 1796, entered the diplomatic service in 1814, and went to Vienna, St. Petersburg, and Madrid. In 1829, he became director of political affairs to the Ministry of Foreign Affairs. Under the July Monarchy, he was made minister in Portugal, Holland, and Switzerland. He was created a Peer of France in 1845, and died in 1863.

been director of political affairs under M de Polignac   I interrogated him closely on the matter , he declares that no engagement whatever has been entered into   Finally, I desired him
to write me a full account of the Algerian affair from this
memorandum I will extract everything that concerns England
and forward it to you, so that you may make what use of
it you think best   I therefore wish, on the one hand, to
have it made plain, that I have not spoken lightly on this
subject, and on the other, I wish to come to a clear understanding with the English Government, as to the value and
nature of these supposed engagements, of which we can find no
trace whatever here, either in the documents, or in the recollection of the persons attached to the department   Be good
enough to speak of this, mon Prince, to Lord Palmerston   I
say again, that I should be very sorry if anyone could
accuse me, with the slightest show of reason, of having retracted
from any engagement made even by M de Polignac .

LORD GREY TO THE PRINCE DE TALLEYRAND

DOWNING STREET, *March* 21st, 1833

MON PRINCE,

I return you herewith, with many thanks, the documents you did me the honour to entrust to me
In them I have found all the good feeling and uprightness
that distinguish M le Duc de Broglie, and I hope that we shall
be enabled to come to an understanding on this Algerian
business, in a manner conformable to the friendly relations of
both Governments and the European interests thereto attached
I pray you

THE PRINCE DE TALLEYRAND TO THE DUC DE BROGLIE.

LONDON, *March* 22nd, 1833

. I have informed Lord Grey of everything relating to
the Algerian question[1]   I have more reason than ever to think
that great importance is attached here to this matter, and I shall
be very glad to get the memorandum you speak of   Lord
Palmerston has instructed the Crown counsel to draw up one

---

[1] Sitting of March 8th   On the occasion of the credits demanded for the army
in Africa, Marshal Soult, President of the Council, made the following statement :—
" .   I have already said that we are not pledged to any undertaking relative to
Algiers, as regards the Foreign Powers   France may deal with that country in any
way suitable to her policy   The measures taken by the Government, and the loans we
now ask for, do not look as if we thought of giving up the country "

on the same subject, as he has no documents, I do not know on what he can base it. Lord Stuart's letters to his Government, reporting some verbal communications, seem to me to furnish but poor arguments to persons of good faith.

I am not surprised at the dissatisfaction which the results obtained by Admiral Roussin have produced on the Russian Government and its agents; it is easy to understand that after having taken the lead in so important a matter, the Russian Cabinet should feel hurt at seeing it put an end to by our intervention. It is however only a question of *amour-propre*, though for that very reason, I think we ought to show more moderation, in our satisfaction at a success which everyone will know how to appreciate.

THE DUC DE BROGLIE TO THE PRINCE DE TALLEYRAND

PARIS, March 22nd, 1833

MON PRINCE,

I am very glad that you are satisfied with the conduct of Admiral Roussin. His instructions were to endeavour by all lawful and reasonable means to prevent the Russians from occupying Constantinople, *with the consent of the Porte*. Should they occupy it *against the wishes* of the Porte, it would at once become a European matter, and we should then have more allies than would be necessary, to make them clear out. Roussin has managed very well. I am quite prepared for an outburst from St. Petersburg, but, after all, what can they do? They can only protest against *the proceeding*, and then I shall make a counter-protest and will complain of the dissimulation with which the whole of this business has been carried on, and the small amount of sincerity in their communication of Mouravieff's mission. Poor Pozzo is in mortal fear of being recalled, and the rest of the diplomatic corps are very anxious.

I am greatly pleased that all this is so much approved of in England. The extreme coldness with which for the last three months the English Government has received all our overtures relative to Eastern affairs, made me fear that we might be abandoned at this juncture, and it is for this reason, that in the short article inserted in our papers of the day before yesterday, no mention was made of the English legation. I feared that the English Government might accuse us of wishing to compromise it in this affair, but now that it shows itself disposed to come forward and join in it, I will have another article drawn up to-morrow, in which the English legation will almost play the principal part I hoped I should have been interrogated this morning in the Chamber of Deputies, when in my reply I should have placed the English legation in the front rank, but our adversaries found the ground too favourable for us, and they voted the money we asked for the armaments in the Mediterranean, without a word and unanimously Would it not be possible for the English to send some reinforcements to their naval station ? Even if they only made a pretence, it would have the best effect

THE PRINCE DE TALLEYRAND TO THE DUC DE BROGLIE

LONDON, *March* 28*th*, 1833

MONSIEUR LE DUC,

In one of the last despatches you did me the honour to send, you spoke of an interview between Sir Stratford Canning and M de Rayneval, the result of which was that England would not be indisposed to treat the Portuguese question on the basis of Dom Miguel's recognition

I have already pointed out to you, the difficulties I have to contend with, in order to procure information as to the precise intentions of the English Cabinet with respect to Spain and Portugal I can, however, inform you that I have several times spoken to Lord Palmerston about the state of the Peninsula, and from what he has said to me on these different occasions, I feel sure England has no settled scheme for putting an end to the condition of affairs in Portugal I am even led to believe, that since the departure of Sir Stratford Canning, and more especially since that diplomat has failed in the negotiation he was to carry out at Madrid, the English Cabinet has rather trusted to the chapter of accidents to solve the Portuguese question It now awaits further information from Sir Stratford Canning, and I think that he has received no other instructions than to act according to circumstances

I am not sending you the note which Sir Stratford Canning sent to M de Zea on February 3rd, nor the latter's reply, dated February 28th, I have them here, but I suppose M. de Rayneval will not have failed to transmit copies of these two documents to you

I again renew the assurance, that I will neglect no means to procure all the information I possibly can, as to the intentions of the English Government with regard to the affairs of Spain and Portugal, and will hasten to forward them to you

MADAME ADÉLAIDE D'ORLÉANS TO THE PRINCE DE TALLEYRAND

TUILERIES, *March 25th*, 1833

I write, mon cher Prince, to inform you of a visit which you will shortly receive in London, namely, from Chartres Our dear King considers that this journey, which he is so anxious to make, cannot fail to have a good effect Lord Granville, to whom the Duc de Broglie spoke about it, is of the same opinion Last night Chartres asked me to write to you about it ; and we shall be very glad to hear what you think of it I believe that it will be most useful and beneficial to our dear boy ; he wishes to make it a matter of instruction, and see all the great manufactories, the improvements, the railroads, &c You will be an admirable guide for him in this journey He proposes to leave here on April 7th Easter day, and return on May 1st, the fête day of the King, who will probably write to the King of England, telling him of Chartres proposed visit What do you think of it ?

THE PRINCE DE TALLEYRAND TO THE DUC DE BROGLIE

LONDON *April 9th*, 1833

MONSIEUR LE DUC,

Lord Palmerston has not been well enough to receive me to-day ; he has not in fact seen anyone I also failed in seeing Sir James Graham [1] the First Lord of the Admiralty, who is also indisposed, but I succeeded in seeing Lord Grey, to whom I made known the contents of the despatch respecting Eastern affairs which you sent me on the 4th of this month

Lord Grey told me that England would not remain inactive under these grave circumstances and that orders had been issued to all the available ships stationed in the Tagus and the various English cruisers in the Mediterranean to proceed at once to Alexandria This naval force has been instructed to support Colonel Campbell's negotiations ; you have been informed of the instructions that officer received when he was sent to Alexandria, you can therefore judge of the line of conduct he will follow

In the event of the Pasha of Egypt refusing to consent to the proposals approved by Colonel Campbell, the English squadron will not permit a single war-vessel of Mehemet Ali's to leave the ports of Egypt, and will also intercept all transport

[1] Sir James Graham born in 1792 member of the House of Commons, was First Lord of the Admiralty in Lord Grey's Cabinet In 1841, he became Home Secretary, and in 1852 Colonial Secretary He died in 1861

of men or ammunition that they may attempt to send to Ibrahim's army

Further, orders have been sent to the commander of the English naval forces in the Mediterranean to act in concert with the French admiral, if Colonel Campbell's negotiations at Alexandria should fall through.

Such is the communication I have received from Lord Grey in Lord Palmerston's absence

It appears, according to the advices you have received from Vienna, and which you did me the honour to forward, that M de Metternich is greatly disturbed at the events that are taking place in the East, and that he is secretly disquieted as to the ulterior projects of Russia The information received in London from Vienna, either by the Cabinet or the Foreign Ministers whom I have seen, is not in this sense On the contrary, both the despatches and private letters state, that M de Metternich tries to reassure all those who are alarmed at the presence of the Russians in the Bosphorus, and that he has full and complete confidence in the assurances given by the Cabinet of St Petersburg, and by the Emperor Nicholas

It is also stated in the accounts you have from Vienna, that public opinion has expressed itself loudly against Russia I am a little surprised to hear the public opinion of Vienna quoted , my recollections and my actual knowledge of that place, led me to believe that there was no such thing as public opinion in Vienna , society there has an opinion, but society is one , it is not divided, and M de Metternich is its leading spirit it would, I think, be a great mistake to count upon finding an ally in public opinion there

However, the general feeling in London is, that the present Eastern affairs will settle themselves, because the four Great Powers (including Russia) who have a more or less direct interest in them, seem all to incline towards the same end, namely, the maintenance of the Ottoman Empire

April 11*th*, 1833

. . By to-day's post, we have received an account of the occurrences that have just taken place at Frankfort, which appear to be rather serious[1] I pray you to consider them in

---

[1] A sanguinary insurrection had broken out at Frankfort, on the 3rd April It was after the Revolution of July The movement was the final episode of the ferment and the disturbances that had arisen all over Germany It was quelled by the troops of the Diet, and the territory of the Republic was placed under the military occupation of Austria

connection with what I have had the honour several times to point out to you, the influence they will have on the Austrian Cabinet M de Metternich only shows perfect confidence in the intentions of Russia, because he is afraid of the influence and the disturbances which a revolutionary spirit may create in Germany and Italy He is, in general, inclined to sacrifice the foreign policy of Austria to what he considers the essential principle of his home policy, and as he now sees in the Russian Government a declared enemy to the spirit of innovation, he is quite determined to ally himself with it, in order to repress any attempts on the part of German or Italian agitators Not that he absolutely neglects the important interests of Hungary and Austria for Eastern affairs, but these are only a secondary consideration with him

I am not surprised at the suggestions thrown out to you by M d'Appony and M de Werther, to open a conference on Eastern affairs in Vienna ; this is another of M de Metternich's inspirations Ever since the existence of the London Conference, he has not attempted to conceal his dissatisfaction at seeing negotiations carried on outside his direct influence, and he uses his best endeavours to bring them back to himself again ; it is, I believe, entirely a question of *amour-propre*   [1]

---

[1] M de Metternich, in fact, earnestly desired to withdraw the centre of the negotiations from London, especially as regards Eastern affairs In January last, he had given indications of this to the St James's Cabinet, but they were ignored In the beginning of February, just when the Courts of Berlin and Vienna sought to improve their relations with France (see p 87 and note), a move, which had the same end in view, was attempted with the Cabinet of the Tuileries When events were precipitated in the East, and an understanding was come to between the Sultan and the Pasha of Egypt (see p 118) M de Metternich's vexation increased He addressed himself to M de Sainte-Aulaire, to whom he repeated the proposition he had already made to Lord Palmerston and the Duc de Broglie The latter, in acquainting the Prince de Talleyrand of these incidents added, ' Prince de Metternich, on learning from M de Sainte-Aulaire the terms of the arrangement concluded on the 5th of this month, manifested considerable excitement and uneasiness He attaches such importance to the territory of Adana, that although fully recognizing that the Powers should unite their efforts to maintain the arrangement arrived at between the Porte and the Pasha he considers it indispensable it should be modified in this respect He spoke vaguely of the necessity of coming to an agreement on the Eastern question, and of establishing for this purpose at Vienna, not a Congress, nor even a regular Conference, but a centre for deliberations All this is very vague and very confused, and singularly manifests the false and uncertain position in which the Cabinet of Vienna has placed itself with reference to Eastern events " (*Despatch of 26th May*) The Cabinet at the Tuileries refused to accede to the Austrian demand Eight days later the Duc de Broglie wrote "We shall not give the slightest encouragement to the Austrian proposal M de Sainte-Aulaire will simply acquaint M de Metternich, that he is authorized to discuss with him, any overtures which the Chancellor considers it necessary to make respecting the condition of the Ottoman Empire ' (*Despatch of 3rd June*)

THE DUC DE BROGLIE TO THE PRINCE DE TALLEYRAND

PARIS, *April* 12*th*, 1833

. MON PRINCE,

I blame myself for not having written to you more fully respecting M le Duc d'Orléans' journey. When the question was first mooted, the various little difficulties to which it might give rise did not, I confess, strike me as they ought to have done It seemed to me quite a simple matter, and to say truth, I had not thought it over sufficiently when I foolishly mentioned it to Lord Granville as a probable and possible event, before it had actually been decided upon He regarded it as a fact, and wrote at once to his Government about it, assuring me that nothing would please the King of England more Nevertheless, on thinking it over quietly, it seemed to me that though it was not a bad idea in itself, it would be well to prepare for it, and to take such measures as would insure its success With this view, I have done my best to defer the journey M le Duc d'Orléans does not wish to go as a Royal Prince, nor as a Prince travelling incognito It still remains to be ascertained, how one can arrange a suitable reception for him in this intermediate position I do not know whether I am right, but, for my part, I have laid great stress, both with the King and with him, on his taking the highest possible stand when he goes to England, and on his not giving a chance to those persons who would ask nothing better than to treat him *en parvenu* I have begged him to think well over this, and then give me his ideas as to the number and description of the people who are to accompany him, and the etiquette to which he wishes to resign himself, in a word, as to all the accessories of the journey as he thinks it ought to be carried out. When he has given me his ideas on this subject, I will write to you, and ask for your valuable advice to aid me in rectifying whatever may be deficient M le Duc d'Orléans has acquired much knowledge I feel sure that his deportment will be admirable , his desire to visit England is caused more by the wish to escape from the idle life in Paris than anything else. Here he is absolutely a stranger to all politics, almost too much so, for it has made him gayer than he would be naturally After all, we have at least a month before us, and between then and now, I shall have time to receive your directions as to what had better be done

Our affairs in the East are becoming somewhat complicated, but I think we shall, nevertheless, succeed in the end.

II 2

THE PRINCE DE TALLEYRAND TO THE DUC DE BROGLIE

LONDON, *April 15th*, 1833

MON CHER DUC,

The delay respecting M le Duc d'Orléans's journey has had this advantage, that he will have escaped the slight epidemic that is prevalent here , Lord Palmerston and M Dedel have been attacked , the King of Holland, who is also ill, has sent no answer

I trust that M le Duc d'Orléans will not quit Paris until after the approaching event at Blaye , it would hardly be suitable for so near a relation, and under such special circumstances, to be abroad at such a period No political interest whatever is felt here in Madame la Duchesse de Berry , but she has inspired a feeling of pity Why then should not M le Duc d'Orléans, who is master of his own time, put off his journey until after the convalescence of his cousin ?

My despatch of to-day is somewhat meagre, for the week that has just elapsed has been very dull, at least apparently so If one were to believe all the reports that are circulated, it has been passed in a sort of intestine war which would threaten immediate changes in the Cabinet But without believing in so serious a result, the Ministry must at present not only experience great Parliamentary difficulties, but also difficulties in the Cabinet from the varied opinions of those composing it I do not think matters have advanced far enough in this direction to be made the subject of a despatch , I must confess, however, mon cher Duc, that I have no great opinion of the importance that is attached by us to secrecy I have several times during the last three years had reason to fear, that what took place at the Council in Paris very quickly became the property of the salons

The storm that threatens here will, in my private opinion, pass away without bursting , but it would not need its recurrence for me to draw your attention to the difficulties of the home administration

April 18th, 1833

I saw Lord Palmerston yesterday In speaking to him concerning matters in the Levant, I made use of the observations contained in your despatch No 47, in order to prove to him the great inconvenience of even an apparent discord between Great Britain and France, in the negotiations that are now being carried on at Alexandria and Constantinople He fully appreciated the importance of these observations, and said that as

Colonel Campbell s instructions laid down that in his conduct, he was, as much as possible, to conform to that of the Consul-General of France, he had no doubt our action on this point would be simultaneous , that with regard to Constantinople, he could not entirely approve of the hastiness which Admiral Roussin had displayed, ever since the commencement of the mission with which he had been entrusted [1] that the English *Chargé d'Affaires*, who had received no instructions, was bound to exhibit a certain reserve, which was better suited to his secondary position, and perhaps also, to the actual circumstances in which he was placed

I am very glad that you have requested Lord Granville to inform Lord Palmerston, of the ideas with which the conduct of England in Eastern affairs has inspired you I have already, more than once, had occasion to point out to you that the English Cabinet, either through pre-occupation by the increase of Egyptian supremacy, or the indifference it feels in questions of foreign policy which do not interest it directly, has always received the various proposals I have brought forward rather coldly I shall therefore be very glad of the support of Lord Granville's opinion with the members of the Cabinet

Lord Palmerston told me that the Austrian *Chargé d'Affaires* had informed him of M de Metternich's project, which you wished to communicate to me, and which consisted in negotiating, the various questions relative to Eastern affairs at Vienna [2] M de Metternich does not want this negotiation to take the form of a Congress or a Conference , he is afraid, no doubt, that he might seem to imitate in some way what is now being done in London Lord Palmerston is not indisposed to adopt M de Metternich's idea, as regards the meeting of the four Powers to regulate the pacification of the Levant , for he thinks, and in this I agree with him, that the best way to neutralise the evil intentions of Russia is to ask her to take part in all the negotiations, and bind her by such engagements as she could hardly refuse to accept Russia, acting alone, will require the utmost vigilance , working in concert with the other three Powers, the danger of her action is greatly lessened But, on the other hand, Lord Palmerston would prefer that this matter should rather be dealt with at Constantinople than at Vienna The apparent reasons he gives are, the necessity for being actually on the spot in an affair of such great importance, and the difficulties caused by distance But I believe the real cause for his preferring Constantinople to Vienna, is the idea that M de Metternich, by

[1] See page 91   [2] See page 98

holding this negotiation at Vienna, might end in attracting thither
the affairs of Europe, and thereby diminishing the influence of the
close alliance between France and England, which now offends
him   In my opinion, Constantinople is decidedly to be preferred,
as there all the inconvenience of delays will be avoided, a serious
evil in the weak state of the Ottoman Empire   I fancy that having
such confidence in Admiral Roussin, the King's Government could
not fail to agree to the choice of that city as the centre of the
negotiation   .

April 23rd, 1833

I have read with great interest M Bresson's letter of April
14th, which you have done me the honour to communicate,[1] and
I confess that I have great hopes as to the results of Comte Matusiewicz's presence in Berlin, in solving our negotiations with the
King of the Netherlands   I think it would not conduce to
the success of the Hollando-Belgian affairs, to show any distrust
just now respecting the conduct of the Russian Cabinet, we
must, on the contrary, make the most of whatever is offered us
My former experience has taught me, that there are circumstances in which confidence, even if somewhat hazardous,
becomes a matter of expediency   This opinion gains still further
strength and value, when one finds a pledge of security in the
separate and well-founded interests of those in whom one trusts

It is on this principle also, that I base the necessity for France,
England, and above all Austria, to claim the co-operation of
Russia in Eastern affairs, for I am fully persuaded that it is to
the true interests of Russia to reassure Europe, *for the present*, as
to the ambitious projects attributed to her   The very conciliatory
language, so full of abnegation, which M de Lieven has never
ceased to hold here, only still further confirms me in this opinion

The last news received in London from Constantinople, has
created some exaggerated alarm here, partly, I think, because no
one was prepared for so rapid a march of events   There has
evidently been a want of forethought on the part of the Government, and for repairing this provision must now be made
The English Ministry, which up to now has taken but little

---

[1] In this despatch M Bresson announced the arrival in Berlin of Comte Matusiewicz, on a mission to invite the Prussian Cabinet to join in the Note of April 2nd   It
will be remembered (see page 62) that this Note had been sent by the Prince de
Talleyrand and Lord Palmerston to M Dedel, in reply to some inadmissible proposals
he had formulated in his project of March 23rd   M Bresson gave an account of the
steps taken by M Matusiewicz, who, he said, had convinced the King of Prussia   He
praised his boldness, for he had acted thus without having specially referred to his
Court   He also spoke of his request on the same subject to the Austrian Minister,
who however had not replied, and had asked for instructions from Vienna

interest in this grave question, is at last beginning to appreciate its just value Lord Grey and Lord Palmerston had both spoken to me with some anxiety respecting the state of the East, even before the arrival of Lord Granville I have no doubt that this ambassador's presence in London, will contribute greatly to draw the attention of the British Cabinet to this matter

I have given much thought as to what really would be the best to do for the East, and though it is very difficult to form any plans with regard to such complicated and uncertain events as those now taking place in Asia, it is at least possible to hold oneself in readiness to lessen their evil effects, by providing for a future teeming with dangerous collisions, or by sanctioning the results of these events, if they really offer some kind of guarantee to the Governments of Europe

As recent events permit the expression of individual opinions, my observations have confirmed me in the idea, that in order to terminate Eastern affairs now in a way most re-assuring to Europe, the joint action of all the four Powers is absolutely necessary This joint action would have to be expressed by some deed, which would contain a formal under-taking on the part of the contracting Powers not to receive any territorial augmentation at the expense of the Ottoman Empire There would be nothing unusual in such an undertaking, it was even recently applied to the Greek question, when the three signatory Powers of the treaty of July 6th, 1827, pledged themselves not to choose a sovereign for Greece from among the members of the reigning families of France, Russia, and England

We should find no difficulty as regards Algiers in such an undertaking, the principle of our expedition having already received the full and entire approbation of Russia and Austria. Moreover, to shelter ourselves completely, it would suffice to choose a time, when there could be no possible doubt as to our right to a permanent occupation of the Algerian territory

I have communicated the opinion I have just had the honour to explain to you, to Lord Palmerston, it will be submitted to a Cabinet Council this evening, and I hope to-morrow to be in a position to acquaint you of a definite resolution

April 25th, 1833

MON CHER DUC,

This Eastern business is becoming too bad It is certainly rather strange that Admiral Roussin should not have assured him-self of the feeling at Alexandria, before taking such a high hand at Constantinople[1] this has led us all astray However, we must face matters as they now stand Here, after a long spell of lethargy, they have suddenly awakened to a sort of alarm, but this fright has not resulted in any expedient, and each in turn has come to talk to me about it and to ask my advice I was able therefore to tell them what, *in my private opinion*, I believe to be the only sound issue You will find the details of it in my despatch of to-day To-morrow I shall be able to tell you more, as my *verbal* project is to be submitted to a Cabinet Council this evening Lord Palmerston accepted it eagerly this morning, but his opinion of itself is not sufficient to warrant taking any action, which this time I hope will not be long delayed, as it is specially a question of expediency So adieu till to-morrow

April 26th

The resolution which I had the honour to mention in my despatch of yesterday, has been adopted by the English Cabinet, which will, I believe, propose to the Russian, Austrian, and French Governments, to conclude a convention containing in about three articles, the following —

1 An undertaking not to consent to any dismemberment of the Ottoman Empire, either in favour of one of the four contracting parties, or any other Power

2 The consent of all the four Powers to be given, in any arrangement between the Ottoman Porte and the Pasha of Egypt in consequence of which the suzerainty and the integrity of the Ottoman Empire would be maintained

3 An undertaking to be given equally by the four Courts, to compel the Pasha of Egypt by such measures as they may mutually agree on, should he not consent to an arrangement, such as that defined in the preceding article

I have here indicated the three points which will be embodied in the draft of the convention, but cannot specify how it will be definitely drawn up and adopted That however will at once be communicated to you

My despatch of yesterday will have reassured you, I hope, on the only question which directly interests France, I insisted on the dates, you will see whether those proposed suit you.

I did not see any objection to the proposal coming from England, who only wishes to have a European interest in Eastern affairs, and who, having up to the present taken no active part in them, finds herself placed in a more impartial position with regard to the other Powers than we are

If such a proposition is not accepted by the Austrian and

[1] See page 91

Russian Governments we might see in this refusal a proof that those two Governments have some *arrière-pensées*, perhaps even some projects of division, for to make use of a common saying, " they are old hands at such work."

I shall await with impatience, your replies to my despatches of yesterday and to-day   . .

April 29*th*, 1833

I learn with great pleasure that you consider the discussion which had arisen between the Court of St Petersburg and the French Government, respecting Admiral Roussin's negotiations at Constantinople, as ended   That is one complication the less, at a time when such are assuredly not wanting

When this despatch reaches you, Monsieur le Duc, the English papers which almost always anticipate our couriers, will have informed you of the serious embarrassment which has arisen for the Government in consequence of the vote on Friday night in the House of Commons, by which the malt tax has been reduced by one half   This reduction will cause a decrease in the receipts of nearly £2,500,000 sterling, and if the abolition of the window tax is adopted to-morrow, as it is quite possible it may be, there will be a deficit of nearly five millions sterling

The Ministry has had several meetings during the last three days, in order to provide for this embarrassment   They find the greatest possible difficulty in meeting the deficit with which they are threatened   . It is a very serious matter , men's minds are greatly excited here , the funds have experienced a considerable change , and the discussions in the papers have redoubled in violence   It is not thought however, that this triumph on the part of the opposition will lead to the resignation of the Ministry , but it will have the unfortunate effect of awakening distrust among its partisans and consequently weakening its strength   It is thought that this evening the Ministry will present to the House of Commons a resolution which the vote of Friday has obliged them to take , its tenor is not yet known, and the state of the tide will, I fear, prevent my sending it you to-day   But I will write to you on this subject to-morrow, by courier

Your despatch of the 25th, containing the copy of a letter from M Bresson of the 18th, caused me great satisfaction, which, however, unfortunately, did not last long   By the last accounts from Berlin, we learn that M Ancillon, when on the point of signing the note agreed upon with Comte Matusiewicz, suddenly changed his mind, under the pretext that the vote of the Cabinet at the Hague, of April 16th, ought to suffice us, owing to the propositions it contains with reference to the armistice. I must say that I cannot understand such a method of doing business; it would be discouraging for the future, were it not that one must always expect some fresh departure on the part of M. Ancillon[1] We have received no intelligence from the Hague since the despatch of our letter of the 22nd,[2] but we expect to hear at any moment; the first accounts will probably not be of much interest. It is greatly to be feared that M. Ancillon's indecisions, the state of the East, and above all the present embarrassment of the English Ministry, will only create fresh difficulties for us at the Hague.

Evening, April 29th, 1833

MON CHER DUC,

An enemy to evil predictions, I refrain from making any as to to-day's results, which nevertheless are of great importance as regards the political and financial interests of the Ministry and the country. I will confine myself to drawing your attention to the *Times* of to-day. Read, I pray you, the *leading article* and the *money market.* You will not fail to see their tendency, and you will then understand England's present position.

The Tories will honestly support the Ministry in the House to-day; but if Friday's vote is not annulled, matters here

___

[1] Comte Matuszewicz's mission at Berlin had passed through various phases. At first it seemed to have great success, so much so that M. Bresson in a despatch of April 24th positively announced that M. Matuszewicz was starting for the Hague, after having drawn up with M. Ancillon the terms of the collective Note which was to be sent to the Cabinet of the Netherlands under two hypotheses, the first, if its reply to the note of October 2nd was negative, evasive, or dilatory, the second, if no reply was received within a reasonable period of delay. If the reply were favourable, action would not be taken, and the Berlin Cabinet would join its efforts to those of the other courts to hasten the conclusion of a definite treaty. Everything seemed in order, when suddenly M. Ancillon changed his mind (M. Bresson's despatch of 22nd April) and declared that there was no reason whatever for sending the collective Note. Notwithstanding this, the French Cabinet returned to the charge and with the assistance of Lord Minto, the English minister, ended in persuading the king. Finally, on the 6th of May, M. Bresson was able to write to Paris, that the Note had been sent off the evening before, to the Hague. He added that M. Ancillon had told him that should the King of the Netherlands refuse, Prussia intended to leave him to himself. [Official correspondence of M. Bresson.]

[2] It will be remembered (see page 62) that M. Dedel had made fresh proposals to the Conference in a Note dated April 16th. These, considered inadmissible in London (see letter on this subject from Lord Palmerston to M. de Talleyrand, Appendix letter No. 9) had provoked a very sharp response from the Conference in the form of a collective letter to the Cabinet of the Hague. It is this letter, dated April 22nd, which is here spoken of.

will speedily assume a totally different aspect, and one will soon see, as Madame de Lieven said yesterday with suppressed delight, that 'England will hardly then weigh in the balance of Europe" Adieu , a thousand greetings

LONDON, *May 1st*, 1833

MONSIEUR LL DUC,

As I had the honour to acquaint you yesterday, the sitting in the House of Commons did not end until 4 o'clock this morning, with a vote in favour of the Ministry By a majority of 154, the House decided to cancel the abolition of the malt tax

It is hoped that this circumstance, which at first caused some serious apprehension, will render the discussion on the budget somewhat easier The funds have risen considerably to-day

THE DUC DE BROGLIE TO THE PRINCE DE TALLEYRAND

PARIS, *April 29th*, 1833

MON PRINCE,

You will find in my despatch sent herewith, the decision arrived at this morning by the King's Council We accept England's proposal as far as its principle goes, reserving to ourselves discussion of the draft when we receive it I trust the matter at Constantinople will be concluded, before the answer from the Courts of Austria and Russia arrives , yet that will be a good reason for the Russians to clear out I am very vexed that England did not make up her mind sooner, but it certainly is not my fault Ever since I took office, I have not ceased to urge her to send an Ambassador to Constantinople I have shown Lord Granville almost daily, all the despatches I sent off as well as those which I received on this subject , I have warned him, entreated him and urged him , I have not left him in ignorance of anything, whenever an incident of the slightest importance occurred , I also entreated you, mon Prince, to renew your overtures on this subject However, better late than never , I still hope we shall come out of it triumphantly , but everything might have been finished, both at Alexandria and Constantinople, if the English Cabinet had liked

I send you a despatch from M Biesson which will show you that M Matusiewicz has failed at Berlin [1] I believe we must begin to show our teeth, otherwise people will fancy that we

[1] See page 106

have reached the summit of our influence, and Holland will
laugh at us Would it not be possible to make the blockades
more stringent, and to press more heavily on Dutch commerce?
The best season of the year is passing, if we do not profit by it,
what will be said of us? Adieu, mon Prince

THE PRINCE DE TALLEYRAND TO THE DUC DE BROGLIE.

LONDON, *May 3rd*, 1833

I often converse with Lord Palmerston as to the means
best suited to France and England in coming to some final
arrangement with King William, and those which you mention
in your despatch, and in your letter of the 29th, have more than
once formed the topic of our conversations, but I must tell you
that we see, at any rate for the present, more than one difficulty
in carrying out the proposed scheme The English Cabinet is
fully occupied with various motions on Hollando-Belgian
matters, with which it is threatened in both Houses of Parliament,
and also pretty strongly expressed demands from the English
commercial world against the imposition of the embargo The
Cabinet therefore fears to increase the dissatisfaction which has
lately been expressed on this question, by any fresh restrictions
brought forward just now Lord Grey and Lord Palmerston still
hope that M Ancillon will come round to us again, and think
that Russia's assistance would be more advantageous to us than
an increase of coercive measures, they are supported in this
opinion by recent letters from Berlin, which represent M Ancillon
as not being indisposed to return to the project of a declaration
from the three Courts at the Hague Finally, we all think that
it is not possible to decide upon anything definite, before knowing
what will be the reply of the Hague to our Note of April
23rd

THE DUC DE BROGLIE TO THE PRINCE DE TALLEYRAND

PARIS, *May 4th*, 1833

You will find in my official despatch, mon Prince, the
résumé of our news from Constantinople The whole affair
at Alexandria only hangs on a thread Ibrahim is retiring, I
have reason to hope that the united efforts of everyone will
have their effect on the Pasha, and that we shall have it all our
own way But this makes it all the more needful now to

influence Russia, who, I hear from Constantinople, is doing all she can to prevent the *dénoûment*, in order to quietly obtain the upper hand in the Levant, thoroughly establish herself there, and not depart without creating a thousand difficulties I suppose that the late occurrences in the English Parliament are the only difficulty to the proposal you mentioned to me, and about which I hastened to reply to you After the victory, I hope we shall take up Eastern affairs afresh, and I entreat you, do not let the English Government go to sleep again

I do not know what we can hope for here from the proceedings of the three Courts at the Hague, M d'Eyragues' accounts are not very reassuring, the affair must, however, be brought to an end

Here, matters are going on very well, everything seems to point to a short and easy session

THE PRINCE DE TALLEYRAND TO THE DUC DE BROGLIE

LONDON, *May* 6*th*, 1833

MONSIEUR LE DUC,

Monseigneur le Duc d'Orléans arrived here the night before last, at ten in the evening, having had a good crossing and a comfortable journey.

I have received the despatch and private letter which you were good enough to send me on the 4th of this month, that which I had the honour to write to you on the 3rd, is virtually an answer to the observation you make on the Hollando-Belgian business I quite feel with you the need there is to terminate this matter, but there are circumstances here which render its speedy accomplishment just now very difficult It seems to me that the argument brought forward in the last paragraph of your despatch, is open to question, for it must not be lost sight of that the first Belgian expedition and the convention of October 22, were acts which, while they strengthened the French Ministry, contributed greatly to weaken the English one, so that there is no parallel between the two situations The imposition of the embargo has already caused much dissatisfaction in England, and the discussion to which it will give rise on Thursday or Friday next, in the House of Commons, cannot fail to produce a bad impression on public opinion As I pointed out to you in my last despatch, the accounts from Berlin still further strengthen the English Cabinet in their determination to await the result of the proceedings of the three Courts at the Hague, and the reply of the Government of the Netherlands to our Note of April 23rd This reply, according to M d Eyragues'[1] letters, will not now be long delayed .

By writing this despatch, I wished rather to lessen the ardour of the French Government, which, urged on by the Belgians, was led to ask for increased severities towards Holland, just when I felt assured that the King of the Netherlands was about to give in, if not on every point, at least on those which were most important to Belgium, and consequently to us My opinion was, as will be seen, soon proved to be well founded

THE PRINCE DE TALLEYRAND TO THE DUC DE BROGLIE

LONDON, May 13th, 1833

MONSIEUR LE DUC,

I had the honour to inform you, that Sir Pultney Malcolm had been appointed to the command of the English station in the Mediterranean He is to start at once, and has been entrusted with more extended powers than his predecessor Sir Arthur Aston [2] will have informed you of this, as well as what has been written to Lord Ponsonby, the English ambassador at Constantinople, on this subject The admiral and the ambassador are to come to an understanding with Admiral Roussin, and it is thought here that this concord between the two Powers will suffice to insure to their policy in the Levant, that influence which it must exercise under the present circumstances

The English Cabinet has abandoned the draft of the convention, which Lord Palmerston promised me should be proposed to the three Courts The Prince de Lieven, to whom he communicated it, made some objections to it, the chief of which somewhat surprised us He thinks that the Emperor of Russia could never consent to enter into a convention, which might constitute an actual act of intervention in the home affairs of Turkey On Lord Palmerston remarking that it seemed to him, the despatch of Russian vessels and troops to Constantinople was a much more positive act of intervention, M de

[1] The Marquis d'Eyragues, a French diplomat, at that time Secretary of the Embassy at the Hague since 1832 He was first sent to Copenhagen (1827) In 1835, he went as first secretary to Constantinople, and was subsequently accredited to Carlsruhe as minister plenipotentiary (1838) , and then to Dresden (1845)
[2] Sir Arthur Ingram Aston, English diplomat, born in 1798 was secretary to the Legation at Paris in 1833 He was appointed minister to Madrid in 1840

Lieven replied that he could not agree to that opinion The Sultan, he said, had asked the Emperor for assistance The Emperor had sent it to him with the firm resolution to leave it entirely at the Porte's disposal, as long as she deemed it necessary for her safety, but also, with equal resolution, to withdraw it as soon as the Sultan expressed a wish on this point Therefore, in this instance, it was a matter of assistance from an ally, not an intervention

However small the plausibility of this reply, Lord Palmerston had perforce to be satisfied with it, and to abandon a project which seemed to him fraught with innumerable difficulties

You will be able to judge for yourself, whether the instructions given to Admiral Malcolm will suffice to bring about a happy solution of Eastern affairs

The English papers will have informed you, of the result of Friday's discussion in the House of Commons on the Dutch embargo and the state of Turkey This result, though favourable to the ministry, does not reassure them, and the very general complaints in commercial circles make them feel the imperative necessity of putting an end to this Belgian affair Nevertheless, it would be very difficult to get them to have recourse to stronger measures, than those which have been employed up to now

THE DUC DE BROGLIE TO THE PRINCE DE TALLEYRAND

PARIS, *May* 13*th*, 1833

MON PRINCE,

There is nothing spoken of here but the magnificence of your *fêtes*. The king is enchanted with the reception accorded in England to M le Duc d'Orléans,[1] and he attributes to you, and with reason, the greater part of this general good feeling I, for my part, am all the more rejoiced, as it gives an answer to the reports which our ambassadors often seek to spread abroad, respecting a coldness between France and England

A still more complete answer to this are Lord Ponsonby's instructions, which Sir Arthur Aston has communicated to me

---

[1] The Duc d'Orléans has arrived, and I dined with him yesterday at Talleyrand's He has marvellously improved since I saw him in Paris in 1830 Even then he was good looking, but now he has become a man, and a very handsome one, and has all the manners and the deportment suitable to his rank He has really quite the air of an hereditary Prince, and from the conversations I have had with him, it struck me that his mind had developed quite as much as his person   [Lord Palmerston to the Honourable William Temple, May 7th, 1833]

this morning, and also those given to Sir Pultney Malcolm by the Admiralty These instructions are almost identical with ours, and I see that we shall begin to act in concert in Eastern affairs I am impatiently awaiting every moment the news from Alexandria, which has been announced by telegraph I trust it will contain the conclusion of the affair at that end Then there will only be the Russians to get rid of

If you can terminate the provisional convention with Holland, honourably and effectually, you will be rendering a great service to the King of the Belgians, who does not know which way to turn In any case, we are quite prepared to go as far as may be wished with coercive measures The Chambers are disposed to be patient, if it is necessary, or to support us in any energetic movement we may wish Home matters are working admirably, and prosperity has never before recovered itself so rapidly Tranquillity has been established everywhere If nothing from abroad occurs to disturb us, in another year there will not be a trace left of the agitation caused by the revolution of July.

You will see in the *Moniteur* of to-morrow, full details of Madame la Duchess de Berry's declaration That matter has ended in a somewhat burlesque and less disgraceful manner than could have been expected . .[1]

THE PRINCE DE TALLEYRAND TO THE DUC DE BROGLIE.

LONDON, *May 17th,* 1833

MON CHER DUC,

Your friendship wishes to attribute some of M. le Duc d'Orléans' success in London to me I may perhaps admit, between you and me, that I am not quite innocent of it ; but, nevertheless, I must say that it would be impossible to be more successful in every way than our young Prince is *The Duchess of Cumberland*[2] has just requested Madame de Dino to ask M. le Duc d'Orléans to go to Kew on Sunday, where she wishes to entertain him at luncheon For once the great bells are ringing and I think this mark of attention which I never expected is greatly due to the liberation of the prisoner at Blaye

---

[1] When about to be confined, Madame la Duchess de Berry declared that she was married to the Comte de Lucchesi Palli

[2] Frederica of Mecklenburg-Strelitz, sister of Queen Louisa of Prussia, born in 1778, married in 1815 Ernest Augustus, Duke of Cumberland, son of George III, King of England subsequently King of Hanover The Duchess of Cumberland died in 1841

When sending you M Dedel's Note [1] yesterday, I omitted to tell you that it would be better not to let M Lehon have a copy   I am afraid that he might make it known too soon in Brussels , on that account also I decided only to let M Van de Weyer read it   Moreover, if, as this Note gives us reason to hope, we shall soon arrive at a preliminary convention, we must protect ourselves against the demands of the Belgians, who will yet give us some trouble

I am delighted that you are satisfied with the instructions given to Lord Ponsonby and to Admiral Malcolm   Under the circumstances, I think it is indeed no small matter to have gained as much as we have

Let us hope that a preliminary and tranquillizing convention may be the result of M Dedel's last Note, to which, it seems to me, very few objections can be raised   You will notice that the title of Grand Duke of Luxembourg has been omitted   Is this done on purpose ?   We are to have a conference with M. Dedel either to-morrow or the day after   I will write to you as soon as anything is decided

May 20th, 1833

I have received the despatch you did me the honour to send, numbered 59, as well as the ratifications of the supplementary treaty, which regulates the order of succession to the Greek throne [2]

We had some conferences both yesterday and to-day, lasting several hours, between Lord Palmerston, M Dedel, and myself, and if I dared to believe in a hope which has so often deceived me, I should tell you that perhaps to-morrow we shall sign the preliminary Convention   M Dedel, whom I have just left, still hesitates about an explanatory article which we proposed to him, and if he does not decide between this and to-morrow, he will refer it to the Hague , that will cause a fresh delay of eight days   If, on the other hand, after a careful examination of his instructions, he considers that he is justified in consenting to the

---

[1] The Note of May 16th, in which, after a long discussion, M Dedel declared that "until a definite treaty had been signed, His Majesty of the Netherlands undertook not to recommence hostilities with Belgium, and to leave the navigation of the Scheldt entirely free "

[2] The object of this supplementary treaty, which was signed on the 30th April, 1833, was to establish and complete the provisions of Article 8 of the Convention of May 7th, which defined the succession to the Greek throne   It declared that the succession to the Crown, either in King Otto's branch, or that of the Princes Luitpold and Adalbert, which had been eventually substituted for that of Prince Otto, should be established from male to male by order of primogeniture   Females were not to be entitled to succeed to the Crown, except in case of the total extinction of legitimate male heirs in the three branches

proposal we have made to him, the Convention will be signed to-morrow

I need not assure you that I am doing all in my power to hasten the solution of a matter of which no one appreciates the importance more than myself I shall have the honour to inform you of the result of the Conference, which we are to have to-morrow

May 21st, 1833.

This time my hopes have not been deceived, and I have the honour to send you the preliminary Convention which I mentioned to you yesterday, and which we have just signed with M Dedel[1] It contains all the stipulations which it seemed to me were essentially necessary to obtain, for the evident result of this Convention is, that Belgium finds herself in a most *favourable* position, whilst that of the King of the Netherlands is so *unfavourable* that he will himself be compelled speedily to ask for a definite treaty The opening of the Scheldt, and the non-payment of the interest of the debt by Belgium, will very quickly force him to do this I think, therefore, that I have completely carried out the wishes of the king's Government, by concluding an arrangement which contains everything it was possible to ask just now from the Dutch Government

You will perceive that we have added a separate Article at the end, which fully explains Article III, respecting which we did not wish there should be any uncertainty We first asked that it might be inserted in the treaty, but M Dedel, whose assent to this Article we only obtained with great difficulty, objected to its forming part of the Convention itself, for a reason which seemed to us fairly founded, namely, that an explanation immediately following Article III, would appear to throw a doubt on the good faith of the proposal made by the King of the Netherlands, and that we owed at least this slight satisfaction both to the King of the Netherlands and to himself, as he feared he had exposed himself to the reproaches of his sovereign

---

[1] By this Convention, King William promised the maintenance of the armistice, the free navigation of the Scheldt and the Meuse, free communication between Maestricht, Brabant, and Germany On the other hand, the embargo on the Dutch vessels was removed, and the prisoners of war were set at liberty The explanatory Article, referred to further on, was as follows —

It is agreed between the high contracting parties, that the stipulation relative to the cessation of hostilities, contained in Article III of the Convention of this day, includes the Grand Duchy of Luxembourg, and those portions of Limburg provisionally occupied by the Belgian troops It is also understood, that until the conclusion of the definite treaty, of which mention is made in the said Article III of the Convention of to-day, the navigation of the Scheldt will be conducted as it was before the 1st November, 1832 The present Article will have the same force and value

by consenting to its insertion as we desired We agreed all the more readily to this, as the question is in itself of no great importance, since the explanatory Article must be ratified at the same time as the Convention, and have the same value

You will no doubt consider it unadvisable to make the Convention public until after the expiry of ten days, the time fixed for the exchange of the ratifications

The king's Government will doubtless deem that the proper time to ask for the disarmament of Belgium will be after the Convention has been ratified It might be advisable to hint at this measure in Brussels ; it would hasten a definite arrangement more than anything else , for if Belgium is once disarmed, the Dutch troops will disband themselves, or will very quickly be dismissed, and the Dutch Government will thus find itself obliged to put an end to a state of affairs which so seriously compromises its existence

M le Duc d'Orléans started this morning for Liverpool and Manchester ; His Royal Highness will return to London on the 28th .

BARON PASQUIER TO THE PRINCE DE TALLEYRAND.

PARIS, *May 18th*, 1833.

I have received your letter of the 14th, mon Prince, and thank you for all the good news it contains The success of the tour, which you have planned so admirably, will have an excellent effect here ; not that we can hope that our *Faubourg St Germain* will as yet listen to reason, but because its evil desires will be at least somewhat restrained thereby, and it will find fewer ears ready to listen to its insipid absurdities

The event at Blaye took place sooner than we expected , but I agree with you that, taking it altogether, the result has been very satisfactory It does not seem to have caused any unpleasantness in England as regards the Prince's position, and that was one of the essential points

I thank you for the support you have been able to give to my earnest desire for an amnesty , this desire, I admit, has become a fixed idea with me, and I cannot understand why every one does not see that it is an indispensable issue, and the only one by which it is possible to come profitably and honourably out of a serious political crisis If the occasion of the Duchesse de Berry's departure is not utilized, I do not see when another such favourable occasion is likely to arise

I need say nothing about our home affairs ; their improvement is visible to every eye, and as for foreign affairs, you know a hundredfold more about them than I do

I certainly neither lent my aid, nor did I approve of the measures taken, in connection with our poor friend Dalberg's death [1]   On the contrary, I was among those who were strongly against it, and even desired to bring about a positive decision, which would for the future afford protection against similar outrages, of which the utter uselessness is, and always will be, their least inconvenience [2]

A great deal is said about the consequences of the July Revolution, it seems to me that this one cannot be denied

Pray accept, mon Prince, with your usual kindness, the assurances of my most sincere devotion

PASQUIER

THE DUC DE BROGLIE TO THE PRINCE DE TALLEYRAND.

PARIS, *May 24th*, 1833

MON PRINCE,

Accept my sincere congratulations, you have effected, as you always do, the very best thing possible   If the King of the Belgians has any sense at all now, he will quietly establish himself under the provisional Convention dismiss half his army, and state plainly that he is quite ready to sign a definite treaty, but that he hopes it will be as late as possible, seeing that the provisional one is all in his favour   If he acts and speaks thus, we shall have the definite treaty before very long

While you have been doing such marvels, we have been running a terrible risk here   the discussion on the Greek loan has been most troublesome, and we only carried it by making it a regular Cabinet question [3]   However, the session is drawing to a close, and in six weeks all will be finished

[1] The Duc de Dalberg died on the 27th April, at the Château de Herrensheim, near Worms, at the age of fifty-five

[2] On the death of the Duc de Dalberg, the Government had sealed all his papers, which they claimed on account of the official positions which the Duc had filled [Note by M. de Bacourt]

[3] After the Convention of May 7th, 1832, by which the Greek throne was given to King Otto, the signatory Powers (France, Russia, and England) had undertaken to guarantee a loan of sixty millions, which the young king was about to raise   The first revenues of Greece were exclusively appropriated for the interest and the sinking fund of this loan   On the 24th January, 1833, the French Cabinet brought in a bill for authority to give its guarantee   On April 4th, it was favourably reported upon by Colonel Paixhans   It did not come up for discussion until May 18th   The bill, which was hotly contested by the opposition, occupied four days in discussion, and was finally passed by a vote of one hundred and seventy-five against one hundred and twelve   Fifteen days after, it was also passed by the Peers, with a majority of ninety-one against nine

THE PRINCE DE TALLEYRAND TO THE DUC DE BROGLIE

LONDON, *May 27th*, 1833

The discussion in the Chamber of Deputies, respecting the Greek loan, has been followed here with great interest, Monsieur le Duc, and I must tell you that public opinion has been quite unanimous with regard to the various speeches you have made on this matter The very clear and at the same time, brilliant statement you have made on the whole Greek negotiation, has been very generally admired Moreover, a very important constitutional question was involved in this business, and you have admirably defined the rights that are given to, and the limits that are imposed on the Chambers, when they intervene in diplomatic transactions concluded by the Government

I have the honour to send you a despatch which arrived this morning from the Hague It will show you the good effect produced there by the Convention which was signed on the 21st We can, I think, find in this a fresh proof of the inconvenience we should have experienced, if we had allowed ourselves to be influenced by any exaggerated reports If we had credited the information received from various quarters during the last few months, we should have been forced to believe that Holland's resistance was insurmountable, and that she was upheld by the three northern Courts Now we see that this information was rather the result of personal impressions, and perhaps inexperience in business affairs, than of a complete knowledge of the actual state of matters there

It is thought that the ratifications will arrive from the Hague on the 29th M Dedel, whom I have just seen, and who has also received most satisfactory accounts from the Hague, expects them on that day

M le Duc d'Orléans returned this afternoon at 4 o'clock from Liverpool His Royal Highness proposes to attend the Queen's drawing-room to-morrow, and then to start for Deal to inspect the French squadron stationed in the Downs

KING LOUIS PHILIPPE TO THE PRINCE DE TALLEYRAND

NEUILLY, *May 25th*, 1833

MON CHER PRINCE,

I do not wish to put off any longer telling you, how very sensible I am of the reception given to my son in England, and how fully I appreciate the part you have taken in preparing the way, and gaining this success, to which I attach the greatest value, both on account of its actual importance, and from my old feelings of friendship for that grand country   This success will confirm these feelings in my son, which will in itself be a great blessing for both countries   He is very sensible of it, and begs me tell you, and especially Madame de Dino, how very grateful he is for all you have done for him in this matter   I hope she will allow me to join in these thanks, until I can repeat them in person to her

I pray you, mon cher Prince, to try and seize an opportunity to express from me and the Queen, to the King and Queen of England, how very sensible we are of the kind reception they have given our son, and all the attention they have paid him Also kindly be my interpreter in the same way, to the Princes and Princesses of the Royal Family, and the other English and foreign magnates, and above all, tell them how greatly I have been touched and rejoiced at the manner in which my son has been received in England

And last, but not least, I must compliment you on the signature of the Convention of May 21st, with M Dedel   I look upon that as assuming a pacific conclusion to the grand task which I congratulate myself on having entrusted to you, and which you have so skilfully brought to a successful issue   I hope and believe that they will be satisfied with it in Brussels, and that it will have the effect there, which I look upon as the decisive point of the question, namely, that the expenses will be reduced within the limits of the revenue   Once this equilibrium is established, we can wait with patience and resignation for the time when the King of the Netherlands will consider it right to sign the definite treaty

You know of old, all my feelings of friendship for you, mon cher Prince

LOUIS PHILIPPE

THE DUC DE BROGLIE TO THE PRINCE DE TALLEYRAND.

PARIS, *May* 26th, 1833.

MON PRINCE,

In the official despatch which I send you by courier, you will find the latest news we have received from Constantinople , it is up to 8th May

The most prominent fact is the decision come to by the Grand Signior, to cede Adana to Ibrahim, and the important part of this fact is, that Lord Ponsonby has advised it ; this pledges the English Government more than I had dared to hope for. Now everything is finished *legally*, and there is no further pretext for the Russians to remain But as a *fact*, it might easily be very different Admiral Roussin has sent me a letter, in which he seems very uneasy respecting the efforts made by Comte Orloff to break up the whole of this business, and establish the Russians, if not permanently, at least temporarily, at Constantinople, he even seems to fear that arrangements are being made to bring fresh forces secretly into the Bosphorus I do not know how much real importance should be attached to these alarms [1] The aspect at Constantinople is so changeable, that things alter from black to white in the same day Nevertheless, his letter is written in such evident perturbation, that it has given us matter for thought I felt I ought to submit it to a special Cabinet Council, which decided unanimously that I should write to you on this subject, and ask you to sound the English Cabinet as to its intentions, supposing that Russia were to partially throw aside the mask, oblige the Porte to break all the engagements entered into under our joint guarantee, and scheme half secretly, to establish herself on the Bosphorus under pretence of protecting the Sultan

The Council was of opinion that it would be well to equip two more vessels at Toulon, and send them to Admiral Hugon, these two vessels will be ready in twenty days, that is to say, about the 15th of June As we do not wish to excite any jealousy in London by this increase of our forces, which will make the French squadron stronger than the English one, we request you to make this known to Lord Palmerston, asking him to similarly increase the English squadron

But the most important point on which we wish to be thoroughly in concert with the English Cabinet, is the alteration to be made in the instructions to the two admirals

At present, Admiral Malcolm's instructions are exactly similar to those of Admiral Hugon [2] They will join their forces

---

[1] An arrangement had in fact been come to on the 8th May, between the Sultan and the Pasha of Egypt, in consequence of which Ibrahim retired beyond the Taurus On hearing this, which upset all his plans, the Emperor Nicholas sent Comte Orloff to Constantinople with very full powers The fears manifested by Admiral Roussin were only too well founded, since, as will be seen in the course of this recital, the Russian plenipotentiary succeeded in effecting an offensive and defensive treaty of alliance with Turkey (July 8th) It was not until after the signature of this treaty, which placed Turkey at the mercy of the Czar, that the Russian fleet quitted the Bosphorus

[2] Baron Hugon, born in 1783, entered the service in 1795, and took part as a commander in the battle of Navarino In 1821, he was made rear admiral, and sent to put down Greek piracy in the Levant He became vice-admiral in 1840, senator in 1853, and died in 1862

near Smyrna everything being now finished in Egypt They have both received orders to await fresh instructions before attempting to pass the Dardanelles, but the distances are so great, that it seems to us there would be much risk in continuing these arrangements. According to our view, it would be better to point out in advance, dating from now, under what circumstances the two ambassadors at Constantinople would be authorized to direct the admirals to secure that spot from being taken possession of by the Russians. It seems to us that this authority ought to be given to them in either of the following events

1 If the Russians, by their movements, give them cause to fear that they wish to obtain possession of the Dardanelles

2 If, after the peace that has now been made and concluded, fresh reinforcements are sent to Odessa and Bucharest, for these reinforcements can have no other object, than to secure to themselves an impregnable position

It must of course be clearly understood that, having passed through the Dardanelles, the two squadrons will lie to, and will not approach Constantinople, avoiding all aggression, and contenting themselves with repulsing force by force, in case of need.

The Council also resolved that our *Chargé d'Affaires* at St Petersburg should be instructed to declare, in measured but decisive terms, that the French Cabinet expects, now that peace is made, that the Russians will not take advantage of any idle pretext to prolong their sojourn at Constantinople, and that they will follow the example set by us this year in Belgium This is the attitude I am taking as regards M Pozzo

Kindly inform the English Cabinet, mon Prince, as to what you think most advisable in this matter, and keep us *au courant* as to its views

THE PRINCE DE TALLEYRAND TO THE DUC DE BROGLIE

LONDON, *May* 29th, 1833

MONSIEUR LE DUC,

I have received the despatch, No 63, which you did me the honour to write, relative to Eastern affairs I have just had a long conversation respecting it with Lord Palmerston, who has received almost similar accounts to yours from Constantinople I fancy that when once the Porte has consented to the cession of Adana, it may be looked upon as definitely settled, and that there will be no longer the slightest pretext for the Russians to prolong their sojourn in the Bosphorus Lord

Palmerston has already written in this sense to the English minister at St Petersburg, and he will renew the orders he gave him, and make them even more positive

Lord Palmerston refuses to believe that the Sultan would, at the instigation of Russia, reconsider the cession of Adana, after the representations that have been made to him on this subject by the French and English ambassadors, nevertheless, he approves the measure adopted by the king's Government, of sending two more vessels to the Archipelago, and he added, that a similar step would be taken by the English Government Two of the vessels, therefore, which in consequence of the Convention of May 21st, will no longer be employed on the Dutch coasts, will at once be despatched to rejoin the squadron under Admiral Malcolm

Lord Palmerston will not however, in any case, consent to giving such ample powers as the king's Government proposes to the ambassadors of France and England at Constantinople, and in this matter I am quite of his opinion In fact, would it not be unheard of, to grant an ambassador the power of coming to a decision, which might lead to a war, without first consulting his government? The inconvenience caused by distance, however great it may be in the present circumstances, could never justify the adoption of such a course I must say myself, that I would not care either to give or to receive such powers

I think that nothing would alter Lord Palmerston's opinion on this point, and all his colleagues, whom he consulted at the Cabinet Council held this morning, fully agree with him.

May 31st, 1833

In the despatch you did me the honour to send on the 27th of this month, you ask me to give you my views respecting M de Metternich's and M le Comte St Aulaire's proposal, on the subject of Eastern affairs [1]

---

[1] M de Metternich had made a proposal to the French Cabinet to hold a kind of congress in Vienna, for the purpose of discussing the Eastern question The Duc de Broglie wrote about this to the Prince de Talleyrand 'The Prince de Metternich, on hearing from M de Sainte Aulaire, the terms of the agreement concluded a Constantinople on the 5th of this month, manifested a very strong feeling of anxiety He attaches so much importance to the territory of Adana, that even while admitting that the Powers must unite their efforts to maintain the transaction entered into between the Porte and the Pasha, he considers it indispensable that it should be modified on this point He talks vaguely of the necessity of coming to some agreement on the Eastern question, and of establishing for this purpose at Vienna, not exactly a congress, nor even a regular conference, but a centre of discussion All this is very obscure, and still shows the effects of the false and uncertain position in which the Vienna Cabinet has placed itself, in connection with the events in the East " (Despatch of May 26th) The French Cabinet refused to accede to Austria's request " We shall not in any way enter into the proposal of Austria," the Duc de Broglie wrote

I must admit, that under the circumstances, I feel a certain difficulty in responding to the confidence you wish to show me The Eastern question has, for the last six months, been regarded in so many ways, both for and against—it has been the subject of so many uncertain and changeable schemes, alternately accepted and refused—it has brought into action so many different interests —that I feel it would be impossible to decide on any really effectual course, as long as the Powers who are called to this work, do not adopt one principle alone, that of the preservation of the Ottoman Empire, which, for the present at least, is assured by the peace that has just been signed

It is easy to understand the confusion that reigns among the various European Cabinets on this point, when one considers the divers feelings by which they are actuated All, with the exception of Russia, regard the state of Turkey according to their relative considerations Thus we see that Austria is influenced by her anxiety with respect to Germany and Italy, France, probably without any very clear reason, first favours the interests of the Pasha of Egypt, and then speedily abandons them ; England manifests a degree of coldness bordering on utter indifference, Russia alone, as I said before, goes steadily on towards a certain aim She has thus by her action (skilfully conducted, one must admit) arrived at a result, which if advantageous for herself, is only all the more dangerous to Europe

I find it necessary, M le Duc, to recall here the different steps I had to take with the English Cabinet, respecting affairs in the Levant, in order to show, that as far as I was concerned, I have never neglected any thing that could bring about a happy solution of these affairs

At the close of last January I communicated to Lord Palmerston, as stated in despatch No 57,[1] which I had the honour to send you, a plan of joint action between England, France, and Austria This plan, which I think offered great advantages, and which was at first favourably received by the English Ministry, was not adopted by M de Metternich, who replied that he had the most complete confidence in the loyalty and the assurances of the Emperor Nicholas Matters therefore remained thus, left to themselves, or rather to Russian influence, which had not gone to sleep)

Towards the end of February, Admiral Roussin concluded

eight days later, "M de Sainte-Aulaire will simply tell M de Metternich, that he is empowered to discuss any proposals with him that the Chancellor may think it necessary to bring forward, respecting the state of the Ottoman Empire" (Despatch of June 3rd) See also p 98 and note

[1] See despatch of January 28th, p 76

an imprudent convention with the Porte, which at first established a baneful security among the Powers   I say imprudent because this ambassador, before concluding it, had not assured himself as to the intentions of the Pasha of Egypt, whom he could not induce to accept his views

The Russians disembarked in the Dardanelles, and with the consent of the Porte occupied several points there   It was then that I proposed a fresh scheme to the English Ministry, which consisted of joint action on the part of the Powers, but this time I considered it would be necessary to seek the concurrence of Russia which, if it exhibited at the end of January all the inconvenience which I then pointed out, had become a necessity since her occupation of Constantinople   You know, M le Duc, that this scheme found no more favour with the English Cabinet than the first, and that they confined themselves to sending fresh instructions which had but slight influence on the chief question, namely, that of maintaining the Ottoman Empire equally free from protectors as from enemies

M de Metternich has several times, I confess, proposed to come to some understanding on this important matter, but one cannot help seeing that all his ideas are equally impracticable with those which he recently confided to M de Sainte-Aulaire

Peace has at last been signed, and whatever may have been the projects up to the present, I think they must now be considered to be annulled by the very fact that peace has been concluded between the Sultan and the Pasha of Egypt, and we must keep to this fact, as one which will for the future rule the whole Eastern question   We must boldly declare that we look upon this peace as putting an end to everything, and not allow the faintest doubt to arise respecting the immediate withdrawal of the Russians

My opinion, therefore, would be to reply to M de Metternich's overtures, that any assembly of the Powers to terminate this matter is now no longer needed, as there is nothing further to arrange, and that the cession of the district of Adana is only the result of an agreement between the Sultan and the Pasha— that is to say, between the sovereign and his vassal, with which the Powers have no right to interfere

I am inclined to believe that this is the best line to take, as that proposed by M de Metternich would throw matters back into uncertainty, encourage the evasions of the Sultan, and serve as a pretext to the Russians not to withdraw from Constantinople   It would certainly deprive the Sultan of the small amount of moral force still remaining to him, and in the present weak state of the Ottoman Empire, would expose it to all kinds of dangers, by provoking the revolt of the Pashas, who could easily excite the people against European intervention

Moreover, the course I propose to follow is quite in accord with the language you have used to M le Comte Pozzo and M d'Appony, and with the instructions you have given to the French *Chargé d'Affaires* at St Petersburg , it equally accords with Lord Palmerston's views, as he, and I think rightly, does not wish to have conferences either at Vienna or Constantinople, where some time ago, under different circumstances, I proposed having them , and we both think, that in the face of the expressed wish of all the Powers, the Court of Russia will not hesitate to recall her troops from Constantinople

June 2nd, 1833

The Prince de Lieven received letters yesterday from St Petersburg, which, while informing him that peace had been signed between the Sultan and the Pasha, announced the formal intention of the Emperor Nicholas to withdraw his troops as soon as he has been asked to do so by the Sultan   This is quite in accord with what we foresaw here, and I confess I am inclined, under the circumstances, to believe in the assurances of Russia

Lord Palmerston and I have to-day sent to M Van de Weyer the Note of which I have the honour to enclose you a copy [1] Its object, you will observe, is to obtain the immediate fulfilment by the Belgian Government of the articles of the Convention of May 21st, which concern Belgium

June 4th, 1833

I have the honour to transmit to you a copy of the Note, in which Lord Palmerston and I communicated the Convention of May 21st, to the Austrian, Prussian, and Russian plenipotentiaries in London, and of the reply thereto sent to me by M de Lieven, which is identical with that of the other two plenipotentiaries

In reading this reply you will see, that the plenipotentiaries do not pledge themselves to any undertaking, which is only natural, as they were informed by the Secretary of the Dutch Embassy, who arrived yesterday in London, that the Dutch Government had addressed itself to the three Governments of Vienna, Berlin, and St Petersburg, with the view of reopening

[1] Note of June 1st M Van de Weyer replied on the 10th of June, by a Note addressed to Lord Palmerston and M de Talleyrand, in which he finally accepted the Convention of May 21st

negotiations with the five Powers [1] The plenipotentiaries therefore must learn the result of this step and the instructions from their respective Courts to which it will give rise, before expressing an opinion, which moreover under the circumstances could only be a personal one Nevertheless, as Prussia was the last to address the Hague in the name of the three Powers, it is possible that the reply from Berlin might suffice to decide the three plenipotentiaries to rejoin the Conference

One must suppose, that in communicating with the three northern Courts, the King of the Netherlands has informed them of the claims he intends to bring forward at the final negotiation, but, be that as it may, we are justified in expecting, that the first communication made to the Conference by the Dutch plenipotentiary, will contain the figures of the Dutch Cabinet, as to the financial points still to be decided If this is not the case, and if the King of the Netherlands raises fresh difficulties which would tend to prolong the negotiations, an adjournment might be proposed This would certainly be displeasing to Holland and would not inconvenience us, for now that Belgium is placed in a much more favourable position than she could be by the definite treaty, she can wait patiently, until the Dutch Government returns to more reasonable views .

In the English papers of to-day, you will find a detailed account of the sitting in the House of Lords last night The Duke of Wellington brought forward a motion to present a petition to the king, asking him to maintain the strictest neutrality in the struggle now going on between the two princes of the House of Braganza This motion, which was opposed

---

[1] A very energetic attempt at reconciliation was made at this period, between the Cabinet of the Hague and the three Continental Courts, especially that of Berlin M Ancillon gave it his adhesion On the 11th of June, M Bresson announced, not without some surprise mingled with anxiety, that Prince Frederick of the Netherlands had arrived unexpectedly in Berlin On the 13th, he sent an account to the Department of an interview he had relative to this subject with M. Ancillon "Prince Frederick," the Prussian Minister told him, "had appeared in Berlin like a bombshell in a house, no one had been more surprised at it than the king himself" According to M. Ancillon, the prince stated that he had come as an envoy from his father, to thank the King of Prussia, and through him the Emperors of Austria and Russia, for the part they had taken in the conclusion of the provisional convention M Bresson added, that he had noticed a change in the Berlin Court It wished, he said, to see the Conference give up its character of arbitrator and take that of mediator He recalled the fact that a few months previously (M. Bresson's despatch of March 12th) he had already drawn the attention of the French Cabinet to a letter of M de Metternich's to M Clam, Austrian agent at Berlin (who had shown it to M Ancillon), which contained the first intimation of this idea He saw in this scheme, the fixed determination of the Continental Courts to intervene in favour of the King of the Netherlands The Duc de Broglie at once sent this information to London, and requested M de Talleyrand, to eliminate all proposals and suggestions which might tend to alter the character of the Conference (Despatch of June 24th)

by the ministers, ended by being carried by eighty-eight votes
against sixty-eight This is a defeat, but it is not thought that
it will affect the Ministry

MADAME ADELAIDE D'ORLÉANS TO THE PRINCE DE TALLEYRAND

NEUILLY, *June 2nd*, 1833

MON CHER PRINCE,

The King of Holland's ratification of the Convention
of May 21st, is indeed a grand, good piece of news ! Now I
have no longer any doubt as to the speedy and happy
termination of this wearisome and difficult Belgian business
Your views, as to the line of conduct to be followed by King
Leopold, seem to me perfectly right and fair , I have therefore
written to Brussels in this sense , but I think they are very well
disposed there and that they will commence the disarmament at
once . .

The accounts from Blaye are excellent , Madame la Duchesse
de Berry is able to go out in the garden, and I hope before long,
that she will be strong enough to travel She has asked Madame
Laurence de Bauffremont [1] to return and accompany her on the
journey to Palermo The latter has accepted, and asked M
d'Argout yesterday for a passport, and permission to go there,
which has been granted I have just seen her brother Raoul,[2]
who told me she was starting to-day for Blaye . .

THE PRINCE DE TALLEYRAND TO THE DUC DE BROGLIE

LONDON, *June 11th*, 1833

Lord Palmerston received news yesterday from Constantinople, which he was anxious to communicate to me Lord
Ponsonby has written to say, that in an interview he had had
with Comte Orloff, the latter gave him most positive and satisfactory assurances of the Emperor Nicholas's readiness to recall
the Russian troops from Constantinople, as soon as Ibrahim
Pasha had effected his retreat These assurances have now been
repeated in so many quarters that it seems impossible to regard
them as unfounded The Russian Cabinet is too astute, not to

[1] Laurence de Montmorency, daughter of Anne de Montmorency, peer of France,
was born in 1802, and married in 1819 to Théodore, Prince de Bauffremont, a major in
the cavalry

[2] Raoul, Duc de Montmorency, a grandee of Spain, born in 1790, entered the
service in 1807, was aide-de-camp to Marshal Davoust, then chamberlain to the
emperor Under the restoration, he became aide-de-camp to the Duc d'Orléans He
died in 1862

recognize that the destruction of the Ottoman Empire is not a matter to be accomplished by a *coup de main* The time for its partition has not yet arrived, and the cautious Cabinets who may foresee it, will have time to prepare for it Russia has at this period gained great moral force by accustoming the Turks to the presence of Russian soldiers, and she will be satisfied with that for the present Poland exhibits only too well the effect of gradual procedure, which Russian policy knows how to utilize even in matters which seem to interest her most

Lord Ponsonby also gives Lord Palmerston an account of a step taken by Admiral Roussin with the Porte, which does not appear to have been very opportune ; it is with reference to the request made by the French ambassador, that the French squadron might be permitted to enter the Bosphorus, simultaneously with the Russian ambassador's undertaking to procure the recall of the Russian troops, as soon as Ibrahim had effected his retreat I am very sorry that this has occurred, as in any case, such a step will be considered as having been made either too soon or too late However, you will no doubt have already heard, that Lord Ponsonby had induced Admiral Roussin to withdraw his request

King Leopold's speech has just been received here It is more noticeable for future requirements than for satisfaction [1] with the present .

June 24*th*, 1833

MON CHER DUC,

I have not disguised from you the difficulties of the English Ministry, but I think I also told you, two months ago, that I did not consider the crisis was as imminent as some people supposed The result has proved I was right ; but if the difficulties disappeared gradually, they have as gradually cropped up again, and it is only too evident that they have now attained a serious degree of gravity It is no longer a mere question of establishing harmony between the two Houses by a fresh and extensive creation of peers, to which the king is averse, as being an abuse of power, but it is also a question of triumphing over the two factions, Tory and Radical, in the lower House, both of which are much dissatisfied with the Church Bill,[2] one side because too much has been taken away, the other because too much has been retained United, these two factions might easily upset the majority in the House of Commons

[1] The King of the Belgian's speech at the opening of the Chambers.

[2] The Bill for the reduction of the Irish Church establishment which for more than two months had been the subject of violent debates in Parliament.

I keep carefully aloof, almost absurdly so, from all these present agitations; but, if as a simple spectator, I cannot help seeing the difficulties that surround the Cabinet, I, nevertheless, cannot yet share the predictions of those who accord it only a very short existence. One must, however, admit the possibility of this; the next three weeks will solve this great question . .

THE DUC DE BROGLIE TO THE PRINCE DE TALLEYRAND.

PARIS, *June 29th*, 1833

MON PRINCE,

The papers will have informed you of the unfortunate fate of the amendment, which we had intended should take place in the Customs law. No sooner was this amendment printed, than it excited a general outcry in the Chamber, the uproar was so great that most of those who had intended to support it lost courage[1]. Saint Cricq, who was to have explained it, was in the room next to the Chamber; he declares on his honour, that he had only gone out for a moment, and that the President spitefully brought forward the amendment for discussion before it was due. However, the fact remains, that the amendment, having been put to the vote before it was explained, was rejected with acclamation by an enormous majority, no one having the hardihood to defend it against such universal opposition. We had against us, besides those interested, of whom there were a great number, and who made a great disturbance, the whole of the Opposition, who declaimed against the power which this amendment would place in the hands of the government. I fancy that the English Ministry will be very vexed at all this, and I frankly express my own great annoyance. The truth is, that both Thiers and Humann are very conservative at heart,

[1] The session of the Chamber was about to close, without having passed the new Customs law containing important reductions in the duties, which were impatiently awaited in England. At one of the final sittings, therefore, on the 18th June, the Cabinet presented, through M. de Saint-Cricq, the following additional Article to the financial law. — ' The king shall, by order in Council, have power from now until next session of the Chambers to put in provisional execution, by extension of the privilege granted by Article 34 of the law of December 14, 1814, such of the provisions of the draft Customs law presented to the Chamber of Deputies on the 3rd December last, as in the interest of trade, agriculture, and manufacture, appear to be urgent. Such orders as may have been issued in virtue of this arrangement shall be presented to the Chamber next session, in order to be converted into law.'

The reading of this Article created loud protestations in the Chamber, and it was thrown out without discussion. Nevertheless, the Cabinet passed, on the 29th of June, irrespective of and after, the close of the session, a royal ordinance, containing numerous reductions of duties, which appeared in the *Moniteur*, it was countersigned by M. Thiers.

and that it is only out of compliance they yield to my importunities and my efforts to modify the Customs tariff; if they did not actually show any bad faith, in the delays created to prevent the discussion of this law, and in the misadventure of the amendment, they probably did not exhibit quite as much zeal as I should have done You must kindly do your best to appease the displeasure of the English Government Meanwhile, I will endeavour to repair the evil, by trying to find in the existing laws some means of doing in part, what the amendment would have given us a right to do. I am working heart and soul, and hope to succeed I rest all my hopes, mon Prince, on your friendly skill to repair our follies Accept. . . .

PARIS, *July 1st*, 1833.

MON PRINCE,

I told you in my last letter of the Customs question, of the rejection of the amendment in the Chamber of Deputies, and of the hope I had of finding in existing legislation some way of repairing this parliamentary mishap We have, in effect, found this way, though not without seriously involving our responsibility I have succeeded in getting my colleagues to adopt it : the order is signed, and will appear to-morrow or the day after in the *Moniteur*, it contains on the silk question, which was not discussed, all that the Customs law bore With regard to cotton, as the proposals of the Commission were not to take effect until two years after the promulgation of the law, the delay is but of slight importance to the English Government It is in fact of little consequence, whether the law is passed this session or not, since its effect would become deferred We shall exercise every care to see that account is taken of this delay, when the Customs law is next drawn up I think the English Government will be satisfied with what we have done ; they will be wrong if they are not, for in truth we are compromising ourselves greatly on this point, and I am not at all sure that we may not repent it yet

I should like to give here, as I did after the recital of the taking of Antwerp in January last, a *résumé*, as short and succinct as possible, of the new phase on which the affairs of Holland and Belgium had entered, consequent upon the Convention of May 21st I will thus spare the reader the details of the long and wearisome negotiations which very shortly recommenced and continued for several months This point once set aside, I shall only have to give extracts from the correspondence concerning those other European matters, which the French Embassy in London had to deal with at that time

As has been seen, King William of the Netherlands had ratified the preliminary Convention of May 21st,[1] which placed Belgium in such an advantageous position, that she had no need to desire the conclusion of a treaty which would definitely regulate her relations with Holland It was not quite the same, however, as regards the other Powers, notably Austria and Prussia, who, when signing the treaty of November 15th, 1831, on which the existence of the new Kingdom of Belgium was based, had, in the name of the German Diet, reserved its rights to the Duchy of Luxemburg It must be remembered that in virtue of this treaty, one portion of the Duchy of Luxemburg had been incorporated with the Kingdom of Belgium, in exchange for a part of the province of Limburg, which in 1790 did not belong to the States-General of Holland The Vienna and Berlin Cabinets were therefore specially interested in resuming the negotiations, in order that a definite treaty might be arrived at between Belgium and Holland, such as had been formerly stipulated for in the Convention of May 21st Article V of this Convention was conceived in the following terms

"The high contracting parties pledge themselves to attend without delay to the definite treaty which is to determine the relations between the States of H M the King of the Netherlands, Grand Duke of Luxemburg, and Belgium They will invite the Courts of Austria, Prussia, and Russia to concur therein"

This invitation, given by France and England to the other three Courts, had been accepted by them, and the London Conference, which had been dissolved, consequent on the adoption of coercive measures, was now again reconstituted

The treaty of November 15th, 1831, concluded between the five Powers and Belgium, had declared that a *direct* treaty between Holland and Belgium would still have to be carried out But what was to be the character of this *direct* treaty?

According to the Note of the Conference of November

---

[1] The ratifications were exchanged in London, May 29th

15th, 1831, the direct treaty between Holland and Belgium ought to have contained the literal reproduction of the twenty-four articles, to be accepted word for word by Holland, as had been done by Belgium But a literal reproduction was no longer possible, because ·

1. The three Courts of Austria, Prussia, and Russia, when ratifying the treaty of November 15th, had made some reservations which entitled Holland, by agreement, to open up a fresh discussion on some of the twenty-four articles ,

2 It had been recognized that some explanation was indispensable respecting such of those articles as were not quite clear ;

3 Lastly, the plenipotentiaries of the five Courts, in default of sufficient information, had been compelled to leave some questions unsolved which it now became necessary to reduce to some definite arrangement

The King of the Netherlands had decided on sending M. Verstolck de Soelen, his Minister for Foreign Affairs, to join his plenipotentiary, M. Dedel ; and the Belgian Government, on its side, had sent General Goblet, Minister for Foreign Affairs, to assist M Van de Weyer The new negotiations were thus opened with an amount of solemnity which seemed to promise their speedy termination

The Conference held its first sitting on July 15th, 1833, and resolved that :

1. The plenipotentiaries of the Netherlands and Belgium should be heard separately and treated exactly alike ,

2 That the negotiations should, as much as possible, be verbal ;

3 That the treaty of November 15th, should serve as the basis for the negotiations ,

4 That the articles of this treaty should be submitted separately to each side, and initialed, in case of adoption, either with or without modifications.

The territorial question was to form the first subject of the negotiations No objections were raised as to the arrangements come to respecting this question by the treaty of November 15th, but there was some hesitation on a secondary point

These arrangements, as has been seen, were based on the principle of an exchange between a portion of the Belgian territory in the province of Limburg, and a portion of the Grand Duchy of Luxemburg, consequently, according to this principle, the ceded portion 'of Limburg ought to have been substituted for that of Luxemburg in all the transactions of this latter country with the Germanic Confederation   But in citing in Article III the co-relation that existed between these two cessions, the treaty of November 15th admitted in Article IV the alternative of the reunion of that portion of Limburg, either to Holland or to the Germanic Confederation, and by Article V reserved to the King Grand Duke, the power to arrange regarding this with the Diet and the agnates of his House   The Cabinet of the Hague, which wished to incorporate the right bank of the Meuse with Holland, instructed its plenipotentiaries to ask, that Articles III and V of the treaty and the terms of Article II, which pointed out the connection between the two cessions, might be eliminated   The Belgian plenipotentiaries, after having referred to their government, consented to this excision, on condition that the King Grand Duke should gain the assent of the Germanic Diet and the agnates of the House of Nassau, before the treaty was signed The Dutch plenipotentiaries on their part, declared themselves authorised to accept this double undertaking

The articles relative to the territorial delimitations were thereupon initialed by both parties, and subsequently also the Articles VII, VIII, X, XV, XVI, XVII., XVIII, XIX, XX, XXI, XXII, XXIII, XXIV, and a twenty-fifth Article was added, which declared that there would be peace between the King of the Netherlands and the King of the Belgians, &c.

The examination of the five articles which gave rise to these demands on the part of Holland was then proceeded with   These were   Article IX, relative to the navigation of the rivers and streams, Article XI, concerning the use of the roads which traversed Limburg, Article XII, concerning the power of establishing a canal or a road through Limburg ; Article XIII, relative to the annual payment of the debt, and to the liquidation of the sinking fund syndicate; and lastly, Article XIV, concerning the arrears of the debt [1]

The Conference for some time, followed both parties in the examination of these questions; but when it became convinced, that the Cabinet of the Hague had taken no steps whatever to obtain the double consent required for the cession of Luxemburg, it considered it ought again to suspend the negotiations, and subordinate their resumption to the accomplishment of the engagement entered into by the King Grand Duke We shall, further on, find mention of this suspension of the negotiations and the reasons which caused it

We will now return to the correspondence

THE PRINCE DE TALLEYRAND TO THE DUC DE BROGLIE

LONDON, *July 4th*, 1833

MONSIEUR LE DUC,

I informed Lord Palmerston of the resolutions adopted by the king's government on the subject of the customs, of which you kindly gave me notice. Lord Palmerston was much pleased, and requested me to express in his own name as well as that of his colleagues, their great satisfaction thereat

I had the honour of informing you that the English Cabinet were about to endeavour, by some conciliatory measures, to escape from the difficulties which had arisen in the House of Commons; in this they have succeeded by means of some concessions in the Bill on the temporal affairs of the Irish Church The difficulties have almost disappeared, and the Ministry now seem to feel that they will reach the end of the session happily, despite the obstacles inseparable from parliamentary struggles The session will probably close about the middle of August

News has been received here, but without any details, of the disembarkation on the coast of Algarve of the expedition organized by M. Palmella and M Villaflor at Lagos This expedition, which only consists of 2,500 men, was not strong enough to venture on landing at Lisbon, where it expected to receive further encouragement.

---

[1] This method of procedure was not approved at Paris The Cabinet of the Tuileries did not desire to reopen negotiations on questions which appeared to it to have been decided by the treaty of November 15th. See Madame Adelaide's letter on the subject, Appendix letter No 10

July 8th, 1833

I am very glad that M de Fréville [1] has come here, he will appreciate the success of your courageous ordinance It will speedily be seen, thanks to your care, that reciprocity is better than reprisals, the former never engenders quarrels In the present state of public opinion, the most cautious will be compelled to acknowledge that no one nation can continue to produce at a cheaper rate than the others The soil never changes, but all industries can be learnt

M Dedel and M Verstolck are expected to-morrow morning It is seven weeks now since the preliminary treaty was made, in this treaty, all the advantages are on the side of the Belgians; notwithstanding this the King of Holland still creates delays It is very difficult to explain this, for money will soon fail him, and it is more than probable that the States-General will not grant him a fresh credit, at least, that is the general opinion I will tell you my first impression as soon as these gentlemen have arrived

July 9th, 1833

Intelligence has just been received of the expedition which left Oporto under the orders of M de Palmella and M de Villaflor The disembarkation took place on the 24th June, at the small port of Villa Real, in the kingdom of the Algarve, close to the Spanish frontier The letters, which are dated on the 28th, state, that immediately after the disembarkation, which was effected with hardly any resistance from the Miguelist governor, M de Villaflor proceeded to Tavira and was to advance thence on Beja, the capital of the province of Alemtigo, where he expected a good deal of support M de Palmella, for his part, went to Faro, where he busied himself in organizing the Kingdom of Algarve; all the towns along the coast have proclaimed Queen Dona Maria

Captain Napier,[2] commandant of the fleet, was to return to

---

[1] French Councillor of State, sent to London to advise as to the application of the Royal Ordinance on the Customs, mention of which is made in the Duc de Broglie's letter of July 1st

[2] Captain Napier commanded the fleet of Dom Pedro, he had taken the name of Carlos de Ponza while in Portugal, because in 1813 he had taken possession of the little Island of Ponza on the Neapolitan coast, with great *éclat*

Sir Charles Napier, born in 1786, commanded a vessel in 1809, took part in the Portuguese campaign, and signalized himself in various enterprises till 1815 He was then placed on the retired list In 1829, he entered the service of Dom Pedro, and contributed largely to the successes of his cause In 1834, he entered Parliament He was made commodore in 1839, rear-admiral in 1846, and vice admiral in 1853 He failed before Cronstadt in 1854, and returned to England, where he died in 1860

the mouth of the Tagus to blockade Lisbon, as soon as he had proclaimed the queen at Lagos . . .

July 14*th,* 1833

The news arrived this morning in London that Queen Dona Maria's fleet, commanded by Admiral Carlos Ponza (Captain Napier), had encountered the squadron of Dom Miguel on the 5th of this month off Cape St. Vincent, and that, after a spirited engagement, Admiral Ponza had captured two of Dom Miguel's line-of-battle ships, two frigates, and one corvette . This news has created great sensation in London ; the Ministry are much pleased, and one cannot but think that this will be very helpful to them, in the important discussions that will come on when Parliament opens this week

M de Bourmont's son has arrived here from France, bringing considerable sums of money with him He has just purchased a large steamer, *The United Kingdom,* which will start for Lisbon during the course of the week, laden, it is said, with ammunition, artillery, and English officers, who have been induced to enrol themselves

July 15*th,* 1833

. . . We have this morning held our first conference on Dutch and Belgian affairs . After the conference, I informed Lord Palmerston of the communication you made to me in your last despatch, on the subject of an offensive and defensive treaty of alliance between Russia and the Porte, which Admiral Roussin had mentioned to you [1] Lord Palmerston has received the same information from Lord Ponsonby, although in a rather less positive manner. Sir Frederick Lamb also writes that when M. de Metternich spoke to him of it, he seemed very much annoyed that anyone should believe in the existence of such a treaty Neither Lord Palmerston nor I, can conceive that Russia would have dared to take such a step ; but my own opinion is, that if the treaty does exist, Austria must be a party to it, for it would be unreasonable to suppose that Russia would, by herself, make a treaty which must necessarily place Austria, France, and England in opposition to her ; besides, the conduct of the Vienna Cabinet would, on this occasion, be quite in accord with many of its antecedents . [2]

July 19*th,* 1833

The discussion in the House of Lords on the second reading of the Bill relative to the temporal power of the Irish Church,

---

[1] See pages 119 and note, also 140   [2] See pages 140 and 141.

which has already lasted two days, will probably be concluded this evening Lord Grey's speech on the first night produced an immense effect, and has been universally applauded The position of the Cabinet has greatly improved during the last few days, there seems no longer any doubt that the Bill will pass its second reading, and it is even thought that only some unimportant changes will be made in committee The calmer and more conciliatory feeling shown just now by the Opposition in the House of Peers, is generally attributed to the moderate stand taken by the Duke of Wellington We have heard nothing from Portugal since the news of Admiral Napier's victory

July 26th, 1833

I can perfectly understand the interest with which you must follow the course of the Hollando-Belgian affairs, I will therefore, as I have done since the negotiations were resumed, continue to keep you *au courant* of all the deliberations of the Conference You always have been, and will continue to be, kept informed of everything that strongly interests us here, and truly, on this point, you ought often to be much wearied by the multiplicity of my letters and despatches The other ambassadors generally wait till we have arrived at some decision in the Conference before writing to their Courts I think I am the only one who writes almost daily, and perhaps this is a mistake, as I thereby draw your attention to mere crude ideas, and so expose your judgment to an uncertainty which might even momentarily lead it astray

I do not think that during the three years that I have been in London, the king has had cause to complain of weakness or imprudence on my part, or that he can ascribe the present delays to any other reason than to that spirit of conciliation, the great advantage of which, experience proves to me more and more each day

I do not believe that this is a time for trying a new system, and the incident at Maestricht, mentioned by M d'Eyrague, confirms this opinion Remember, that in order to terminate the Belgian affair, we have at last obtained the friendly joint action of the northern Powers, that we owe the present calm to them, and that it would be as easy as it would be dangerous to compromise their present good feeling, *so little due to natural impulse*, by unlimited complaisance towards Belgium The real interests of the Belgians will be secured, but their fancied needs must not be allowed to obstruct our course and prejudice the good feeling existing in Europe, which is of such importance just now   .

THE DUC DE BROGLIE TO THE PRINCE DE TALLEYRAND

PARIS, *July* 25*th*, 1833

MON PRINCE,

Whenever any difficulties arise, we are always obliged to have recourse to you   I am therefore most anxious to acquaint you at once of the Portuguese business, and ask your advice as to what course to pursue, if Lisbon should shortly surrender to the Marquis de Palmella.

Without doubt we shall rejoice at this event, supposing it does take place ; but we cannot conceal from ourselves that it will certainly cause us some serious embarrassment   The very precarious position in which Spain is already placed, will become still more so, and every day we are brought face to face with fresh complications consequent on the attempts made to bring about a revolutionary state of affairs in the Peninsula   These difficulties will be more or less numerous, or more or less urgent, according as the establishment of the young queen is directed by Dom Pedro or by Palmella, and according as the Brazilian Charter is or is not, set aside   I fancy that it is quite as important to the English Government as it is to us, that Dom Pedro and his Charter should be removed from Portugal as soon as possible, and for this it is necessary that the two governments should understand each other, and agree in good time as to the line of conduct they intend to pursue   We learn from Oporto, that Dom Pedro has forbidden Palmella to enter Lisbon without him   We also know that Palmella has decided not to obey him   Lastly, we are also aware, that the empress has received secret orders not to permit the young queen to embark, until Dom Pedro himself writes to say that he wishes to have her sent to him   It seems to me, that we cannot too soon endeavour to frustrate his design to take exclusive possession of the whole affair. I should like to know what measures you consider most efficacious to arrive at this end, and at the same time those you deem most easy to arrange with the English Government

Be so good as to give me the benefit of your advice on this point, as well as on all the others, and accept   .

THE PRINCE DE TALLEYRAND TO THE DUC DE BROGLIE.

LONDON, *July* 27*th*, 1833

MONSIEUR LE DUC,

M Bresson will no doubt have informed you, that H M the King of Prussia was obliged to go to Toplitz from the 22nd to the 24th of this month, accompanied by M Ancillon, another of his ministers, and one of his private secretaries Prince Felix de Schwarzenberg [1] was to be there at the same time as his Majesty It appears that H M the Emperor of Austria, who just at this time is staying at his estates in Bohemia, has invited the King of Prussia to visit him there Prince Metternich will go from Konigswerth, and it is believed that the meeting of the two sovereigns will take place on the 20th of August It is not yet known in London whether the Emperor Nicholas will be present at this meeting

MON CHER DUC,   *July 30th*, 1833

I reply, with the least possible delay, to the very friendly and flattering letter you have written to me, respecting our position and that of England with regard to Portugal I have seen Lord Palmerston on this subject ; I think he seems fully to recognize the advantage there would be, in separating Dom Pedro from his daughter's cause and recognizing a regency excluding the Duc de Braganza, but of which Palmella would be the centre and the head While Lord William Russell for example, might be accredited to it The two other members (because matters only require three) would be M de Villaflor on the one side, and a moderate Miguelite, if it were possible to secure one for the cause of the young Queen, on the other It would be a very fortunate thing if the Miguelite in question was M le Duc de Cadaval [2]

I am too ignorant as to the actual state of feeling in Spain, and as to your language at Madrid respecting Portugal, to be certain whether you would care to follow the course I have just pointed out to you ; but in case it should meet with your approval, I think it would be useful to send a French envoy to Portugal in the same position as that of William Russell, to act in concert with him there, point out, when opportunity occurs, the advantages of the regency, and recognize it at once in the name of France This plan would certainly have the

[1] Felix Louis Jean Frederic, prince de Schwarzenberg, an Austrian General and Statesman Born in 1800 He followed simultaneously a military and diplomatic career, was attaché at the Embassy at St Petersburg in 1824, then in London (1826), at Rio de Janeiro (1827), at Paris, and Berlin He was then appointed Minister at Turin, whence he was transferred to Parma and to Naples (1846) In 1848, he became head of the Austrian Cabinet, and held this high office till his death (1852)

[2] Minho Caetano-Alvarez Pereira de Mello, duc de Cadaval, born in 1798, was descended from a younger branch of the house of Braganza Dom Miguel nominated him in 1828, President of the Council of Ministers He was an energetic supporter of the absolutist cause, and after Dom Pedro's triumph he fled to Paris, where he died in 1838

advantage of establishing a government in Portugal, which would act in the name of the young Queen, without her presence being absolutely necessary, at a time when you might fear that her stepmother, in obedience to Dom Pedro's orders, would place some obstacle in the way of Dona Maria's departure I think that the regency should abandon Dom Pedro's constitution, that great terror of Spain , this in my opinion would not be difficult to do, and it would allay all the irritability of Europe It will not be an easy matter for you to select some one to send to Portugal, as above all he must not be a party man You will no doubt talk all this over with Lord Granville Lord Palmerston is to-day writing fully on this question to him , it has occupied us the greater part of the morning   .

July 31*st*, 1833.

It is midnight, the sitting in the House of Peers has just ended ; the ministers have had a majority of fifty-three votes.[1] You may consider the session as concluded The Ministry will have no more real difficulties to contend with

The Duc de Broglie to the Prince de Talleyrand.

Paris, *July* 30*th*, 1833

A thousand thanks, mon Prince, for your kind letter of the 26th, and for all the admirable work you have done It seems to me that, thanks to you, this Belgian business is in a very fair way, and I am beginning to hope that we shall see the end of it at last I pray you to believe that my opinion of the Belgians is the same as yours, and that my sole idea in mentioning them to you, is to endeavour to deprive them of any pretext for committing some folly, which would either spoil your work or cause you fresh embarrassments

Our *fêtes*[2] went off admirably, and I really think if you were to return here a few weeks hence to spend part of the autumn, you would hardly recognize us . . .

The Prince de Talleyrand to the Duc de Broglie

London, *August* 2*nd*, 1833

Lord Palmerston has just communicated to me the following news from Lisbon —

[1] This was the Bill on the Reform of the Irish Church Establishment. It was carried in the Peers by 135 votes against 81
[2] The *fêtes* on the anniversary of the days of July   They were signalized this year by the replacement of Napoleon's statue on the Vendôme column

"Queen Dona Maria was proclaimed at Lisbon on the 24th July   There has been an engagement, south of the Tagus, on the 23rd between General Villaflor and Tellez Jordaô , the latter was killed and his troops were defeated , the Spanish minister [1] who was fighting with the Miguelites was taken prisoner by Villaflor   On the morning of the 24th the Duc de Cadaval retired from Lisbon with the garrison   The people immediately and unanimously proclaimed Dona Maria Queen   In the afternoon of the same day, Villaflor crossed the Tagus with fifteen hundred men   On the 25th, the fleet entered the Tagus   On the evening of the 26th, the Emperor Dom Pedro embarked with all his ministers on board a steamer for Lisbon, leaving Saldanha [2] as civil and military governor of Oporto.   The besieging army were beginning to retire."

August 2nd, 1833

You will already have received the news which reached London to-day, and of which I have this moment been informed   They have just heard that the treaty between Russia and the Porte has been signed at Constantinople,[3] and although it is stated to be purely defensive (which even we might admit), experience proves that in similar circumstances, a defensive treaty when it suits can very easily become an offensive one

Such a matter demands the full attention of the king's Government, and it is because I feel the importance of prompt

---

[1] Louis Fernandez de Cordova, Spanish General and Diplomat, born 1799, one of the staunchest partisans of King Ferdinand VII , whom he supported unceasingly against the constitutional party   He was Secretary of the Embassy at Paris in 1825, then Minister in Prussia   In 1832, he was accredited to Dom Miguel, whose cause he energetically supported   He took part in the civil wars of Spain and sided with Queen Isabella   He died in 1840

[2] Joao Carlos, Duc de Saldanha Oliveira e Daun, a Portuguese statesman and General, grandson of the Marquis de Pombal, born in 1780 . in 1810, he accepted the French rule and was taken prisoner by the English , he then went on to Brazil   On his return to Portugal, he was made Minister of Foreign Affairs to King John VI   On the king's death, he became head of the Liberal party, and upheld the cause of Dom Pedro   Created a Marshal in 1834, he was made War Minister and President of the Council in 1835   He retired from office in 1846, and was for the next fifteen years mixed up with all the civil struggles in Portugal   In 1851, he again came into power, which he retained for five years   The Marshal later on became minister plenipotentiary in London   He died in 1875

[3] This was the treaty of Unkiar-Skelessi, signed on the 8th July, between Comte Orloff and the Ottoman Government   By this treaty, Russia and Turkey contracted an offensive and defensive alliance against any attack at home or abroad whatsoever   Russia promised to assist Turkey with all the help she might need, either by land or sea   Finally, by a supplementary article, it was agreed that in case of necessity, the Porte would close the Dardanelles, that is to say, that she would allow no vessel to enter there under any pretext whatever

This treaty was to hold good for eight years

and vigorous action, that I do not hesitate to send you the result of some reflections suggested to me by the situation

It seems to me that France ought to act in concert with England, and you will no doubt deem it advisable to make known your views to Lord Granville with regard to this ; I on my side will make use of any directions you may think fit to send me

According to the letters received from Constantinople, the ratifications of the treaty are not to be exchanged for two months · this is valuable time, of which we must make the most.

In the present state of affairs, France and England have to choose between St Petersburg, Bohemia, where M de Metternich is, and Constantinople, and use all their influence in order to prevent the ratification of the treaty just concluded.

It is more than probable, that it was only after very mature reflection, and in consequence of a persevering policy, that they decided at St Petersburg to draw the Porte into this alliance ; there is therefore every reason to fear that the proceedings of the two courts will have no influence with a Cabinet fixed in its resolutions, and, one moreover which does not usually show itself very well disposed towards France and England

As for M de Metternich, judging from his language to M. de Sainte-Aulaire and Sir Frederick Lamb, we must suppose either that he is himself deceived, or that he wishes to deceive us[1] In the former case much time would be wasted in disabusing him , in the second, he would only seek to increase our embarrassment still further by the tortuous measures of the policy he has adopted Although I do not lay much stress on the efficacy of any attempts that may be made with him, still I think they must not be entirely neglected

[1] M. de Sainte-Aulaire wrote to the Duc de Broglie on the 5th of July, giving him an account of an interview he had had with M. de Metternich on Eastern affairs . M de Metternich, he said, " pretends that he knows nothing of this treaty (Unkiar-Skelessi), but he declares that if it exists, it has been conceived and accomplished not only without Austria's participation, but without a single circumstance occurring to arouse the suspicions of the Vienna Cabinet This would, however, according to him, be one more reason for working together in the future, and the greater the importance attached to this fresh danger against the independence of the Porte, the greater reason will England and France have to unite with Austria and Russia, in order to substitute a common protectorate, in place of an exclusive one " M de Metternich gives reiterated assurances, that Austria will not permit Russia to acquire either an increase of territory or an exclusive protectorate of the Porte Prince Metternich's distrust and ill-will towards Russia are very strong Nevertheless, he would not at any price decide to break with her abruptly, but he is very anxious to organize mutual negotiations M de Sainte Aulaire added, that on the 14th July he had come to an agreement with M de Metternich, as to the necessity of the four Powers notifying to the Porte that they all took an equal interest in her preservation, and that they intended to protect the integrity of her territory [Official correspondence of M de Sainte-Aulaire Extracts]

But it is at Constantinople, above all, that we must concentrate our means of action ; it is there that the French and
English ambassadors must represent to the Sultan the danger
into which he is rushing ; they must entreat him, even menace
him, if necessary, and above all, they must endeavour to secure that
large party in the Divan and the Ministry, which refused the
Russian alliance   It is not possible to believe that just when
the Russian troops have quitted Constantinople, and when,
consequently, the Sultan has recovered some sort of independence,
the united voice of France and England should not make itself
successfully heard

Our sole aim must be to prevent the ratification of the treaty,
and in my opinion the way to arrive at this is by a prompt and
energetic declaration from both Powers, in order to assure the
Porte of a support which may have become necessary to her, and
in default of which she has allowed herself to be led away

It seems to me that the English and French representatives
have acted prudently, in not taking any steps before the departure
of Comte Orloff and the Russian troops

August 2nd, 1833

MON CHER DUC,

I send you some very important news from Lisbon,
which I believe is quite true   It appears that Dom Pedro has
gone thither   By this time the regency will have been established ; my views of the day before yesterday are therefore
out of place   But if, in consequence, England and France have
not been enabled to take part in establishing the regency, they
now remain in a position either to recognize it or not   I cannot
at this moment tell you which side England will take with
regard to this, and perhaps, under these circumstances, the course
to be pursued by us must not depend entirely on that which she
will adopt   England has direct interests with Portugal ; our
direct interests are with Spain   Portugal has only a *second-hand*
interest for us   The conditions under which it might suit us
to recognize the regency, could therefore not be identically
the same as those which would suit England   I think I
ought to draw your attention to all this, when the time for a
decision seems so near . .

August 5th, 1833

I have received the despatch No 85[1] which you did me the
honour to send, and I notice with great satisfaction from its
contents, that my opinion is quite in accord with yours con-

[1] See Despatch of 1st August   Appendix letter No 11

cerning the serious matter that has just taken place at Constantinople

I have been urging the English Ministry for the last few days, to take in this question the line which I pointed out to you in my last despatch, and I can now tell you the resolution they have adopted

An English courier will start to-morrow for Constantinople, taking Paris on his way. Lord Granville will be instructed to communicate to you the despatch that has been sent to Lord Ponsonby. This despatch will express, in a very clear and pronounced manner, the astonishment and dissatisfaction experienced by the English Government on hearing of the alliance concluded between the Ottoman Porte and Russia, accompanied by an order to make this known to the Ottoman Government, at the same time pointing out the dangers of the situation in which it has placed itself Lord Ponsonby will have to make it plain that the Porte, in accepting this treaty, renounces her independence, which henceforth will be submissive to the wishes and requirements of Russia ; that by this one act, her power has become annihilated in the eyes of Europe, as well as in those of her own people He will specially insist on the dangers that such a treaty must occasion, in the existing relations between the Sublime Porte and her old allies , that England can only recognize her as a dependent of Russia, and that in the event of a war with this latter Power she would be obliged to treat the Ottoman empire as an enemy ; that such a result, which nevertheless is inevitable, would annul all the Porte's relations with old and faithful allies such as England and France, and would deliver her up to the power of Russia, her persistent enemy.

This is about the summary of what is being sent to Lord Ponsonby ; you will probably deem it desirable to transmit somewhat similar instructions to Admiral Roussin I think it very important that both the ambassadors should be in accord in the steps they take, and work in conceit on all points

If you adopt this course, you will no doubt communicate to Lord Granville the instructions you send to Admiral Roussin It would also, I think, be advisable, that the French courier who takes your orders should start at the same time, and perhaps together with the English courier, so as to furnish, even in actual execution, a fresh proof of the community of views between France and England

There is no time to lose, for the exchange of the ratifications between Russia and the Porte is to take place on the 8th of September, and all our efforts must be directed to prevent this exchange

You will see that in all this I make no mention of Austria. As I had the honour to inform you in my last despatch, any overture made to Austria just now would hamper instead of help us. But after the departure of the couriers, it might be as well to allow some observations on the present circumstances to reach Vienna, so that later on we may be enabled to represent to the Austrian Cabinet that we did not neglect to make known our views to it, and that it rested with them to join us ; for we must equally avoid being hampered, or accused of want of confidence

August 5th, 1833

The English Cabinet has decided to recognize Queen Dona Maria's Government officially. This recognition will be expressed simply by accrediting an English envoy to the regency. Lord William Russell, who, as you are aware, is already at Lisbon, will be charged with this, which will have the character of a special mission.

Lord Palmerston will write at the same time to Mr. Addington,[1] the English minister at Madrid, to tranquillize the Spanish Government as to the consequences of this recognition, by letting them understand that in thus acting, England has only made use of the same right that Spain exercised when she recently recognized Dom Miguel. Mr. Addington is also to give the further assurance, that it is the firm intention of England to prevent any sort of reaction in the Peninsula.

When the return of Queen Dona Maria comes into question, would you not deem it advisable that she should be escorted by a French as well as an English frigate ? I believe the English Government would regard this with pleasure.

August 6th, 1833

I have just seen Lord Palmerston, who told me that the departure of the courier for Constantinople has been delayed until to-morrow. The disposition displayed by the English Government in always bringing forward fresh delays in the decisions on Eastern affairs, induces me sometimes to think that it does not sufficiently realize their importance. However, the king's Government will thereby have one more day, for deliberating on a matter which certainly merits the most serious attention.

[1] Henry Unwin Addington, cousin of the minister of that name. Born in 1790, he entered the diplomatic service, was Secretary of Legation at Berne and at Copenhagen, *Chargé d'Affaires* at Washington (1822), then Envoy Extraordinary at Frankfort (1828), and at Madrid (1829). In 1833, he was Under Secretary of State at the Foreign Office, and became Privy Councillor in 1854.

The steamer which is to take Lord William Russell's credentials, starts for Lisbon to-morrow   I think there is no reason for you to hasten the despatch of a minister to Portugal Such action taken by France would be much more marked than when taken by England, who only accredits some one who is already on the spot   You, however, will have information on this point, which ought to place you in a position to judge much better than I can, as to the most opportune moment for taking such a step. . .

August 8*th*, 1833

. . . . Lord Palmerston sent Lord William Russell his credentials yesterday, but at the same time authorized him not to make known his position, if any disturbances or other circumstances seemed to him to render this step unadvisable.   This information may, in case of need, be useful to you

The night before last, the English Government asked the shipowners in the city for fifteen transports of three and four hundred tons, whose services they would require for three months   A report got abroad that they were intended for the conveyance of troops to Portugal, which did not seem at all improbable   However, it appears this is not the case, at any rate for the present, since they have confined themselves to receiving the shipowners' offers, without giving any positive replies ; it is probable that they only desired to assure themselves as to the facilities available in case of urgency.

Moreover, the English Government is fully assured as to the views of the Madrid Cabinet ; the ministers acquainted me that Mr. Addington had informed them that in his last interviews with M. de Zea. he found him much more conciliatory and moderate, and that he even seemed to wish to reject any project of intervention on the part of Spain in the affairs of Portugal

Mr Aston will have made known to you the instructions that were sent from here yesterday to Lord Ponsonby.   Lord Palmerston has received the draft of the formal protest to Constantinople, of which you informed Mr Aston ; he entertains it very favourably, and I may tell you, that it is quite in accord with the views of the English Cabinet   . .

August 10*th*, 1833

We have to-day exchanged with the Bavarian minister the ratifications of the explanatory and supplementary article to Art VIII of the Convention signed in London on the 7th of May, 1832, for the final settlement of Greek affairs [1]

During this assembly of members of the Conference on Greek affairs, a question arose as to the demand that will be immediately made to us by the Greek Government, in order to obtain the guarantee of the three Powers to the third part of the loan   Lord Palmerston and Prince de Lieven told me that they were authorized to accord this guarantee, and I have promised to obtain your instructions on this point ,   I therefore pray you to inform me of the wishes of the king's Government, and whether or not, I am authorized to accede to this Greek demand   ..

August 10th, 1833

I herewith send you an extract of the news received here to-day from Portugal , it is dated up to the 31st July, and is, on the whole, very satisfactory as regards Queen Dona Maria's cause

The Emperor Dom Pedro entered Lisbon on the 28th, and a great number of people of the higher classes, among them several grandees of the kingdom, hastened to do homage and make their submission to the young Queen   The Patriarch of Lisbon, not wishing to follow the Duc de Cadaval, had already ordered the names of the Queen and the regent to be inserted in the church prayers

In the action that took place on the 23rd, against Tellez Jordão, the Duc de Terceira took eight pieces of cannon , the enemy lost 300 men and two squadrons of cavalry   M de Cordova, the Spanish minister, was actually taken prisoner during this business , but although he had been seen directing and encouraging the Miguelist troops during the fight, the Duc de Terceira at once ordered him to be set at liberty   On his return to Lisbon, M de Cordova had all the arms of the legation removed from his hotel, and retired to Coimbra ..

Several diplomatic and other despatches have been seized, which throw a good deal of light on the intrigues of Dom Miguel's agents, friends, and protectors   According to letters from Oporto, dated July 29th, the enemy is said to have lost five thousand men in the action of the 25th   Among the list of dead are General Cardozo, M de Bourmont's son, and M Duchâtel, and it is also affirmed that a number of other important persons have

[1] See page 113

been killed M. de Bourmont [1] *père*, M. Clouet, and M. Lemos are among the wounded . . .

THE DUC DE BROGLIE TO THE PRINCE DE TALLEYRAND

PARIS, *August 7th,* 1833

MON PRINCE,

To-day I confine myself to replying to your communications concerning the treaty between the Porte and Russia. To-morrow I will write to you about the Portuguese business. Let every day bear its own burden

The first thing that strikes me in reading over this treaty again is that the Eastern question is drawing to its close, and that whatever we do, we must avoid reopening and starting it afresh. You approve the conduct of our ambassadors ; you consider that they have done well not to compromise the evacuation of the Bosphorus, by trying to place obstacles in the way of the signature of the treaty. I fully agree with you, and the conclusion I draw therefrom is, that any action on our part which might have the effect of raising fresh difficulties and reproducing complications at Constantinople, would cause greater inconveniences than advantages

Another consideration which also influences me is that the treaty does not materially change anything in the existing state of affairs

The Porte undertakes to give aid to Russia if the latter demands it This is a mere farce It is no real advantage to Russia ; she has no need of it, and the Porte is not in a position to carry out her undertaking, if she were put to the proof

Russia undertakes to give aid to the Porte if the latter demands it, and in such proportion as she may require This is not more serious either Treaty or no treaty, Russia will always be ready to send her ships into the Bosphorus and her troops to Constantinople, and from the moment that she no longer acquires the right by treaty to send them there, *without awaiting a request from the Porte,* (as the Porte, in like manner, reserves to

---

[1] Louis Auguste-Victor, Comte de Ghaisnes de Bourmont, born in 1773, was an officer in the French Guards at the time of the Revolution He emigrated, served in Condé's army and then in Vendée He was arrested during the Consulate, but managed to escape Returned to France in 1810, and re-entered the service He became a General of Division. His conduct in 1815 will be remembered In 1829, he was for a short time War Minister, and in 1830, commanded the expedition to Algiers, which won him a Field Marshal's baton He refused to swear allegiance to Louis Philippe, followed the Duchess de Berry into Vendée in 1832, and then placed his services at the disposal of Dom Miguel, whose troops he commanded. He returned to France in 1836.

herself the right of asking for them or not, and deciding the
extent and the nature of the aid she may seek,) Russia has
gained no positive right, and I say again, that *actually*, matters
remain pretty much as they were

But, if the treaty does not assure any material advantage
to Russia, it will produce a great moral effect, to which she
is quite right to attach some value, and which we must not
ignore

First, by concluding this treaty, under the very eyes of
France and England, Russia *has had the best of it*, if I may so
express myself, she has concluded the matter to her own profit,
and proved herself in the ascendant

Secondly, the treaty has the air of sanctioning and in some
way perpetuating, what has been done   the intervention of Russia
in the quarrel between the Porte and her Pashas, the occupation
of the Bosphorus and Constantinople, instead of being something
extraordinary and unheard of, on which all eyes have been fixed,
becomes a simple and natural matter, an aspect quite habitual
to the Ottoman Empire

The power of the Divan to resist the Sultan, when his fear
or his fancy induces him to invoke the aid of Russia, will thus
be diminished

The Emperor of Russia, likewise, will acquire the facility of
interfering again, without being obliged to take so many precautions, engagements, and considerations with reference to the
Western Powers of Europe

This, if I am not very much mistaken, is the real result of the
treaty   This is what we must guard against, while at the same
time taking care not to disturb the state of tranquillity in which
the departure of the Russians has left Constantinople

This once established, if we did make any effort to
prevent the ratification of the treaty, I fear, either that we
should not succeed, or that we should be obliged to do more
than we wish

The treaty is to be ratified in two months, or sooner *if
possible*, it will probably be sooner   When our instructions
arrive, matters will probably be so far advanced, and the ratifications so near being exchanged, supposing it has not already
been done, that our chance of preventing them will be very
small, and if, after attempting it, we fail, the triumph of
Russia will be all the greater, her power more affirmed, and her
success more complete   Admitting that we succeed, we should,
as matters are at present, embroil Russia hopelessly with the
Porte, consequently, we should be pledged implicitly to support the latter in all her difficulties, to assist her in her troubles,

and to protect her in every way—in a word, to take charge of her. This is a good deal for Powers so distant from the Porte as France and England. And troubles would not be long in making themselves felt. Russia is so mixed up with Turkish affairs, the treaty of Adrianople has given her such great advantages, the war contribution, (the greater portion of which the Porte still owes,) the occupation of the principalities, the troubles in Servia,[1] and numerous other circumstances, afford so many means of complicating the Sultan's position, that her work will always be ready to her hand, while we shall be obliged to keep soldiers and vessels constantly at the service of the Porte, if we do not want her to elude us, and again throw herself into those arms from which we have only with difficulty rescued her.

This would, if I mistake not, create more trouble than need be, and the remedy might end in becoming more dangerous than the evil. What then should be done?

The following is my view of the matter. Both the legations of France and England should on the same day send a note to the Porte, couched as nearly as possible in the following terms: after announcing that the existence of the treaty has become known to them, they should complain of it to the Porte (but in very measured terms) as showing a want of confidence towards those governments with whom the Porte has always had reason to be well satisfied, who have constantly given her proofs of their interest and friendship, and are still ready to do so. They should point out that as the existence of the Porte is not menaced by any foreign Power, but, on the contrary, the maintenance and integrity of the Ottoman Empire are urged, upheld, and demanded by all the Powers with whom this empire comes in contact, the treaty could only have one aim, namely, that of establishing, as a fact, the habitual intervention of Russia in the home affairs of the Ottoman Empire, that is to say, of placing that empire under the protection of Russia, and making the occupation of the Bosphorus, if not a constant fact, at any rate a simple and by no means extraordinary one. It must then be stated, that such an arrangement could never be admitted either by France or England; that if individuals have the right to give up their independence, such is not the case with States, their independence being of consequence to other States and a matter of public right; that the interdiction of the Bosphorus to armed vessels of all nations is a principle founded on treaties; that the existence of the Porte, as a state *sui juris*, is a common

[1] In virtue of the treaty of Adrianople, Turkey had obtained certain portions of Servia. This incorporation had not taken place without protest. The inhabitants of the ceded districts rose, and, aided by the Servian troops, drove out the Turks.

interest ; that, consequently, neither France nor England could recognize or respect the treaty in question, inasmuch as it would be in violation of this ; and that when the time for the execution of this treaty arrived, they reserved to themselves the right of acting as if it did not exist, believing that they could not possibly be opposed, either by the Porte or by Russia, in their just demands, which they would know best how to support, if necessary

This note, after having been remitted to the Porte, without asking for any reply, and merely as a simple declaration, should then be communicated also to Russia by the two legations at St Petersburg and likewise without asking for any reply

It seems to me that this mode of proceeding has the advantage of not opening up the Eastern question again, or entering into fresh discussions It leaves it undisturbed and at the same stage at which it has arrived Moreover, we shall have the last word in this affair instead of Russia

Whatever answer we may receive, we shall reply that we can only refer to our declaration

Finally, this will be sufficient to annul the moral effect of the treaty On the one side, the anti-Russian portion of the Ottoman Government will be made aware that it is supported by France and England ; that it can offer opposition without running the risk of finding itself standing alone ; and that as by the actual terms of the treaty, aid from Russia must be *asked for*, it can make a struggle to prevent this demand, as though the treaty did not exist On the other hand, the Emperor of Russia is warned that if he attempts to send his vessels a second time into the Bosphorus, he will be subjected to the same treatment as before ; that he is being watched ; that the treaty will not be accepted as an excuse ; and that the very existence of this treaty is only a further reason for vigilance and disquietude

This, mon Prince, is how I look at the matter, its consequences, and the remedies it is possible to apply to it To do more than this would, I think, lead us into a path strewn with rocks, and with a very vague and uncertain ending Have the goodness to tell me how far you deem these ideas feasible, and wherever you find them faulty, kindly point out to me the means of rectifying them

As for M de Metternich, I confess I do not count much on him If he is really sincere, I think if he takes offence it will only be short-lived and of little consequence Nevertheless, it is unfortunate that he should just now be away from the influence of M de Sainte-Aulaire and Sir Frederick Lamb ; but as neither of them is invited, I do not see any means of their going to

Bohemia in attendance on the Emperor of Austria   I will, however, endeavour to learn what takes place there from Maison, who is at Carlsbad, and who has received an invitation from the Emperor of Austria, a means of rendezvous of which he intends to avail himself . .

THE PRINCE DE TALLEYRAND TO THE DUC DE BROGLIE

LONDON, *August* 12th, 1833.

MON CHER DUC,

I should like my answer to your confidential and frank letter to be equally full and useful to you   Your last letter showed me the need, if I required any further stimulant, for earnestly wishing that your Ministry, already so fortunate in many respects, should be equally fertile in good results, amid all the numerous complications which arise each day.

The Eastern question is undeniably the most serious of the whole range   The very fact of a treaty between the Porte and Russia, apart from the other Powers, so evidently upsets the equilibrium, that it seems to me it must be put a stop to before anything else   Like yourself, I fear that we may be too late, but I also think that we ought at least to attempt what later on, we might be reproached for not having tried   The other considerations so clearly developed in your letter, necessarily escaped me, as in default of a mass of information which can only be obtained at the Foreign Office, I could but take note of isolated facts.   I have been particularly struck by the encroaching, though measured and slowly progressive, policy of the North , by her uniformly persevering and cautious action, which never becomes rapid except when it is a question of availing herself by promptitude and skill of the actually opportune moment   This has alone occupied me, as being the real danger against which civilized Europe demanded the close and simultaneous union of France and England.

But collateral considerations might, I admit, paralyze this action.   I therefore yield to those which you have been good enough to bring to my notice.   I cannot, however, understand the Sultan's monetary difficulties as regards Russia, for the Greek loan furnishes him with the means of acquitting himself of the tribute imposed by the treaty of Adrianople[1]   I am not aware

---

[1] The Treaty of Adrianople imposed upon Turkey a tribute of 137 millions , but Greece only owed Turkey the sum of 12 millions, levied upon her by the Convention of 16th September, 1832, which determined her northern frontier   It is evident therefore, that although Turkey had her tribute materially reduced by the Treaty of 29th January, 1833, a considerable difference still existed between the amount due by the Porte to Russia, and that which was due to her from Greece

whether there exist any special and pecuniary exigencies on the part of the Russians for the period of their occupation of Constantinople

However, the great distances will of themselves have resolved one part of the question, for the English courier, as well as yours, will probably only arrive in time to protest against an accomplished fact. The protest of England, which Lord Ponsonby is ordered to make use of if the ratifications have been exchanged, is drawn up in the same spirit as that of which you speak in your letter to me, and which has served as a guide and model here. There is therefore nothing further to be done just now, we must wait for the replies from Constantinople

In my despatch to-day, I send you all that is known here about Portugal, the news is up to the 31st

The refractory spirit of the Belgian Cabinet is such, that the whole Conference is half inclined to grant King William the delays he no longer dares ask for

August 16th, 1833

The last accounts from Portugal have by no means reassured the English Government, which, for the last fortnight especially, shares the apprehensions you expressed to me, in the last despatch you did me the honour to write respecting the claims of the Emperor Dom Pedro. The English ministers would like to set aside this Portuguese prince altogether, but have not as yet found any suitable means of attaining this end. For the peace of the Peninsula, they dread the influence which the very advanced men who surround Dom Pedro may exercise over him ; and they have no confidence in anyone, except the Duc de Palmella and the Duc de Terceira. The instructions sent to Mr Addington and Lord William Russell, which have been communicated to you, will have been useful to you in directing the conduct of the King's Government in an affair which needs the greatest possible care. . . .

THE DUC DE BROGLIE TO THE PRINCE DE TALLEYRAND

Paris, August 15th, 1833

MON PRINCE,

Eight days ago Mr. Aston, the *Chargé d'Affaires* in Lord Granville's absence, showed me, by Lord Palmerston's wish, the instructions he has sent to Lord William Russell, which appeared to me very judicious, very reasonable, and completely adapted to the present state of affairs in Portugal. Lord Palmerston at the same time informed the French Cabinet, that the intention of the English Cabinet was to accredit Lord William Russell to the regency of Dom Pedro, but as an envoy extraordinary, entrusted with a special and provisional mission ; it being the intention of the English Cabinet not to defer establishing diplomatic relations with Queen Dona Maria's Government Nevertheless, the organization of an ordinary and permanent mission is to be considered as a favour which Dom Pedro must first merit by his wisdom, prudence, and his good conduct.

The English Cabinet has avoided the formal recognition of Dona Maria's Government, by referring to the recognition which had taken place in 1826, and making the present recognition consist in the simple fact of resuming diplomatic relations

Mr Aston asked the French Government to associate itself with him, both in the nature of the steps to be taken, and in the choice and position of the agent who would be entrusted with them.

I at once observed that the English Government had the advantage of having its agent already established there on the spot, whereas if we were to send a man of the same rank and position as Lord William Russell as our envoy to Portugal, it would be a much graver step and pledge us much further. Nevertheless, as Mr Aston urged it, I promised him I would take the King's directions and the advice of my colleagues on this subject

The advice of the Council was to satisfy the English Government, as far as it was in our power, by recognizing Dona Maria, supposing that the English Government recognizes her ; to make this recognition, as it has done, consist in the resumption of diplomatic relations ; and to send a man of the same rank and position as Lord William Russell, to Portugal, as a minister charged with a special and provisional mission In order however that we should not do more than the English Government, I proposed and the Council adopted, the following expedient . that this official should go with Dona Maria, without any title, as if to take her back and do honour to her, reserving to ourselves not to send him his credentials until after his arrival in Lisbon, and when he would be already there for another reason

The King had already designated M de Flahaut for this post, his relations with England and Portugal seeming to point him out as more suitable than anyone else

In the midst of all this, we heard of the Marquis de Loulé's[1] arrival at Brest. He had come from Dom Pedro, but had to

---

[1] Dom Pedro's Minister, who had married his sister, the Princess Anne.

undergo quarantine for ten days   It was thought that at the end of two or three days he would send on his despatches, and that we should then know what he had come for, but until this evening he kept, or rather they kept, the object of his mission a profound secret   Only it was easy to see that there was some mystery at work   The King, having visited the Duchess de Braganza, with the view of offering her a French frigate, if she wished it, to carry her to Portugal, found her very cold and reserved

At length, last night, when the Duchess de Braganza went to see the Queen, she incidentally mentioned that she intended leaving at once, that some Portuguese vessels would be at Havre on the 25th to convey her, that she would not therefore require a French frigate, and further, that she meant to take her brother, the Duc de Leuchtenberg, with her and had written to tell him to meet her at Havre

That was the key to the enigma   It is clear that Dom Pedro and his wife intend to endeavour, at once and openly, to bring about a marriage between Dona Maria and the Duc de Leuchtenberg

I need not point out to you, mon Prince, the foolishness of this project, and how very offensive this proceeding is to the King

It is also quite plain now, that if the success of Dona Maria's cause has been so difficult to accomplish, if even now it is still somewhat doubtful in Portugal, it is not because the Portuguese like Dom Miguel, but because Dom Pedro has done his best to denaturalize this cause, and to deprive it of everything national and Portuguese, by identifying it with himself, his follies, his freaks, and his idiotic Constitution, and in confounding it with the cause of all the disturbances, all the fire-brands, and all the *fuor usciti* of Europe   Now, there certainly is no more direct and certain way of achieving this in the minds of the Portuguese, and at once disgusting the moderate party as well as the masses, than by endeavouring to make Dona Maria marry an adventurer, whose sister Dom Pedro married, when despairing of his cause, and when none of the reigning families in Europe would contract an alliance with him   Nothing would more completely shock the pride of the Portuguese than such an alliance, or ruin all hopes of even the semblance of a peaceful future.

Moreover, what could we say to Spain in such a case?

In 1831, we declared that we could not tolerate the Duc de Leuchtenberg on the Belgian throne, because that throne would necessarily become the hot-bed of all the Buonapartists' intrigues, and all the authors of disorder who follow in the wake of every claimant   How can we now tell the Spanish Government that it must not mind seeing the Duc de Leuchtenberg on the throne of Portugal, when that throne must inevitably become the *rendezvous* and centre of all the *Josephinos*[1] and all the malcontents of the Peninsula ? Add to this the Constitution, the liberty of the press, the tribune and the refugees How could we contest the right of the Spanish Government to defend itself against a state of affairs which would so manifestly threaten its existence ?

Lastly, the matter is also very serious from another point of view It shows that Dom Pedro evidently intends to go his own road, to gratify his whims, and conduct his daughter's affairs at random to the same point to which he has so happily brought his own, without any regard for the other Powers whose support is necessary to him If England and France give in to him now, if they do not at once take a very high hand with him, I believe that all chance of exercising the slightest ascendency over him, will disappear entirely

As for the king, how unbecoming, I might almost say insolent, it was, to take such a resolution without informing him of it—without consulting him—and only telling him about it incidentally and by chance as it were !

Under these circumstances, mon Prince, the French Government considers that it ought to ask the English Cabinet to act energetically with it, to thwart so senseless and disastrous a scheme It thinks that a joint step should be taken by both Governments towards Dom Pedro, which would consist in sending him a despatch couched in the plainest and most categorical terms, pointing out the danger and folly of such a project, and concluding by stating that the French and English Governments did not intend to compromise themselves in Dona Maria's cause, except in so far as the sensible conduct of those who directed it, gave a reasonable hope of success, and that the moral and material support, which they were expected to accord, would be regulated by the deference paid to wise and prudent counsels

In conclusion it should be demanded that the Duc de Leuchtenberg should depart, and the projected marriage be absolutely abandoned.

In thus proposing a joint action to the English Government, mon Prince, you will see that we do not renounce the idea of at once establishing diplomatic relations with Dom Pedro's Regency. Nevertheless, the conduct of the Duc de Braganza,

---

[1] This was the name given to the Spanish partizans of King Joseph during the French occupation Later on, this term was extended and applied to all liberals and revolutionists

is on this occasion so offensive to the king, that it would be impossible for him to send any person of distinction with Dona Maria, or to have her escorted by a French frigate   He owes it to himself to resent the insult offered and to show it plainly. We shall content ourselves by sending credentials to M de Lurde,[1] the Secretary of Legation at Oporto, who will reside provisionally at Lisbon, not exactly as a *Chargé d'Affaires,* (which would indicate a permanent mission,) but as *charged with the affairs of France*   He will second Lord William Russell in all his efforts to restrain and moderate Dom Pedro   If the English Government is of opinion that the course I have indicated above should be carried out, I will communicate the despatch which I shall send to M de Lurde to Mr Aston, so that he may inform Lord Palmerston of its contents, and I will also send you a copy, mon Prince   It would I think be well, that the language should be as much alike as possible

It is moreover not necessary for me to remind you, that this is not the first time the question of Dona Maria's marriage has been the subject of correspondence between England and France   The English Government is already quite in accord with us as to the impossibility of tolerating the Duc de Leuchtenberg ; and it also agrees with the French Government, that it would be well for Dona Maria to marry a prince of Naples, which according to the information we have received, does not seem at all impossible   In any case, there can be no question of her marrying one of our princes.   It is quite enough to have to defend Belgium, and please Heaven we may never have another such task to carry out [2] . . .

THE DUC DE BROGLIE TO THE PRINCE DE TALLEYRAND.

PARIS, *August 17th,* 1833

MON PRINCE,

Events succeed each other very rapidly, but their daily progress it seems to me, shows more and more the necessity of acting with prudence and decision in Portuguese affairs   If we allow matters to take their natural course, everything before long will have reached such a state of confusion that even the most skilful will not be able to put them straight

---

[1] The Comte de Lurde, Secretary of the Legation in Portugal since 1833, had been previously on a mission to Rio de Janeiro (in 1830)   In 1838, he became first Secretary of the Embassy at Constantinople, then Minister at Buenos Ayres

[2] Since the preceding February, M de Talleyrand, who had probably felt his way in Paris on this question, had received from Madame Adelaide a most categorical reply See Appendix, letter No 8

The following, if I am not mistaken, is the object we ought to have in view.

1. To exclude Dom Pedro and Dom Miguel from Portugal.

2. To adjourn putting the Constitution of 1826 into operation, until more peaceable times will allow of its revision and adaptation to the customs of Portugal and the interests of all parties.

3. To marry Dona Maria to some prince, who would not excite either the anxiety of Spain or the jealousy of any one

Looking at it in this light, I do not think the proposal made by M de Zea to M de Rayneval, is quite to be despised.[1]

If by guaranteeing the exclusion of Dom Pedro and the adjournment of the Constitution, subject to its revision later on, we could obtain from the Spanish Government its recognition of Dona Maria, and aid in negotiating a marriage between this princess and a prince of Naples, we should I think be doing a wise action, and one not exceeding the measure of possibility

The Spanish Government is evidently in great perplexity ; it has little hopes of upholding Don Miguel ; it is dissatisfied with his conduct as regards Don Carlos ; it feels the necessity of returning to friendly relations with the Court of Naples, with which it had almost become embroiled over the question of the succession ; there would be an opportunity of doing so by offering it a crown for the second or third prince of the house of Naples

By taking this line, the French and English Governments would not only have Spain on their side, but also the whole of Europe, as well as the greater part of Portugal , they would have no adversaries, so to speak, except Dom Pedro and the train of blunderers who follow in his suite

It will then remain to be seen how the two Governments will proceed in order to dispossess Dom Pedro and succeed in driving out Dom Miguel, without intervening openly and with an armed force in the affairs of Portugal

---

[1] The Spanish Cabinet was extremely excited about Dom Pedro It feared that England would openly take up arms in his favour, and declared that it should consider such an act as a declaration of war, for the fall of Dom Miguel, would, they said involve that of the Spanish monarchy itself (*M de Rayneval's despatches of 13th and 15th July*) When the news of Dom Pedro's entry into Lisbon on the 2nd of August, reached the Government, Madrid became more and more anxious M de Zea proposed to M de Rayneval to exclude Dom Pedro and instal Dona Maria with a Regency, from which her father should be left out (*Despatch of August 12th*) Mr Addington was also sounded as to this On the 9th August, M de Rayneval confirmed the preceding information, and added that M de Zea consented formally to recognize Dona Maria, provided he received a complete guarantee against Dom Pedro and his Constitution (*M. de Rayneval's official correspondence*)

As for Dom Miguel, his fall will be greatly accelerated if Spain abandons him, it will result naturally from the course of events and from the success of the opposite party

As regards Dom Pedro, however, the matter is much more difficult.

The true way, as far as I can judge, is to separate Dom Pedro from the cause of the Constitution, and to turn, if I may so express it, his Constitution against himself According to the terms of article ninety-two of this Constitution, the Regency devolves on the nearest heir to the existing sovereign Dom Pedro is not a Portuguese, Dom Pedro is not an heir, his regency is a usurpation, the regency belongs to the Infanta Maria Isabella, who administered it in 1826, in default of Dom Miguel [1]

This is the ground upon which we can take a stand

If the two Governments formally declare, that they resume affairs at the exact point they occupied when the summons of Dom Miguel to the Lieutenant-Generalcy upset everything, that they will not give any moral or material support except to Dona Maria's Government, as it then existed, it is probable that they will create a Portuguese party at Lisbon which will awe Dom Pedro and end by forcing him to retire from affairs In acting thus, they might, if it is absolutely necessary, deviate more or less with the approbation of every one from the system of neutrality, and from the moment that their efforts are directed simultaneously against both princes, and with the object of benefiting Spain, it is quite certain that no objections will be made Their arbitration would in fact be admitted, similarly to that of the whole Conference in the affairs of Belgium

Dom Pedro once expelled, it would be easy enough to come to an understanding about the Constitution, and to modify it in the manner most favourable to the peace of the Peninsula

I am writing these views rather hurriedly, mon Prince, as they come into my head, for I have not had time since the morning to think them over I submit them, or rather hand them over to your experience Adopt from them as much as you desire, or nothing at all, if they do not appear to you capable of execution We shall however adhere to the resolutions taken with respect to the Duc de Leuchtenberg, and I now confirm all I said to you in my letter of the night before last   .

---

[1] Dom Pedro was no longer a Portuguese, as Brazil had been separated from Portugal He was no longer heir to King John VI, as on becoming Emperor of Brazil, he had resigned his right to the Crown of Portugal The Regency therefore devolved upon the Infanta Maria Isabella, daughter of Dom Pedro, who was Dom Miguel's elder brother

THE PRINCE DE TALLEYRAND TO THE DUC DE BROGLIE

LONDON, *August 17th*, 1833

MON CHER DUC,

Your letter of the 15th reached me this morning. After reading it carefully and thinking it well over, and likewise the admirably drawn up documents accompanying it, I went to see Lord Palmerston My despatch of to-day will give you the general and very satisfactory result of our interview Here are a few more details

The Belgian question has been suspended for the last ten days, this wearies every one. In Brussels they do not fail to prolong this state of affairs Strong in an advantageous provisional arrangement, confident, more than they ought to be, in the ties of a French relationship, the Belgians give but little thought to peace, equilibrium, and a *recognized* existence which can only be arrived at by a definite arrangement The Conference cuts but a sorry figure in face of this Belgian silence, which, to say truth, is quite as impertinent as the abuse of the Dutch You are quite right to set aside all these family interests which are grafted on a foreign policy. It was this which ruined the Emperor Napoleon, it is what is now embarrassing us at Brussels, and what would have caused Portugal to become a thorn in the side of France, if they had tried there to bring about a marriage with one of our princes I pray you to do your very utmost with regard to the Belgians, for matters are becoming urgent

England quite understands our objections to the Duc de Leuchtenberg, as well as our just indignation at the unbecoming conduct of the Duke and Duchess of Braganza Lord Palmerston agrees with us that Spain should not be exposed to so disturbing an influence as this marriage would become Instructions will be sent from England to Lord William Russell to place serious obstacles in the way of such a project The marriage as well as the Constitution, would disappear with Dom Pedro ; but a more decided course should have been adopted here, and diplomatic agents should only have been accredited to a wise and responsible Regency. Palmella and Villaflor appear to have been quite set aside by Dom Pedro However, we are without news from Lisbon for some days, and it is impossible to know exactly what is happening there The English seem to think that for the present, M de Luide is a very sufficient representative ; when matters are a little cleared up, M de Flahaut will no doubt do admirably

The despatch relative to Switzerland, which you have

addressed to Vienna and Berlin, appeared so conclusive to Lord Palmerston, that his letters on this subject, will only be as it were, paraphrases of yours [1]

August 17th, 1833

This morning I received by courier, the despatch No 89, which you did me the honour to write, and I profited by the opportunity I had of meeting Lord Palmerston to-day, to discuss the various subjects which you recommended to my notice.

When I spoke to him of the Duc de Leuchtenberg's journey, and the scheme of a marriage with Queen Dona Maria, which might have been the Emperor Dom Pedro's object in inviting his brother-in-law, Lord Palmerston did not hesitate to reply that England could never give her assent to such a project, and that she fully agreed in all the considerations you had so clearly brought forward, in order that France and England might oppose its execution He added that he was quite ready to give such instructions to Lord William Russell, as would in reality be similar to those you had pointed out The difference that existed between the position of France and England with regard to Portugal, might perhaps necessitate some slight alteration in the actual form sent, but this would in no way influence the result You can therefore arrange about these instructions with Mr Aston, and transmit them to whatever agent you may accredit to Portugal Lord William Russell will receive orders to come to an understanding with this agent, in order that their action may be simultaneous

I could not help noticing, from Lord Palmerston's language during this interview, how well founded was the information I had the honour of sending you yesterday, as to the discontent with which Dom Pedro's conduct has inspired the English Cabinet . .

THE PRINCE DE TALLEYRAND TO THE DUC DE BROGLIE

LONDON, *August 19th*, 1833

I received your despatch No 90, this morning, and hastened to see Lord Palmerston, to whom I at once communicated it, with certain portions of M de Rayneval's letters [2] He then gave me Mr Addington's second despatch to read, which was dated the 11th, that is to say, one day later than M de Rayneval's

[1] See in Appendix the despatch in question, which the Duc de Broglie sent to M Bresson, letter No 12
[2] See page 159

In this despatch Mr Addington gives an account of a conversation he had just had with M de Zea, the tenor of which was very different to that held with M de Rayneval

Instead of proposing, as he did to the latter, to endeavour to come to some understanding, and find means of securing the pacification of the Peninsula by conciliatory measures, M. de Zea on the contrary, declared to Mr. Addington that Spain would in no way swerve from the line of conduct she had followed up to the present in Portuguese affairs, and that for his part, he intended to hold to it

Neither Lord Palmerston nor I, could help being struck by this contradiction in the reports of two ambassadors, in whom their Governments, and rightly so, place full confidence, and we were obliged to conclude that M de Zea was double-tongued, and that he wished to deceive either one or the other of the ambassadors.

I also told Lord Palmerston that we should expect the English Cabinet to show more determination in its communications, both with Lisbon and Madrid

You will have learnt from my despatch, No 159, that Lord William Russell is to act in concert with the agent whom you may accredit to Lisbon, to oppose the marriage projected by Dom Pedro   Lord Palmerston is equally decided to support the scheme of marrying Queen Dona Maria to one of the Neapolitan princes, and he is quite prepared to take any steps you may deem advisable in this matter

As to the expulsion of Dom Pedro from Portugal, and the suspension of the Constitution of 1826, he fully shares in your views, and is only held back by the difficulty in finding some means of accomplishing it, without having recourse to violence He dreads anything that might even have the semblance of interfering with the home affairs of the country ; he does not even care for a solemn declaration by both Governments, which would tend to re-establish, under their auspices as you proposed, the state of affairs that existed in Portugal before the usurpation of Dom Miguel

Lord Palmerston does not conceal from himself the inconvenience of Dom Pedro's presence in Portugal, or the dangerous effect of the faulty Constitution in 1826[1] on the peace of the Peninsula ; but, as I had the honour of telling you, even while desiring the end, he recoils from the means   I omitted

---

[1] The Constitution which Dom Pedro, had given Portugal, on assuming the Regency in the name of his daughter Dona Maria after the death of King John VI It conferred legislative power upon two Chambers, one elective, the other nominated by the King

none of the many weighty arguments you brought forward in
your different letters, but I could not get him to make up his
mind to any of the bold measures which England ought to
adopt under these circumstances

Lord Palmerston also told me that after Mr Addington's
reports, it would be impossible for him to take any steps whatever with the Madrid Cabinet, until M de Zea had made fresh
overtures to the English Government, of a nature somewhat
similar to those recently made to M de Rayneval

As I found him quite determined on this point, I thought it
best not to urge him further, reserving to myself, however, to
speak to Lord Grey about it, I went to him as soon as my
interview with Lord Palmerston was ended I did not find him
in, I will therefore go there again to-morrow, but I do not wish
to delay in sending you information, which it may perhaps be
useful to forward to Madrid   .

LORD GREY TO THE PRINCE DE TALLEYRAND

DOWNING STREET, *August 21st*, 1833

MON PRINCE,

I return you, with many thanks, the Duc de Broglie's
very interesting letter, with which you did me the honour to
entrust me

I think there is great justice in the Duke's views and reasons,
though I do not share all his fears respecting the marriage of
the Duc de Leuchtenberg I shall be delighted to have an
opportunity of talking this over with you on my return from
Windsor

THE PRINCE DE TALLEYRAND TO THE DUC DE BROGLIE.

LONDON, *August 22nd*, 1833

.   I could only see Lord Grey for a few moments
about Portuguese affairs, he is absorbed by Parliament and
has also been over to Windsor for a day He certainly shares
your dislike to the marriage projected by Dom Pedro for his
daughter, but, nevertheless, he hardly appreciates the very
serious consequences it may have on the future of the Peninsula,
and I have found both in Lord Grey and Lord Palmerston, if
not actual indifference, certainly a hesitation, and indecision
concerning the Portuguese question, which might have very
serious results, if it were prolonged I should advise you to be
perfectly frank as to this with Mr Aston

August 23rd, 1833.

. . . . Lord Palmerston seemed quite to understand our objections to the Duc de Leuchtenberg's marriage, but I have noticed with pain, that several other members of the Cabinet look at this question with a sort of sentimental policy, which to me seems quite misplaced Meanwhile, nothing is really being done Dom Pedro is establishing himself more firmly in the Regency, which he claims as his own, he is leading it to the devil, and unfortunately each day makes it more difficult to turn him out; it is greatly to be feared now that a civil war alone will upset him . .

August 26th, 1833.

. . . . The instructions which you have sent to M de Lurde seem to me admirably drawn up, they apply equally to emergencies wisely thought out, and to facts which we know exist already

I must congratulate the King's Government more and more, on the line of policy it has adopted in its relations with Spain, and of which your despatch to M de Rayneval furnishes me with a fresh proof

I am inclined to agree with you, that M de Zea's overtures to our ambassador at Madrid were made with the intention of following suit, and assuring peace to the Peninsula, jointly with France and England Whether this novel tone on the part of the Madrid Cabinet has been dictated by fear as to the result of the different events at Lisbon, or by some other feeling, it is perhaps as well not to inquire too closely I have therefore not neglected any arguments, which might induce the English ministers to see the necessity of our coming to an understanding with Spain, in order to arrange the future of Portugal to the advantage of everyone . .

I had the honour to inform you of the bad impression produced here by Mr Addington's last despatches; but I do not think that the unfavourable disposition of the English Cabinet towards the Spanish Government is entirely due to these reports, for people go so far as to say, that there is a general feeling of animosity against M de Zea, which might lead to some very troublesome complications The recent nomination of Mr George Villiers [1] in

---

[1] George William Frederick Villiers, Earl of Clarendon, born in 1800, was in 1833, appointed Minister at Madrid In 1833, he became Lord Privy Seal; Chancellor of the Duchy of Lancaster in 1840, Lord-Lieutenant of Ireland from 1847 to 1852; and then Secretary of State for Foreign Affairs He resigned in 1858, was again made Chancellor of the Duchy of Lancaster in 1864, and resumed the ministry of Foreign Affairs in 1855.

place of Mr Addington seems rather to give point to this feeling, and although full justice is done to the high character of this new envoy, a fear is expressed as to his views, which are much more pronounced than those of Mr Addington, in a way which is hardly in accord with the policy of the Madrid Cabinet Mr Villiers' nomination is all the more unfortunate, since M de Zea only very recently expressed a wish that Mr Addington should remain at Madrid

I must further cite, as a fact in support of the reproaches addressed to the English Government, the publication of the letters which were intercepted at Lisbon—a publication which I have deplored quite as much as you, M le Duc, and which the English Government will have some trouble in justifying [1] Some portions of these letters might have been made use of advantageously, either in the hands of some English members of Parliament, or such foreign governments as were more or less compromised by them, and whom the fear of indiscreet revelations would certainly have made more reticent and careful What seems to me to make this imprudent publication still more to be regretted is, that the English Government has not known how to profit by the sole advantage which it had gained thereby, in being able to

[1] During the war in Portugal, a certain number of letters addressed to Dom Miguel's Government had been intercepted and communicated to the British Cabinet The *Times* obtained possession of them and published them Amongst this correspondence the most curious are, reports addressed to the Duc de Cadeval and Vicomte de Santarem by a man named Antonio Ribera Saraiva, secret minister of Dom Miguel in London, seriously compromising many influential members of the Tory party and representatives of continental courts The letters of 14th July, 1833 (reproduced in the *Débats* of 20th August), speak of secret conferences which had been held in London by Marshal de Bourmont with Lord Beresford, M de Neumann, Austrian Chargé d'Affaires, and M Viel, Spanish Minister The Portuguese agent thus writes "The Baron de Neumann told me that, not only he himself, but a number of other persons, and among others the Duke of Wellington, would be delighted to learn that Marshal de Bourmont had gone to Portugal He added that the three powers had praised his Majesty's resolution to take the Marshal into his service, and that in fact Bourmont ought to look upon his departure for Portugal not as being a mission to save the Portuguese cause only, but that of legitimacy in the whole Peninsula in Europe, and in the world" After receipt of the news of the destruction of Dom Miguel's fleet on the 17th July, Ribera wrote again "I have no longer any hope I have spoken on this subject with the ambassadors of the great powers and other exalted personages All consider our cause, if not entirely lost, at least very seriously compromised, and the sole hope of those who are interested in us is, that Marshal de Bourmont may be maintained at the head of the land forces" The publication of this correspondence caused a lively sensation in England Lord Palmerston was questioned on the subject by Mr Murray in the House of Commons He asked him if these letters were authentic, or not "As far as I can judge," added the honourable member, "this correspondence is very strange, and it is annoying to see certain persons therein spoken of as agents of the most detestable government that ever was If the letters are authentic they do but little honour to English character, but I am ready to believe that the noble Viscount is prepared to deny them" Lord Palmerston refused to reply to the question, which leaves but little doubt as to the authenticity of the documents published

pronounce itself energetically with reference to Portuguese affairs
After these letters, it might have considered itself authorized to
interfere at Lisbon, in order to expel Dom Pedro and facilitate
the reconciliation of Dona Maria's Government with that of
Spain. It would have been quite easy for it to have concealed
this intervention in the home affairs of the country, under some
pretext or other, and besides, success in such cases justifies everything All the Cabinets would thereby have been satisfied, silence
would have been imposed on the Tory party in Parliament, and
tranquillity thus re-established in Portugal (notwithstanding the
suspension of the Constitution of 1826, until the majority of
Dona Maria) would have given the Government the most
powerful means of defence against that fraction in Parliament
which holds the most exaggerated opinions As you authorized
me to do, I have just communicated to Lord Palmerston
the instructions you sent to M de Lurde He was very
sensible of this mark of confidence, and desired me to tell
you that he fully approved of these instructions, and that he
intended writing to Lord William Russell to instruct him that
in his measures generally, he was to act in concert with M de
Lurde. . . .

August 26th, 1833

MON CHER DUC,

I have taken away the official character of the despatch
I am sending herewith, so that you may, if you think proper,
only look upon it as a private letter I think I ought to
forward the information it contains to the Government. You
will besides find in it some arguments, which you could, of course
without citing me, turn to account with Mr Aston I need not
point out to you what very serious unpleasantnesses would
arise from any direct indiscretion as to the contents of this
despatch

The English Government is very dissatisfied with its minister
at St Petersburg, who has for no reason whatever compromised
Lord Minto with the Berlin Cabinet I have done all in my
power to prevent injury to Lord Minto in his position, through an
indiscretion on the part of one of his colleagues My opinion is
that the Ministry will strain every effort to hush up this affair in
order to keep Lord Minto at Berlin . .

August 27th, 1833

The following news arrived in London to-day from Lisbon
and Oporto :—

Lord William Russell presented his credentials to the regent
at Lisbon, on the 15th.

On the 16th, Saldanha defeated the Miguelites before Oporto, the siege of which is completely raised, and in such a manner that a great many trading vessels have entered the Douro. The Cortes have been convoked at Lisbon, and the elections are to commence on the 1st October

Another piece of news, which also reached London this morning, and for which no one was prepared, is the arrival of the Emperor of Russia at Stettin [1] We heard this from a courier who had been sent to the Prince de Lieven

THE COMTE DE RAYNEVAL TO THE PRINCE DE TALLEYRAND

MADRID, *August* 19*th*, 1833.

MON PRINCE,

I thank you much for your letter of the 27th July I can quite understand how very little attraction a stay in Paris has for you now, and for my part, I frankly admit that I do not consider it any privation to be away from it   There are moments when I should much like to put in an appearance there, such as the present for instance, for I should meet you, which would be both a very great pleasure, and an immense help to me   You would, I feel sure, dispel a cloud of

---

[1] The Emperor of Russia went to Munchengratz, where he was to meet the Emperor of Austria on the 9th September (see page 181). M Pozzo had just informed the Duc de Broglie of this officially, and he had told it to the king   "M Pozzo," he wrote, "has shown me a long despatch from M de Nesselrode in which he gives as the reasons for this journey, the long standing wish of the three sovereigns to meet again and exchange mutual tokens of friendship   Political circumstances have hitherto prevented this   the war in Poland, the cholera, and the general state of agitation everywhere   Now that Europe is at peace, that Poland is tranquil, that Eastern affairs are ended, Belgian matters on the point of being so, and all else too insignificant to disturb the peace of Europe, there is nothing further to stand in the way of the wishes of the three sovereigns, and their interview must therefore not be looked upon as anything alarming   It has no hidden designs for its object, nor has it been arranged in order to attain any such ends   It is merely a proof of affection they wish reciprocally to give each other, and no other motive should be looked for   Such, Sire, is the substance of this despatch, to which I listened without comment, either for or against, as something perfectly indifferent to France and without showing the least curiosity as to the details of the interview   Time will show whether this interview conceals any profound mystery   I think not   nevertheless it is as well to be on one's guard and to watch everything "—(*The Duc de Broglie to King Louis Philippe, August 30th*)

A similar step was taken by M de Lieven with Lord Palmerston, who wrote on this subject to his brother   "The reason for the meeting of the three sovereigns in Bohemia will explain itself later on   Nesselrode writes to Lieven so that he could show me the letter, that it was only '*an epanchement de cœur*,' and that politics had nothing to do with it   How can anyone take up his pen to write such stuff !   It is truly as if they wished us to disbelieve every word they said "—*Lord Palmerston to the Hon William Temple, 3rd September, 1833 —Private Correspondence of Lord Palmerston*

doubts which constantly presents itself to me, and you would show me the path I ought to follow, to enable me to extricate myself from the ever increasing difficulties of my present position here   The Ministry ought really to send for me, even if only for a few days   It seems to me that there are some points in the affairs of this kingdom for which writing is not sufficient, they must be talked over

One might believe in a speedy *dénoûment* of the drama that is being enacted here, if Dom Pedro would resign himself to disappearing from the scene   But he no doubt has some idea that they are only too eager to set him aside, and has taken his precautions accordingly   Dom Miguel and his adherents are pretty nearly *hors de combat*.   Is there not some fear, however, that a fresh conflict may arise and that the country may be divided between Dom Pedro and Dona Maria ?   Spain would, I think, in a manner, accept the sovereignty of this Princess ; but dreads the father   The hasty measures he has adopted against the clergy, cause him to be regarded here as a most violent revolutionary.[1]   Notwithstanding this, if he humours Spain she will leave him in peace   The Government of Madrid knows its own weakness and will undertake nothing, unless driven thereto by desperation   It is very anxious to be assured as to the views of England , Mr Addington's recall, although foreseen, seemed to augur ill , the dread is that he will be replaced by an ardent and prejudiced man   Much can be done by humouring the Spaniards, but if they are roughly handled or threatened, they fire up at once and will not only decline to act with you, but you may even cause them to rush into the most dangerous follies

M. de Zea thanks your Highness for remembering him   He trusts you will endeavour to conciliate Lord Palmerston, who he fancies is not over well disposed towards Spain.

King Ferdinand is in a very sad condition   It is feared he may not live through September   I believe that Don Carlos's determination to remain in Portugal, notwithstanding the war and the cholera, is entirely due to the accounts of the king's

[1] Dom Pedro on entering Lisbon on the 28th July had at once assumed the reins of Government   He suspended the Charter until after the close of the war, and dismissed from the Ministry the Duc de Palmella, who had the confidence both of France and England, in order to surround himself with people who were well known for their advanced democratic views.   He also ill-used the clergy, who were the firm supporters of Dom Miguel   The Pope's Nuncio was forcibly compelled to embark for Italy, and the Jesuits were expelled   It was strictly forbidden to pay the revenues due to other Miguelist corporations   Decrees were issued, dismissing all the bishops nominated by Dom Miguel, and forbidding all novices, who were then in convents, to enter Holy Orders   Lastly, Dom Pedro claimed for the Crown all presentation to benefices

health His death under present circumstances would, I feel sure, throw this country into terrible confusion, and I do not think that even the tranquillity of Europe, which your care has so miraculously preserved up to now, would be able to withstand this shock

THE PRINCE DE TALLEYRAND TO THE DUC DE BROGLIE

LONDON, *August 29th*, 1833

I have the honour to send you herewith, the speech made by the King of England at the prorogation of Parliament to-day You will notice the paragraphs which relate to the Dutch, Portuguese, and Turkish questions

The Chancellor leaves London this evening for two months. and Lord Grey starts in a few days for his country seat in the north of England, where he also hopes to pass a couple of months

THE COMTE DE RAYNEVAL TO THE PRINCE DE TALLEYRAND

MADRID, *August 24th*, 1833

PRINCE,

We are in a sort of crisis here While Lord Palmerston is giving reiterated assurances of England's neutrality to the Madrid Cabinet, and requiring more imperiously than ever that Spain should do the same, declaring that if *a single* Spanish soldier sets foot on Portuguese territory England will look upon it as a declaration of war, Lord William Russell announces that he has decided, in order, as he says, to protect the English subjects, to land not *one* soldier, but two thousand of those who are with Admiral Parker's [1] squadron, and to occupy with them not only Fort St Julian, which defends the mouth of the Tagus, but also Fort St George, which commands the town of Lisbon Lord W Russell communicated this decision to M de Cordova, in a letter dated 13th This, as you may imagine, has created a very strong impression on the Government here, which only two days before had received the reassuring communication above mentioned It is at a loss to know whether this idea of disembarking the British troops is due to Lord William or to his Government It is rather inclined to believe in the former than in the latter

[1] Sir William Parker, born in 1781, entered the navy very young, became a captain in 1810, and rear-admiral in 1830 In this capacity, he commanded the English squadron sent at this time to the mouth of the Tagus He was appointed a Lord of the Admiralty in 1834, and again in 1841 Commanded, at this latter date, the English naval force in the Chinese seas , was promoted admiral in 1863, and died in 1866

hypothesis, which would seem to be too directly opposed to what the English Cabinet had stated   In the uncertainty in which M de Zea, is placed, he is hastening to send a courier to London to ask the Government not to pass the bounds which it has itself established, and not to force Spain, in spite of herself, to quit that line of conduct, to which at the request of England she has so faithfully adhered   He assures me that the Note on this matter, which will be transmitted to Lord Palmerston, is couched in such terms as could not possibly be taken in bad part.   He asks our Government to support this pacific measure, and he would be most grateful, if you would use your personal influence to endeavour to change a decision of which it is impossible to calculate the results.   But I very much fear that this request will arrive too late   On the 16th, M de Bourmont quitted Coimbra to join his army, *en route* for Lisbon   It consists of 5,000 or 6,000 men, not including some detached corps on the Tagus and the coast of Torres Vedras   With this force he can certainly attempt to relieve the capital, and with success   Lord William will no doubt be obliged to carry out his plan, or else relinquish it, without awaiting instructions from his Government   The whole future of the Peninsula therefore, depends upon what resolution he may come to

We cannot conceal from ourselves that these wretched Portuguese affairs are taking the most vexatious possible turn   A bloody anarchy is preparing for the whole country, and Dom Pedro offends all opinions and all interests by the decrees he is constantly issuing, and renders return to order all but impossible. It is now only necessary that Spain and England should take part in the struggle to make matters completely hopeless, not only for the Peninsula, but for the whole of Europe   .

MADAME ADELAIDE D'ORLÉANS TO THE PRINCE DE TALLEYRAND

St. Cloud, *August* 30*th*, 1833

I cannot let M Thiers start for London without a few words from me to you, mon cher Prince , he asked me to write last night, and I am charmed to be able to tell you how greatly our beloved king appreciates and is fully satisfied with, his ability and his devotion ; he is doing admirably, and is an excellent little man.

The most satisfactory accounts have reached us respecting the king's journey [1] ; it appears to be a regular triumph.   I am

---

[1] The king had gone on a tour into Normandy on the 26th August   Fêtes took place on his passing through Cherbourg, where the rest of the royal family joined him. The king returned to Saint-Cloud on the 12th September

going with the Queen, my nieces, and my two youngest nephews
to join him at Cherbourg, whence I hope to send you further
news I am writing this in haste, as I am just going out for a
drive

THE PRINCE DE TALLEYRAND TO THE DUC DE BROGLIE

LONDON, *September 4th*, 1833

I only received the despatches yesterday, which you did me
the honour to write on the 29th and 31st of last month Their
arrival has been greatly delayed owing to stress of weather

The Marquis de Rezende arrived here a few days ago from
Havre, charged by H I M the Duchess of Braganza to ask
H M the King of England for permission for herself and her
daughter, Queen Dona Maria, to await in England the arrival of
the Portuguese vessels which are to convey them to Lisbon   In
making this communication to the English ministers, the Marquis
de Rezende complained bitterly of the manner in which the
Duchess of Braganza had been received at Havre, and especially
of the very bad treatment experienced by M le Duc de Leuchtenberg at the hands of the authorities at Havre [1]

Lord Grey, who informed me of M de Rezende's mission,
told me that he had received a copy of the protest made by the
Duc de Leuchtenberg before leaving Havre, which had been
remitted by him to the Sous-Préfet He seemed to me to be
greatly struck with the manner in which this document was drawn
up, though he could not show it to me as he had left it with the
king Lord Grey added that he had received His Majesty's
orders respecting the Duchess of Braganza's request, and that
the king had told him to inform M de Rezende that he would
be very pleased to see Queen Dona Maria and the Empress in
England, and that if there was an available vessel he would send
it to Havre, so that they might make use of it

When Lord Grey informed me of what I have just had the
honour to communicate to you, I had not yet received your

---

[1] The Duc de Leuchtenburg arrived at Havre under an assumed name The king's
Government having pointed out to him that he could not, without inconvenience,
prolong his stay in France, which he had only entered by means of an irregular passport, he was at first not inclined to give in to this suggestion, but he soon changed
his mind, and wrote to the Sous-Préfet that he had gone at once to Havre, as he had
expected to find the vessels there which were to convey Dom Pedro's family to
Portugal, but that as the arrival of these vessels appeared to have been deferred, he
would himself proceed to Munich —(*The Duc de Broglie to the Prince de Talleyrand,
August 31st*)

despatch of the 31st, which contained the explanation of what had occurred at Havre, relative to the Duc de Leuchtenberg , nevertheless, I was enabled to assure him that the recital of the Marquis de Rezende must have been greatly exaggerated, for it was impossible for any one to believe, that after a sojourn of two years in France, during which T I H the Duke and Duchess of Braganza and Queen Dona Maria had always been treated with every possible consideration and respect, they should, just at the moment of their departure, be subjected to any unbecoming proceedings so foreign to the Court of France   Nevertheless, here again, as on several other occasions, I found that Lord Grey was rather surprised that we laid such stress on rejecting the Duc de Leuchtenberg, and could not understand that this was a question of maintaining the dignity of Portugal and the tranquillity of the whole Peninsula, a point on which I specially insisted

I have to-day had an interview with Lord Palmerston respecting the Note which is being sent to him by the Spanish Government, relative to the occupation of the forts at Lisbon by English troops   He had not yet received the Note, but M Vidal, the Spanish minister, had mentioned it at the king's *levée*   I took the opportunity thus offered me, to renew the urgent entreaties which I had already so frequently made at various times, as to the necessity of friendly relations between Spain and England   I pointed out to him, that by working in concert with the Madrid Cabinet to prevent revolutionary disturbances in the Peninsula, he would win over those foreign cabinets which intrigues might have alienated, and would thereby gain an influence beneficial to the whole of Europe ; that the best method of satisfying Spain just now, would be to renounce the occupation of the forts at Lisbon and to reject unhesitatingly the marriage of Dona Maria with the Duc de Leuchtenberg, which could only result in bringing on a civil war both in Portugal and Spain

Lord Palmerston listened to all my remarks with great attention, and gave me his promise that, as soon as he received the Note of the Spanish Cabinet, he would endeavour to see how he could best enter into friendly relations with Spain   I think he quite recognized all the importance of the matter, and even assured me, as Mr Aston had already informed you, that the directions for the English troops to occupy the forts at Lisbon had been cancelled, and that Lord William Russell had received instructions to act in conformity with the previous orders that had been transmitted to him, of which you are cognizant

THE DUC DE BROGLIE TO THE PRINCE DE TALLEYRAND

PARIS, September 5th, 1833

MON PRINCE,

I herewith send you a despatch which I received from Madrid this morning. It is not quite so satisfactory as I had hoped. It is very plain that as the crisis in Portuguese affairs still continues, the Spanish Government hopes that Dom Miguel may yet be successful and is not therefore prepared to be quite open with us, while the English Government, looking upon Dom Miguel as ruined, thinks more about its grievances against Spain than about its own real interests. If Lisbon is taken by assault and if Dom Miguel is defeated in the attack, each Government will I fear follow its own course, and remain perfectly intractable. But if I am not mistaken, neither of these events are at all probable. Unless Dom Pedro has entirely lost his head, he will not risk fighting in the open country, and as long as he keeps on the defensive, it will take more than De Bourmont's fifteen or twenty thousand men to enter a city like Lisbon by force. As the bad season of the year is approaching, it seems that the future of this unhappy country will be to see both its capitals occupied by the Pedrists, and the rest of the territory by the Miguelites, or delivered up to their ravages, and that without any apparent limit, or any early or probable termination. How can such a state of affairs continue?

I for my part do not think it possible. I much respect the principle of non intervention. Every man for himself and by himself is only fair and right. But this principle, like all others, has its limits; it presupposes, that the country to which it is applied possesses within itself the means of suppressing anarchy and preventing civil war; it presupposes, that the country has a majority and a minority, a majority too sufficiently strong to overcome the minority, no matter how much it resists, and to protect it without giving into it when it has succumbed. But when after a long, patient, and sincere trial, it has been proved that the country in question does not possess any of the means necessary to re-establish order within itself, that there is no real majority on any side capable of coming forward and making it-self obeyed; when, in fact, it is quite evident, that the struggle cannot end in the absolute triumph of any party, then it appears to me that humanity, reason, and common sense demand, that those neighbours who have any sort of interest in the pacification of the country in question, should agree to intervene, in order

to make the combatants lay down their arms, and should subsequently bring about a compromise between the opposing
parties, apportioning the mutual advantages as much as possible
to the respective strength of the parties

This, according to my view, is Portugal's position at present

The more I think over it, the more I look into it, the more am
I persuaded that this unfortunate business can only be ended by
the friendly intervention of France, Spain and England—an
intervention more or less pronounced, more or less direct, and
more or less active, according to the exigencies of the case and
the requirements of the circumstances, but an intervention without which this affair will drift into a war between Spain and
England, each side pledging itself deeper and deeper in support
of its *protégé*, and making fresh appeals every day to public
opinion in each country, until men's minds get so excited, that
they lose all power of choice or of holding independent views

I trouble you with these reflections, mon Prince, not with the
view of asking you to take any actual steps just now, so much
as to pray you to prepare beforehand, those measures which events
may soon render necessary   If some sort of convention should
be established between the three Governments to act simultaneously in this affair, you will be the person to settle the
basis on which it should be founded   Your wisdom and your
experience will be relied upon by the English Government.
I feel that I alone could have but little hope of being listened to
Moreover, I count above all on receiving some assistance from
your advice and will not hasten anything without your approval . .

THE PRINCE DE TALLEYRAND TO THE DUC DE BROGLIE

LONDON, *September 9th*, 1833

MONSIEUR LE DUC,

Queen Dona Maria and H I M the Duchess of Braganza
disembarked yesterday at Portsmouth, having come from Havre
by a steamer, chartered by one of Dom Pedro's agents   The
young queen was received with great honours on her arrival ·
the Lords of the Admiralty who were then at Portsmouth
hastened to present their respects to her, as well as all the civil
and military authorities in the place.   She has been invited to
stay at Windsor, where it seems she will spend three or four days
There is an evident desire of display in this very friendly reception of Dona Maria in England, it is easy enough to guess the
reason, and *The Times* in an article this morning leaves no
possible doubt on this point

September 9th, 1833

MON CHER DUC,

Parliament is dissolved, the English ministers are all in the country and the Conference has been adjourned, until it pleases the King of Holland to reply and to give in   At present he does not seem disposed to do either one or the other, and we are not doing anything here   I therefore think this is a good time to obey the doctors' orders, who consider that change of air is absolutely necessary for me to throw off the terrible cold I am suffering from   My family are anxious that I should come to Paris, where the sad state of my brother's health requires my presence to carry out certain measures which cannot be done without me ; and, in addition, my private affairs have suffered so much, since the death of the man who managed them for twenty-five years, that I cannot any longer leave them as they are

As the state of matters here does not seem to require my presence specially just now, I beg to request leave of absence, the length of which would depend upon the greater or less importance of political affairs   I beg you will kindly grant my request with as little delay as possible, as I feel that my health sadly needs some repose

I am inclined to think that the King of the Netherlands will find means to let us wait sometime for his decision ; but even if he should shortly give in, it will not now be by more or less skilful negotiations that he will accede ; the pressure of events, the evident advantages that we have assured to Belgium by our Convention of May 21st, which will continue as long as the provisional arrangement remains in force, will alone decide King William to sign   The course taken by the Frankfort Diet at the Hague, and our refusal here to continue a useless negotiation as long as the King of the Netherlands has any *arrière pensées,* were two excellent measures   Everything therefore is well prepared   All that was difficult and needful to do has been done ; now, time and time alone can bring matters to a conclusion   My presence here will neither hasten the progress nor the conduct of affairs

If, which is very improbable, the first answers from Holland were sufficiently favourable to give me any certainty that the definite treaty might be concluded in September, I would consider it my duty not to make use of my leave until after the signature of the treaty ; but this chance is so very remote that it is hardly worth while taking it into consideration. . .

September 11*th*, 1833

. . . . I have read with great interest M le Comte de Rayneval's despatch of August 30th, of which you kindly sent me a copy, and I have already made use of its contents in my conversation here [1]

Mr. George Villiers, on his way through Paris, *en route* for Spain, will have communicated to you the views of his Government respecting the state of the Peninsula, he was told by Lord Palmerston to do so. He is entrusted with the reply of the English Cabinet to M de Zea's last Note, which, as you are already aware, only contained two points: the occupation of the forts at Lisbon by English troops, and the disembarkation of these same troops, for the protection of English subjects, in the event of a conflict at Lisbon itself when such protection would be necessary. As to the first point, the Spanish Cabinet, as you know, is quite satisfied As to the second, Lord Palmerston has replied, that the English admiral was bound to use every means at his disposal to protect British interests if they were threatened, and that he had received formal instructions relatively to this To the two articles above indicated, M de Zea added some earnest protestations of friendship, to which Lord Palmerston has replied in the same spirit However, you will be much better informed on these questions by your conversation with Mr Villers than by my correspondence

The news from Portugal, which you will have seen in the English papers of to-day, shows that matters in that country are approaching if not a decisive, at any rate a very important crisis The forces of Dom Pedro and Dom Miguel are pretty evenly balanced, and it is impossible to foresee the result of the struggle Queen Dona Maria remains at Windsor until the 15th, when she will return to Portsmouth; it is said that she will almost immediately leave that port for Lisbon; but she will probably

[1] M. de Rayneval in this despatch gave an account of an interview he had just had with M de Zea as to the contingency of an Anglo-French mediation in Portugal. Our ambassador did not conceal from M de Zea that the two mediatory Powers had expressed some doubts as to the sincerity of the Spanish Cabinet in this matter. The minister protested vehemently, nevertheless, although closely pressed by M de Rayneval, he refused to point out the conditions he would propose as to the arrangement for intervention in Portugal. If Dom Miguel triumphed, Spain promised not to allow any interference with English interests, but she required the same guarantee on the part of England, if Dom Pedro was successful M de Zea insisted on the great moderation of the Spanish Government, which with its thousands of men could easily weigh down the scale in favour of its candidate M de Rayneval concluded by saying that the Spanish Cabinet had given up the idea of excluding both brothers at once, as the success of Dom Miguel seemed to them assured He thought a rupture between Spain and Portugal imminent

not depart until intelligence has been received that it will be safe for her to return to her capital

I believe, without attaching any exaggerated importance to the Emperor Nicholas's journey, that it would be useful to watch the results carefully. The return of M. de Metternich to Vienna and M. Ancillon to Berlin, will put M. de Saint-Aulaire and M. Bresson in a position to give you some information on this subject; I shall be much obliged if you will kindly forward anything fresh to me

September 10th, 1833.

I am in receipt of your letter, telling me that His Majesty is pleased to grant me leave to return to France I should like at once to profit by this permission, and had intended to start on the 20th, but as H. M. the King of England has done me the honour to invite me to Windsor for three days, I have been obliged to delay my departure I shall only return from Windsor on Sunday the 22nd, and will leave on the 24th, so as to be in Paris on the 27th I will take care before leaving London to present M. de Bacourt, as *Chargé d'Affaires,* to Lord Palmerston as you wish

No other news has reached London from Portugal, except that which came *vià* France; it is just twenty-one days now since there has been any direct communication between London and Lisbon The uncertainty existing as to the state of the latter city has not prevented the embarkation of Dona Maria, who left Portsmouth the day before yesterday in very bad weather

MADAME ADÉLAÏDE D'ORLÉANS TO THE PRINCE DE TALLEYRAND

St. Cloud, *September 16th,* 1833

On my arrival here, mon cher Prince, I found your letter of the 9th awaiting me, and I at once spoke to the king as to your wish to return here He is always delighted to do what he can to please you, and he immediately wrote to the Duc de Broglie, from whom you will ere this have received the answer you wish I know how painful one of your reasons for returning to Paris is, and you have my full sympathy in this, as in everything else that affects you, but I shall be very glad to see you again and to be able to chat quite freely with you . I regret exceedingly that the King of Holland's obstinacy still retards the conclusion of Belgian affairs However, the Belgians are not of my opinion, as they find the Convention of May much more advantageous to them than another which would oblige them to pay the debt ; this I feel quite sure they do not see at all

You have the young Queen of Portugal and the Duchess of Braganza in England just now   The conduct of the latter, and that also of Dom Pedro, towards our king is incomprehensible, most ungrateful and highly improper   The duchess left here as soon as she heard of Dom Pedro's entry into the city, without thanking the king for the offer he made her of a frigate so that she might take the young queen to Lisbon, or even informing the Government of her departure.   Not only has Dom Pedro never written to the king since his entry into Lisbon, but he did not even entrust M. de Loulé, who came to see the king on his own account, with a word or message for the king, notwithstanding all the kindness the latter has shown to him and his family It is right you should know, that Madame de Loulé (Dom Pedro's sister) has had sixty thousand francs during her sojourn in Paris ; she is very grateful, but I think Dom Pedro also owes something to the king   All this is very unpleasant, but I none the less sincerely wish every success to the cause of the young queen.   Good-bye, mon cher prince, till we meet. . . .

The Prince de Talleyrand to the Duc de Broglie.

LONDON, *September* 19*th*, 1833.

. . . . While speaking to Lord Palmerston this morning respecting the news from Constantinople, of which you kindly informed me, we went into the question as to the line to be adopted towards the Russian Cabinet with regard to the treaty of July 8th, which it has made with the Porte   After the declaration transmitted to the Porte, we both think that some steps should be taken by the ambassadors of France and England at St Petersburg.   It is a question, whether this step should consist of a simple notification of what has been done at Constantinople, or of a declaration somewhat of the same nature as that addressed to the Porte   I incline to the latter measure, which seems to me plainer, and fairer, and would at the same time give a higher character to our policy.   It would, in any case, certainly be better and more appropriate, after the meeting of the three northern sovereigns, to give some very marked proof of the union of France and England   I beg you to consult with Lord Granville about this, and arrange with him what steps the two Governments ought to take under these circumstances.

We are still without news from Portugal . . .

September 23rd, 1833

Lord Palmerston has begged me to thank you for your kind reception of Mr George Villiers. He is also perfectly satisfied with the last instructions you have sent M de Rayneval, and he thinks they ought to produce a very good effect on the Madrid Cabinet

I still hope to sleep at Dover to-morrow, and embark the day after .

I did finally leave London on the 24th September and reached Paris on the 26th

END OF PART XI

PART XII.

THE REVOLUTION OF 1830

(1833—1834.)

Talleyrand almost decides not to return to England—Fresh complications arise—He is urged to return by the King and the Ministers—Results of the meeting between the three Northern Sovereigns, planned by Metternich—The Duc de Broglie's reply to the communication of the three Courts—Talleyrand returns to London—He proposes to England to form a defensive alliance with France—The Duc de Broglie's scheme for the basis of such a treaty—Lord Grey considers such a step unadvisable, as giving Metternich material for discussion at the Congress of German Powers then convoked at Vienna—Russia desirous to reassure France and England as to the projects of invasion attributed to her—Reference in the *Augsburger Gazette* to a treaty between Russia and Austria guaranteeing the existence of the Ottoman Empire—Anxiety in England at the Duc de Broglie's illness and reported resignation—De Broglie's explanation of the scene in the Chamber—Louis Philippe refuses to accept his resignation—Talleyrand's reply—He encloses a note from Lord Grey expressing satisfaction at the Duc's remaining in office—Talleyrand's *résumé* of the state of Europe—Martinez de la Rosa replaces M. Zea as Prime Minister at Madrid—Annoyance of Lord Palmerston at M. de Nesselrode's despatch to Prince de Lieven—Talleyrand condemns Lord Palmerston's habit of allowing his personal feelings to influence his business relations—Cites the instance of Sir Stratford Canning's nomination to St. Petersburg—The Emperor Nicholas declines to receive him—Palmerston refuses to send any one else—Prince de Lieven is recalled and both Embassies remain vacant—Formidable riots break out in Paris and various parts of France—Dom Miguel's troops beaten by Dom Pedro's forces—Spain sends troops into Portugal—The Duc de Broglie resigns, consequent on the French Chamber rejecting the treaty between France and the United States—He is succeeded by Admiral de Rigny—Fresh insurrections break out in France—Very serious riots in Paris—Orangist demonstrations in Brussels—Diplomatic fencing between Talleyrand and Palmerston respecting the Spanish and Portuguese treaty—End of the Manuscript of the *Memoirs*—Talleyrand does not quit London till August.

Further letters and despatches up to the conclusion of his Embassy—King Leopold's wish to establish a Coburg succession, failing his having a son, opposed by France and England—The War in Portugal is brought to a close—Don Carlos lands at Portsmouth—Retirement of Lord Grey—The King sends for Lord Melbourne—Don Carlos returns to Spain—Lord Londonderry's speech in Parliament on the affairs of the Peninsula—Text of the additional Convention of the Quadruple Alliance—Talleyrand tenders his resignation—Louis Philippe's reply—Appendix. Memoir of the Duc de Choiseul

ON quitting London in September, I had almost decided not to return again   I felt that I had left affairs there in such a position that my presence was no longer necessary, and in addition to my great age, my infirmities and the condition of my personal affairs, greatly deranged by my long absence, made me think that it was time to retire into private life

I should probably have persevered in this determination if I had not received urgent solicitations recalling me to Paris

These entreaties began early in November, at first I resisted them, putting forward the reasons above stated, but the king and the Ministry urgently insisted, and I went to Paris at the commencement of December, to learn the reasons which rendered it so desirable that I should return to my post in London

It was not merely a question of the negotiations respecting Belgian affairs, which they hoped would soon be resumed, consequent on the steps which the King of the Netherlands had taken with the Diet at Frankfort, and the agnates of his house, in order to obtain their assent to the conditions imposed by the London Conference [1]

---

[1] The King of the Netherlands had, in fact, determined upon this step at the pressing solicitation of the Courts of Russia, Austria and Prussia   Prince Felix of Schwartzenberg had for this purpose been sent to the Hague, bearing autograph letters from the three sovereigns pointing out the uselessness and danger of a further resistance (*Letter from M. Bresson to M. de Talleyrand of 29th September*, 1833)   In consequence in November following, the King of the Netherlands applied to the agnates of the House of Nassau and the Diets, for their consent to the cession of the Walloon portion of the Grand Duchy of Luxemburg The Diet replied that it would require a territorial equivalent in exchange   The King replied that he had made too many sacrifices already, and that the Germanic Confederation, not having known how to protect Luxemburg, had no right to compensation of any kind, and the matter remained in abeyance   As for the Duke of Nassau, he formally refused his consent. The negotiation, therefore, fell through on these two points

The king and his Government were very uneasy respecting the meeting that had taken place during the autumn in Bohemia, between the sovereigns of Prussia and Austria, as well as the events that were occurring in Spain and Portugal, which gave rise to the fear, either of a revolutionary movement, or of the continuance of a civil war, inconvenient and perhaps even dangerous to our Pyrenean frontier.

Immediately on my arrival in Paris, I had several long interviews with the king and his ministers, and I was shown the whole correspondence relative to these three questions, so as to put me completely *au fait* as to what had occurred during my absence.

As to the first point, I did not share in their hopes that serious negotiations respecting Belgian affairs would be resumed in London, and I must confess, that if it had only been a question of these, I should not have considered it necessary for me to return to England. The other two questions seemed to me much more serious. I will first speak of the meeting between the Russian, Austrian and Prussian sovereigns, and the impression this had left on me.

This meeting, it appears, had been first suggested by Prince Metternich The Austrian chancellor, filled with recollections of the Ancona Expedition, and dreading that Austria's liberty of action in Italy might be interfered with, in consequence of the doctrines professed by France and England, on the right of non-intervention, had proposed to the Russian Government to come to an agreement with him on this subject, and prepare jointly a statement of the principles according to which the two Governments intended to regulate the exercise of this right.

The desire to come to some decision on this point, initiated the idea of a meeting, either in Silesia or Bohemia. This idea, brought forward by the St Petersburg Cabinet, was eagerly welcomed at Vienna They thought themselves sure of Prussia's concurrence, and the Emperor Nicholas, who had to pass through his father-in-law's country, to reach the spot designated for the interview, never doubted but that he would obtain his consent

He was not however completely successful At Schwedt, where a preliminary meeting was held, the overtures made by the

Emperor failed in part The King of Prussia declined to enter into
any formal engagements, which might compromise his Government in German public opinion, the liberal tendencies of which
were well known The Emperor Nicholas was therefore obliged
to go on to Bohemia alone, and meet the Austrian emperor at
Munchengratz There, questions of general policy such as those
of the East and Poland, which interested both countries equally,
were first discussed The Austrian Cabinet, swayed by the fears
with which the general feeling in Germany, and the precarious
situation of Italy inspired it, and abandoning its old traditions,
would have consented to admit in principle the almost exclusive
supremacy of the Russians in Constantinople It would also
have agreed to the measures adopted by the Russian Government, to take away from Poland the remaining vestiges of a
national and independent existence

Once agreed on these two points, M de Metternich would
then have proposed to conclude a Convention, which laid down,
on the basis previously recommended by Austria, the principle
of a new right of intervention, in virtue of which no Power
would be allowed to intervene in the home affairs of any other
state, unless it had been formally called upon to do so by that
state , but at the same time assuring to the Power whose aid
had been invoked, the exclusive right of intervening, without any
other Cabinet taking part therein or opposing it

The Russian Cabinet, which in this Convention saw the assurance of having the power to intervene whenever it pleased at
Constantinople, as the treaty of 8th July with the Porte permitted it to do, would not have hesitated to agree to this

M de Metternich, not content with having obtained for
himself the right to intervene in Italy, with the certainty of
Russia's support in that case, would then, in addition, have proposed to convene the heads of the Cabinets of the various states
of the Germanic Confederation at Vienna, and to induce them,
by an Act drawn up conjointly, to annul all the concessions
made since 1815, by those constitutional German states who
objected to the repressive measures which it was proposed to
employ against the propagation of revolutionary ideas The
Emperor Nicholas would have eagerly approved this project.

When all these points had been arranged and drawn up be-tween the sovereigns of Russia and Austria, M de Nesselrode and M. de Fiquelmont[1] would have been sent to Berlin, to persuade the Prussian Government to enter into the views of the two allies After a sufficiently prolonged resistance, and much hesitation, the King of Prussia would have ended by giving in to the urgent solicitations made to him, and would have signed the Conven-tion, but under the formal condition that it was to remain secret.

This is as near as possible, a *résumé* of the information con-tained in the correspondence of our diplomatic agents which was sent to me. I would not venture to guarantee its being perfectly correct, but that the treaty of 8th July, 1833, was im-posed on the Porte by Russia, and that a collective step was taken in Paris during the last days of October by the Austrian, Prussian, and Russian ministers was perfectly true and correct They had successively presented themselves to the Duc de Broglie, to read a despatch to him from their Court, which in substance contained the following: I cite the Austrian despatch

M. de Metternich began by pointing out that the three sovereigns who had met in Bohemia had found, during the explanations they had had together, the most undeniable proofs of the strength of the ties of friendship which united them, as well as the friendly dispositions which they all equally felt towards the other Powers.

After this preamble, the Austrian chancellor proceeded to develop the principles which the sovereigns had agreed to recognize as the only ones that could possibly guarantee the peace of Europe.

According to M. de Metternich, or rather, according to the Cabinets of which he here represented himself as the mouth-piece, each Government was naturally disposed to favour those

---

[1] Charles Louis, Comte de Fiquelmont, an Austrian general and statesman, born in 1777, was the son of a French *émigré* killed at Marengo He became major-general in the Austrian army, and was made Minister Plenipotentiary at Stockholm, Florence, Naples, and St Petersburg In 1840, he became War Minister, and then Minister for Foreign Affairs In 1848, he was for a short period Prime Minister He died in 1857.

doctrines on which its existence rested This kind of proselytism is too common for any one to dream of condemning it, as long as it is carried out in a pacific manner, and by moral influence only There is, however, a system of propagandism which, extending its action over the whole of Europe, tries to upset existing institutions everywhere, in order to substitute violent and dangerous innovations Such a system, equally hostile to all established governments, must necessarily be opposed by their joint efforts Should the French Government, which has known so well how to defend itself against the aggressions of revolutionists, not be able in future to equally baffle the machinations which are being practised in its territory against foreign states, interior disturbances and disorders might result to some of these states, which would oblige them to ask for the support of their allies Such support would not be refused, and every attempt which aims at opposing this, will be looked upon by the three courts as an act of hostility directed against each

The communications made by the Russian and Prussian ministers differed slightly in the doctrine expressed, but were fully in accord as to the summing up, and thus proved that there was an actual joint responsibility between the three Cabinets in the course they had taken

The Duc de Broglie answered these communications with as much firmness as tact [1] He informed the three foreign ministers, that if the documents he had just heard of were only intended as a profession of faith, more or less open to dispute, he thought it superfluous to discuss them, but that as he presumed that this communication was somewhat more than a useless expression of principles, he was bound to endeavour to seek its object

Was it intended, he asked, to insinuate that the French Government favoured revolutionary propagandism? he fancied not, but if there was the least uncertainty on this point, he wished at once to refute by the most positive denial, even the semblance

---

[1] In consequence of the course adopted by the ambassadors of the three courts towards the Cabinet of the Tuileries, the Duc de Broglie addressed a circular to all the French agents abroad, of which the lines that follow are an analysis and almost a literal reproduction This circular has been published by M d'Haussonville in his *Histoire de la Politique extérieure du Gouvernment Français*, T. 1, p 47.

of an imputation, in which the King's Government could only see a gratuitous insult, which it was quite resolved not to submit to.

It will soon be seen that the French envoy at Stockholm had quitted that capital, in accordance with orders he had received, and without taking leave of King Charles John, because that prince thought he could make allusions to the policy of the King's Government similar to those above referred to [1]

The Duc de Broglie thus replied to the sort of intervention referred to in the end of the three despatches : " There are some countries, such as Belgium, Switzerland, and Piedmont, in which, as we have already stated, France would not suffer intervention by foreign troops at any price   There are other countries again in regard to which, without approving of an intervention, she could not oppose it under given circumstances, in so absolute a manner as she would under other conditions. This was the case when the Austrian army entered the Romagna. The conclusion to be drawn therefrom is, that each time that a foreign Power enters the territory of an independent state, we shall consider ourselves *legally entitled* to follow such a line of conduct as our interests may demand   Such would be any occasions on which the rule of common right no longer being applicable, each one would act on either side, at his own risk and peril."

This answer, transmitted to the three Cabinets, had been received by them without their making any reply [2]   Thus far had matters arrived when I returned to Paris, that is to say, one month after the reply sent by the Duc de Broglie

I must also not omit to mention that during my absence

[1] Charles John, King of Sweden, had been much vexed at the revolution of July. On the arrival of M de Saint-Simon, the new French Minister, he complained bitterly of the conduct of the French Government towards the other Powers.   He accused it of favouring revolutionary propagandism, and even reproached the king himself as wanting in good faith and sincerity (M de Saint-Simon's despatch of 6th October, 1833)   The Cabinet of the Tuileries immediately ordered M de Saint-Simon to ask for his passports , the King of Sweden was somewhat embarrassed ; he denied the conversation which had led to this rupture   Nevertheless, friendly relations were not re-established until 1835, when M de Mornay was accredited to Stockholm

[2] The Berlin Cabinet especially, which had unwillingly allowed itself to be led away by M de Metternich, was greatly astonished and taken aback by the Duc de Broglie's reply   (See in Appendix, letter No 13, a letter of M Bresson's on this subject)

from London the English and French Governments had, through their agents at St Petersburg, sent a formal and identical protest against the said treaty of Unkiar-Skelessi, signed on the 8th July between Russia and the Porte, which protest wound up by a declaration that the above treaty was looked upon by the Paris and London Cabinets as non-existent.

It was evident that the three courts of Austria, Russia and Prussia, were offended that France and England, by separating themselves from them in the Hollando-Belgian question, had succeeded by their joint action in conquering the obstinacy of the King of the Netherlands; it was, I say, perfectly evident, that these three courts had intended to make a demonstration, which would cover the defeat of their policy   But was it only a demonstration, or had a resolution been adopted to take action together should an occasion present itself?   I thought not ; nevertheless such symptoms ought not to be neglected, and it became necessary either to reply to threats by threats, which would be puerile and do no good, or to resolve on some measure, which would prevent the three courts advancing any further on a course perilous to the maintenance of peace, and at the same time announce the determination to resist all offensive action on their part

After carefully thinking over this question, I proposed to the king and to the Duc de Broglie, to try and induce the English Government to form a treaty of alliance with us, couched in sufficiently liberal terms not to inconveniently bind the two Governments, but which might, if necessary, be made use of according to circumstances   And with this view, I cited the precarious situation of the Ottoman Empire, and the state of the Peninsula, which at this moment caused the greatest possible disquietude, in consequence of the troubles that had arisen in Spain between the Infant Don Carlos and Queen Isabella ; and also, in Portugal between Dom Pedro and his brother Dom Miguel   It was impossible to conceal from one's self that if these troubles were prolonged, of which there seemed every likelihood, the time would arrive when French interests in Spain, and English interests in Portugal would oblige the French and English Governments to take some kind of action in the Peninsula to put an end to the civil war In my opinion, this action ought to be concerted between the two Governments, and I thought that it would have been useful to connect it with a preliminary treaty, which would at the same time have the advantage of showing to every one, the intimate union between France and England. I considered that such a measure would be the best reply to the Russian treaty of July 8th, and to the unusual communications of the three northern courts

I succeeded in inducing the king and his Government to agree to my views ; they, however, were all the more urgent that I should return to England I was forced to give in to their solicitations, even while declaring that I was very far from believing that I should succeed in inducing the English Government to adopt my opinion. Nevertheless, I considered the results to be of sufficient importance to be worth the trouble of endeavouring to obtain them

I therefore started for London, having arranged with the Duc de Broglie that he should send me a detailed exposition of his views on the subject of the treaty, the conclusion of which I wished to propose to the English Government It was with this object that he wrote me the following letter, which I will give in its entirety, despite its length, as it brings forward admirably all the arguments in favour of the political measure, which I deemed it so important for my country that England should adopt. The rest of my correspondence will follow later.

THE DUC DE BROGLIE TO THE PRINCE DE TALLEYRAND

PARIS, *December* 16*th*, 1833.

MON PRINCE,

The idea of a defensive alliance between France and Great Britain is yours ; and it is doubly so, as you were the first to mention the subject to me two months ago on your way through Paris You were the first to speak to Lord Granville about it ; I have only thought over and developed your own arguments Nevertheless, you wish me to sum up, in a purely confidential letter, those which, during your absence, had

appeared to me of value   You will not, I fear, find anything
fresh, but the least I can do is to defer to your wish

It is a question of a defensive alliance

It is a question of a treaty, by which the enemies of one
country would become those of the other, in the event of unprovoked and gratuitous aggression against either   In no case could
there be, for example, a question of allowing England to incur
dangers caused by a just or an unjust attack on the part of
France against some other country, or of making her responsible
for the consequences of a reprisal which France had drawn on
herself

In the hypothesis of a purely defensive alliance it might at
first sight be asked, whether England would have the same
reasons for subscribing to it as France ?   It might be questioned
whether the advantages were equal for both countries, that is to
say, is the danger the same, and is England threatened equally
with France ?   Looking at it from this point of view, the answer
would be unfavourable   The safety of France is evidently more
threatened than that of England   Although both Governments
have the same foundation—I mean a revolution, just in its
principles and moderate in its results—and although there is an
analogy between the institutions of both countries often approaching to identity, France is exposed to dangers from which
England is exempt   Our Government is new, the English
Government dates back for a hundred and fifty years   We have
a claimant to contend with, there is no longer any claimant to
the English throne   We are a continental country, and consequently vulnerable at many points, England is an island, and
the English are masters of the sea   The enumeration of the
differences might be extended much further

But either I am all wrong, or this view is purely a superficial
one.

It is not necessary when two countries enter into an alliance
that the advantages should be equal, nor is it necessary that
they should find therein the same advantages   All that is needed
is that each should find what they counted upon   The advantages may be greater for the one than for the other, they may be
different, not only in degree, but in nature, that is of little consequence   Provided they exist, and provided they are sufficient,
it would be puerile and unreasonable to insist on this difference,
and make it a ground for refusal   That would be injuring one's self,
through dread of benefiting others

That France has great interest in the treaty in question is so
self-evident that I need not pause to demonstrate it

That England also has a real and great interest in it, the

more I think it over the more I am convinced of, for the
following reasons

I will first suppose that the alliance exists, no matter whether
it has been committed to paper or not I will suppose that if
France became the object of an unprovoked and gratuitous
aggression—if France were attacked by the north of Europe, as
Spain was attacked by France in 1823—England would defend
France, and make common cause with her. The English
Government could not prevent this, even if it wished, and it
would not desire it, even if it could.

The revolution of 1830 was, from the very commencement,
very popular in England, so popular, indeed, that when it was
represented by Lord Stuart, certainly not in the best light, to
Lord Aberdeen and the Duke of Wellington, who had no reason
to view it favourably, they neither of them ventured either to
blame or disavow it. And not only was the revolution of 1830
popular in England (popularity is but fleeting), but it was a
national matter ; by this I mean, that the revolution found men's
minds in that country in conformity with the ideas and sentiments which originated it ; public opinion was ripe for a great
political change and prepared to run the risks, although at the
same time resolved only to proceed with justice and caution, and
not to trust either to excitement or chance What France saw
herself obliged to obtain through the perils of a revolution,
England also desired to have, but more fortunate than her neighbour, she was able to obtain it without going beyond constituted
authority The aim was the same, and both countries have
equally attained it The revolution of 1830 was not the cause
of parliamentary revolution , but it was the signal for it, and
this signal once given, both nations have advanced side by side
along the same path There has been a community of desires,
interests, and conduct ; the enemies of the one, both at home
and abroad, have become the enemies of the other ; and before
this complete and joint liability all the old enmities, all the
ancient jealousies, all the inveterate prejudices have disappeared.
This is not the work of any particular person, no one man, no
single Cabinet can claim the merit of it France and England
have naturally taken their stand side by side in the face of the
other European Powers, not because they are the only two
great nations who enjoy political liberty, but above all because
they have simultaneously made a great stride in the career of
political liberty, another great stride taken together. This
double event has, in the same degree, roused against both the
distrust and the enmity of the absolute governments, and
it has created for these governments, in the very heart of both

countries, auxiliaries whom it suits us equally to restrain—in France the vanquished Carlists, in England the Tories, who are out of power

I therefore repeat, that I hold it to be impossible that France, such as the revolution of 1830 has made her, should be attacked in her honour and her safety, without England, such as Parliamentary reform has made her, feeling her own honour, and up to a certain point also her safety, equally attacked   I hold it as a certainty, that in such a case, no matter what Ministry was in power, it would be bound to defend France, and that if (which heaven forefend!) Lord Aberdeen should find himself at the head of the Foreign Office in England, it would only be under such conditions as would oblige him to act thus, whether he liked it or not, and that he would be compelled to defend the revolution of 1830, even more imperatively than he was forced to recognize it

I say therefore that what public feeling and national impulse would oblige any Ministry to do in such a case, the most ordinary common sense, and the most evident self-interest would equally counsel them to do

It is to England's interest to maintain the *statu quo* of Europe

England performed her part in 1815, it is only justice to say that she did it splendidly Every country in Europe passed beneath Napoleon's yoke, she alone resisted him   Her resistance saved Europe from the scourge of tyranny and a universal monarchy   I repeat, that England played a grand part, and the position which she created for herself in Europe is proportionately great and strong   Any important changes which might henceforth occur in Europe, more especially if they take place without her concurrence, would be very disadvantageous to her, and would necessarily turn against her

Now, supposing that France was attacked by the rest of Europe, one of two things would happen, we should either be conquerors or be conquered.

I have the firm belief that we should be the victors; but in order to become victorious, we should be obliged to stir up frightful passions both within and outside of France. We should be reduced to making terrible sacrifices, we should run great risks   The passions thus roused would have to be satisfied, and we should require compensation for all our sacrifices and our dangers   We should have to fall back upon making conquests, and England, who in this hypothesis had done nothing for us, would have neither the right nor the power to oppose us

If, on the other hand, we were vanquished, the result would be precisely the same, but in an opposite sense France would be mutilated, dismembered, and under military occupation, in every part that was still left of her

Is it possible to imagine England looking on unmoved at such a spectacle, or coming forward to demand her share of the decimated and crushed spoils of the revolution of July ?

The great fact once admitted that the alliance really does exist, that a defensive treaty of alliance between France and England would not bring upon England any danger which she has not already necessarily to contend with in the existing state of affairs, it remains for her to see what will be the surest way for her to escape from eventual dangers, and provide for those chances which she cannot completely avoid

This way, I believe, is to be found in carrying out the treaty, and not waiting for events, but forestalling them.

As long as the union between France and England exists, as long as it exists not only tacitly and in reality, but outwardly and visibly, all hostile demonstration on the part of the northern Powers is impossible. The six hundred thousand men at the disposal of France joined to the English army, the combined French and English navies, the French credit added to that of England, and the means of action possessed by both Governments in Italy, Germany and Poland, are all matters which the northern Powers dare not face But the real, and in fact indestructible union between France and England may be impaired in a thousand ways from a merely apparent point of view. Nothing will be left undone by the violent parties in both countries, no matter what their inclination, or by the foreign Governments abroad, to provoke, to foster, and turn to account, every possible cause for estrangement In free countries politics are more or less changeable ; during the course of the last session the London Cabinet, and likewise that of Paris, was several times on the point of being dissolved and giving place to others. Other men mean another system—at least that is what would be thought ; all the slight coolnesses would spread, increased by the violent language of the press ; a thousand insignificant circumstances would cause it : questions of custom dues, the affair of Algiers, or anything, may furnish fresh pretexts, and pretexts, as soon as they acquire the slightest consistency, are quickly changed into real misunderstandings. All this, I repeat, would be nothing in reality ; when the time for action arrived, all these worries would disappear before an inevitable joint responsibility, and an evident community of interests. But meanwhile, supposing action has become necessary ;

the northern Powers will have regained courage, they will have plunged into a course which must prove fatal to them, but which would none the less press heavily on France and England, namely the scourge of a universal war.

If, on the contrary, a treaty of alliance is concluded, say for five, eight, ten years, more or less, it matters little, all such ideas will pass away from the Holy Alliance of Munchengratz, the secret and open enemies of both Governments, both at home and abroad, will be deprived of all hope, all the accidental difficulties to which events may give rise will be reduced to their just value, their solution will be foreseen by every one, and people's minds will be at peace

But this is not all.

An attack on France is not the only danger which just now threatens the *statu quo* of Europe   There is more than one way of impairing it   It is quite possible to prepare such changes in the midst of peace, as would only need a breath to complete them

I will explain my meaning

There exists among the three northern Powers a joint responsibility of interests, similar to that which exists between France and Great Britain, although based on directly opposite principles   This joint responsibility keeps them united, and each day we have fresh proofs of this union   The past year furnishes them in abundance.

This situation may lead to two results

The first would be the temporary abandonment of all ideas of aggrandizement, of all increase of territory or of preponderance, the sacrifice of any purely Prussian, Austrian or Russian policy, to a conservative European one   This is what happened in 1830 and 1831, when the danger of revolutions was great and imminent

The second is a sort of compromise between the ambitions and the claims of the three Powers, it is a compact, by which they mutually give up to one another certain parts of Europe, in exchange for other parts

This is what is happening now, when anxiety has decreased, and when hopes of aggrandizement may again rise to the surface.

Russia says to Austria   In heaven's name do not let us quarrel, let us remain united against the common enemy; but, meanwhile, let me do with Turkey as I list   To this Austria replies   I am agreed, we will not quarrel, but if I permit you to dispose of Turkey, you must second me in the dominion I wish to establish in Italy, and thus the bargain is concluded

Prussia in her turn says to Austria. I am quite willing to

lend you a hand in your projects about Italy, but then you must let me introduce my system of custom duties[1]; allow me to establish my frontier custom houses as far as the shores of Lake Constance, impose my tariffs on the whole Confederation, put down the opposition of all the refractory States, and lay the foundations of a united Germany, which later on will bear fruit.

And Austria allows Prussia to have her way.

In Turkey, Italy, and Germany, they have only arrived at an increase of power, protectorates and guardianships; but any one who has read history, or who has the slightest knowledge of the progress of events, knows to what all this leads and what all these protectorates become

Now, it must be one of two things Either France and England must quietly look on at this great alteration in the equilibrium of Europe, this successive demolition of the independence of States of secondary rank, or they must seize the opportunity and oppose it In the first case, these States will be considerably diminished, as might be expected In the second case, both nations will be obliged to act in common, and we think that already in truth, as far as Turkey is concerned, both Governments are on the point of making some arrangement to check the enterprises against Constantinople If both Governments act in concert, they will be obliged to mutually guarantee the consequences resulting from this common action Here then is the defensive treaty which appears imperatively necessary; but as it stands at present it is only for the purpose of settling the consequences of war, whereas if concluded and made public at once, it would have the effect of preventing them

Let us suppose, in fact, that a defensive treaty exists now between France and England, it is not necessary that there should be any other undertaking than to mutually support each other in such events as shall be judged by both parties to be in accordance with the letter of the treaty Behind this general stipulation, the other Powers will conjure up all kinds of secret articles intended to anticipate any encroachments they may meditate Each time England raises her voice, there will be seen behind her the six hundred thousand men at the disposal of France Each time France raises her voice, the power and ascendency of England will be there to back her up It will be

[1] It will be remembered that Prussia at this period had entered into a long series of negotiations, for the purpose of establishing the customs union of Germany—the Zollverein A preliminary treaty had already been signed on the 22nd March, 1833, between Prussia and eight of the States, among which were Bavaria and Wurtemburg Saxony joined on the 30th March All the other German States by degrees joined this union, which ever since 1871 has become the Constitutional law of the Empire.

enough for them to speak in order to disconcert those schemes, which, by adopting another line of conduct, they would probably find themselves obliged to thwart

I may add, that this alliance would become the natural *point d'appui* of all those sovereigns who feel an inclination to resist the King of Naples in Italy, against the Austrian dominion, the duchy of Baden, the duchy of Nassau, the city of Frankfort against the Prussian customs duties, all the small German princes against the prepotency of the Diet   It would become the centre of a fresh group of interests, it would be, in my opinion, the sole efficacious counterpoise to the union of the three great northern monarchies

Lastly, there is a final consideration which, although but of secondary interest, still has its importance

As long as the union of France and England only exists as an understanding, it will be liable apparently to variation and eventualities   On the one hand, each Government will be forced to hold itself in readiness for any event, just as if it had to support alone the whole weight of the chances of the future, on the other hand, the commerce and industry of each country will only pursue their natural course in a doubtful and hesitating manner   If, on the contrary, we suppose the union to be public, indissoluble and founded on a treaty, the power of both Governments will be doubled by this fact alone, and they will be able, without any inconvenience, to reduce their military and naval armaments   Then, as regards the home policy of each Government, the possibility of such reductions is in itself a matter not to be despised   In addition, all men's minds will calm down, confidence in the future will increase tenfold, national wealth will be doubled, whilst expenditure will be diminished   There is not a single Ministry under a representative Government that would not realize the value of such a result

These, mon Prince, are the considerations I have put before Lord Granville   Either out of friendship for me, or interest for France, and I do not know of which of these two sentiments I was most sensible, he seemed to consider them worthy of being carefully weighed   The obstacle which appeared to him the most serious was the difficulty of making the English public understand them, and of procuring their adoption by Parliament   This is an obstacle the power of which it is not for me to estimate, much less indicate the means of overcoming it   You, mon Prince, are on the spot, it is for you to enlighten the French Government on this point   As long as you do not give me any hope that my ideas have been welcomed by the English Cabinet, I shall abstain from speaking about them to my colleagues or

taking any official steps This will remain a secret between you
and me Accept   . .

I am very glad to be able here to show the great political
capacity of the Duc de Broglie If the recollections I am now
writing ever see the light of day, justice will be done to the
clearness and firmness of the views which inspired this letter, and
I feel sure that herein will be found the true basis of a close
alliance between France and England, which has been my most
ardent wish from the beginning to the end of my political career,
convinced as I am that the peace of the world, the confirmation
of liberal ideas, and the progress of true civilization, can only
be founded on such a basis

THE PRINCE DE TALLEYRAND TO THE DUC DE BROGLIE

LONDON, *December* 24*th,* 1833

MONSIEUR LE DUC,
          I have thought a good deal both during my journey
and since my arrival here, about the question which was the
principal subject of the last conversations I had the honour to
have with you before my departure from Paris I have not
wavered in my opinion as to the importance and benefit that a
defensive treaty of alliance concluded with England would be
to the king's Government I have gone carefully into the
manner in which such a treaty might most advantageously be
brought forward, which would offer the best chances of success
with the English Government, and at the same time approach
sufficiently near to the views of some of the continental Govern-
·ments, as to encourage the hope that they might some day be
induced to join it
          After having carefully weighed all the considerations which
you lately placed before me, and compared them with the facts
which my own experience has shown me to be my best guide
in so very serious a matter, I have come to the conclusion that
the *statu quo* as it now exists in Europe should be our point
of departure, and that its maintenance is the best basis to
select for a defensive alliance between France and Great
Britain
          To France, the *statu quo* presents nothing that has not been
already recognized and admitted by her , it does not militate
against our real interests at any single point, and has moreover

O 2

always formed part of the policy upheld ever since its origin by the present French Government

As for England, it is incontestable that she should wish to see the present state of affairs in Europe maintained ; it guarantees her all the advantages of the treaties of 1815, and, as you very justly remarked, these advantages were immense It is unnecessary to say that they have lost nothing in strength since 1830 It is possible that I may be mistaken, but I do not see what difficulties could be raised in Parliament, if the English Government entered into a defensive alliance with us, based on the maintenance of the European *statu quo* It seems to me that such a treaty would be justifiable in every respect, and before changing my opinion on this point, I must wait to see objections raised such as I at present cannot conceive

On looking round the different continental Cabinets, it is impossible to see how a treaty such as I speak of could cause them alarm ; nay more, it is quite in accordance with the views of the most reasonable amongst them Is not the *statu quo* M de Metternich's fixed idea, so to speak ? Has not the Prussian Cabinet perpetually shown its desire, to see universal peace guaranteed by the stability of the existing state of affairs ? Does not Russia herself emphatically declare, that the treaty of 8th July with the Porte is the plainest proof of her friendly intention to preserve the Ottoman empire ? Which of all these Powers would dare, with any show of reason, to declare itself hostile to a union between France and England, proclaimed for the purpose of maintaining the *statu quo* of Europe ? If there still remains some hope of bringing round those Cabinets whose more moderate policy offers a means of reconciliation, I do not doubt that a treaty, drawn up according to the principles I have just indicated, would but hasten their return to us

It was therefore on this ground, that I conceived I ought to take my stand, in order to place most advantageously before Lord-Grey and Lord Palmerston the treaty about which I had the honour to speak to you Both these ministers listened very attentively to my explanations on this matter, and, I thought, were greatly impressed by it Nevertheless, as I expected, they could only promise me to think over the scheme, to discuss it with their colleagues, and then let me know what resolution the British Government had come to

I impressed upon both English ministers that this resolution should be in accordance with the position of affairs, that is to say, it should be noble and high-minded " A simple expedient," I said to them, " would be very dangerous ; it would only seem to be the result of some intrigue, or the indirect expression of our ill-feeling, which we must above all avoid. The true way for us to succeed is by frank and energetic action, without any doubtful colouring or mental reservations"

I do not think I shall be in a position for some time to send you anything positive as to the views of the English Cabinet on this question   Lord Grey and Lord Palmerston both leave either to-day or to-morrow for the country, and the other ministers will not be in London before the beginning of January. The matter will not be dealt with in council until then . . .

On the same day, in addition to the despatch, I added the following in a private letter ·

I arrived here at the same time as your letter of the 16th   I have read it with the utmost attention, and it was not until I had thoroughly mastered it that I went to see first Lord Grey and then Lord Palmerston   My despatch will tell you the impression made on both ministers by the overtures I made to them   These seemed to me to have the small merit of having been unexpected, at any rate as to the form, even if not as to the idea, of the treaty itself .   .

THE DUC DE BROGLIE TO THE PRINCE DE TALLEYRAND

PARIS, *December* 30*th*, 1833

MON PRINCE,

According to your wish, I am sending you a draft of the treaty[1]   It is a simple, rough sketch, on which the king asks your advice   I have endeavoured to carry out your own ideas ; and in order to make it as general as possible, and to admit of the amplest construction being put upon it, I have reduced it to a preamble and one article, the article stating nothing beyond the simple fact of a defensive alliance, and consequently referring all executive measures to be decided by a special convention, circumstances requiring it   It seemed to me, on the one hand, that this single article would give the impression that there were a number of secret articles, and on the other hand, I considered that by only tying down the English Government to the beginning of the measure, and leaving it at full liberty with regard to the rest, it would facilitate the admission

---

[1] This treaty stipulated purely and simply for a defensive alliance   It added, that the two parties undertook to act in concert on all occasions, whenever the peace of Europe and the independence of the States composing it, seemed to them to be threatened

of the principle of the treaty   By reducing the treaty to its
moral effect, the objections that may be brought against it would
to a great extent be eliminated

I founded the preamble, as you wished, on the *statu quo*, but
I thought this *statu quo* ought to be called *la foi des traités*
It would be very unpopular in France, if we were ostensibly
to pledge ourselves to renounce all right to the departments we
have lost, but there is not a single soul bold enough to come
forward and declare that we ought to violate, nay, even that we
ought not to respect, the good faith of treaties   The remainder
of the preamble is, I think, very conciliatory and irreproachable,
as far as the foreign Powers are concerned

The separate article is only a measure of negotiation with the
English Government   We do not wish it to be inserted in the
treaty, but in the event of the English Government wishing us
to join to some extent in the Eastern question, or if it should
make its consent the price of a future engagement, or should the
Russians return to Constantinople, we would have no objection
to this article being then inserted, as it gives extended liberty to
both parties, and is quite in keeping with the character of the
defensive treaty itself   Meanwhile, as I said before, it is but a
rough sketch, respecting which we ask your advice .   .

THE PRINCE DE TALLEYRAND TO THE DUC DE BROGLIE.

LONDON, *January 3rd*, 1834

MON CHER DUC,

I thank you for your letter and the draft of the treaty
which accompanied it, and which I think admirable   I trust
that we shall ere long be able to make use of it, and that we
shall succeed in obtaining a recognition of its advantages by
the English Government   Just now, however, I think we must
let it lie dormant, that at least is the impression I have gained
from the frequent conversations I have had lately with Lord
Grey and Lord Holland, the only members of the Cabinet who
are in London   You know the dislike the English ministers
have always shown to be fettered by ties, which have no special
or decided aim

Setting aside the parliamentary difficulties, which will be
very serious here in questions of foreign policy, the English
Government is strengthened in its desire to do nothing
hurriedly by the last despatches received from Vienna and
Berlin

They have heard from Vienna that M de Metternich is

greatly embarrassed by his Congress, not knowing what proposals to submit to it[1] Lord Grey concludes from this, and I think with reason, that if we were just now to bring forward an arrangement, no matter of what nature, between France and England, we should give cause for some action at Vienna, and thus relieve M de Metternich from his embarrassment This objection, which seems to me very plausible, would be still further strengthened, if, as Lord Minto writes from Berlin, Prussia seems disposed to separate herself from the Courts of Austria and Russia, in the event of their proposing to her some joint arrangement on Eastern affairs, which might be displeasing to France and England

I therefore think, mon cher Duc, that this is not an opportune moment for urging the English Government You may rest assured that I will carefully watch the tendency of feeling here, and will eagerly seize the first occasion I may deem at all favourable The meeting of Parliament next month, will necessarily give occasion for discussion on Eastern affairs, as it is probable that the speech from the throne will refer to it It is quite possible that this may oblige the Ministry to come to some definite resolution, and moreover, by that time, M de Metternich's Congress will have come to an end, and we shall no longer require to disquiet ourselves as to his machinations . .

January 7th, 1834

. . Lord Palmerston only arrived in London this morning, and I have not yet been able to see him , but I have just come from Lord Grey, with whom I had a long talk about Eastern affairs, and particularly as to the relations of Austria and England with regard to this question This last point you

---

[1] A Congress of the representatives of the German Powers had been convoked at Vienna by M de Metternich, for the purpose of discussing the general interests of the Germanic Confederation They were to deliberate on five groups of questions

1 On the principle that sovereignty belongs entirely to princes and not to nations

2 On the publicity of legislative assemblies

3 On schools and universities

4 On the press

5 On the accord of special legislation with general laws

M de Sainte Aulaire kept the French Cabinet informed as to the course of these deliberations, which however did not make much stir "There is no doubt," he wrote on the 28th November, "that a scheme has been drawn up between Austria and Prussia , but these two Powers, and especially Austria, desire that the small States should take the initiative, as their independence would thus seem to be respected The secondary Governments, on their part, though quite disposed to make a good bargain at the cost of their own Constitutions, nevertheless desired to avoid the reproach of having voluntarily sacrificed them, and wished to shelter themselves from responsibility as regards their people " (M de Sainte-Aulaire's official despatch)

specially drew my attention to, in your despatch of the 2nd of this month

Lord Grey told me that Prince Esterhazy had in fact been to see him several times lately, especially about ten days ago, to discuss with him, in the name of his Court, the very important matter which was just now so earnestly occupying all the Cabinets of Europe, and had spoken in the most satisfactory manner on this subject, assuring him that M de Metternich's aim was one with that of England, namely, the maintenance of the Ottoman Empire

Prince Esterhazy having added that he feared, on this occasion, the English Cabinet had shown itself too distrustful of Russia, Lord Grey replied, that it might also be feared that Austria had shown herself too confiding in Russia, that the English Cabinet, moreover, was liable to constant questions in Parliament respecting Eastern affairs, and that public opinion had pronounced itself so strongly in England against the ambitious projects of Russia, that he, Lord Grey, would require very strong testimony of that Power's moderation in order to allay an irritation the cause of which he was quite aware was not without foundation

In reply to this, Prince Esterhazy having asked what proofs were necessary to give weight to the repeated assurances of the St Petersburg Cabinet, Lord Grey, without wishing specially to indicate them, pointed out the immediate and complete evacuation of Moldavia and Wallachia, and the relinquishment by Russia of all that Turkey still owed her, consequent on the treaty of Adrianople

Prince Esterhazy promised to make the details of this conversation known to M de Metternich, and even added, that he hoped his Government would entertain these ideas, which appeared to him most reasonable Prince Esterhazy's courier, conveying this information to Vienna, left some days ago

Since then, despatches have been received from Sir Frederick Lamb, which, from what I hear, are quite in conformity with the language held by this ambassador to M de Sainte-Aulaire [1] According to these despatches, he states, that in the course of a

---

[1] The despatches of M de Sainte-Aulaire confirmed those sent by Sir Frederick Lamb to his Government He wrote on the 12th December, that the Austrian Cabinet had been much satisfied with Lord Palmerston's overtures that he had replied that Austria and England had the same interests in and the same views on the Eastern question, but that Austria sided with Russia, whom England distrusted, and that England sided with France, of whom Austria was suspicious, that consequently, England ought to accept Austria's guarantee with respect to Russia, and that then Austria would have to accept England's guarantee with regard to France (M de Sainte-Aulaire's despatch to the Foreign Office)

conversation he had had with M de Metternich, the latter, even while repeating the assurances of moderation so often renewed by Russia, nevertheless declared that Austria was quite determined not to consent to a single village being ceded by Turkey to Russia   This declaration, M le Duc, coming as it does from M de Metternich direct, appears to me of very great importance, especially if, as Sir Frederick Lamb writes, it was made in a very positive manner

I must add, that in all this there was not, I am told, the slightest idea of separating France and England, and that if the king's Government was less frequently mentioned, it was only because the Cabinet of Vienna seemed assured of its concurrence in everything that tended to the maintenance of an honourable peace, and lastly, that it was in London where irritation with regard to Eastern affairs had lately manifested itself in a marked manner, and, I repeat again, that there was never a thought expressed as to separating us from England

Lord Grey also informed me of the despatches he received a few days ago from Sir John Bligh,[1] the English minister at St. Petersburg   It appears that this minister has been much made of lately by the emperor, M de Nesselrode, and most of the influential people, and that he has been asked to express the emperor's complete disinterestedness in the Eastern question   On this occasion, also, the former declarations were repeated as to the treaty of 8th July, that it would never have been made but at Turkey's earnest request, and that the emperor's sole aim was the maintenance of the Ottoman Empire

The Prince de Lieven, whom I saw frequently during my late sojourn at Brighton, always spoke to me in the same sense, and I cannot fail to remark, that the Court of Russia attaches great importance just now to assuring France and England as to the projects of invasion which are attributed to her

It appears to me from all these facts that, without sharing M de Metternich's blind confidence in Russia, one may conclude that it would be as well not to repulse the advances which that Power seems disposed to make

However, M de Lieven did not conceal from me, that he rather feared the effect produced in St Petersburg by the articles against Russia lately published in the French and English newspapers   He said as to this   "The emperor is young, and but little accustomed to put up with abuse of this kind

---

[1] Sir John Bligh, born in 1798, was Attaché to the Embassy at Vienna in 1820, then Secretary of Legation at Florence   He went subsequently to the Hague, then to St Petersburg as *Chargé d'Affaires*, became Minister at Stockholm, and finally at Hanover (1833)

He will probably be at Moscow when these papers reach him, and as this city is the centre of that powerful party which is in favour of war, it is to be feared that the insults of these papers may raise great difficulties in the path of the moderate party, at the head of which is Comte de Nesselrode, who always tries to return to moderation

I could only regret with M de Lieven, that the liberty of the Press was so badly understood in Russia, as it was only fair to acknowledge that Constitutional Governments had but little influence over it

January 10th, 1834

I have read with great interest despatch No 2, which you did me the honour to write as well as the copy of that from M de Sainte-Aulaire which was enclosed[1] This latter contains some curious details and valuable hints I have judiciously made use of some of them in my interviews with Lord Palmerston and Lord Grey, and by impressing upon both these ministers the exact state of the relations of their Government with that of Austria relative to Eastern affairs, I have called forth some explanations which appear to me very satisfactory

The conviction left on my mind by them is, that for the last three months there have been a good many *pourparlers* and attempts at closer relations between the London Cabinet and that of Vienna, and that the Eastern question has been the principal topic,[2] but that until the last conversation between

---

[1] Despatch from the Comte de Sainte-Aulaire of 25th December The ambassador gives an account of an interview he has had with M de Metternich The latter thinks that the treaty of 8th July between Russia and the Porte opens the door to a terrible catastrophe, which Europe ought to try and prevent, and which she only can do by joint action and joint consent He therefore proposes to open a Conference M de Tatischeff, on the contrary, will not hear of anything except joint action at Alexandria, to intimidate Mehemet Ali, and M de Sainte-Aulaire concludes from this, that Austria and Russia are completely at discord respecting Eastern affairs Austria, he adds, calls Europe to her aid, she will accept the first help that is offered her M de Metternich said to him in M de Tatischeff's presence "You can assure Admiral Roussin that there is not the slightest dissent between us, and that Austria's policy is identical with that of France in Eastern affairs" M de Sainte-Aulaire then stated, that Sir Frederick Lamb had been directed by M de Metternich to propose to his Government to agree to a profession of faith by the four Powers relative to Eastern affairs, which would either take the form of a treaty or a joint declaration, and become the basis of a European public right

[2] M de Sainte-Aulaire also wrote to Paris, as to the growing influence of Sir Frederick Lamb at Vienna (*Despatch of 12th December*) He declared that, in conformity with the orders of his Government, he tried to place England between France and Austria (*Despatch of 25th December*) Finally, on the 5th January, he stated that he was sure something was going on between Sir Frederick Lamb and M de Metternich, which they wished to keep from him (As to this, see also despatch of 2nd January from the Duc de Broglie to M de Talleyrand, appendix, letter No 14)

Lord Grey and Prince Esterhazy, of which I had the honour to inform you in my last despatch, no attempt has been made to give shape to the views shared by both Governments

By mentioning, as it were casually, to Lord Palmerston, that I was aware of the more intimate relations that had recently taken place between Sir Frederick Lamb and Prince de Metternich, I led him on to tell me of the last despatches from that ambassador, and after our conversation he ordered, in my presence, that copies of these despatches should be sent to Lord Granville, who will show them to you You will find them the same in substance as those sent by M de Sainte-Aulaire

This very frank and open conduct was accompanied by the reiterated assurance, that everything in this business would be done conjointly with France, with respect to this, I have also received separately Lord Grey's promise and likewise that of Lord Palmerston It seems to me more than probable that the document mentioned by M de Sainte-Aulaire as having been shown by Sir Frederick Lamb to the Emperor of Austria, is a copy of the instructions sent to Lord Ponsonby It was no doubt intended thereby to convince the emperor that England's views on Eastern matters are in accord with those of Austria.

However, I am induced to think that the first steps in this business should be taken in London, and what makes me fancy this, are the complaints which have been made to me against M de Metternich and against the coolness he has so long shown concerning the Eastern question, the direction of which he seems inclined to abandon entirely to Russia Moreover, it is not at all impossible that Lord Palmerston, whom the Cabinets also reproach for having, in some circumstances, held rather haughty language, should deem it advisable to approach the Vienna Cabinet, which was one of those not the least irritated by the tone of his communications On the other hand, I think that the English Cabinet recognizes the justice of the reproaches now addressed to it relative to its conduct last year in Turkish affairs It feels that had it adopted the project we suggested to it before the arrival of the Russians at Constantinople, much harm might have been avoided This project, as you may remember, included Austria in our joint efforts to prevent the evils which then threatened the Sultan, you will find the outlines of it in my despatches of the 8th, 28th, and 31st January, 1833 [1]

I believe that the English Government, swayed by the effect of this political error, will follow the line it has now adopted with all the greater zeal and perseverance

[1] See pp 76 and 78 The despatch of 8th January has not been transcribed in these Memoirs

The overtures made by Lord Grey, in reply to Prince Esterhazy's communications, will necessarily induce M de Metternich to explain clearly his actual intentions He will no doubt appreciate at its full value the course adopted by England, which has been entirely dictated by expediency, for Lord Grey told the Austrian Ambassador frankly, that England wished that the demand for guarantees which she claims from Russia, should pass through the Vienna Cabinet, as such an indirect course would remove anything that might wound Russia's *amour-propre*

It seems to me, M le Duc, that we shall have to congratulate ourselves if they decide at St Petersburg to give in on some of the points advanced by Lord Grey, such as the disbanding of the army in Wallachia and Moldavia, and the breaking up of that in the Crimea The king's Government will find means to defend these facts before the Chambers, as will also the English Cabinet before Parliament, should it be attacked, and besides, they will give us breathing space, the better to concert such measures as the unsettled state of the East will, in a short time, render inevitably necessary

I think that now we must not neglect any opportunity of convincing the Court of Austria, that it is our intention to act together with her and Great Britain in this affair, and not let it be supposed that we fancy any proposals had been made without our knowledge M de Sainte-Aulaire's despatch describes M de Metternich as being disposed to enter into a joint alliance of the four Courts Perhaps later on, Russia's refusal, if she does not accede to the guarantees that are now asked of her, will induce the Chancellor to agree to a triple alliance We are on the right track, which cannot fail to improve

January 12th, 1834

On reading the French newspapers of the 9th of this month, I noticed an article, taken from the *Augsburger Gazette* of the 5th, which will not have escaped you, and which has been repeated by all the English papers The correspondent of the *Augsburger Gazette*, referring to the treaty concluded between Russia and Austria for the purpose of guaranteeing the existence of the Ottoman Empire (even in the event of the reigning dynasty becoming extinct, but to the exclusion of Mehemet Ali), adds that the Prince de Metternich has informed Sir Frederick Lamb of the provisions of this treaty, and that he has approved of them fully [1]

[1] This is the article The Eastern question has latterly taken a turn which seriously threatens the peace of Europe The treaty concluded between Russia and the Porte has caused great disquietude to England, whose policy

However reassuring I may have felt the declarations of the English Ministers, of which I sent you an account in my last despatches, the condition excluding Mehemet Ali, which I knew was of a nature to affect the English Cabinet, has raised some doubts in my mind, and I deemed it necessary to obtain some fresh explanations from Lord Palmerston and Lord Grey I therefore saw them again yesterday, and I may assure you that their language was quite as frank and explicit as in our previous interviews But although there was no mention made between us then respecting the Pasha of Egypt, I cannot refrain from telling you that the king's Government should not fail to use every care to allay any suspicions on the part of the English Government as to the nature of any relations it might have with the Pasha I feel almost certain that here we are always supposed to have *arrière-pensées* on that point

Lord Palmerston told me that he had sent Sir Frederick Lamb's despatches to Paris to be shown to you ; but he also gave me a later one to read, which had arrived this morning, in which that ambassador states that after the conversations which he as well as M de Sainte-Aulaire have had with Prince de Metternich, he has arrived at the conclusion that the Austrian Chancellor was only trying to separate the Courts of France and England I do not know how far this remark of Sir Frederick Lamb's may be well founded, but it seems to be an indication well worth attending to

In the *Globe* of this evening you will find a long article, which all throughout gives a fresh proof of the sincerity of the assurances that have been given me for the last three days This ministerial organ insists, with truly remarkable vehemence, on the necessity of England's union with France . . .

is principally directed by the interests of its commerce and industries, while France dreads to lose the influence it has gained at Constantinople in consequence of the energetic actions of Admiral Roussin Hence has arisen the coolness in the relations of Russia with France and England In order to avoid such a conflict, the Vienna Cabinet, which during these last few years has acted with so much energy in order to preserve the general peace and the *statu quo* in Europe, has addressed itself to the Cabinet of St Petersburg, with which, ever since the negotiations at Munchengratz, it has been in close and friendly relations, recalling those which existed between them at the time of Napoleon's wars The reply of the Russian Cabinet has been most satisfactory in every way, and it is stated that a treaty has been concluded between the two Courts, by which they will guarantee the existence of the Turkish Empire, even should the existing dynasty die out, but to the exclusion of Mehemet Ali We are also assured, that Prince de Metternich, two days ago, communicated the substance of this treaty to the English ambassador, Sir Frederick Lamb, and that the latter has fully approved, in the most positive terms, a negotiation which can only produce the happiest results, and which entitles the great statesman, who directs the affairs of Europe with such ability, and who has so long preserved us from the horrors of anarchy and war, to the fresh gratitude of all the friends of order and peace

Confidential

LONDON, *January* 13th, 1834

MON CHER DUC,

The newspapers declare you are ill The *Times* even goes so far as to speak of retirement Pray reassure me as to your health ; the retirement I do not believe in, and do not wish to do so Write me a few lines which I can show to Lord Grey, as he seemed somewhat surprised at what had passed from the tribune between you and M Bignon [1] The English Cabinet fears being hampered in Parliament by utterances on the Eastern question which are not identical in Paris and London It is therefore absolutely necessary that I should be able to satisfy Lord Grey by some clearer explanation than that given in the *Journal des Débats*, and which it will be easier for you to send through me than to give from the tribune

THE DUC DE BROGLIE TO THE PRINCE DE TALLEYRAND

PARIS, *January* 16th, 1834

MON PRINCE,

Here are the facts I submit them to your wisdom On Wednesday, January 8th, the discussion came on relative to paragraph 8 of the address This paragraph, we had been informed, was specially directed against the Ministry In my opinion, on the contrary, nothing was easier than to show that it contained the most complete approbation of our policy for the last three years M Bignon rose, *in the name of the Commission*, to explain his paragraph in a perfectly reasonable manner and quite in conformity with my views ; he then proceeded to make a long speech on the general state of Europe, in which, as you will have seen, there was much that was quite reasonable, and more that was utter folly

I ascended the tribune after him, and, in so doing, I agreed to to what he had said, *in the name of the Commission*, intending to make use of it the following day, and show that our policy prevailed by common consent over that of our habitual adversaries As regards M. Bignon's speech itself, I took no notice of

[1] Louis-Pierre-Édouard, Baron Bignon, born in 1771 He entered early into the diplomatic service, was Secretary of Legation at Berne in 1797 then at Milan (Cisalpine Republic) in 1799, and at Berlin in 1800 In 1802, he was made *Chargé d'Affaires*, then Minister in 1804 In 1806, he was entrusted with the administration of the Prussian provinces In 1809, he was nominated Administrator-General of Austria From Vienna he went to Warsaw as Minister Plenipotentiary During the Hundred Days he was Under-Secretary of State for Foreign Affairs, and had charge of this department for some days in June M Bignon was elected deputy in 1817, and was regularly re-elected until 1837 He was then created a Peer of France, and died in 1841

it ; seeing that it contained no attack on the Government, there was no occasion for me to make any reply to it   I concluded by thanking M Bignon for the moderation of his language *towards us*

The next day I was seriously unwell, so much so, that I hesitated for some time whether I should go to the Chambers Nevertheless, I decided to make the effort   On my arrival, I found the whole Chamber in a state of uproar   The adhesion which I had given to the explanations of the Commission had been taken as given to M Bignon's speech, to which I had not replied at all Men's imaginations had been fired, and every one was firmly convinced that we should go to war with the whole of Europe in a week !   Being violently attacked by M Mauguin, I was obliged to rectify this general error, and to point out what I really had agreed to and thus endeavour to reassure men's minds , unfortunately, as I said before, I was too unwell to have full possession of my own   Just when about to speak, I suddenly turned so faint, that I was compelled to grasp the tribune to support myself   Under these circumstances, I hurried on as fast as I could   I replied, without really knowing what I said , I particularly explained the treaty of 8th July, respecting which a great deal of nonsense had been talked, but while endeavouring to show that neither its meaning nor its intentions had been understood, I failed to make them see its real dangers and its true character   I was obliged, I repeat, to cut short my speech and finish abruptly, lest I should lose consciousness completely   On leaving the tribune, I had to go to bed, and was profusely bled

The result of all this, I do not conceal from myself, is very vexatious, both for me and for business   Although I have not said or done anything really reprehensible, I think it would be better that the king should have another Minister for Foreign Affairs ready at his hand   But as this is not the case, and as my retirement would upset the whole Ministry, I have consented to remain   If you will read the *Moniteur* of the 9th and 10th, you will now perfectly understand what has occurred   I should have done better not to have entered into the explanations given by M Bignon in the name of the Commission, as I already felt unwell on the 8th   It would have been better to avoid all discussion   Such has been my fault, I do not pretend to excuse it All the rest was unfortunate and inevitable   If I had been master of myself the next day, the discussion, instead of ending in my failure, would have resulted in the most signal defeat our adversaries have experienced for a long time

You may make what use you like, mon Prince, of all these details.   I have nothing to conceal, nothing to dissemble, nothing

to justify I was wrong, feeling as ill as I did, to play for such
high stakes ; I was wrong to lose That is all I can say

THE PRINCE DE TALLEYRAND TO THE DUC DE BROGLIE

LONDON, *January 20th*, 1834

MON CHER DUC,

There is a certain candour, which, to be perfectly true,
requires no little skill Your admirable letter of the 16th is the
best proof of this You will see the effect it has had on Lord
Grey from the note which he wrote to me, and which I enclose

I am induced to think that we shall have a very good
paragraph about France in the King of England's speech on the
4th February I have done my best to secure it I cannot sufficiently urge you to impress upon all those journals that depend on
you, not to recur perpetually to the incident of the Address ; it
should be buried in oblivion

(Note inclosed in the above letter)

LORD GREY TO THE PRINCE DE TALLEYRAND

DOWNING STREET, *January 20th*, 1834

MON CHER PRINCE,

I return you with many thanks M le Duc de Broglie's
letter, which you were kind enough to send me last night

I find in his explanations fresh proofs of his candour, and of his
upright and honourable character The matter has no doubt been
very annoying, and I feared that it would give Russia some advantage in her future discussions with us, however it is impossible
to impute any other motives to the Duke than those which he
himself acknowledges But this is of little consequence, as long
as both governments maintain the close union which has been so
fortunately established between them

I am greatly rejoiced that M de Broglie has given up all idea
of sending in his resignation ; it would have been an irreparable
loss to France as well as to us, as we trust so entirely to his
loyalty and his honour

Pray accept .

THE PRINCE DE TALLEYRAND TO THE DUC DE BROGLIE

LONDON, *January 20th*, 1834

MONSIEUR LE DUC,

I wrote to you somewhat hurriedly the night before
last telling you that the reports which had got abroad as to the

resignation of the English Cabinet were entirely without foundation   I am still of this opinion ; but although there is no question of a change of Ministry, it is none the less certain that a very decided difference of opinion has arisen among some of its members, and it seems that a proposed English intervention in Portugal is the cause of it   Several of the Ministers thought that an immediate intervention had become imperative ; but the majority having voted against this measure, it has for the present been abandoned   This matter was the cause of Lord Grey's last journey to Brighton, and I am told that the king shares the opinion of the majority of the Council   However, you will find a full, and I think fairly true, account in to-day's *Times* of the principles on which the partizans of intervention in Portugal lean

It will have been seen, from the extracts of these despatches, that I had been obliged to put off any attempts to persuade the English Cabinet to conclude a defensive alliance between France and England   The difficulties I had to encounter were various   First, I was assured that there was no hope of any closer relations with Austria, whom such a treaty could not fail to alarm and throw still further into the Russian alliance   Nearly the same objection had been raised with regard to Prussia   But these were not the only obstacles I had to encounter   There were some who upheld the foreign relations of England, others the home position of the Cabinet, and they feared that by pledging themselves to us, they might lose their independence as regards Portuguese matters, which England watched with a jealous eye, and with the firm resolution of acting independently of us in that portion of the Peninsula !   It was also feared that if we permitted her full liberty in this respect, she might, in return, be obliged some day to grant us the same liberty of action in Spanish affairs   And it is well known that ever since the peace of Utrecht, England has always sought to oppose our influence in Spain   This is a species of political axiom which, I am inclined to think, is taught at the Universities of Oxford and Cambridge   Finally, the existence of the English Cabinet was somewhat shaken , there was a diversity of opinion on several subjects among its members, and, not to conceal any reasons which might prevent its forming the alliance I had suggested, I must admit that it was not at all confident as to the continued existence of the French Ministry The incident which happened to the Duc de Broglie maintained distrust on this point, and I saw plainly that I must give up my scheme of an alliance, if not altogether, at any rate until some event, either in the East or in the Peninsula, made England recognize the importance of such an alliance

There was besides, at this time, a series of complications in the policy of Europe, which would require to be unravelled before the English Cabinet would feel disposed to entertain the scheme I had proposed to it in the name of my Government

The fall of the Zea Ministry at Madrid,[1] was regarded as a success for England, as the latter looked upon this Ministry as entirely submissive to France, and therefore rejoiced at seeing it replaced by that of M Martinez de la Rosa,[2] whom she hoped to lead

On the other hand, the Russian Government at this time tried to approach France, and specially England, in order to prevent the latter from allying herself too closely with us[3] The following letters will enable the reader easily to follow the course I have indicated, as well as the events resulting therefrom

---

[1] M de Zea had fallen in consequence of the action of several Captains-General, who addressed a *statement* to the Queen Regent, begging her to dismiss her Ministry The question was submitted by the Queen to the Council of Regency, which decided that M de Zea's retirement was imperative The Cabinet, in consequence, resigned on the 16th January

[2] Francisco Martinez de la Rosa, born in 1789, Deputy to the Cortes in 1812, had become one of the most influential members of the Liberal Party He became head of the Cabinet in 1822, but was exiled after the re establishment of absolute power in 1823 He returned to his native land in 1830, and became President of the Council in 1834 In 1840, he was Ambassador at Paris, and at Rome in 1842 In 1844, he joined the Narvaez Cabinet was again accredited to Paris from 1847 to 1851, then became President of the First Chamber of the Cortes, Chief Secretary of State in 1857, and President of the State Council in 1858 He died in 1862

[3] Marshal Maison in his correspondence drew, the attention of the government to the reaction in the St Petersburg Cabinet On the 31st December, he wrote that M de Nesselrode had expressed himself perfectly satisfied with the attitude adopted by France relative to the Eastern question "When one takes so nearly the same views," he had said, "one must end by a thorough understanding " On the 3rd January, the Marshal again recurred to the same subject, and stated that M de Nesselrode had shown the greatest satisfaction at the efforts France was making to consolidate her government and repress revolutionary propagandism On the 6th January, the ambassador gave an account of an interview he had had with the emperor, during which the latter had expressed himself with great violence regarding England. He thought that the Russian Government, after having sought for the last eighteen months to embroil England with France, was now trying to embroil France with England

THE PRINCE DE TALLEYRAND TO THE DUC DE BROGLIE

LONDON, *January 25th*, 1834

MONSIEUR LE DUC,

The English Ministers are entirely of your opinion respecting the advances recently made to the King's Government both by the Emperor Nicholas and the Cabinet of St Petersburg, they quite recognize with you, that these fresh advances made to France have no other object than to try and separate the Paris and London Cabinets They are very glad here to see that we are not duped by these demonstrations, and I have reason to believe that they will give you credit for this when occasion requires

The steps taken by the Russian Government at Stockholm and the precautionary measures it has deemed it necessary to take in the Baltic, point to some anxiety, which will not be allayed by anything done here [1]

Lord Grey spoke to me this morning about M Martinez de la Rosa He considers him by far the best suited to conduct Spanish affairs I fancy that the praises lavished on M Martinez are greatly due to the dissatisfaction felt by the English Government against M de Zea This will not surprise you

I thank you for the memorandum you sent me relative to the conspiracy which lately broke out in Greece [2] I shall find it of great use when we are called on to take the affairs of that country in hand, which, as far as we are concerned, is not very urgent, but which will no doubt become so as soon M Tricoupis [3] arrives in London

[1] The St Petersburg Cabinet had sounded the Swedish Government as to the attitude it would take, in the event of war breaking out between England and France on the one side, and Russia on the other M. Billecocq, our Charge d'Affaires at Stockholm, had an interview on this subject with M de Wetterstedt, the Swedish Minister (see page 222), of which he sent an account to Paris in a despatch, dated January 4th M de Wetterstedt declared " with extraordinary energy, ' that Sweden had made no engagement, that she had entered into no alliance, and that Russia had left her the power of remaining perfectly neutral A few days later, the Minister declared that if such a war should take place, Sweden would throw open her ports to the ships of both parties (despatch 20th January) Two months after, in an interview with the English Charge d'Affaires, M de Wetterstedt admitted that Sweden had been formally asked by Russia to enter into an alliance with her against France and England, but that she had only promised to remain neutral (M Billecocq's despatch of 7th March)

[2] A conspiracy against the Greek Government had been discovered at Nauplia in the month of September 1833 Its object was to overthrow the regency, proclaim the king's majority, and the conspirators would have then seized the reins of power in his name The arrest of the ringleaders caused the enterprise to miscarry

[3] Spiridion Tricoupis, born in 1791, a Greek statesman and historian He took an active part in the Wars of Independence On the accession of King Otto, he was accredited to London (1835-1838), and returned in 1841 He was Minister for Foreign Affairs in 1843, then Envoy at Paris 1850, and again in London He was Minister at various periods between 1855 and 1862, and died in 1873

P 2

January 28th, 1834

I was with Lord Grey and Lord Palmerston yesterday when they received the news of General Saldanha's entry into Leiria It is looked on here as a matter that cannot fail to have important results , but the details received are so characterized by ferocity, that one cannot help wishing to see the end of the struggle now going on in Portugal It seems quite evident that General Saldanha[1] will not stop at this success, and that he intends to march at once to Coimbra, in order to combine his forces with the *corps d'armée* of the Duc de Terceira This news is the best possible augury for the solution of a question which, as you are aware, has greatly occupied the English Cabinet for some time It replies to the fears of the partizans of an immediate intervention in Portugal, and has for the time, caused the English Ministry to give up all idea of any direct and material action in the affairs of that country

February 1st, 1834

As I had the honour of telling you in my despatch of the morning, I went to Lord Palmerston last night at ten He gave me a despatch to read, the original which M de Lieven had received the night before, having been entrusted to him I read it through twice very carefully, and he then allowed me to take some notes . .

This despatch seems to be a reply to one written from London by the Russian Ambassador on December 27th M de Lieven therein stated, that Lord Palmerston had expressed the wish that a frank explanation should be come to between England and Russia To this entirely conciliatory overture, Russia replies by eager protestations of her desire to entertain only peaceful and friendly relations A few lines lower down are these words *England is the natural ally of Russia* Then it is remarked, that in her intercourse with England, Russia has always followed and will continue to follow such forms as she has *continuously* employed with her In proof of this the Note of October 27th[2] is cited, to which Russia made the only reply she felt consistent with her dignity and thereupon an apologetic remark is made, that the Notes were not called forth by her After this observation, they endeavour to show that wherever the English Government has made any communication,

---

[1] General Saldanha had taken possession on the 15th January of the fortified town of Leiria, situated at an equal distance between Lisbon and Oporto Of the 500 men who composed the garrison, barely a handful succeeded in escaping from the conquerors

[2] Note of October 27th 1832, which notified the Anglo-French Convention of 22nd October to the Russian Government Russia sent an answer in reply, which will be found on page 30 in a foot note

which was moderate in its views and conciliatory in form, they had at once hastened to reply in the same spirit, and that when England had expressed a desire to have more extended information, Russia had gladly lent herself to remove everything that might complicate the relations between the two countries or prejudice the friendly feeling

Looked at from this point of view, the request of the English Government does not present any objections to the Russian Government, which is quite willing to accede thereto

M de Nesselrode then proceeds to give some exact particulars relative to military arrangements He declares that the information the English Government has received is not correct, and he tries to point out the errors. The military measures that have been notified to England could not in any way be considered as indicating an offensive policy on the part of Russia, and still less so towards England than towards any other power.

Then come some details He assures the English Government

First, That the Russian fleet in the Black Sea, is in exactly the same condition as it was when it returned from Constantinople, and that no fresh vessels have been added since that period (As regards this, Lord Palmerston remarked to me, that no explanation was given, as to why, when the expedition was ended, so large a force was kept there, and that it naturally gave the impression of some ulterior object in view)

Secondly, That the division encamped in the Crimea, was simply that which had returned from Constantinople last autumn on board the Russian squadron, that no reinforcements had been sent there, and that all the troops in the southern provinces of the empire, did not exceed the number that had been quartered there for the last fifteen years

Thirdly, The Russian Government did not hesitate to declare that the reports spread abroad as to the increase of its maritime forces in the Baltic, were utterly without foundation M de Nesselrode computes the number of vessels at twenty-seven This number, he said, is far less than the Empress Catherine had in those same waters, and the fortifications on the Aland Isles were merely a fortified barrack intended to hold two battalions No naval establishment had been formed there Those islands, moreover, had only harbours of refuge, which were of use to all the world, and which could not disquiet Sweden, who alone might feel alarmed

Fourthly, That the object of the fortifications in Poland, was solely for the proper security of the empire, which, as will be remembered, might have been seriously threatened two years ago in that quarter

His Government might find very just cause for alarm in Lord Palmerston's own words   These words, according to the despatch, run as follows   ' That it would be to the interest of England, to prefer seeing the Sultan's throne occupied by Mehemet Ali, a change which would substitute Arab supremacy for Ottoman rule "

There is a great want of accuracy in this quotation   Lord Palmerston might have said that he would prefer seeing the throne occupied by Mehemet Ali, rather than by the Emperor of Russia   That certainly is the meaning of the expression used by Lord Palmerston, and from what he has told me, it is what he did express

M de Nesselrode then makes some observations on the subject of the words attributed to Lord Palmerston, and says that the policy they advocate aims at replacing a powerful ally of Russia by a power hostile and dangerous to the maintenance of peace in the East   He admits, however, that England has not acted in the sense that has been gratuitously attributed to her, but declares the admission that such an idea could have existed exhibits greater hostility to the interests of Russia, than is displayed by the forts on the Vistula against the interests of England

From that he goes on to say, that the treaty of 8th July should be looked upon less as an offensive weapon placed in the hands of Russia, than as a moral guarantee against the projects of invasion and conquest which an Arab Power would endeavour to extend over European Turkey

As a summing up to all these reasons, he gives the assurance that the separate act of 8th July, does not give the Russian flag any exclusive privileges to the prejudice of the other Powers, and that in that respect, no alteration has been made in the usages established by the Porte , for, it is added, Russia is as far removed from the idea of wishing to infringe them herself, as she is interested in their not being misunderstood by any other power

Then follow some explanations, relative to the reproach of secrecy towards the other Courts when this treaty was made The reason for this, given by M de Nesselrode is that the secret did not belong to Russia, that it pertained solely to the Porte , it was the latter who felt the necessity of a treaty and who had a direct interest in this transaction, and that therefore it was for her to decide when it would suit her to give legal publicity to this document, Russia according the most absolute liberty to the Divan either to publish it or keep it secret

In proof of this, the Convention of 22nd October is cited (only they are not happy in their citations) relative to the measures concerted between France and England with respect to Holland

They quite forgot, in recalling this circumstance, that when the plenipotentiaries of the five Courts were assembled, two of them asked the other three whether they would take part in coercive measures, and that when they refused, France and England considered themselves free to act independently of them There certainly was no secrecy there

The best thing in this Note is at the end, where there is a question of the present *pourparlers* which are going on at St Petersburg between the representatives of the Porte These are the terms generally

The result of the mission to the Porte, which we may look upon as near its end, will plainly prove that Russia, in pursuance of the conservative policy she has adopted towards the Ottoman Empire, will make a point of honour of respecting its integrity and independence, and of strengthening the Sultan's authority rather than making the slightest attempt to lessen it "The arrangements we are now making with Achmet Pasha" (these are M de Nesselrode's last words) "will give fresh weight to the frank explanations which form the subject-matter of the present despatch "

This, Monsieur le Duc, is the somewhat lengthy analysis of M de Nesselrode's despatch to the Prince de Lieven, but I do not wish to miss the opportunity of making known to you, if you have not already heard it from the Comte de Pozzo, Russia's reply to the reproaches addressed to her with reference to the line of policy she has adopted in the Levant

To conclude it appears evident to me, that this lengthy Russian document is specially intended to allay the anxieties of the London and Paris Cabinets , it even shows a disposition to satisfy them To estimate the degree of confidence that should be accorded to these expressions is somewhat difficult , but to doubt them altogether would I think be imprudent There are certain characters, and I believe the Emperor Nicholas is one of them, who feel themselves pledged in proportion to the confidence placed in them

I have the honour to transmit to you the despatches from the Hague You will see that the King of Holland has not yet exhausted his dilatory *ruses*, and that he attributes language to one of the members of the Conference which is evidently in opposition to the engagements entered into by all the members at their last meetings There could have been no ambiguity in Lord Palmerston's explanations to M Dedel, and I cannot think that the plenipotentiaries representing the three Northern Courts would have shown anything but the conciliatory spirit which has always distinguished them.

The Conference, when it separated, decided not to meet again until it had received positive and acceptable overtures for a final arrangement from the King of Holland, or until one of the plenipotentiaries made such a proposal. This latter course has been adopted to resume negotiations, and we shall no doubt have a meeting either on Wednesday or Thursday. It will, to all appearance, lead to no results.

I was obliged to give this long extract from the despatch of the St. Petersburg Cabinet, as later on it had a most serious effect, and reveals a trait in Lord Palmerston's character which I have already alluded to in other circumstances; I mean, that he so often allowed personal feelings to enter into the conduct of public affairs. Thus, this Russian despatch made him so angry, that he was led to adopt a measure which I considered most ill-judged, to say nothing more. The English Court had at this period to nominate an ambassador to St. Petersburg to replace Lord Durham,[1] who had asked to be recalled on account of his health. Lord Palmerston had decided to replace him by Sir Stratford Canning, knowing well that such a choice was the most disagreeable he could make for the Court of Russia. In fact, when it was announced to M. de Nesselrode, he hastened to make it known in London that the emperor would be very displeased if Sir Stratford Canning was sent to St. Petersburg, because that diplomatist, while English ambassador at Constantinople, had always exhibited the most hostile feelings towards Russia, and that he therefore considered him but little calculated to foster the friendly relations, he was desirous of establishing between the two Courts. Lord Palmerston replied with his usual haughtiness, that it was very possible that an English ambassador might have displeased the emperor by conscientiously fulfilling his duties and the instructions of his Government, but that he did not consider this a sufficient reason for not giving him an appointment to which his great services had entitled him, and that if this choice was not accepted, the English Government would leave the post of ambassador at St.

[1] Lord Durham was not ambassador at St. Petersburg; he had been sent on a special mission for the purpose, it was said, of offering to the Emperor Nicholas the mediation of England in favour of the Poles. This mission however led to no results. As for the English Embassy in Russia, which was then without a head, the duties were carried on by Mr. Bligh, the *Chargé d'Affaires.*

Petersburg vacant   The Emperor Nicholas in his turn showed
himself greatly offended at this, and decided to recall his ambassador, the Prince de Lieven, who had been accredited to
London since 1812   The two embassies remained vacant for
some time, and the relations between the two Courts naturally
felt the effect of this

I did not share Lord Palmerston's views, or rather his feelings,
I thought Russia's explanations ought to have been accepted
for what they were worth, and a watch kept on her, but that
we should not embroil ourselves, unless it was seriously resolved
to go to war with her

I therefore wrote —

THE PRINCE DE TALLEYRAND TO THE DUC DE BROGLIE.

LONDON, *February* 3rd, 1834

MONSIEUR LE DUC,

I have received your despatch No 8   I thank you
for having sent me the document enclosed therein   After
its perusal, I was still further confirmed in the opinion I had
formed as to the line which the king's Government ought to
take with regard to Russia, at a time when that Power seems
disposed to be friendly   Our position is good, we ought to
believe in the sincerity of the Russian Government's protestations   The language uniformly held by the ambassadors
in London and Paris and the Russian ministers at St Petersburg,
proves the desire and almost the necessity, of convincing us
Knowing all we do, what danger can we run by appearing
to be convinced ?

The truth is that Russia's course is arrested just now, she
will have to seek for some time ere she finds a fresh pretext for
meddling directly in the affairs of the Ottoman Empire, it
is to these we must direct all our attention   The English
Government seems to take the same view, if, as I have reason
to believe it will, the speech from the throne expresses itself
relative to Turkey in this way

" Since the arrangement with Mehemet Ali, the peacefulness
of Turkey has been uninterrupted, and will not be menaced by any
other danger, the English Government will do all in its power, to
prevent any change in the relations of this empire with those
Powers which can insure its future stability and independence "

I am also induced to believe, that there is a paragraph in
this speech which concerns us alone, and which is conceived as
nearly as possible in the following terms :

"The constant aim of my policy has been to insure to my people the continued enjoyment and blessings of peace, in this I have been greatly aided by the good feeling that has happily been established between my Government and that of France; the continued assurances I receive of the friendly disposition of the other Continental Powers, gives me full confidence in the success of my efforts."

February 4th.

I have just returned from the opening ceremony, it was most brilliant I hasten to send you the King of England's speech France is mentioned separately from the other Powers, the king wished this to be understood, by the way in which he uttered the passage which concerns us specially; he even made a pause before pronouncing those words "*the assurances which I have received*"[1]

February 7th.

Our conference on Dutch affairs took place at the request of Lord Palmerston It was very long, because in discussing the various opinions, we were carried back far into the past

The Austrian plenipotentiaries took the initiative, and declared that their Court, not wishing to neglect anything that could bring about a speedy settlement of the Hollando-Belgian affair, had charged them to express to the plenipotentiaries of the other Courts the desire that the negotiations which had been so long interrupted should be resumed, they assigned as the reason for their request the action taken by the King of the Netherlands, the pledge he had given, the steps he had taken to obtain assent to the territorial arrangements from the parties interested, and moreover the fresh instructions he had sent to the Dutch plenipotentiaries to renew the negotiations of those matters still in dispute

Lord Palmerston then spoke, and taking up the question where it had been left on the 30th August, when the Conference separated, he proved that nothing had really changed since that period, that the Germanic Confederation had not acquiesced in the demand of the King of the Netherlands,[2] that

---

[1] The King of England's speech at the opening of Parliament The following is the passage alluded to by M de Talleyrand "   The constant aim of my policy has been to insure to my people the enjoyment of the uninterrupted blessings of peace In this I have been fully seconded, by the good feeling so happily established between my Government and that of France, and the assurances which I have received of the friendly disposition of the other Continental Powers, gives me full confidence that my efforts will continue to be crowned with success   "

[2] It will be remembered that the negotiations relative to the Hollando-Belgian question had been suspended in the month of August, in consequence of King William's

the Austrian and Prussian ministers, trusting to their influence, had led us to believe in the success of such a course, but having been mistaken, the important difficulty as to the boundaries was not removed, and that thus the principal guarantee (without which it was impossible to foresee the issue of this negotiation) had not yet been given, and was as far off as ever from being so It was the same also with the question as to the powers of the Dutch plenipotentiaries, he had seen M Dedel, and after pointing out to him that the delays of the Diet deprived the Conference of the guarantee it had asked for, in order to conclude the territorial arrangements, he had told him, that looking to the difficulties which had succeeded each other for the last three years, he must ask him whether he had at last got a guarantee to give us for example, had he received powers authorizing him to sign the articles initialled by M Verstolck himself, among others, Art IX and the paragraphs it contained, M Dedel replied that he was not authorized, and could not take it upon himself to sign Lord Palmerston then added, that he was compelled to come to the conclusion that fresh conferences would lead to nothing, and that the negotiation was just at the same point now which it had reached five months ago

The Prussian minister, M de Bulow, tried to answer, and insisted that the Conference ought to assemble, giving as a convincing reason that the King of the Netherlands would represent our refusal to the Dutch nation and the different Cabinets of Europe, as the cause of the negotiation not being brought to a close

I was then enabled to show, by going on with several of the arguments so ably brought forward by Lord Palmerston, that to proceed with the negotiations, when there was no prospect of arriving at any definite conclusion, would be placing the Conference in a very unsuitable position, that we ought always to be agreed among ourselves, that the division of territory, the actual basis of the Belgian Kingdom, had been settled without any reservation by the Powers, in this respect, therefore, we were bound, if M Dedel had no powers to sign with us what we were pledged to, there was no use in any negotiation, and that therefore my opinion coincided with that of Lord Palmer-

refusal to authorize the Diet and the Princes of Nassau to take the necessary steps to cede that portion of Luxemburg to Belgium, which the treaty of the twenty four articles had given her When the King of the Netherlands had at last determined to act (see p 180), he had met with a double refusal Nevertheless, he thought that having shown such goodwill, the Conference would agree to commence negotiations again, and had given his plenipotentiaries powers accordingly It will be seen what reception his proposal met with in London

ston, that matters must for the present be allowed to remain as they were, and as action had not proved successful, we must fain trust to the power of inaction

After a silence of some minutes, we all separated, and as I had foreseen and told you, this Conference ended in nothing The Austrian and Prussian plenipotentiaries carried out to the letter the instructions of their Governments,—they could not well seem to agree to our observations, but their silence made us think that they found our reasons unanswerable We separated without any adjournment, as is the case when a matter is quite given up

February 14th, 1834

At the request of M Skinas, Grecian *Chargé d'Affaires*, the Conference assembled to-day to discuss the proposal he was directed to submit to us, viz, to give our guarantee to the third portion of the Greek loan M Skinas laid before us the embarrassed state of the Greek finances, and entered into full details on this matter We, that is Lord Palmerston and I, were aware that the Prince de Lieven had received instructions, which did not permit him to consent that the guarantee asked for should be granted We therefore allowed him to estimate the difficulties raised by his Government as to granting this guarantee The difficulties are as follows Russia wishes to have detailed accounts as to the real state of the Greek finances, and M Skinas having promised to furnish these in a very short time, we listened to M de Lieven's further observations, which only pledged us to a delay

I need hardly point out to you, that the visible reason given by M le Prince de Lieven was not the real one on which the objections were founded Russia does not wish to lose a means of interference in Greek affairs, which she still possesses. Perhaps she has some special schemes, which the present difficulties would render easier of execution The information which you will have received, will enable you better than anyone else, to judge as to the value of the conjectures we have formed here, and will probably explain to you how it is that Russia, who a year ago was the first to ask for a guarantee of the three Powers, should now have raised a difficulty on this point

LONDON, *February 23rd*, 1834

Accept my thanks for sending me Marshal Maison's despatch, in which he gives you an account of the new Convention concluded at St Petersburg on January 29th, between the Porte and Russia[1] This Convention somewhat ameliorates the conditions which the treaty of Adrianople had imposed on Turkey, but it is not difficult to recognize, that the renunciations of Russia are not nearly so extensive as they seem Turkey is really her insolvent creditor, if therefore she remits any part of the loan, the sacrifice is not so very great The evacuation of the Principalities is an incomplete measure, for the occupation of Silistria and the military route across the provinces which are to be evacuated, are almost as good guarantees for Russia, as those she gave up by the treaty of January 29th In all this, there is neither much abnegation or generosity What is to be regretted more than all, is, that the Turkish plenipotentiary did not stipulate in the Convention as to what number of troops were to form the garrison of Silistria That is a most important point, which the Porte and Austria ought not to have neglected to arrange in accordance with their joint interest You know what an occupation of eight years means Austria appears to have forgotten that only two months ago, she declared she would never allow Russia to take possession of even a Turkish village, she would find it difficult to show in her own annals that an occupation of eight years had not become a possession It would, I think, be a grand and beneficial stroke of policy for France and England to unite in making a loan to the Porte which would free her at once, and enable the Principalities, as well as the Porte herself, to resume their sovereign rights Never would the credit of our country and that of England have been more nobly and politically employed

February 24th

On reading over what I had the honour of writing to you in my despatch of yesterday, as to the benefit which would accrue were the Porte to be freed by a loan, from the obligations she has lately contracted with Russia, I found, that in order to make this idea complete, it would be necessary to endeavour to associate

---

[1] Despatch of 1st February, 1834 The Convention of 29th January stipulated for the evacuation of the principalities by Russia, before the end of May following It settled the organization of those provinces, the quota of tribute to be paid to the Porte, the mode of nominating the Hospodars, who were to be chosen by the Sultan from a list presented by the Boyards The Principalities were to have their army, their fleet, and their flag

The Sandjacks of Tcheldir and Pasken were to be definitely united to Turkey

It granted the Porte a deduction of two million ducats, on the six million which the treaty of Adrianople had assigned to it as a contribution The payment of the remaining four millions, to be accomplished in eight years, and until Turkey was completely free, Russia was to occupy the fortress of Silistria, communications between it and the Empire being kept open by a military route through the Principalities

Austria in the scheme I suggested to you the security of her eastern frontiers, the free navigation of the Danube, (which is commanded by Silistria) and also her German interests, make it her duty, so it seems to me, to use all her efforts to take from Russia the position which that Power is endeavouring to preserve in the Principalities I should think therefore, that this would be a favourable time to make this proposition to her, and that if she accepted it, we for our part should find the immense advantage of breaking up the united policy, followed for the last three years by the three northern Powers I think this matter is worthy of your careful attention

The Swedish minister spoke to me yesterday, relative to some advances made to his Government by General Suchtelen,[1] the Russian ambassador at Stockholm, for the purpose of finding out what Sweden intended to do, if a war should break out between France, England, and Russia The Government had replied by a memorandum, that it would remain neutral, and had instructed its minister at St Petersburg to notify this to the Russian Government I thought I ought to advise you of this fact, although I do not believe it will have any con-sequences

MADAME ADÉLAÏDE D'ORLÉANS TO THE PRINCE DE
TALLEYRAND

TUILERIES, *February 27th*, 1834

What happened at Marseilles, Lyons, and St Etienne, and what occurred here at Paris, were all from the same cause, an affair got up by the same factions, the republicans and the associations and secret societies The working-classes of Lyons and St Etienne fortunately did not wish to take any part in these riots, and everything has again settled down in those towns Here, not only did the populace take no part in these wicked attempts at disorder, but they were most indignant, the National Guard was much exasperated, and likewise the regular troops, they were brought about by a mere handful of wretches, which could not cause any serious anxiety In fact, it has been an

---

[1] Jean Pierre, Comte de Suchtelen, born in 1759, formerly a Dutch officer who entered the Russian service in 1783, rose to be a General and was then sent as Ambassador to Stockholm He took part in the campaign of 1813 on the staff of Bernadotte, returned to Stockholm after the peace, and remained there until his death in 1836

[2] Some disturbances had broken out in various parts of the country, consequent on the law relative to public auctioneers The law of February 16th, obliged them to first apply for authority This produced most violent scenes, especially in Paris and Lyons, on the 21st, 22nd, and 23rd February

evil resulting in a benefit, by proving the necessity of having a law to repress all these associations and secret societies, and thus causing everyone to desire it There is no doubt now that this law will be passed in the Chamber [1] . .

The king agrees with you, that the new Russo-Turkish treaty is a great improvement, but that it cannot materially change the relative position of Russia and Turkey, which is that of strength and nonentity What the king therefore considers most important, is the disarmament of the fleet in the Black Sea, for as long as it remains equipped, it can transport the Russians to Constantinople in three days Once this fleet is laid up no rapid movement is possible As for the evacuation of the Principalities, that no doubt is a good measure, but with a military route and Silistria, it is more apparent than real

The essential point, the Gordian knot of this whole affair, is Austria's policy Russia will not move unless she is assured of Austria's assent, and in this case I should call the certainty of her inaction assent The question is to know what is being done as to this England is in every way in a better position than we are, to find this out, and it is for her to tell us Try and get her to do this .

LE COMTE DE RAYNEVAL TO THE PRINCE DE TALLEYRAND

MADRID, *February* 21*st*, 1834

MON CHER PRINCE,

I did not wish to disturb the rest which I thought you would like to enjoy, during your sojourn in France I thought you would not take it amiss if I allowed you to forget the affairs of the Peninsula for a brief period But I was unable to resist the too tempting opportunity of recalling them to you, offered me by M de Florida-Blanca's departure [2]

We heard here yesterday officially, Lord Palmerston's reply to the request for aid addressed to the English Government by Dom Pedro The feeling experienced by the new Spanish Cabinet, at the assurance that England will not depart from her policy of inaction, is one of deep consternation Spain is, and will be for a long time, unable to intervene effectively in Portugal, and as long as Dom Miguel and Don Carlos support each other, there can be no peace or safety for the young Queen's Government

---

[1] This law was passed the following March in the Chamber of Deputies, by a majority of 246 to 154
[2] The Comte de Florida-Blanca was leaving for London, whither he had just been accredited

M. de Florida-Blanca is instructed to enlarge on this text and endeavour to effect a change in England's decision It is thought here, that even if the English Government cannot actually become the auxiliary of its ally Dona Maria, it might at least aid her indirectly by granting subsidies to Spain But I fancy the time for subsidies is passed

They are talking seriously here of convoking the Cortes It is a dangerous experiment, of which no one can foresee the result, but it has become impossible not to do so When one comes to think of the work to be accomplished by those who govern this country, one almost feels inclined to despair These are a few of the tasks imposed on them—altering the order of succession, changing the form of government, reforming the finances and the administration, putting down the civil war, and pacifying a neighbouring country—all this to be done too during a regency, and that regency entrusted to a woman !

M. de Florida-Blanca trusts that your Highness will honour him with your goodwill and assist him with your advice He knows how valuable it is, and that it is only by following it, that he can hope to succeed in the difficult mission that has been entrusted to him [1]

THE PRINCE DE TALLEYRAND TO THE DUC DE BROGLIE

LONDON, *March 4th*, 1834

MONSIEUR LE DUC,

The English Ministry have received news from Portugal, announcing that a serious engagement has taken place near Santarem between the troops of Dom Pedro and those of Dom Miguel [2] Baron Mortier's despatches, which I transmit to you to-day, will give you fuller and more circumstantial details than I could send you But I must warn you that the reports which have reached the British Ministry, and even the letters from persons attached to Dom Pedro's party, all agree in stating that this affair so much boasted of at first, was anything but decisive,

---

[1] The Duc de Broglie wrote at the same time to M. de Talleyrand " The French Cabinet continues to see in the prolongation of this struggle [in Portugal] one of the greatest dangers that could threaten the throne of Queen Isabella, and as it believes that the intervention of England can alone put an end to it, it does not yet give up all hope of inducing the London Cabinet to forego her neutrality M. de Florida-Blanca who is momentarily expected to arrive in Paris, has instructions to urge this point most vehemently with Lord Palmerston There is no need, Prince, for me to beg you to accord your support and advice to the Spanish Legation, whenever you think you can be of the slightest use to them "

[2] The battle took place on February 18th, the Miguelite troops beat a retreat after a desperate struggle

for Dom Miguel's army, according to the latest accounts, was four leagues in advance of Santarem

Although Dom Pedro's partizans consider his military forces sufficient to insure success to the cause of the young Queen, a great many enlistments are nevertheless being made in London, as well as purchases of arms and warlike stores

LONDON, *March 10th*, 1834

I have received your despatch, No 19 I will certainly not delay in offering my services to M de Florida-Blanca as soon as he arrives in London I should hope that the British Government, when better informed as to the real interests of the Peninsula and freed from the obstacles which home affairs impose on it, will at last recognize the necessity of renouncing the neutrality they have maintained in Portugal I have always endeavoured to lead it in that direction, and I will continue to do so after M de Florida-Blanca's arrival, but I must confess that, so far, I have but little hope we shall attain the end so greatly desired by the present Spanish Government

March 18th.

I think I ought to draw your particular attention to the account of the Parliamentary sitting last night in the House of Commons, reported in the English papers to-day A motion of Mr Sheil's,[1] requesting that all the documents relative to Eastern affairs should be laid before the House, gave rise to a very important discussion[2]

You will no doubt notice with pleasure those passages in Lord Palmerston's and Mr Stanley's[3] speeches, which referred specially to the political relations so happily established between France and Great Britain[4] The King's Government cannot fail

[1] Richard Lalor Sheil, born in 1791, an Irish writer and politician He entered the House of Commons, became Vice-President of the Board of Trade in 1839 and Master of the Mint in 1846. He was nominated Minister at Florence in 1850, and died the following year

[2] Mr Sheil's motion, which amounted to a vote of censure against the Cabinet, was rejected, notwithstanding the intervention of Sir Robert Peel

[3] Edward John, Baron Stanley of Alderley, born in 1802, entered the House of Commons in 1831, was Secretary of State for the Colonies from 1833 to 1834, Lord of the Treasury in the Melbourne Cabinet (1835-1841) Under-Secretary of State for Foreign Affairs in 1846 In 1852, he succeeded his father in the House of Lords, became Vice-President of the Board of Trade in 1853, and was made Privy Councillor in 1855 He became Postmaster General in 1860

[4] Lord Palmerston " The relations between France and England become each day more friendly As both Governments know each other better, they appreciate one another more, and it is, I must confess, a real matter of pride and satisfaction to me, to think that the prejudices which divided both countries have almost entirely disappeared "

to be satisfied with the language of both ministers, which was not only honourable to France, but which proved to the eyes of Europe in a manner very favourable to us, the union of the two countries   This union should be the aim of all our efforts   its realization has already procured us and promises also (so it seems to me) still further good results   .

March 27th

I gave Lord Palmerston the letter to read which you wrote to the French *Chargé d'Affaires* at the Hague, requesting him to ask some explanation from M de Zuylen, respecting the movements that have taken place in the Dutch army.[1] Lord Palmerston approves of this step so thoroughly, that he will cause a similar request to be made at the Hague, and has sent a memorandum to the English *Chargé d'Affaires*, which he is to give to M de Zuylen   This memorandum is worded almost in the same terms as the letter of which you were kind enough to send me a copy.

I did not suggest any alterations in the form of his representations to the Hague, but I think that your letter to M Drouyn de l'Huys[2] is preferable, and that it is better to avoid the use of a diplomatic Note, the formality of which may sometimes offend   I am induced to think this from the example I have just seen. You are aware that the Vienna Cabinet sent an evasive reply, somewhat like that from Berlin to the Note of the English ambassador, relative to the events which have taken place at Luxembourg.[3]

[1] This incident resulted in nothing   The Duc de Broglie wrote on the 31st March : " The anxiety manifested by the Belgians did not actually rest on any positive facts   It has entirely disappeared now, and the Brussels Cabinet itself admits, that it gave too ready credence to the reports of its agents."   (Despatch of the Duc de Broglie to M de Talleyrand)

[2] Edward Drouyn de l'Huys, born in 1805, entered the diplomatic service and was attached to the Embassy at Madrid in 1830, was then for three years *Chargé d'Affaires* at the Hague   and in 1836 First Secretary at Madrid   In 1840, he became Director of Commercial Affairs at the Foreign Office   and Deputy for Melun in 1842   Re-elected in 1848, he became Minister for Foreign Affairs the same year, Ambassador to London (1849), again Minister in 1851, and later on Vice President of the Senate   He again entered the Ministry in 1852, left it in 1855, and came in once more in 1862.

[3] A fresh incident had just occurred at Luxembourg.   The Belgian Government, relying on the treaty of May 21st, which had guaranteed the territorial *statu quo* of Belgium   had commenced the usual sale of felled timber   and the levy of the militia in the German part of Luxembourg   General Dumoulin, who commanded the fortress of Luxembourg, objected to this, and the Government anxious to avoid all conflicts, desisted   Nevertheless, as the notices relative to the militia levy had been posted up by the Communes, General Dumoulin carried off M Hanno, the Belgian district commissioner, notwithstanding that he was outside the strategic radius   and made him his prisoner (January 15th)   The Belgian Cabinet appealed to France and England, who made representations to the Diet   This latter at once gave orders for the Belgian commissioner's release and repudiated General Dumoulin's action.

But M de Metternich at the same time instructed the Austrian ambassador in London to give fuller explanations to the English Cabinet   These explanations refer to the two facts which had served as a pretext for the arrest of M Hanno, that is to say, the levy of the militia and the sale of the felled timber within the strategic radius of the fortress of Luxemburg   With regard to the first of these points, M de Metternich maintains that the Belgian Government was in the wrong, because the levy of the militia is entirely a military question, and on that ground the commandant of the fortress could oppose the measures of the Belgian administration   As to the sale of the felled timber, the chancellor believes that Belgium had the right to claim that privilege, and adds somewhat ironically, that on this point he cannot share the opinion of Lord Palmerston, who, at the outset of the discussion, had condemned the Belgian action   M de Metternich makes use of this last circumstance, to show the impartiality he has brought to bear on the facts, and he winds up by expressing the astonishment felt at Vienna at the course adopted by the English Cabinet, for which he says there was no ground whatever, as England had a minister at Frankfort and Belgium had one at Vienna, and that the proper course would have been to instruct one of these agents to act, and not the English Embassy in Austria[1]   Throughout the whole of M de Metternich's communication, there runs a tone which plainly shows how little goodwill he bears to the English Government, or it may be to Lord Palmerston alone, and one perceives that the chancellor has eagerly seized the occasion to condemn the memorandum, remitted perhaps somewhat too thoughtlessly, by Sir Frederick Lamb to the Austrian Cabinet

I have communicated the news from Madrid which you transmitted to me, to Lord Palmerston   He was very pleased to hear of the entry of eight thousand Spaniards into Portugal, and I did not think it was necessary to enter into further explanations[2]

---

[1] France had intervened at Vienna, simultaneously with England, respecting the occurrence at Luxembourg   M de Sainte-Aulaire wrote about it stating that he had found M de Metternich very ill-disposed as to this matter, and that this ill-feeling was due to the Note which Sir Frederick Lamb had transmitted to him   M de Metternich declared that Austria could not interfere in this more than the other Powers   When pressed by the ambassador he at last admitted that General Dumoulin's proceeding had been indefensible, and that if he had been in the Austrian service, he would have been recalled at once   (M de Sainte-Aulaire's despatch to the Department, March 9th)

[2] Spain's intervention in Portugal had been provoked by Dom Miguel's attitude   Having taken refuge near the frontiers of the two countries, he had refused to recognize Queen Isabella, and had welcomed Don Carlos as King of Spain, aiding him in every way   The Government of the Queen Regent took advantage of these facts to send General Rodil with 8,000 men into Portugal, with orders to assist Dom Pedro   (April 16th)

The English Cabinet only looks at the Portuguese side of the question in all this, and are in favour of everything that may lead to its solution. Nevertheless, we are both surprised that the Spanish Queen Regent should, in her present position, be able to dispense with eight thousand men; it would lead one to suppose, that her difficulties were in reality less great than one imagined, but that I find in your despatch more than one reason for modifying this opinion.

March 31st

At the last interview I had with Lord Palmerston and Lord Grey, before the departure of these ministers for the country, they spoke to me about a despatch they had just received from Vienna, in which Sir Frederick Lamb gave them an account of a conversation he had had with the Prince de Metternich. It appears that in this conversation, the chancellor brought forward one of those questions which he loves to uphold and enlarge upon. The one referred to was respecting the Ottoman Empire, whose speedy downfall he predicted. As a reason for this he assigned the Mohammedan religion, which had placed the Turkish race under the yoke of an absurd fanaticism, an enemy to all progress in the midst of European populations, whose tendency was perpetually to modify it. Applying this view to the Arab race and without caring a straw for the contradiction ...... bold enterprises of the Pasha of Egypt, M. de Metternich declared this latter race to be equally incapable for the same reason of becoming fit successors to power in Turkey, and he added, that it would be necessary to seek for a fresh combination to avert the catastrophe which was brewing in the East, or at any rate to take advantage of what might happen there.

To this extent, at any rate on that day, the chancellor limited his confidences, but both English ministers, desirous of still further ascertaining the Chancellor's views, strove to discover what the Vienna Cabinet proposed to substitute for the present state of affairs in Turkey; and having put on one side the idea of a European Prince at Constantinople, they concluded that the *arrière-pensée* which dominated M. de Metternich, was a division of the Ottoman Empire. I have not attempted to oppose this conviction on the part of Lord Palmerston and Lord Grey, although I think they have allowed themselves to be too much influenced by what M. de Metternich, probably with that fickleness to which he is prone, has said; but I thought I ought to inform you of the chancellor's conversation, and the impression it has produced on the English Cabinet.

The ministers will be out of town until April 7th, on account of the Easter holidays   .

Matters had arrived at this stage, when an unfortunate incident occurred which momentarily disturbed the confidence which the English Government seemed at last to have placed in our Cabinet   I refer to the resignation of the Duc de Broglie, which he considered it necessary to tender in consequence of the vote in the Chamber of Deputies rejecting the treaty concluded between France and the United States of America [1] This treaty settled the compensation claimed twenty years before by the United States for depredations committed by the French Navy during the wars of the Empire

France undertook to pay twenty-five million francs to the United States, and on account of this clause the treaty was submitted to the Chamber of Deputies   It had been signed by General Sebastiani when Minister of Foreign Affairs, but the Duc de Broglie generously assumed the responsibility of it   An intrigue was raised in the Chamber to defeat the proposal of the Government   It succeeded, and the Duc de Broglie tendered his resignation   Some letters which I received from Paris on this occasion, are sufficiently interesting to induce me to give them a place here

MADAME ADELAIDE D'ORLEANS TO THE PRINCE DE TALLEYRAND

PARIS, *April 2nd,* 1834

MON CHER PRINCE,

I feel sure that you would like to hear from me just now, therefore, although I know nothing as yet of what is probably being now decided at the Council, which our king has been holding ever since half-past ten this morning (and it is now half-past two), after having been in Council last night till midnight, I sit down to lament with you over the deplorable vote passed in the Chamber yesterday   It is very serious and very unfortunate

---

[1] Treaty of 4th July 1831   The question dealt with in this treaty had been pending ever since 1812   The United States demanded seventy millions , they ended by accepting the sum of twenty-five millions offered by France, and conceding in addition several reductions in the wine and silk duties   This treaty, which was submitted to the Chamber on the 28th March, was rejected after a discussion lasting five days, by 176 votes to 168   The Duc de Broglie at once tendered his resignation

I understand that the Duc de Broglie and Sebastiani will not remain in, and what other sad consequences may not arise from this rejection of the American treaty! What ignorance and what folly on the part of this Chamber, which acted so wisely with respect to the law of the associations

3 o'clock The king is still in Council, but General Sebastiani, who has just come from there, tells me that M de Rigny will probably be nominated Minister of Foreign Affairs I do not yet know who will replace M de Rigny in the Marine In other respects the Ministry remains the same, which is what one would wish under the present circumstances

It is said that already there is a reaction, and regret concerning the vote in the Chamber Unfortunately, it is too late .

4th April

I hoped, when I wrote to you on the 2nd, to be able to tell you yesterday that the arrangement in the Ministry had been accomplished as I thought, namely, with the least possible change, –for that very reason alone, and under present circumstances, the best thing that could be done This also was the opinion of Marshal Soult, Sebastiani, and at first, of the majority of the Council The first stumbling-block was M Molé, to whom there was some objection on your account and that of England In truth as you observed in your letter, nothing but the king's authority, his forbearance, and his conciliatory spirit could have succeeded in keeping his Ministry together so long, Men become tired of working together, and what satisfied them at first does not content them after a time The king has the most difficult task, for he has to reconcile and keep everyone together , but, thank heaven, he is one who, for the sake of his country, can face anything It needs his patience, his strength of mind and determination, to stand up against it Nothing has yet been decided about the Ministry Meanwhile, everyone remains at his post . .

5th April

The great business of the Ministry was at length concluded yesterday evening I send you enclosed the *Moniteur*, which will give you the entire new Cabinet [1] They are men of ability, and I hope matters will work well I am very thankful that it is settled, as our king sadly needed some rest after all the

[1] The new Ministry was formed on the 4th of April Marshal Soult, M Humann, and M Guizot kept their posts, M Thiers went from Commerce and Public Works to the Home Office , M de Rigny, Minister of Marine, to the Foreign Office M Duchâtel took Commerce, and M Persil was appointed Keeper of the Seals Admiral Jacob became Minister of Marine after the refusal of Admiral Roussin, to whom the post was offered

fatigues and anxieties of every kind he has had lately There is one omission in the *Moniteur* which I send you, but it will be corrected, namely, that Sebastiani has been made ambassador at Naples, where he will do excellently

One thing has greatly vexed us, namely, that several of the English papers, and others also, desire to attribute the close union between France and England and the idea of the alliance, to other causes than the influence of the king and yourself, whereas, as the king says, he is the father of it, and you are the godfather ! You must lay claim to this honour, both for yourself and for him .

LORD HOLLAND TO THE PRINCE DE TALLEYRAND.

HOLLAND HOUSE, *April 4th*, 1834

What vexatious news ! May one not hope that M de Broglie will take back his portfolio ? Why will they not attend to the wise counsel of the ancient monk, who said :

" In omnibus tuis cogitationibus semper caveto de resignationibus " ?

Tell me, I pray you, all you know about it

LORD BROUGHAM TO THE PRINCE DE TALLEYRAND

April 4th, 1834

MON CHER PRINCE,
A thousand condolences on the resignation of our good friend in Paris Nothing could have been worse just now But we must redouble our efforts so that nothing shall injure the ties so happily established between our two countries. That is the point on which nearly all my foreign policy turns, and yours likewise, as I well know .

THE DUC DE BROGLIE TO THE PRINCE DE TALLEYRAND

April 6th, 1834

MON PRINCE,
I have delayed writing to you until the crisis we have just come out of was over I had not the courage to do so while it lasted Although I was fully resolved, and though I was convinced that the resolution I had taken was indispensable, my anxiety was intense when I saw that power threatened to pass into the hands of those who would deliver it up to our enemies I feared I should not be able to conceal this from you Thank heaven, everything is ended, and happily so The Council has been reformed , it is more united, stronger, and more firmly seated than

the preceding one , nothing will be changed in its working , every-thing will be done more unanimously and with greater vigour and speed The impotency of our adversaries has again been forcibly proved , they are very much ashamed of themselves and much put out

I have therefore only to congratulate myself on what I have done , but even if matters had turned out differently, I could not have acted otherwise

A Minister of Foreign Affairs is obliged every day to pledge the faith of his Government, and to do so, more often than not, without consulting his colleagues or taking the king's orders Every word he utters is at once taken hold of, and sent to the four quarters of Europe , it is not only necessary that his language should be sincere, but that it should also be guarded One ought to be able to rely on it, not merely as being frank, but as being a reality He must not merely have the desire, but he must have the power of fulfilling what he has promised But from the moment it is seriously established, that the Minister for Foreign Affairs is not in a position to obtain the respect of the Chamber for a pledge given in the name of the Government, he is bound to retire , the interest of the country requires it, and his own honour demands it One of the reasons, which more than anything else contributed to the rejection of the American treaty, was that the Government would in fact have been very glad if its hand had been forced , I therefore felt I could no longer hesitate in giving the most public denial to such baseness

Another reason also left me no liberty of choice The Chamber did not see what would be the result of its action , it imagined, no matter what was said to it, that the rejection of a treaty was quite a simple matter , that a treaty might be put aside like an amendment to a law of local interest , it fancied, that in warning it of the consequences, I, as it were, overrated them , that in stating that I attached my own ministerial existence, and probably that of the entire Cabinet, to the vote, was merely a form of speech , that I was a sort of Marshal Soult, first threaten-ing to leave, and then accommodating myself to whatever posi-tion fate chose to assign me I was therefore obliged to prove the contrary, and to evince to the Chamber that there are things and men in the world whom one cannot lightly treat with impunity The lesson has been a severe one, and the anxiety of the majority has been very great during the last few days I trust this anxiety will bear fruit Nevertheless, it is quite certain that at present the Chamber is greatly humiliated at its conduct, and that the treaty will now be passed by four-fifths of the votes

You have always been so kind to me, mon Prince, but more

especially during the last eighteen months, that I feel bound to
acquaint you with my reasons for the step I took As for my
successor, you know him as well as I do , the king and my colleagues insisted, so to speak, that I should name him myself I
feel sure that he will follow the course I have hitherto pursued
under your auspices and according to your advice This he is
fully resolved to do He has great talent and is very able I
believe he is sincerely attached to me, in fact I am sure of it ,
whatever good I could have done he will do, and do it even
better than I, because the accession of M Duchâtel,[1] as
Minister of Commerce, will furnish him with the means I count
greatly on the excellent principles and feelings of this young
man, in drawing still closer the alliance between France and
England He is a man of distinguished ability My only and
real grief is, that the friendly intercourse which I have had with
you, and through you with the English Ministry, among whom
I count several friends, is interrupted But I trust they will not
quite forget me, and will consider, that neither by entering the
Ministry, remaining there, nor leaving it, have I falsified the impression they had formed of me

Pray mon Prince, kindly remember me to Madame de Dino,
and count for ever on my sincere and unalterable friendship

ADMIRAL COMTE DE RIGNY TO THE PRINCE DE
TALLEYRAND

PARIS, *April 6th*, 1834

MON PRINCE,

A political hurricane has cast me, in spite of myself,
on a platform, where I feel my complete insufficiency I foresee
all that awaits me

In order to overcome my reluctance, they have repeatedly
assured me that I should not be personally disagreeable to you,
and that my advent would not be ill-received by those who are
around you

Driven into a corner, urged on by my colleagues, and perceiving that if I refused, the king had only one desperate
resource left, I accepted a burden, which the near and pressing
discussions make me dread

Allow me to count on your support and advice , on receiving
this assurance from you, I shall feel encouraged, and of this I
have great need

[1] Charles Marie Tanneguy Comte Duchâtel, born in 1803 was made Councillor
of State in 1830, and elected a deputy in 1833 He was Minister of Commerce from
1834 to 1839 , finally, he was made Minister of the Interior from 1840 to 1848 He
retired from public life after the Revolution of February, and died in 1867

I cannot to-day give you all the particulars of the last few days, but I did not wish to lose a moment in adding a fresh expression of my devotion to the official announcement.

THE PRINCE DE TALLEYRAND TO THE DUC DE BROGLIE.

LONDON, *April 7th*, 1834

MON CHER DUC,

Nothing can be more honourable than your resignation ; this opinion can however only suffice for you ; it leaves us room for deep regret, the expression of which is evinced by the entire English Ministry in a variety of ways. You cannot for a moment doubt my feelings, or my devoted friendship. Pray offer my kindest and most respectful homage to Madame de Broglie. Adieu.

LONDON, *April 10th*, 1834

MON CHER DUC,

If your admirable letter of the 6th still further increased the regret which your actual retirement from office caused me, it has also occasioned me a great pleasure, namely, that of reading it to Lord Grey, Lord Brougham and Lord Holland, and of seeing the deep and keen impression it made on them. They found a fresh motive therein for rendering you all honour, and welcoming M. de Rigny, whose name is already well known and greatly appreciated here. They read with great pleasure what you wrote to me relative to the invariability of the system, the sentiments, and the principles of our Government. This, mon cher Duc, you will be as glad to hear as I am to tell it you, both for the general good and your own personal satisfaction. Do not entirely cease writing to me, and give me accounts sometimes of yourself and of France. Your letters may be most useful to me : I trust to you to write when you have time. A thousand best wishes. P.S.—Keep what I am now going to tell you to *yourself.* Your admirable and *useful* letter has been to Windsor, where it had a most excellent effect in every way.

THE PRINCE DE TALLEYRAND TO THE COMTE DE RIGNY

LONDON, *April 7th*, 1834

MONSIEUR LE COMTE,

I have just heard, in an indirect way it is true, that the King has called upon you to assume the direction of the Foreign Office, and I will not wait to receive the official confirmation of the news, in order to express to you how greatly pleased I am. I have not the slightest doubt that it will be equally well received by the English Government, and from what I have gathered in the various conversations which I have had with His Britannic Majesty about you, I feel convinced that the king's choice will, in present circumstances, be personally agreeable to the King of England

The English ministers have not yet returned to town, and consequently I have not been able to see Lord Palmerston to-day, or converse with him respecting the matters mentioned by the Duc de Broglie in his despatches Nos 26 and 27 [1] I will not fail to give you an account of the successive results of my interviews on everything in these despatches relating to Spain, Portugal, and the Germanic Diet , but I lose no time in calling your attention to a question which, it seems to me, greatly needs it I refer to Turkish affairs, and especially as they affect our position with England

The honourable and important command which you have so long held in the Greek Archipelago, the thorough knowledge of the interests and the situation of the various Eastern Powers which you have acquired, the position which you have for some years occupied in the Government, and by which means you have been kept informed of all the political relations of France, obviate, Monsieur le Comte, my having to recall facts and events which are vividly present to your memory I shall therefore only confine myself to what has more recently taken place

If you will have the goodness to look over the despatch which I had the honour to send M le Duc de Broglie on the 24th December last, [2] you will find the details of a draft treaty for a defensive alliance, which I had submitted to the English Cabinet This treaty between France and England, which in my opinion ought to be based on maintaining the European *statu quo*, had the advantage of being applicable not only to Eastern affairs, but also to any complications that might arise elsewhere The despatch referred to contains full particulars The proposal was not welcomed by the English Government, and if I did not then insist on carrying it through, I was none the less convinced of its immense utility

More than three months have elapsed since that period, and the events which have happened meanwhile have only still further confirmed me in the opinion, that a defensive treaty of alliance, such as we drew up, has, one might say, become an actual necessity, to England as well as to France

---

[1] These despatches related to Spanish affairs (see despatch, in Appendix, letter No 15)

[2] See page 195.

In fact the discussions both in the English Parliament and in the Chamber of Deputies, have plainly revealed an anxiety, which neither Russia's explanations, nor those of the Porte, have tended to allay completely. The efforts of the Northern Governments on the one hand, and those of the periodical press on the other, have been redoubled in order to rupture, or at any rate to weaken, the close union that exists between France and Great Britain, and we must not conceal from ourselves, that these attempts have not failed in making some impression in this country. The change that has just taken place in the French Cabinet has already been interpreted in this sense, and for all these joint reasons I think it would be very advisable just now to renew the unsuccessful attempt of last December, and propose to England to form a defensive treaty of alliance with us.

Not only would it be the best possible answer to those who accuse us of having withdrawn from the English alliance in order to curry favour with Russia, but likewise the best means of dispelling the distrust of the English Cabinet, if by chance it has conceived any as to our good faith.

If the English Government, better disposed this time, should enter into our views, there is no doubt that we should gain immense advantages. A treaty of alliance between the two Governments would consolidate our position in Europe. It would offer to everyone a guarantee for security and the maintenance of peace, because it would put a complete stop to all the intrigues of the other Cabinets who are endeavouring to separate us.

You may feel quite assured, Monsieur le Comte, that by placing the king's Government on this line of conduct, I do not in any way wish to isolate it in Europe, or compel it to espouse all the well or ill-grounded quarrels of England; such a result would be quite opposed to my idea. I am fully convinced that a striking exhibition of the union of the two countries could only tend to draw the other Cabinets nearer to us, for being compelled to accept an accomplished fact, they would only attach a still higher value to it as lessening the consequences of what might befall them.

If the views I have just expressed strike you as strongly as they have done me, and if you think them sufficiently important to determine the king's Government to make a fresh attempt at an alliance with the British Government, you should not lose any time in speaking about it to Lord Granville, and also to Lord Durham during his sojourn in Paris. I, on my side, will not neglect anything that may make our proposal acceptable here, as

soon as I receive your authority You will understand, that
in that case it will also be necessary to send me a general
scheme of the conditions you desire should be contained in the
treaty

But whatever is decided, allow me to urge upon you the
necessity of choosing a successor to Admiral Roussin at Constantinople without delay,[1] and of selecting an able and prudent
man and one well versed in diplomacy By so doing, we shall
avoid such reproaches as were showered on the English Ministry,
owing to the long-delayed departure of Lord Ponsonby for
Constantinople

April, 9th, 1834

I received the despatch yesterday, which you did me the
honour to write, and I was at once enabled to make use, in my
interviews with Lord Palmerston and Lord Grey, of the explanations it contained, with reference to the change that has
just taken place in the French Ministry These explanations
were very well received by both ministers, who, as I had already
foretold in my despatch of the day before yesterday, consider
your appointment to the Foreign Office as a guarantee that the
king's Government will continue that system of moderation
and firmness which has already produced such advantageous
results

At the interview I had with Lord Palmerston, there was some
conversation relative to the last Notes received from the Porte.
Lord Palmerston, while stating that no definite resolution had
been come to by the English Government with regard to this,
told me that he had thought it best to let this matter stand over
for the present, and that later on, we might jointly arrange such
a course as might be considered necessary, either at Constantinople or elsewhere I did not wish to insist upon this point,
before hearing your answer to my despatch of the day before
yesterday

. The recent advent of M le Comte de Florida
Blanca, who came to see Lord Palmerston while I was with him,
afforded me a good opportunity of speaking to the latter as to the
state of the Peninsula He gave me some details, very similar
to those contained in M de Broglie's despatch No 26,[2] as to what
had taken place in Madrid, after the arrival in that capital of M de

---

[1] Admiral Roussin remained at Constantinople As he had been nominated
Minister of the Marine, M de Talleyrand thought he would have quitted his post, but
one can quite understand that the Admiral refused the portfolio and preferred retain-
ing his Embassy
[2] See this despatch in Appendix, letter No 15

Sarmento, the Portuguese minister It appears that Mr Villiers, nevertheless does not yet despair of obtaining a frank and open declaration from M Martinez de la Rosa on the part of the Spanish Government, against Dom Miguel Lord Palmerston proposed to urge M de Florida Blanca to write in a similar sense to his Court I was then enabled to question him as to the communications which had lately been made by Lord Howard de Walden to Dom Pedro's Government According to what Lord Palmerston told me, the scheme for the pacification of Portugal, is not so far advanced as was thought at Lisbon, and the articles which were sent to our Foreign Office by M Mortier, would appear only to be suggestions for the points on which the English minister has been requested to sound Dom Pedro's Government The English Cabinet always prefers limiting its relations with the Portuguese Government to official steps, and is very far removed from any idea of intervening by sending troops to the Peninsula

I do not know how far this declaration by Lord Palmerston is true, I will try to verify its exactness by other means, which are not available just now, and I shall have the honour of informing you of the result of my researches   .

THE COMTE DE RIGNY TO THE PRINCE DE TALLEYRAND

PARIS, *April 10th*, 1834

MON PRINCE,

I am very sensible of all the kind things you have said to me I know how much I am in need of your counsel and support which I shall not fail to claim

Maison's despatches show a growing irritation on the part of Russia against England I do not know whether I am mistaken, but I think the English Cabinet might perhaps be induced by this situation to favour the idea which you suggested at a certain period, and which the new Congress at Vienna might revive again[1]

Home affairs here will feel the recoil of what is happening

---

[1] M de Sarmento had asked the Spanish Cabinet to intervene in Portugal in favour of Dom Pedro M Martinez de la Rosa had refused to assist him, but he had freely offered to induce Portugal to disperse the Carlist forces who had taken refuge there He did not point out so with the Miguelites It was, in fact, though under a veiled or disguised and less decisive form, the intervention sought by M de Sarmento.

Charles Augustus Ellis, Baron Howard de Walden, English diplomatist born in 1779 Under Secretary of State for Foreign Affairs in 1824, Minister at Stockholm in 1832 Paris in 1834 and at Brussels 1840

at Lyons We expect news this morning That received last
night states that the troops had charged with spirit and carried
the barricades [1] It is absolutely necessary that this success
should be maintained, so as to put a stop to the plots at Stras-
burg, Dijon, and Châlons After that the course of the law as
regards the associations will be easier or less necessary'

We shall soon close this session, probably about the 10th of
May, and the elections will take place in June Dupin will
be away at that time

Disturbances would recommence again at Brussels, if the
presence of the troops did not keep them in check [2] La Tour-
Maubourg thinks that in order to bring matters home to the *indifferent townsmen* of Brussels, it will be necessary for him to come
to some arrangement with Sir Robert Adair, as to the steps to
be taken in case fresh troubles break out ; he will be authorized
to do this with the English minister . .

The difficulties caused by the retirement of the Duc de
Broglie from the Cabinet had barely been surmounted, when a
formidable insurrection broke out at Lyons, Paris soon following
suit All possible measures were quickly taken to repress it,
and I had no doubt that they would be successful ; but this
deplorable occurrence was not calculated to facilitate my negotiations in London I have already had occasion more than
once to state in these Memoirs, how little calculated such
accidents were to inspire confidence in foreign Governments
I should probably under these circumstances, have experienced
much greater difficulties had not the affairs of the Peninsula
obliged the English Government to approach us The following
correspondence will, I think, justify this remark —

[1] Insurrections at this period broke out afresh in different parts of the country, in
consequence of a general strike of the workmen at Lyons Six of the principal leaders
had been arrested , the commencement of their trial on the 5th April, was the signal for
a fierce struggle, which lasted five days The troops at last succeeded in re-establishing
order in the city Revolutionary movements had at the same time disturbed Marseilles,
Saint Étienne, Perpignan Chalons, and several other towns In Paris, a riot broke
out on the 12th April The cloister of Saint Merry was the scene of a bloody struggle
Quiet was not established until the 14th

[2] Orangist demonstrations, not however of any serious consequence, had recently
taken place in Belgium In Brussels great excitement prevailed, and this city became
the scene of serious disturbances on the 5th and 6th of April Bands of rioters
pillaged the houses of all the known partizans of the Prince of Orange But the disturbance was promptly and energetically put down

MADAME ADÉLAIDE D'ORLÉANS TO THE PRINCE DE TALLEYRAND

PARIS, *April* 11th, 1834

The terrible anxieties of the last fortnight have not left us a moment's peace. That about the Ministry was speedily followed by the one at Lyons. I hasten to let you know the news received this morning, which announce a complete success. The troops are masters of every position, and according to what the *préfet* wrote on the evening of the 9th, the result is assured; but one has always to lament the disasters which these successes bring upon those unfortunate persons who are their victims. The insurgents have retreated and barricaded themselves in some small streets, where however they will be at our discretion; it is impossible for them to hold out there. It seems that they have broken the telegraph near Lyons, at least we suppose so, as no telegraphic despatches have been received here since yesterday morning.

THE PRINCE DE TALLEYRAND TO THE COMTE DE RIGNY

LONDON, *April* 13th, 1834

MONSIEUR LE COMTE,

Lord Palmerston asked me to go and see him this morning, in order to discuss a subject which, he wrote, merited all our attention. I have just come back from this interview, which has been a pretty long one, and hasten to send you an account of it.

Lord Palmerston informed me that he had received, some days ago, a memorandum from the Comte de Florida Blanca, the new Spanish minister. This memorandum, which he showed me, contains a statement of the present condition of Spain, and invites the English Government to join the Spanish Government in putting an end to the agitation which has spread itself all over the Peninsula, by an active war made jointly against Dom Miguel and Don Carlos. It is a formal request for an English armed intervention in Portugal.

Lord Palmerston, after he had read this document to me, added, that M. de Sarmento, the Portuguese minister in London, had urgently supported this step on the part of the Spanish Cabinet, only verbally it is true, but insisting equally strongly on the necessity of an English armed intervention.

In the face of this simultaneous demand on the part of Spain and Portugal Lord Palmerston said, that His Britannic Majesty's

Government did not think they could any longer refuse to take a step which had been forced on them by circumstances, and that he was directed to reply to M de Florida Blanca's and M. de Sarmento's proposals, by a draft treaty to be signed between England, Spain, and Portugal By this treaty Spain undertakes to carry out actively, by every means in her power, the expulsion of Don Carlos and Dom Miguel from Portugal, and to retire from Portuguese territory as soon as this end has been attained Dona Maria's Government, on its side, will join Spain in this undertaking, and will consent to grant a general amnesty in Portugal, and make a suitable allowance to Dom Miguel at the expiration of the struggle   Lastly, England undertakes to send ships to the coasts of Spain and Portugal, to assist the Spanish army and that of Dom Pedro, but with the reservation, that she is in no case to be called upon to disembark English troops on any part of the Peninsula

"The draft of this treaty, which is already drawn up," continued Lord Palmerston," contains in addition an article, by which it is understood that the three Powers will agree to ask France to approve it; and it was for this purpose that I begged you to come and see me, in order to hear your opinion as to this proposal, and to ask whether you would be seriously disposed to give your adhesion to the treaty in question"

I did not hesitate a moment Monsieur le Comte, in replying to Lord Palmerston, that my Government would not refuse to agree to such a treaty, if England would, in return, consent to sign one of a nature similar to that which I had proposed to him in the end of December last, and of which all others would in future only be the natural result, but for my part, I did not think one was possible without the other, and that I would use my utmost efforts to prevent the king's Government from giving its consent to an act which would place it relatively in an inferior position

In reply to this, Lord Palmerston said that we should bear in mind that England's position with regard to Portugal was entirely different to ours, that she was united by special treaties to Portugal, and that this quite explained the different part we should take in this matter

But I in my turn then remarked, that our position as regards Spain was the same, that we had joint interests of neighbourhood, frontiers, and family ties with that country, and that these would most certainly be compromised if we played a part which, from no possible point of view, was suitable either to our dignity or our influence in Europe

I then proceeded afresh to impress on Lord Palmerston all

the weighty reasons which should decide the English Government to enter into a general defensive treaty of alliance with France, from which it would be perfectly easy to elaborate a complete and definite arrangement for the pacification of the Peninsula   In vain he tried to entrench himself behind the dangers England would run, by binding herself to an undertaking with our Cabinet, whose existence, he said, was not yet assured, and which might not even perhaps remain in power after the coming elections   I replied that there was the same danger for us, as we also might later on have to do with another English Government, that, moreover, the French Government, as now constituted, could never change its policy as regards England, and that if any alteration took place in its formation, the English Government would by this very fact, be freed from all engagements it might have contracted under other circumstances   In this way I combated this final objection, which seemed to me as futile in appearance as in reality

Not wishing, however, to reject Lord Palmerston's overtures entirely, and to allow it to be supposed at Madrid that we objected to an arrangement by means of which it might be possible to accomplish the pacification of the Peninsula, I concluded by proposing to him a medium course between his project and mine, should this latter be absolutely rejected by his Government   This consisted of a treaty between the four Powers, France, Great Britain, Spain, and Portugal   I made him see that it would be possible to draw up this act in such a way, that each of these Powers would preserve its own liberty of action

It was on this understanding that our conversation ended. He then went to attend a Cabinet Council, and promised me that he would make an exact statement of what had passed between us   He did not however conceal from me, that he, personally, had great objections to forming an alliance such as I had suggested   I replied, that I regretted this all the more earnestly, as I feared each day would only still further confirm the necessity of such a treaty for the peace of Europe

April 14th   Ten o'clock at night

As I informed you yesterday, a Cabinet Council was held immediately after my interview with Lord Palmerston. The proposal I had made of a general defensive treaty of alliance between France and England has not been accepted by the English ministers, notwithstanding that they admitted the force of the arguments I brought forward on this point   They persist in their scheme of a treaty between the Courts of England, Spain, and Portugal, to which we shall be asked to assent

I saw Lord Palmerston twice yesterday In our first interview he informed me of the resolution of his Government I did not therefore insist any further on the defensive treaty of alliance, which had still been in question between us the evening before, on that head I could not possibly hope for success I therefore objected to the treaty which he had communicated to me ; I disputed it with him and refused to sign it, as it was In consequence of the observations I made, he was obliged to have another consultation with his colleagues and the Spanish and Portuguese ministers, in order to submit the modifications which I demanded, according to which France would form one of the contracting parties to the treaty, instead of being merely a consenting one I must however tell you, that I had to sustain a lengthened struggle ere arriving at this concession

I have just seen Lord Palmerston, again, he has given me the new scheme, of which I have the honour to transmit you a copy

I did not pledge myself that this scheme would receive the approbation of the king's Government, and while merely promising to send it to you, I obtained the introduction of several alterations Among others, you will find that part of Article IV has been drawn up in two ways It has been agreed that in the event of the French Government consenting to my signing this treaty, it will choose whichever of the two renderings of Article IV will best satisfy it In the present state of affairs, I cannot see any real difficulty to the king's Government joining the treaty as it is, on the contrary, it appears to me to present some great advantages

I have not time to add a single remark to this simple narration I must not delay the departure of my courier Lord Granville is receiving instructions to come to an understanding with you, you will therefore be able to make known to him your reasons for granting or refusing your consent

I have to inform you that M de Florida Blanca and M de Sarmento, while taking upon themselves to affix their signatures to this treaty, which does not quite accord with their instructions, have requested that nothing should be said about it to the Spanish or Portuguese ministers in Paris—this has been promised them They are afraid that a premature disclosure, made either at Madrid or Lisbon, might compromise the success of the treaty, the ratification of which, they say, could not well be refused, after it has once been signed by the French and English plenipotentiaries

As they are very anxious here to arrive at some decision, I

R 2

pray you to send me your earliest reply as speedily as possible, and by telegraph

April 15th, 1834

The Prince de Lieven showed me this morning a despatch he had just received from St Petersburg, in which the Comte de Nesselrode informs him, that the Imperial Government of Russia is perfectly satisfied with the last explanations given by France and England respecting Eastern affairs The Vice-Chancellor also expresses the desire to see all the discussions which have unfortunately arisen on this question during the last few months, buried in oblivion, and gives the assurance that his master, the emperor, wishes to retain no recollection of them

MADAME ADELAIDE D'ORLÉANS TO THE PRINCE DE TALLEYRAND

April 14th, 1834

I had not the slightest idea, mon cher Prince, when I wrote to tell you yesterday that everything was over at Lyons, that a few hours later we should have barricades raised in a corner of Paris[1] This was however but a snare for committing some assassinations, for not one was defended , a band of assassins and cowardly wretches has been let loose on Paris We have passed a terrible night, and even up to now are in the most cruel anxiety while our beloved king is out walking through the city, and also Chartres and Nemours, who both went out into the Rue St Martin this morning, with the wretches firing down on them from the windows of a house Thank heaven all is over now The Chamber of Deputies have just come in a body to testify their indignation to the king, and assure him afresh by the mouth of their President of their attachment to his person The Chamber of Peers are also coming The people are admirable and filled with indignation The National Guard behaved splendidly, as also did the regular troops , unfortunately, several of them fell victims to these ruffians

THE COMTE DE RIGNY TO THE PRINCE DE TALLEYRAND.

PARIS, *April 14th,* 11 *o'clock,* 1834

MON PRINCE,

It is now eleven o'clock , the whole night has been passed under arms , the insurgents, barricaded inside the houses, fired individually on the troops, the affair degenerated into

[1] See page 239

partial assassinations, there was no other organized resistance, and it was impossible to make use of artillery The troops and the National Guard have also lost several officers, who were picked out   There is therefore no public danger, but individual assassinations   The day will pass in this way ; the soldiers have been aroused to the extreme limit, and have given no quarter wherever they have effected an entrance [1] We are just now deliberating as to the measures to be proposed to the Chambers

At Lyons, matters have pretty well come to an end , there have been some sanguinary executions there At Châlons, Dijon, and St Etienne, several attempts were made, but the troops remained firm everywhere, and likewise the National Guard in Paris ; but one cannot say as much for it in other places

Upon the whole, the event, or rather the events, are of a nature to strengthen the Government   I will continue to keep you informed up to the time of the courier's departure

The same Day, 3 *in the Afternoon*

The streets are almost quiet again , some houses are still being searched, and I am unable to give you full details which can only be gradually collected

We are greatly exercised in trying to find means to make the most of this, in order to consolidate all that has been so terribly shaken   Unfortunately, we can do nothing with the Press   To-morrow something will be brought before the Chambers—*what*, will only be decided this evening   It will probably consist in an effective increase of the army

The National Guard has been increased considerably   We are sending it out in all directions, for we must be in advance everywhere   I pray you to pardon my being so brief and so hurried

THE PRINCE DE TALLEYRAND TO THE COMTE DE RIGNY

LONDON, *April* 17*th*, 1834

You will have seen from my previous despatches, that I had forestalled the instructions you sent me in your letter No. 30, by working by myself with the English ministers to induce them to conclude a defensive treaty of alliance with us.   The fact of the treaty respecting the affairs of the Peninsula appeared to me too important a matter not to take advantage of, and if I did

---

[1] It was during this riot that the bloody episode of the Rue Transnonain occurred

not succeed in my attempt, I am at least certain that I have not compromised the dignity of the king's Government, which I had not time to consult, when I was asked to sign the treaty between the four Powers Here everyone is impatiently awaiting your decision respecting this last treaty, all the members of the Cabinet whom I saw this morning, eagerly questioned me on this subject, and I could only promise them a speedy reply

The occurrences at Lyons and Paris, at present preoccupy everyone, to the exclusion of all other matters I have already made use of the information contained in your despatch No 31, and it was not difficult for me to show the advantages which England, probably more than any other country, would gain by the prompt and energetic repression of excesses, such as those committed at Lyons It will have all the greater effect here, as for the last few days some serious disturbances are going on among the workmen in several of the manufacturing districts in England, caused by associations of a similar nature to those we are trying to put down in France I may tell you, that public opinion, which is of some value here, is quite with us in this matter, notwithstanding what some of the periodical Press organs may say, all sensible men are grateful to the King's Government for restraining the revolutionary inclinations of those who only wish to disturb the peace of Europe, by first delivering France up to anarchy . .

THE COMTE DE RIGNY TO THE PRINCE DE TALLEYRAND

PARIS, *April 17th,* 1834, 4 *o'clock*

MON PRINCE,

I am as much grieved as I am troubled, that I can only send you observations in place of a positive affirmative

I have found many scruples among my colleagues, not as to the fact for your idea of a defensive alliance is adopted by all, but as to the form The King shared these scruples, and was somewhat put out at finding himself in a preamble, which appears again in the middle of the treaty

However secret this convention may be kept for a time, it will leak out, and you can understand what would be said, if Art V allowed it to be too apparent that at the requisition of the three Courts, we would furnish arms and troops, not that we should be pledged to do this by your wording, but we might be accused of it, and these accusations, although unjust, would weaken the effect of this Convention, even with regard to the result to be gained therefrom, namely, a more visible union with England

We here fully recognize the serious difficulty you have had to overcome, in order to obtain even a first concession; the present was against us, the future appeared equally so—the riots in Lyons, and those in Paris, general feeling, everything was against us Now the position has improved, though I dare not venture to say, mon Prince, that you can profit by it, as probably in London they hardly as yet judge us as we here judge ourselves

All this will notably influence the elections, for it is especially the *bourgeois electoral class* that is threatened by these agitations, it feels it, and the effect in Paris is undeniable If therefore we can hasten the dissolution of the Chambers and the Convocation, our policy will be strengthened This is the opinion of reflecting men

I have just come from Lord Granville, and have given him all the reasons I intend to bring forward at the Council this morning He is writing to Lord Palmerston by our courier, and seems inclined to side with us

I have endeavoured to assist you, by having the official despatch drawn up in such a way that it can be shown to Lord Palmerston

If, in adopting the principle of our idea, there should only arise the question of changing or otherwise transposing the wording of the two articles which remain intact in the counter project, we do not think, mon Prince, in that case and in view of the urgency, that it would be necessary for you to return them to us here

We see that this is pressing, and that we must not allow England to take action alone with Spain We have availed ourselves of a former Memorandum of Martinez de la Rosa, which is almost similar to that which was accepted when we intervened in the treaty of 6th July, 1827, relative to Greece, consequent on a request from the Greek Government

After all, whatever noise may be made over the treaty in the north, we need not be afraid if we can succeed in obtaining credit for it at home You alone, mon Prince, can solve this problem, and the King entrusts himself with full confidence to your great influence and solicitude

THE PRINCE DE TALLEYRAND TO THE COMTE DE RIGNY

LONDON, *April* 19*th,* 1834

MONSIEUR LE COMTE,

I received the telegraphic despatch yesterday, which you did me the honour to send on the 17th, and this morning your despatch No 32, to which is attached the draft of the modified treaty between the four Powers

I had great difficulty yesterday in restraining the impatience of the plenipotentiaries of the three Courts, by the aid of your telegraphic despatch, as they had quite persuaded themselves that your assent was not at all doubtful

Immediately on the arrival of my courier this morning, I sent Lord Palmerston the packet Lord Granville had enclosed for him, and requested him to grant me an interview in the forenoon In the course of an hour he sent me the letter, a copy of which I have the honour to transmit to you herewith [see further on Memorandum No I] so as to enable you to judge of the nature of the opposition that I had to encounter I went to him at the hour appointed, and fully prepared as I was to find him excited over this business, he was even much more so than his letter had led me to expect One difficulty, which I could not have foreseen, still further increased my embarrassment—they had written from Paris that the King's Government approved the treaty, just as I had sent it, and it might therefore be concluded that the objections raised by me came from me alone I was then obliged to make use of your despatch No 32, I read part of it to Lord Palmerston, and while enlarging on the views it contains, I confined myself distinctly to the resolution of not signing anything but the conditions given me by you As to the personal remark about myself, I said that it could not be true, seeing that everything which related to France in this treaty, being the outcome of public opinion, I, placed as I was, could not judge of its disadvantages, and that the King's Government alone was in a position to estimate them

When I left Lord Palmerston, he went to the Cabinet Council, where I learn that the discussion was very hot, and that our observations were not very readily received After the Council was over I went to see both Lord Palmerston and Lord Grey. They were still far from convinced of the importance of our objections, but after a conversation of more than two hours, I at last obtained a promise that some signal changes would be made in the draft of the treaty Lord Palmerston's letter, which I received in the evening, and of which I enclose a copy together with the note which was added to it [see Documents Nos II and III,] will give you an idea of the progress I have already made There was only one preamble in which France and Great Britain were not placed on the same footing as regards Spain, which, according to my views, and I think yours also, Monsieur le Comte, was the essential point But there still remained two difficulties the article which concerns us in the treaty was relegated to the end, after the articles relating to the amnesty in Portugal and the allowance to the Infant Don Carlos, and, what was still more serious, they wished this article to be drawn up as follows —

" In order to attain the end proposed by the present treaty, His Majesty the King of the French undertakes to furnish such aid as may be jointly decided upon between him and the three other contracting parties, *when he shall be asked to do so by them* "

I have just written to Lord Palmerston, returning him the draft of the treaty, and asking him to eliminate the words, *when he shall be asked to do so by them*, as being a repetition of the same idea in the same article   I also demanded several other amendments   I cannot get his answer till to-morrow morning, for it is now eleven o'clock in the evening, therefore I have decided to delay the departure of my courier, in order to acquaint you with the definite result of the negotiation, which will probably be concluded some time to-morrow

April 20th

This morning I received a letter from Lord Palmerston of which I here enclose a copy [see Memorandum No IV], and I hastened to reply that I must insist on the elimination of the words I had asked for yesterday, or at all events an alteration in the wording of the article   He has sent me an amended article, which you will find in the copy of the treaty which accompanies this despatch ⸱ I have accepted it, because it seems to me to have no disadvantages, and because I had come to the end of all the objections I could with decency bring forward   You may therefore consider the treaty as drawn up in the form in which I send it you   It will be necessary to submit it for approval to the King, who is now at Windsor, and to have it copied in the four languages, which makes me fear that it will not even be signed to-morrow   I will forward it to you as soon as it is, but do not let it get noised abroad, lest it should be known at Madrid before the Spanish minister has had time to send it there

I must draw your attention to the fact that I have only sent you Lord Palmerston's letters to enable you to get an exact knowledge of the course of the negotiation   It is most important that these letters should remain completely secret , the slightest indiscretion with regard to this would seriously compromise our relations with England, and render my position here extremely unpleasant and difficult   I trust to you to destroy the copies of the letters as soon as you have read them   .

¹ See page 255

(Documents accompanying the above letter)

No. I.—LORD PALMERSTON TO THE PRINCE DE TALLEYRAND

STANHOPE STREET, *April 19th* 1834

MON CHER PRINCE,

I received the packet you sent me this morning with much regret. It is very unfortunate that so many difficulties should have arisen where we had not expected any. It seems that in Paris they have but imperfectly understood the principles and object of the treaty in question, and the alterations proposed to us would tend to denaturalise the whole transaction.

We hear that your Government has received a Note from Martinez de la Rosa of the same tenor as that remitted to me by M. de Miraflores,[1] I confess this has surprised me greatly, first, because M. de Miraflores' Note was not presented according to instructions received from his Court to that effect, but at my request, and in consequence of a conversation I had with him, and finally, in order to enable me to bring the arguments he had used to me verbally more faithfully before my colleagues. Again, what was the object of M. de Miraflores' Note? It was to tell us, that the Spanish Government, being aware that the Portuguese Government had asked us for material aid against Dom Miguel, would be glad if we would consent to send troops to Portugal, because the interests of Spain suffered from Don Carlos' presence in Portugal. But the Portuguese Government had not addressed a similar request to you, how then could M. Martinez ask you to accede to a request which had not been made to you?

Your Government may have received a communication from M. Martinez, as in the past it had received from M. de Zea, relative to a French intervention in the affairs of Spain, but it is not a question now of the home affairs of Spain, but of Portuguese affairs. But even if, as your Government appears to think, it was a question of a foreign intervention in the affairs of Spain, we should not hesitate to declare, that in asking you for such an intervention, M. Martinez would fail to recognize the

[1] Don Manuel de Pando, Marquis de Miraflores, Comte de Florida Blanca born in 1792, afterwards envoy extraordinary in London, was ambassador in Paris in 1838. He subsequently became head of the Cabinet, then Governor of the Royal Domains, and Senator in 1848.

real interests of Spain, and that your Government, in acceding to it, would, it appears to me, fail to recognize the true interests of France But in any case, so far from joining in any such request, or sanctioning it by an article in the treaty—as it is now proposed we should do—we should certainly protest against it as a matter injurious to all parties

Consequently, as regards the alteration in the basis of the treaty desired in Paris, you must surely feel, mon Prince, that we cannot possibly adopt it

As to the alteration in the wording, it has already cost the ministers of Spain, Portugal, and myself sufficient trouble to bring our polyglot production into harmony, and I must beg of you not to impose a fresh task on us Time is passing , we have lost two days, Wednesday and Thursday, on account of the Court, and we hope that you will consider yourself authorized to sign the document as it stands Try and come here, if you can, before one o'clock, as the Cabinet Council meets at two Always yours   .

No II —LORD PALMERSTON TO THE PRINCE DE TALLEYRAND.

FOREIGN OFFICE, *April* 19*th*, 1834

MON CHER PRINCE,

We will agree to substitute the paragraph, a draft of which I now enclose, in place of the existing paragraph in the treaty, and the last article will therefore undergo the slight change I have made in it If this suits you, I will propose these alterations to the King and to the Spanish and Portuguese plenipotentiaries Kindly send me a reply this evening

No III —(*Enclosed in the above*)

In consequence of this article, T M the Regents have addressed themselves to T M the King of the French and the King of Great Britain, and their said majesties, taking into consideration the interest they must always take in the safety of the Spanish Monarchy, and being moreover animated with an earnest desire to assist in establishing peace in the Peninsula, as well as in all other parts of Europe, and H M the King of Great Britain, also bearing in remembrance the engagements resulting from his former alliance with Portugal, Their Majesties have consented to become parties to the proposed engagement

No IV.—The Prince de Talleyrand to Lord Palmerston

Hanover Square, April 19th, 1834, 9 P M

DEAR LORD PALMERSTON,

I have just read your fresh scheme with great care. Since you persist in not accepting the draft of the French Cabinet for the latter part of the preamble, I submit to your view of looking at this matter

As to Article VI I consider it, first of all, wrongly placed. It ought to follow Article III and so form Article IV of the treaty, seeing that Articles IV and V of your scheme are mere accessories ; it is besides only logical and the proper way of drafting a treaty, that the articles forming the treaty should precede those which are only the result of it

I have also another remark to make respecting this same Article VI, with regard to which it will be easy for you to satisfy me, for it is merely to eliminate a few words   I ask you to suppress the words *when he shall be asked to do so,* and simply to conclude with the words   *such aid as may be jointly decided upon between him and his august allies*   The suppression I here ask for is quite grammatical, for the first draft was redundant, and moreover, it carries out the spirit of the entire draft, in which the same idea is already established

If you assent to my slight modifications, kindly acquaint me of the hour at which you will sign to-morrow, and I shall be at your orders, for I shall then take it upon myself not to refer the matter to my Cabinet   Ever yours

No V.—Lord Palmerston to the Prince de Talleyrand

Stanhope Street, April 19th, 1834, 11 P M

MON CHER PRINCE,

I am quite ready to assent to the transposition of Article IV. which you propose, and I agree with you that this change is a great improvement in every way

As regards the suppression of the last words of this article, I must beg of you to take our sensitiveness into consideration, equally as we have done yours   I agree with you that those words do not add anything really essential to the meaning of the article, and that what they express is already contained in what precedes them ; but we lay *great* stress on them, and when

I say *we* I mean many persons. You must remember, that in the treaty it is solely a question of an armed intervention in the affairs of *Portugal*, and that we have precedents for this point

As for ourselves, not only have we not intervened without being specially invited to do so, but we have not accepted the invitation given us. You must not blame us, therefore, if we are a little inclined to be stiff on this subject

I was just writing an account to the King of the changes with which I believed you were satisfied, and for which I have to obtain his sanction, when your note arrived. Now however I must wait for your reply to this letter, and consequently I shall not be able to send my courier to Windsor till to-morrow. There is another day lost again. Be satisfied, I pray you, mon Prince, with the great changes you have already effected in this draft, which may now be looked upon much more as your child than mine. Ever yours.

No. VI.—THE PRINCE DE TALLEYRAND TO LORD PALMERSTON

HANOVER SQUARE, *April 20th*, 1834, 8 A.M.

DEAR LORD PALMERSTON,

We are now in complete accord on all points excepting on the elimination of three words which our *amour-propre* asks of you. It seems to me that yours cannot be involved in this question, for it is evident, that even without these three words, we can do nothing in the affairs of the Peninsula except in concert with you and the two other Powers. A repetition of the same idea in the same article could only therefore express distrust. It is this which we must avoid in the interest of both our countries and the position of our Governments with regard to one another. The slightest symptom of distrust in our treaty would be more dangerous in its consequences than the fact itself, for when it becomes public, the Opposition both with us and with you, will not fail to take hold of, and certainly utilize it, to the detriment of the close alliance which it is so necessary to encourage. Pray therefore only see in my insistence a desire to be consistent with our point of departure. Your clear mind will perfectly grasp this and arrange everything, in such a way that your next note will tell me at what hour to call and sign at your house. I am almost ashamed of the trifles to which, according to my instructions, I am obliged to attach so much importance. Ever yours . .

No VII—Lord Palmerston to the Prince de Talleyrand

Stanhope Street, *April* 20*th*, 1834

Mon cher Prince,

Upon my word, you are very difficult to satisfy! I agree with you, however, that we should fail in the principal aim of our treaty if, instead of showing unanimity and confidence, we were to proclaim defiance and suspicion. I have therefore endeavoured to draw up Article IV in such a way as to satisfy all parties. Tell me if I have succeeded as far as you are concerned.

You propose to come here to-day to sign, as if preparing a treaty were as simple a matter as writing a letter. But I shall have to submit all your alterations for the King's approval, who is at Windsor, and introduce them into the Spanish and Portuguese text, after having obtained the assent of the Spanish and Portuguese ministers; that will be a nice little task. Ever yours.

No VIII—The Prince de Talleyrand to Lord Palmerston

Hanover Square, *April* 20*th*, 1834, 2 a m

Dear Lord Palmerston,

However difficult I may be to please, I now lay down my arms, and will this time confine myself to a simple grammatical remark. Do not you think that the article would be expressed better in French, if the meaning were not interrupted by a number of incidental and useless phrases. I think therefore that we should strike out the words *by the high contracting parties*, which cut up the first part of the article and obscure its meaning. M. de Voltaire said that of all the alterations in his works suggested to him by his friends, the only one he never repented doing was, cutting out. You will send for me when you want me. Ever yours   .

No IX—Lord Palmerston to the Prince de Talleyrand

Stanhope Street, *April* 20*th*, 1834

Mon cher Prince,

I am very sorry, but I really cannot meet you any further. The alteration you propose, might perhaps improve

the style, but would certainly destroy the sense Voltaire's
saying is a true one, as far as books are concerned, but when
it is a question of treaties, I think the contrary ought rather to
be affirmed, and that one might well say that many a dispute
between States would never have taken place had the treaties
been drawn up with greater care and exactness Can I send
the article as it is, for the King's approval? Send me a *yes*, and
speedily, for truly time presses

THE PRINCE DE TALLEYRAND TO THE COMTE DE RIGNY

LONDON, *April* 23*rd*, 1834

MONSIEUR LE COMTE,

I found it impossible to send you by the despatch bag
yesterday, the treaty which I have the honour to transmit to
you to-day[1] The transcription of the four originals, each in

---

[1] The following is the text of the treaty as it was signed in London, April 22nd,
1834

"Her Majesty the Queen Regent of Spain   , and His Imperial Majesty the
Duke of Braganza   firmly convinced that the interests and safety of both crowns
require the immediate and energetic employment of reciprocal efforts to put an end to
the hostilities, which, if at first intended to overthrow the throne of His Portuguese
Majesty, now furnish support and protection to the subjects and malcontents of Spain,
then said Majesties, wishing at the same time to provide the means necessary to re-
establish peace and happiness at home, and place the future of both countries on
reciprocal and solid bases, have agreed to unite their forces for the purpose of com
pelling the Infant Don Carlos of Spain and the Infant Dom Miguel of Portugal to
quit the dominions of this latter kingdom

"In consequence of these Conventions, the Royal Regents, have addressed themselves to their Majesties the King of the French and the King of Great Britain and
Ireland These latter princes, feeling the interest they must always take in the
safety of the Spanish monarchy, and animated by an ardent desire to contribute to the
establishment of peace in the Peninsula as well as in Europe, His Britannic Majesty
feeling also, the special obligations arising out of his former alliance with Portugal,
have agreed to become parties to the said treaty With this view these sovereigns have
named their plenipotentiaries .   and the plenipotentiaries have agreed to the
following articles

"I H I M. the Duke of Braganza, in the name of Queen Dona Maria II , undertakes to put in action all the means in his power to drive the Infant Don Carlos out of
the Portuguese dominions

"II Her Majesty the Queen of Spain, prayed and invited by H I M the Duke of
Braganza, having besides very just and serious cause of reproach against the Infant
Dom Miguel for the assistance he has given to the Infant Don Carlos of Spain, under-
takes to send into Portugal such a number of Spanish troops as will suffice to co-oper-
ate with those of H M for the purpose of driving Don Carlos of Spain and Dom
Miguel out of Portuguese territory

"III H M the King of Great Britain undertakes to co-operate by sending a naval
force to second the necessary operations and decisions consequent on the present
treaty

"IV In the event of the co operation of France being considered necessary by the
high contracting parties H M the King of the French undertakes to do whatever he
and his august allies shall mutually agree upon

"V The high contracting parties have agreed that in consequence of the powers

four languages, occupied some time, and we were only able to
to sign them an hour ago

My correspondence will have enabled you to judge pretty
accurately of the difficulties we had to encounter in negotiating
this treaty. I think they should now be entirely buried in
oblivion, and that we should only occupy ourselves with the
results.

I am convinced that the King's government appreciates the
advantages of the treaty which has just been concluded between
the four Powers; but you must allow me to point out to you
succinctly, the reasons which decided me to enter this alliance.
I have looked at it from all points of view, and it was only after
mature reflection that I considered it offered us real advantages
without any danger.

This quadruple alliance cannot fail to make some noise in
Europe; I do not say that it will not even excite some jealousy
on the part of the great Northern Powers; but I do not believe
they will think sufficiently about it, to cause us further embarrassment than they have done during the last three years. I
should rather feel disposed to think that they will work more
energetically to separate us from England, and consequently
be more friendly with us. Our treaty will certainly not contribute to strengthen still further the ties which unite the Cabinets
of Vienna, Berlin, and St Petersburg; we have seen lately that
these ties are as strong as they can be. It will be easy for us to
justify the principles and the object of this quadruple alliance
to them, since the state of the Peninsula was a question that
appealed specially to the Anglo-French policy. On the whole,
I cannot bring myself to believe that the alliance which we have
just concluded, which binds us still closer to England, and which,
so to speak, makes Spain and Portugal dependent on us, will
not result in inspiring the Northern Cabinets with some respect

contained in the preceding articles, a declaration shall at once be made to the
Portuguese nation, announcing the principles and the object of the present treaty, and
H I M the Duke of Braganza, animated by the sincere wish to efface afresh all
recollection of the past, and desiring to unite the whole nation around his daughter's
throne, declares his intention of proclaiming a complete and general amnesty in favour
of all the subjects of H M   who, within such period as shall be determined
on, will return to their allegiance; and the said Regent further declares his intention
of assuring to the Infant Dom Miguel, as soon as he shall have quitted Portuguese
territory, an allowance suitable to his name and birth

"VI. H M the Queen of Spain, in virtue of the present article, declares her intention to assure to the Infant Don Carlos, as soon as he shall have quitted the Spanish and
Portuguese dominions, an allowance suitable to his rank and his birth

"VII. The present treaty will be ratified and the ratifications exchanged at London,
in one month, or sooner if possible

"FLORIDA BLANCA,   PALMERSTON,
"TALLEYRAND,   MORALS SARMIENTO"

They might, in their own minds, add Belgium and perhaps Switzerland to the circle of our alliance, and supposing they only wish to look upon all this, as the reunion of nations, at present agitated by a revolutionary spirit, they will only fear still more to provoke the attacks of a mass sufficiently formidable in itself and rendered more so by reason of the good feeling it maintains with all the other nations

Looking at the treaty especially in its relation to Spain, we may do ourselves the justice that we have not in any way compromised the interests of that Power, they having been more especially entrusted to us   In fact, the treaty only stipulates for conditions useful and honourable for Spain, and if these conditions should not have the results we anticipate (which is quite possible in the present state of Spain) no one will be able to accuse us of having brought down another scourge on that unhappy country, by adding a foreign war to the civil war   The Spanish territory will remain inviolable, and that must be one of the fixed principles of our policy in the Peninsula

If we may judge of the importance which the English Cabinet attaches to our participation in this treaty, by the difficulties it has raised as to its form, we ought to think it very great, and it seems to me that we should not be wrong, for now it is evident that the English Ministry has submitted its policy in the Peninsula to our control, and even if this should not in reality be so much as it seems, it will suffice us if it is so apparently in public opinion [1]

There was still another point of view from which it was necessary to examine this treaty, and one I considered most essential, namely, the influence it would have on France   I must confess that in this respect, also, it appeared to me quite as satisfactory as in all the other relations   Is it a question of our material interests ? We are not pledged to anything by the fact, for if our allies call upon us to join in the execution of the treaty (which is not at all likely, with England's consent) we are masters of our

[1] The following letter from Lord Palmerston to his brother Sir William Temple, April 23rd, is a *piquante* counterpart of M de Talleyrand's despatch —" I have been very busy since the 4th of this month elaborating my quadruple alliance between England, France, Spain, and Portugal, to compass the expulsion of Carlos and Miguel . . . . I carried it at the Council by a *coup-de-main*, not allowing them time to raise objections   I was not so fortunate with old Talley (*sic*) and the French Government, for they made innumerable objections , but these objections were all based on the manner in which I proposed to them to join us   Finally, however, I succeeded in satisfying their vanity by giving them the place in our midst they seemed to desire.   I look upon this as a great stroke   Firstly, it will decide this Portuguese matter, and also serve somewhat to arrange those of Spain   But what is of pre-eminent and general importance is, that it establishes a quadruple alliance among the Constitutional States of the West, which will serve as a counterpoise to the Holy Alliance of the East " (Private Correspondence of Lord Palmerston)

own actions, and can refuse to take part in any armed intervention, the terrible possibilities of which are incalculable   If it is
only a question of the national *amour propre*, how could that
ever be hurt by a treaty in which we play politically an equal
part with England, without employing an additional soldier or
spending a sou ?

I repeat again, Monsieur le Comte, I do not see anything in
this treaty of the quadruple alliance which is not justifiable and
honourable both as regards our enemies and our friends   If its
results are not as satisfactory as we hope, it can never at any
rate be brought up as a reproach against the King's Government,
and we shall have done everything that circumstances permitted

You will see that the ratifications are to be exchanged in
one month or sooner if possible   you must not forget that it
will be necessary to send three ratifications in the three different
languages, Spanish, English and Portuguese

I am sending to-day a copy of the Convention to M de
Rayneval at Madrid, and another to M le Baron Mortier at
Lisbon

———————— — — ————

Here ends the manuscript of the *Memoirs* M de Talleyrand, however, did not quit London until the month of August,
and during those last months he had still some very important
matters to deal with   We therefore considered we ought to
continue the work, which he had himself commenced during the
preceding years, to the termination of his Embassy   All the
materials were at hand   official despatches and private letters
We have confined ourselves to classing them according to rational
order, as M de Talleyrand had done during the last volumes

The prince's private correspondence during this period,
was published, two years ago, under the superintendence of
Madame la Comtesse de Mirabeau   It would therefore have
been superfluous to re-edit it here   We have however been
obliged to reproduce some of the letters, in order to show the
course of the negotiations as fully as possible , they will be
found on pages 268, 269, 279, 300, 312. 313, 314

THE COMTE DE RIGNY TO THE PRINCE DE TALLEYRAND

PARIS, *Sunday, April 27th,* 1834

MON PRINCE,

I am taking advantage of the Duc de Frias'[1] courier
Our latest news from Madrid is up to the 19th   The press there
was unfavourable to, and public opinion generally in favour of,
the Royal Statute[2]   Burgos[3] has been replaced by Moscoso de
Altamira[4]

As a rule the news from Germany now shows a disposition on
the part of the Northern Courts to throw the blame of all the
delays on the Duc de Nassau and exonerate King William,
they evidently would like to bring the London and Paris
Cabinets round from their resolve, not to recommence the
Conferences, they complain bitterly, and take advantage of the
events in Brussels

Memorandums are being showered upon Switzerland, the
Canton of Berne will however give in, on the matter of the
refugees who took part in the movement in Savoy[5]

[1] Spanish Ambassador in Paris at that time

[2] The Constitution granted to Spain by the Martinez de la Rosa Cabinet   It was
promulgated on the 12th June

[3] Don Francisco Xavier de Burgos, born in 1778   Having accepted some employment under King Joseph, he was exiled at the Restoration of Ferdinand   He returned
to Spain in 1817, and made a name for himself as a debater on the Liberal side   He
became Intendant of the Council of Customs in 1827   then Chief Councillor of
Finance, Minister of the Interior at Ferdinand's death, and finally Minister of
Finance

[4] Don José María de Moscoso de Altamira had already been Minister of the
Interior in 1822   A few months after, he and his colleagues were dismissed and im-
prisoned   Again made Minister of the Interior in 1834, he was replaced by Don
Diego Medrano in January 1835

[5] Switzerland at this period was the refuge and centre of reunion of all the
revolutionary spirits in Europe   In the beginning of January 1834, about a thousand
refugees of all nations assembled in the Canton de Vaud, for the purpose of entering
Savoy and proclaiming a republic there   The Polish General Romarino headed the
movement   On the 2nd February, several armed bands crossed the frontier and got
as far as Annecy, but without exciting any interest among the inhabitants   They were
quickly attacked and completely routed by the Sardinian troops   In consequence of
this skirmish, Sardinia demanded that Switzerland should take some steps against the
refugees, she insisted that the Directory should expel them and that those Swiss who
had taken part in the enterprise should be brought to trial   Several states individually supported the course of the Sardinian Cabinet, and the Swiss Government received
similar demands from Austria, the Grand-Duchy of Baden, Bavaria, Wurtemberg, the
Germanic Confederation, the Kingdom of Naples, Prussia, and even Russia   It
resisted at first, declaring that such a summons affected the independence of Switzerland   Nevertheless it ended by giving in, so far at least as regarded the expulsion of
the foreigners, even the Canton of Berne, which appeared the most rebellious, and
which had welcomed the Polish refugees with great friendliness, expelled them from
her territory   This incident, which for a moment startled diplomatic circles, was not
brought to a close till the end of July

At home, we shall only have the increased effective force asked for 1835, for the first six months. We shall have to obtain the remainder from the new Legislature, as we have been obliged to compound with the Commission, which only wanted to allow for three months in 1835 [1]

Quesada has just been beaten by Zumalacarreguy [2] and obliged to retire to Pampeluna ; he has lost three or four hundred men

Rodil ought to have taken Don Carlos, who got off with the loss of his baggage

I cannot assure you too often, mon Prince, of the very favourable impression made by the treaty here, and how greatly you are applauded for having brought it to a conclusion. Appony is the only one among the foreigners who has not yet said anything. I wound up some explanations by telling him, that we had not forgotten that Dona Maria was the granddaughter of the Emperor Francis

Pozzo seems in a bad humour. I think nevertheless the general tendency all round is to look upon the matter as of very slight importance

THE PRINCE DE TALLEYRAND TO THE COMTE DE RIGNY

LONDON, *April 28th*, 1834

MONSIEUR LE COMTE,

Lord Palmerston has gone to Windsor for two or three days ; this prevents my seeing him as soon as I should have liked, respecting the question of Luxemburg and the conduct of the Prussian Government towards General Goblet [3] mentioned in your despatch

As soon as the Minister for Foreign Affairs returns, I will see him, communicate to him your observations on these two points, and arrange with him as to the best measures to be adopted by the French and English Governments under the circumstances.

[1] On the 16th of April, the War Minister had submitted a scheme to bring the army up to an effective force of 360,000 men. He therefore asked for supplementary loans for the military exercises of 1834-1835. The Commission only granted him half the loans asked for, and the Chamber ratified the decision of the Commission, May 13th

[2] Thomas Zumalacarreguy, born in 1788, entered the service in 1808 at the time of the French invasion ; after the death of Ferdinand VII , he sided with Don Carlos and became one of the generals of the insurrection. He held the country for two years, gained numerous advantages, which rendered his name famous as a party leader, but he was mortally wounded at the siege of Bilbao in June 1835

[3] General Goblet had been made Minister at Berlin, but the King of Prussia at the instigation, it was said, of the Cabinet of the Hague, had refused to receive him, although he had previously agreed to his nomination

The proceeding of the Prussian Government seems to me, M le Comte, as it does to you, perfectly inexplicable, I may even say more, it is perfectly unbearable   We cannot allow it to pass unnoticed without exposing ourselves to seeing some fresh insult, either gratuitously or otherwise, offered to Belgium every day, which eventually would recoil on the two Governments which specially protect her   The choice of General Goblet for the Berlin Embassy may have been very ill advised, but, if so, the Prussian Government ought to have intimated its dislike to receiving him before his departure from Brussels, which was known long beforehand   In the present state of things, one cannot admit the right of the Berlin Cabinet to reject the Belgian envoy, for so insulting a reason as that which it puts forward, more especially when there is an accredited Prussian Minister at Brussels, who is always treated with great consideration by the Belgian Government

I cannot say, as yet, what line Lord Palmerston will take in this matter, but I will urge upon him to come to some decision promptly

As to the proposals made by Prussia and Austria for a fresh arrangement in the affair of Luxemburg, I do not think it will suit us to entertain them. As you truly observe, they would modify the treaties of 1815, and would also possess the objection of renewing the discussions on the territorial question of the Hollando-Belgian treaty, a question which it is very important that we should consider, and also prevail upon the other Powers to consider, as irrevocably decided and determined by the treaty of November 15 . .

I am convinced that we for our part did very wisely to keep the treaty secret   We can only regret its premature publication by the English newspapers   It is always better in all such cases not to have to reproach oneself for any indiscretion I suppose those journals over which the King's Government possesses some influence, will be instructed to point out the moral and political use to France of this treaty, when the time for announcing it has arrived . . .

THE COMTE DE RIGNY TO THE PRINCE DE TALLEYRAND.

Thursday, May 1st, 1834

MON PRINCE,

I am sending you a few lines, in the midst of all the turmoil of the 1st of May   Goblet has been recalled   M de Mérode's[1] note is very firm.   Bresson took rather a high hand in

[1] Comte Felix de Mérode was at that time Minister for Foreign Affairs

this matter at Berlin, and he has done right I believe King Leopold was in fault, for not replying to a private letter of the King of Prussia's before despatching Goblet I have communicated the tenour of this letter to Lord Granville

Marshal Maison has to-day given me some explanation respecting the preparations in the Black Sea, which our Consul at Odessa had announced, but which do not exist Mr Bligh having probably on the same authority, transmitted similar information to London, it might be as well to acquaint Lord Palmerston of this exaggeration

Switzerland is taking action with regard to her refugees You will have read the proclamation of the Bernese Police in the *Débats*, that was my suggestion I think that the Foreign Legations are now rather taken in by being relegated to Zurich

Our newspapers are commencing to chatter about the treaty Diplomacy has not yet attacked us, but I know it is all astir, the Carlist party especially, is furious

Excepting Quesada's defeat, the news from Barcelona, Valencia, and Murcia is very good The Royal Statute has had a great success everywhere The *Gazette de Madrid*, of the 23rd, announces the reciprocal despatch and reception of the Ministers accredited between Madrid and Lisbon, here we have the formal recognition'

Don Carlos has been closely pressed a second time, and has again lost some equipment

M Sontag[1] has already returned from Brussels, to which place M Périer[2] is now going

THE PRINCE DE TALLEYRAND TO THE COMTE DE RIGNY.

LONDON, *May 1st*, 1834

MONSIEUR LE COMTE,

· I was able to see Lord Palmerston yesterday, and to speak to him respecting the two chief subjects in your despatch No 33 He thoroughly agrees with you as to the conduct of the Prussian Government with regard to General Goblet, and he has written to Berlin, directing Lord Minto to make some representations on the subject

So many and such varied proposals have been brought forward lately, on the subject of Luxemburg, that Lord Palmerston thinks we ought not to exhibit too much interest in that affair, and should wait until some positive proposal is

[1] Second Secretary to the Embassy in London
[2] Auguste Casimir Victor Laurent Périer, son of M Périer, at that time Secretary of Legation at Brussels

submitted to us, which France and England will then be at liberty to accept or refuse

Lord Palmerston also informed me of the despatches he had received from Vienna, in which Sir Frederick Lamb gave him an account of several interviews he had had with the Prince de Metternich, respecting the resumption of the Conferences in London to conclude the Hollando-Belgian affair   All these conversations were simply a long series of arguments on the part of the Chancellor, to prove the necessity of re-assembling the Conference, and although on the whole they bring forward nothing fresh, Lord Palmerston proposes to instruct Sir Frederick Lamb to reply to them, and announce the intention of the English Government to accede to the wishes of the Austrian Cabinet, as soon as it has received the assurance that the King of the Netherlands agrees to sign the first seven Articles of the treaty of November 15th, respecting which the Austrian, Prussian, and Russian Governments have never raised the slightest question   He thinks with me, that the King of the Netherlands' refusal or acceptance will plainly show whether he does or does not desire to bring matters to a conclusion

Lord Palmerston's despatch will be transmitted to Vienna *viâ* Paris, and Lord Granville is to communicate it to you.   .

THE COMTE DE RIGNY TO THE PRINCE DE TALLLYRAND.

PARIS, *May 3rd*, 1834.

MON PRINCE,

Matters are in a complete state of disorder on the northern frontier of Spain, nevertheless I do not see that Madrid is much disturbed thereby   Rayneval does not say a word about it

Pozzo was to have an interview with the King this morning. I strongly cautioned His Majesty, more especially impressing upon him not to make any excuses to Pozzo, still less to tell him that it was in order not to allow the English to act alone in the Peninsula, and to enable us *to keep an eye on them*

I fancy he was rather inclined to take that line, but I did all in my power to prevent his doing so

THE PRINCE DE TALLEYRAND TO THE COMTE DE RIGNY.

LONDON, *May 9th*, 1834

MONSIEUR LE COMTE,

I think it would be as well if you were to send me, as soon as possible, the ratifications of the treaty of April 22nd.

Those from Portugal may arrive at any moment, and as we can count on those from Madrid, a first exchange will probably be made with the Portuguese minister, that is, however, if Dom Pedro's Government does not refuse to ratify the treaty, as some people here seem to fear, which I must confess would certainly be a greater act of folly on the part of that Government than any they have yet been blamed for

I will get Lord Palmerston to delay no longer in sending the necessary instructions to Copenhagen to conclude the treaty relative to the slave trade[1]

You will have seen in the English papers the announcement of the arrival of the Comte de Montfort (M Jerome Bonaparte) in London This is quite correct ; M Lucien and M Joseph Bonaparte are also living here

Accept

LONDON, *May 15th*, 1834

M Feuillet has sent me the ratifications of the treaty of 22nd April

The two documents, of which I herewith send copies, will show you that Dom Pedro's Government has decided to ratify the treaty signed by its plenipotentiaries in London We are not yet aware what day the Portuguese ratifications will arrive here, but that is not of so much consequence now that we know what are the intentions of the Regent of Portugal with regard to this treaty I think, however, that all will be completed in three or four days, unless the Portuguese and Spanish ratifications are not quite in order, which might be the case, owing to their having been sent off so hurriedly from Madrid and Lisbon

I was not able to see Lord Palmerston to-day , I shall not omit to tell him your wishes respecting Swiss affairs when next I see him

LONDON, *May 18th*, 1834

In thinking carefully over the draft of the declaration referred to in Art V of the treaty of April 22nd,[2] which M.

---

[1] Negotiations were at this time being carried on between France and England on the one part and Denmark on the other, in order to obtain the assent of the Cabinet at Copenhagen to the treaty concluded on the 30th November, 1831, between the Cabinets of London and Paris, (and completed by the Convention of 22nd March, 1833) for the repression of the slave trade Denmark joined it on the 26th July, 1834

[2] Art V It is agreed between the high contracting parties that in consequence of the stipulations contained in the preceding Articles a declaration shall be published at once, announcing to the Portuguese nation the principles and the 'object of the engagements of this treaty

Martinez de la Rosa desires should be made by a joint act signed by the four plenipotentiaries, I find there are several difficulties, which I must point out to you as I have already done to Lord Palmerston First of all, I see in this a direct intervention in the purely home affairs of the Peninsula, and we should pledge ourselves, it seems to me, by the very first step, much more than we are bound by the treaty itself For in this latter, I took care that we should only be the guarantors to the conditions of Art. V and that we should not be asked to execute them If, through the inevitable consequences of a war, such as that being waged in the Peninsula, it should come about that in the different towns and fortresses occupied successively by both parties, the declaration of the four Courts becomes subject to all the evil chances of an act drawn up in the name of one of the two combatant parties, would not the dignity of France and Great Britain find itself compromised by the insults which would immediately be heaped upon a declaration emanating from them ?

I do not moreover, under the circumstances, recognize the necessity of the step demanded by the Madrid Cabinet It seems to me that it ought to suffice if, after the publication of the treaty, the Portuguese Government makes the declaration mentioned and guaranteed by Art V

These are the observations I communicated to Lord Palmerston and to which I wish especially to draw your attention, Monsieur le Comte You will have time to let me have your definite opinion on this matter, for we cannot decide on the form of the declaration until after the ratifications have been exchanged, which will not be for some days yet

Lord Palmerston told me that he would positively send the necessary instructions to Copenhagen to complete the negotiation relative to the slave trade

By the time this letter reaches you, you will already have learnt that the English Cabinet had forestalled your wishes respecting the Frankfort affairs [1] Lord Granville will have informed you of the despatch which Lord Palmerston has written to the English minister in that city, directing him to make some representations as to the occurrences which have just

---

[1] In consequence of the revolt of the 5th April, 1833, the Diet had ordered Frankfort to be occupied by a garrison, consisting of half Austrian and half Prussian troops, this became the source of daily quarrels and conflicts with the town militia When more serious riots broke out afresh on the 2nd May, the Diet passed a second resolution, by which the police and all the military authorities were placed under the Austrian commandant The Senate of Frankfort protested vehemently against this measure, which deprived the Republic almost completely of its independence It was this same abuse of power on the part of the Confederation which called forth the intervention of the Powers

taken place, and as to the schemes attributed to the Diet I thought Lord Palmerston's letter rather too strong and fear it will overreach its aim I hope it will make the same impression on you that it has done on me, and that the King's Government, keeping to the sensible views so well expressed in your despatch No 42, will confine itself to making reservations expressed in terms sufficiently moderate not to cause any irritation We must as much as possible humour the susceptibilities of the small German States and show our strength by our moderation towards them You may remember that, only very lately, the somewhat aggressive tone of the English agents in Germany has not greatly served our interests there

THE COMTE DE RIGNY TO THE PRINCE DE TALLEYRAND.

PARIS, *May 19th,* 1834.

MON PRINCE,

Roussin has just refused [1] he will I believe be replaced by Admiral Jacob I left the Council completely free to nominate either a Minister for Foreign Affairs or a Minister of Marine

We have a number of letters both from Constantinople and from Vienna Roussin informs us that the Russian naval preparations are enormous and are being much pressed forward it has been announced that the Emperor is going to make a journey to the Crimea Mehemet-Ali is getting uneasy on his Divan, and believes himself threatened, but he is sufficiently troubled with Syria and Candia, and does not think of occupying himself with anything else except the intrigues in the Divan itself

Sainte-Aulaire thinks that the three Northern Courts will form a separate arrangement with Holland, if the Conferences are not resumed

M de Metternich cannot digest the treaty but outwardly, he takes the matter very quietly M Ancillon is more vehement We are just now having a slight Ministerial agitation, which will not result in anything, but it takes up my time, as well as some of that which I require for writing to you

M de Lafayette is sinking rapidly —this evening, to-morrow or the day after at latest [2]

[1] The portfolio of the Marine Department
[2] M de Lafayette died on the 20th of May His obsequies took place on the 22nd, amid an immense concourse of people

The Prince de Talleyrand to the Comte de Rigny.

LONDON, *May 22nd,* 1834

MONSIEUR LE COMTE,

The Portuguese ratifications have not yet arrived, we cannot account for this delay, except by the bad weather at sea, which for the last few days has been most unfavourable for any arrivals from Portugal

The Prince de Lieven, Russian Ambassador in London for the last twenty years, has just been recalled by his Court to fill the post of Governor, or, as the Russians call it, curator to the hereditary Grand Duke, whose majority was celebrated a few days ago at St Petersburg The letter informing M de Lieven of his appointment is worded in the most flattering and honourable terms

This piece of news produced a very lively sensation yesterday at the Exchange in London, and some people thought they saw in it evidence of a speedy rupture between England and Russia, they have however already recovered from this groundless fear The Prince de Lieven will be much regretted in England, he had won the esteem of all those who for so many years have had the opportunity of estimating the loftiness and nobility of his character

Lord Palmerston, to whom I spoke this morning about the project he has sent to Mr Foster[1] at Turin, relative to Sardinia's joining the Convention on the slave trade treaty, confessed to me that it was entirely through forgetfulness that you had not received this project, and he promised to repair the error as speedily as possible, by directing Lord Granville to transmit a copy to you at once

I hope to send you by the next courier the Order in Council which has removed the embargo laid upon Dutch vessels in 1833

The Comte de Rigny to the Prince de Talleyrand.

PARIS, *May 26th,* 1834.

MON PRINCE,

The King has been greatly excited by a letter from King Leopold, announcing his scheme for establishing an order of succession in Belgium[2] Lehon started yesterday, and I

---

[1] Augustus John Foster, born in 1780, English Minister Plenipotentiary in Sardinia
[2] The Prince Royal of Belgium only a few months old, had just died King

begged him most earnestly not only to postpone all decisions, but if possible all discussion on this subject, which is not much relished in France

Lord Granville has received nothing from London about it, I fancy I have reason to believe, that this announcement by King Leopold will surprise the London Cabinet as much as it has ours

From Madrid we have heard nothing since the 14th The insurrection in Navarre is spreading rapidly, but the other provinces are taking no part in it

MADAME ADELAIDE TO THE PRINCE DE TALLEYRAND

NEUILLY, *May 23rd*, 1834

Who would have believed, mon cher Prince, that King Leopold, who is only forty-three years of age, and with a young wife in perfect health, has allowed himself to be so carried away by grief at the loss of his child, that he himself wishes to assure the succession to the Belgian throne to his nephews, though he never thought of so doing at the time of his marriage, nor before it, and surely he has less reason for doing so now than before the birth of the dear infant whose loss we deplore Our dear Louise has shown that she can have children, and at three-and-twenty, fresh and in good health, it is quite likely that she will have others You will not be surprised that our King (in the letter of which I herewith send you a copy, should impress upon him at once, that he cannot *alone* and of *himself* come to a resolve of such an important nature, without first consulting England and France, and that we cannot consent to Belgium becoming Germanized, nor allow her to be smothered by a host of agnates like those of Luxemburg, who have already caused us so much trouble and difficulty, which you, mon Prince, know better than any one else. The King thinks that it is both advisable and necessary that you should be made aware of this business, so that if they make it known in England and you hear it spoken of, you may, with your usual skill, avert the dangers and difficulties which might arise therefrom for the general peace, by causing them to be thoroughly understood in England to their fullest extent We trust this entirely to your high sense of justice and your great zeal for the good of France

Leopold, who had no other children, wished to assure the inheritance of the crown to his family by getting the Belgian Chambers to proclaim the contingent rights of his relations, the princes of the House of Coburg This determination on the part of the King of the Belgians provoked the intervention of King Louis Philippe

King Louis Philippe to King Leopold

My very dear Brother and excellent Friend,

I am writing to you separately on the very important portion of your letter of the 19th, which I have just received What you have communicated to me is of so serious a nature, that I do not think it is solely in order that I should not hear it through others, that you have informed me of it Resolutions of such a nature must not only be arranged with England and ourselves, but you cannot take them without our concurrence and approbation Neither the act which called you to the throne, the Belgian Constitution, nor the treaties which guaranteed it to you, conferred this right It is necessary therefore, before going any further in this *strange* matter, that you should make it the subject of an official negotiation from your Government to both ours. I say *strange*, my dear brother, for in truth I cannot conceive that at your age, with a wife like yours, grief at the loss we have just sustained, should lead you to believe that it is imperative for you to provide for the chances of your succession, and overwhelm Belgium with a host of agnates like those of Luxemburg

1 I am far from believing that such an act would be a guarantee for the solidity of your throne, and I should rather be inclined to think that, in consequence of the difficulties of all kinds which would arise therefrom, the idea would please those who do not desire its solidity I do not think that it is necessary to remind Belgium of the danger involved in the return of the Nassau family, or the establishment of a Republic, for every one knows that France would never permit either one or the other

2 No one is ignorant of what we want, namely, the real and *not the nominal* independence of Belgium , that we do not wish her to be dependent either on us, on England, or on both , that we still less wish her to depend upon Prussia, the Germanic Confederation, or Germany Not only have we desired Belgium to be independent, but we have established her neutrality for ever, so that she cannot be bound by such ties

The independence of Belgium is also of importance to us for another reason, of which you are well aware it is the basis, the bond of our alliance with England, which is so valuable to us, and is the guarantee for universal peace and social order We shall therefore resist to the utmost everything that could possibly injure it or *Germanize* Belgium, either by uniting it with the

Germanic Confederation, or becoming dependent on any of the States composing it

I therefore hope my dear brother, that you will put a stop to the message to the Chambers you speak of in your letter to me, and that you will not take any further steps in this matter, before informing the London and Paris Cabinets of it and receiving their replies

After all this, my dear brother, please accept every expression of my affection I am just starting for Neuilly, and remain always and for ever, your dear brother, affectionate father-in-law, and faithful friend,

LOUIS PHILIPPE.

THE PRINCE DE TALLEYRAND TO THE COMTE DE RIGNY.

LONDON, *May* 26*th*, 1834

MONSIEUR LE COMTE,

I saw Lord Grey yesterday, and spoke to him about King Leopold's idea of regulating the succession to the Belgian throne, in concert with the Belgian Chambers I easily made him see the objections to such a scheme I must do Lord Grey the justice to say, that he, like you, at once perceived the difficulties of more than one nature which would result from King Leopold's scheme He gave me a positive assurance, that England would oppose any decision come to respecting the succession to the Belgian throne without the concurrence of France and England Instructions to this effect will be sent to Brussels, and I may also add, that Lord Durham, to whom I have spoken, and whose advice is generally very well received by King Leopold, stated, that he would inform him of the opposition which the execution of his scheme would meet with in England

LONDON, *May* 29*th*, 1834

I generally refrain from telling you of the English Parliamentary debates which specially refer to the home affairs of the country, as I know that the papers which are forwarded to you from here, afford you in this respect quicker and more exact details than I could do I must however give you an account to-day of a very serious incident occasioned by the discussion of a bill in the House of Commons

This bill, the first reading of which took place more than a fortnight ago, relates to the redemption of the tithes of the

Protestant clergy in Ireland   It was thought that the financial results produced thereby would eventually leave a surplus, the distribution of which would have to be arranged for   Lord John Russell, one of the members of the Cabinet, who supported the Bill in the House of Commons, had spoken perhaps somewhat injudiciously at the first reading, maintaining that the funds should be used according to the wishes of the Government   This proposal excited strong dissent in the Cabinet, several members of which, sharing the opinion of a considerable portion of the House of Commons and certainly of the majority in the House of Peers on this subject, declared they could not assent to it   The ministers who most strongly opposed Lord John Russell's proposal were Mr Stanley and Sir James Graham   They declared it would be a spoliation of the Anglican clergy, and claimed that if there remained a surplus, after all the provisions of the Bill had been carried out, such surplus should be handed over to the Anglican clergy in Ireland, who should decide as to its appropriation .

Lord John Russell, on his side, persisting in the opinion he had enunciated, declared he must resign if it was not adopted   He was however persuaded to withdraw his resignation, and the Cabinet were endeavouring to put an end to this difficulty when a motion, which Mr Ward[1] is to bring before the House of Commons to-morrow, has revived all the difficulties which it was hoped were dispersed   Mr. Ward will propose, that the funds in question should be employed for the benefit of the Irish Dissenting and Roman Catholic chapels, and it is impossible to foresee the end of this motion   Whatever it is, however, they declare that it must result in the resignation of several of the Ministry   If Mr Ward obtains a majority in the House, Mr Stanley and Sir James Graham have announced their positive intention of retiring , if the contrary is the case, Lord John Russell and probably some other members of the Cabinet will resign

For the last three days a succession of Cabinet Councils have been held, without so far finding any means of reconciling the various opinions expressed   Mr Stanley's retirement would be a very serious loss to the Ministry, of which he is the most reliable and undoubtedly the most able supporter in the House of Commons   Lord John Russell's resignation and that of several

---

[1] Henry George Ward born in 1798, an English diplomat and politician   He was successively Secretary of Legation at Stockholm, the Hague, and Madrid, and was nominated Minister to Mexico in 1825   In 1832, he became member of the House of Commons   In 1849, he was made High Commissioner of the Ionian Islands, Governor of Ceylon in 1856, and died in 1860

of the other members might also produce some unexpected results

Lastly, Monsieur le Comte, you will perceive that this is a very critical time so that if some arrangement is not come to, the existence of the present Cabinet is seriously compromised

You must excuse my here expressing any opinion as to the Government which might be called to succeed this one, predictions would certainly be useless in the presence of such changeable and uncertain circumstances as may arise at any moment   I will confine myself therefore to keeping you fully informed of everything that comes to my knowledge

LONDON, *May* 27th, 10 P M.

Mr Ward has brought forward his motion in the House of Commons , it was seconded by Mr Grote [1]

Lord Althorp, the Chancellor of the Exchequer, in a very able speech, proposed the adjournment of the House till Monday next   Mr Grote hastened to support the minister's proposition, by referring to the serious matters in connection with it   The House adopted it amid loud and very decided acclamations ; so matters, as far as that is concerned, are still undecided   Nevertheless, the Ministerial majority has thereby certainly obtained great moral support, and it appears that Mr Stanley, Sir James Graham, the Duke of Richmond, and perhaps Lord Ripon will retire.

It is said that the King is determined to support Lord Grey and the Cabinet ministers who side with him.

LONDON, *May* 29th, 1834

The Portuguese ratifications arrived in London this morning. I believe the exchanges will be effected this evening or to-morrow morning   As soon as I receive the English, Spanish, and Portuguese ratifications, I will remit them to M Feuillet

I have the honour to send you herewith a copy of the Note, in which Lord Palmerston announces the conclusion of the treaty of the quadruple alliance to the foreign legations accredited in England

The Duke of Richmond and Lord Ripon have positively ten-

[1] George Grote, historian and an English politician born in 1794, entered the House of Commons in 1832, where he sided with the Whig party   He retired in 1841, after which he devoted himself exclusively to historical research   He wrote a history of Greece, a large work, which established his reputation   In 1868, he succeeded Lord Brougham as President of the Council of the London University   He died in 1871

dered their resignations, which have been accepted This will render the fresh Ministerial arrangements somewhat more difficult, but it is hoped nevertheless that all will be settled by Monday, the day fixed for the re-assembling of the House [1]

I am not losing sight of the Eastern question, and I will again bring it before Lord Palmerston and Lord Grey, as soon as the organisation of the new Cabinet allows them time to think about it

Accept .

6 o'clock in the Evening

P.S I have just come from the Foreign Office, to which I had gone to carry out the exchange of the ratifications , this however has not been accomplished, for the document from Lisbon is so incorrect, that it is almost impossible to accept it Among its many irregularities, I will confine myself to pointing out to you the abridgment of the preamble We are trying to find some means of providing for this difficulty, but up to now we have not succeeded This delay, which is unpleasant for us, and which I beg you to keep secret, is a very serious matter for the English Cabinet, as it hoped to be in a position to lay the treaty before Parliament on Monday

LONDON, *May* 31*st,* 1834

M Feuillet, who will have the honour to hand you this despatch, also bears the three ratifications of the treaty of April 22nd

After carefully weighing the inconveniences which the delay in the exchange of the ratifications of this treaty would occasion, we have decided to accept the Portuguese draft despite its incorrectness

We have, moreover, endeavoured to obviate the evil results of our decision by means of two memorandums, copies of which I have the honour to enclose herewith

The first is a declaration by the Portuguese minister in London, as explicit as possible, and the second, a counter declaration by the plenipotentiaries of the three courts, by which they take upon themselves the solemn engagement undertaken by the Portuguese plenipotentiary—that the errors committed in the

---

[1] As a result of this alteration, the English Ministry lost four of its members Lord Stanley, Secretary for the Colonies and War Minister, was succeeded by Mr Spring-Rice for the Colonies, and by Mr Ellice in the War Department ; Sir J Graham, First Lord of the Admiralty, by Lord Auckland , the Duke of Richmond, Postmaster-General, by the Marquis of Conyngham , and Lord Ripon, Lord Privy Seal, by the Earl of Carlisle.

execution of the Portuguese ratifications shall be rectified as quickly as possible

When reading these two documents, you will, I think, agree with me Monsieur le Comte, that under the circumstances we could not have done better

Our refusal to ratify would have caused a delay of not less than a month, during that time, and even long after, the operations of the Spanish army would be suspended, since they would have had to await the necessary orders from London authorising the Spanish Government to take action Moreover, the request we have transmitted to the three ministers of Spain, France, and Great Britain at Lisbon, gives us the certainty that the order to advance will not be accorded to the Spanish Government until they have received the ratified ratifications

You will find herewith, a copy of the despatch I have just written to M le Baron de Mortier on this subject, and I venture to hope that you will consider I was justified in sending him his instructions without awaiting your orders Speed, at the present juncture, outweighs all other considerations

After the exchange of the ratifications, we discussed the projected amnesty, of which mention is made in Article V of he treaty, and we drew up the draft, a copy of which I have the honour herewith to enclose

The reason which specially decided me, Monsieur le Comte, to consent to the arrangement of which I have just informed you, was, that it seemed to me very urgent to give all possible weight to the treaty of April 22nd   The Ministerial difficulties that have arisen here lately, which, although happily arranged for the time, may arise again, make it a matter of the highest importance to us that this treaty should be ratified by the present Ministry or at least recognised as having been so

I think the King's Government, in realising this consideration, will approve the resolve I have taken

You will already have been made aware by the papers, of the names of those who have been summoned to replace the retiring members of the English Cabinet As soon as it was certain, as I had the honour of informing you, that Lord Grey would remain at the head of affairs, the names of the new ministers did not excite much interest

It now remains to be seen what effect the Ministerial changes will have on the two Houses of Parliament. The most generally accepted opinion is, that the Cabinet has not strengthened itself by the addition of those it has summoned to join it   I fancy this opinion is pretty well founded

THE COMTE DE RIGNY TO THE PRINCE DE TALLEYRAND.

PARIS, *June 1st,* 1834

MON PRINCE

In order that you may be fully acquainted with our reasons for sending you a copy of the fresh instructions for M Périer at Brussels, I must inform you, that in consequence of a conversation M Van de Weyer had with Lord Palmerston, the latter wrote a private letter to King Leopold, in which he approved of his plan of naming a successor King Leopold sent a copy of this letter to his father-in-law, which he showed me yesterday, we thereupon at once wrote to Brussels, not relying on this *very confidential* information, but on Périer's last letter, which announced a renewal of this scheme

As it is evident from this, that Lord Grey and Lord Palmerston must have expressed themselves very differently, I felt that I ought to inform you of this, I pray you to consider it strictly as between you and me, even the King is not aware that I have mentioned it to you.

We are anxiously awaiting the result of the London Ministerial arrangement

The Portuguese are exceedingly clumsy with their abbreviated ratifications I fear we shall not get any further

M DE RAYNEVAL TO THE PRINCE DE TALLEYRAND

ARANJUEZ, *June 2nd,* 1834

PRINCE,

This will probably be the last despatch that I shall send you, relative to the events of the Portuguese war, for behold! this war, which, only a few days ago, was looked upon as interminable, has come to an end, as if by magic! You are the real conqueror in this affair The treaty has done it all The co-operation of the Spaniards no doubt produced some effect, but had it not been known that we were behind them, like a reserve corps, the Miguelites[1] would certainly not have laid down their arms so promptly.

[1] The civil war had in truth nearly come to an end in Portugal After the battle of Santarem, February 18th, and the repeated successes of Admiral Napier and the Comte de Villaflor in the North, the Miguelist troops were completely disorganised The Spanish intervention still further hastened matters Dom Miguel, completely beaten near Thomar (May 16th), retired on Evora, where he was shut up and obliged to capitulate unconditionally, May 26th Don Carlos, who had joined forces with him, shared the same fate The following day, May 27th, Dom Pedro proclaimed a general amnesty Don Carlos was released and permitted to retire without any conditions he embarked at Aldea Gallega together with his family and came to England As for Dom Miguel, he was obliged to sign an engagement to quit the Peninsula, in con-

The agreement signed by the Secretary of the British Legation in Portugal and Dom Pedro's generals, relative to Don Carlos, does not impose on that prince any of the conditions required of Dom Miguel. This greatly displeases the Cabinet here, which had just made a request, that before allowing the Spanish pretender to embark, the signatories of the Convention of April 22nd should decide the place where he would be permitted to live. Such a wish was perhaps hardly in accordance with this Convention; nevertheless, here they fully hoped it would be granted. Now they fear that it may be too late, but if they do not receive satisfaction on this point, they will only insist all the more on the necessity of obliging Don Carlos to give the same pledges as Dom Miguel, before receiving the pension which has been assured him. This is easier of compliance, but it is not all: the Spanish Cabinet at the same time proposes that its allies should declare, that, if the same circumstances which rendered their union necessary for the purpose of pacifying the Peninsula, should recur, the treaty would immediately resume all its strength and vigour.

M. Martinez de la Rosa has hastily drawn up and addressed a Note to me and Mr Villiers, in which the three points I have indicated are dealt with, the whole tenor being to ask France and England to assure to Spain the guarantees which she considers indispensable for her future tranquillity. I should like to have sent you this document, on which your Highness and Lord Palmerston will have to deliberate, but I am obliged, for want of time, to ask you to request that minister to let you see it.

THE PRINCE DE TALLEYRAND TO THE COMTE DE RIGNY

LONDON, *June 5th,* 1834

MONSIEUR LE COMTE,

I was only able to see Lord Palmerston for a few moments this morning, but long enough nevertheless to speak to him about the resumption of the scheme to provide by some special measure for the contingent succession to the Belgian throne. He admitted, that after having at first entered into King Leopold's views on this subject, he had given in to the opinion that an indefinite adjournment of this question was

salvation of which, he received a pension of 375,000 francs. After Dom Pedro's death, the Portuguese Cabinet took very stringent measures against the claimant. He was declared to have forfeited all his civil and political rights, and any attempt on his part to return to Portugal was to be punished by death within twenty-four hours. The Cortes however refused to ratify whatever was too Draconian in these measures.

preferable He promised me he would to-morrow, in accordance
with this, transmit instructions to Sir Robert Adair   He moreover showed me a letter, dated the 3rd, which he had just
received from that Ambassador, which stated in a few lines, that
the adjournment we wish, appears to have been adopted by the
Brussels Cabinet

I have the honour, M le Comte, while sending you a copy of
the Note in which Lord Palmerston proposes to communicate
to the diplomatic body here the treaty of the quadruple alliance,
to inform you that this communication was to have been made
at once   This however has not been done, and in accordance
with the opinion expressed by the Crown lawyer, the English
Cabinet has resolved to keep back the publication of this treaty,
until it has received the fresh ratifications from Lisbon.   If there
is still time, I think it would be as well for you also to suspend the publication, to which I was wrong to pledge you
prematurely

I may tell you that the English Squadron which quitted
Malta, has received no other instructions than to proceed to the
coast of Smyrna, where it habitually takes up its station in
summer

Letters have been received here to-day from Lisbon, dated
May 27th, which state that the Infant Don Carlos will not
embark in the same vessel as the Infant Dom Miguel   It appears
that the former of those two princes has asked to be taken to
Plymouth and thence to Holland

The new ministers, Lord Auckland,[1] Mr Spring-Rice,[2] and
Mr Ellice,[3] kissed hands at the King's *levée* this morning

The success of the Ministry in the House of Commons on
Monday[4] has not yet completely reassured the public mind
Lord Grey himself is not free from grave anxiety, which is plainly
traceable in his speeches and in the letter he wrote to the

---

[1] Lord Auckland was in the preceding Cabinet, as President of the Board of Trade

[2] Thomas Spring-Rice, born in 1790, entered the House of Commons in 1820, was Under-Secretary in the Home Office in 1827   In 1830, he was Secretary to the Treasury in Lord Grey's Cabinet, and in 1834, Minister of the Colonies   In 1835, he was made Chancellor of the Exchequer   He retired in 1839, and was created a peer under the title of Baron Monteagle

[3] Edward Ellice, born in 1781, an English manufacturer and statesman   After holding several important posts in the Hudson's Bay Company, he entered political life, was elected member of the House of Commons in 1830, was made Secretary to the Treasury in the Grey Cabinet, then Secretary of War from June till November 1834   In 1836 he was sent on a special mission to Paris.   After this he retired into private life until his death (1869)

[4] This was the sitting at which Mr Ward's motion was discussed (see pages 271 and 272)   It was rejected after Lord Althorp's speech on the previous question, by 396 votes against 120

deputation of 150 members of the House of Commons, who had sent him a petition, urging him to continue in the Ministry Accept

THE COMTE DE RIGNY TO THE PRINCE DE TALLEYRAND

PARIS, *June* 11th, 1834

MON PRINCE,

It seems to us here, that Sir John Grant[1] has been very officious and very prompt with regard to Don Carlos If he had allowed him to be threatened twenty-four hours longer by Rodil, we should have got him to agree to a Convention, similar to that subscribed to by Dom Miguel

Anyhow, the treaty has well attained its object—the expulsion of both Pretenders, and it appears to us that, with the exception of some written undertakings, Don Carlos is in exactly the same position as Dom Miguel

It was not possible to fix their future residence in a treaty, it is better to do this in a supplementary treaty As for making the treaty permanent, I hear that Martinez de la Rosa desires it as a perpetual moral restraint on the partisans of Don Carlos, but we must not take upon ourselves the necessity or obligation of a continued intervention that would become very troublesome Rayneval and Villiers however seem to agree that something further will have to be done If they wish this in London we shall make no objection, but we should not like it to result in any fresh obligations on our part outside the terms of the treaty, of which you have so admirably attested the fitness and calculated the effects

The Duc de Frias received instructions to press the matter on us, but I simply replied this morning, that it was a matter which must be settled in London

THE PRINCE DE TALLEYRAND TO THE COMTE DE RIGNY

LONDON, *June* 12th 1834

MONSIEUR LE COMTE,

I thoroughly understand the necessity under which the King's Government finds itself, of having to refute the attacks of some of the French papers with respect to the exchange of the ratifications of the treaty of April 22nd It

[1] Sir John Grant (1804 1850) was Secretary of Legation in Portugal He acted as *Chargé d'Affaires* in Lord Howard de Walden's absence The conditions of the capitulation of Évora had been discussed in a Conference between him, the General in command of the Miguelist troops, and the Comte de Saldanha

could not act differently, and I do not think it will cause any inconvenience to the English Government, no remark whatever has as yet been made to me on this subject, and I am quite able to reply to any that may be brought forward

I had the honour to transmit to you the day before yesterday, the same day on which I received it, a copy of the Note addressed to Lord Palmerston by the Marquis de Miraflores I had not time to think over and decide what reply should be sent to this Note, neither was I able to talk to Lord Palmerston about it, we were only able to discuss it yesterday [1]

I pointed out to him that we ought not to reply to this communication from the Spanish Government, except by refusing to mix ourselves up in the matter he brings to our notice, that, being in no way bound to this question by the treaty of April 22nd, there would, in my opinion, be something very objectionable, in the French and English Governments wishing to decide the future fate of the Infants Don Carlos and Dom Miguel, after they have been expelled the Peninsula

These two Princes are now in exactly the same position respecting Spain and Portugal, as all the other pretenders with regard to the countries to which they claim a right England, France, and Sweden, have not asked the other Powers for guarantees against the pretenders who might disturb them, and if the Spanish and Portuguese Governments think they have just cause to dread the two Infants in future, it is for the Cortes to ask for rigorous measures against any attempts that these Princes might make which would be of a nature to disturb the tranquillity of the Peninsula

I think Lord Palmerston shares my views on this question He will however ascertain the opinions of his Cabinet, and I for my part will await the instructions which I have the honour to request you will send me

MADAME ADELAIDE TO THE PRINCE DE TALLEYRAND

TUILERIES, *June* 12th, 1834

. . .

P S My brother has just told me of the idea they have in Spain, of making a fresh declaration, in connection with the treaty of the quadruple alliance According to his view, if we want to preserve its strength and effect, nothing should be said, especially

---

[1] The Madrid Cabinet would have liked the signatory Powers of the treaty of April 22nd to agree, that the two exiled Princes, Don Carlos and Dom Miguel, should be interdicted from returning to the Peninsula, and if need be, that their persons should be secured, this was the object of the step taken by M de Miraflores

at a time when its *efficacy* has been so conspicuously proved, and we must abstain from all confirmatory or explanatory declarations, for any such action would invalidate instead of consolidate it, and might, moreover, be attributed to regret that the affair should have been settled without the need of troops or French armies, or to a desire to make use of pretexts for sending them later on

He directs me to tell you that he spoke about it yesterday with Lord Granville, who seems quite satisfied with the arrangements which our beloved King explained to him, which was all the more satisfactory, said the King, because at Madrid a little hitch has occurred in the matter which each delay makes more difficult to remove   .

THE PRINCE DE TALLEYRAND TO THE COMTE DE RIGNY

LONDON, *June 13th*, 1834

MONSIEUR LE COMTE,

I have the honour to send you a telegraphic despatch together with this, it tells you of Don Carlos' arrival at Portsmouth, about which, as yet, I have no further details to give you

I have this morning received the despatch which you did me the honour to write on the 11th, and I hastened to see Lord Palmerston and Lord Grey to confer with them on the various points mentioned therein They had received letters from Mr Villiers, which were quite in accord with M de Rayneval's despatch, of which you kindly sent me a copy Both ministers, therefore, were fully informed as to the wishes and claims of the Spanish Government when I went to see them

We entered thoroughly into the question as to what it was possible to do under the circumstances, and I was soon able to perceive that your prognostications had been verified, and that the English Government did not wish to go beyond the stipulations of the treaty of April 22nd Lord Palmerston told me positively, that when the new ratifications of this treaty are once exchanged, he would consider the treaty as completed in its execution as well as in its form, and that he did not think the action of England ought to extend further than the engagements entered into by the act of April 22nd He added that he intended to reply to M de Miraflores' Note, and to the request sent to Mr Villiers by M Martinez de la Rosa, stating that the English Government could not intervene in the questions submitted to it, and if the Spanish Government considered that it had any engagements to carry out with the Infant Don Carlos, they must instruct a Spanish negotiator to treat directly with the Prince

In accordance with the instructions you have done me the

honour to send, I did not think I ought to urge the demands of Spain upon the two English ministers, I therefore confined myself to telling them I should inform you of my conversation with them

My opinion, of which you will have been able to judge from my despatch of yesterday, Monsieur le Comte, quite agrees, I confess, with that of Lord Grey and Lord Palmerston, and if I regret, with you, that some more positive conditions were not laid upon Don Carlos, I am no less persuaded that now that Prince can only be dealt with by agreement

M DE RAYNEVAL TO THE PRINCE DE TALLEYRAND

MADRID, *June* 14*th*, 1834

PRINCE,

The Queen Regent desires to show her gratitude to you for the treaty of April 22nd M de Florida-Blanca has therefore been directed to send you, in her name, the insignia of the order of Charles III I feel highly honoured by becoming in this way your brother in chivalry, but as it is wrong to deprive any one of what belongs to them, I must state that this royal decision was not in any way owing to me The honour is due alone to M. Martinez de la Rosa, if it is not entirely her Majesty's own idea

That minister receives also the same decoration.

I have to thank you for sending me the documents relative to the Portuguese ratifications Has there been gross ignorance or bad faith? Fortunately, the speedy conclusion of the sad drama played in Portugal removes any occasion for investigating this question. You will have noticed that the amnesty arranged at Evora-Monto, is almost identical with that drafted by you in London

The Spanish troops have already returned to Spain; they are being sent towards Biscay. It is to be desired, though one can scarcely hope for it, that on their approach, the insurgents will throw down their arms, as did the Miguelites If this should be so, it will be another miracle effected by the treaty

We have to-day learnt the success gained by the ministry in the House of Commons It is a good omen Here, as with us, nothing is talked of but the elections. Heaven grant that they may be satisfactory in both countries!

I believe that the Comte de Toreno[1] will continue to be Minister of Finance

[1] Jose Maria Queipo e Llano, Comte de Toreno, Spanish statesman and historian Born in 1786, became one of the leaders in the War of Independence in 1808 in the

THE PRINCE DE TALLEYRAND TO THE COMTE DE RIGNY.

LONDON June 16th, 1834

MONSIEUR LE COMTE

I have seen with pleasure that the King's
Government has adopted a course with respect to the last
proposals of the Madrid Cabinet, quite in accordance with
the views of the English Ministry   You will have seen by
my last despatches, that with regard to this I have always
confined myself within the bounds you prescribed for me,
and within which I continue to think we shall do well to hold
ourselves

I made known to M de Miraflores, in reply to the Note he
addressed to me, the opinion I had the honour to express to you
in my despatch No 63, and as the Spanish minister had
received a similar reply from Lord Palmerston he has decided
to go down to Portsmouth in order to negotiate directly with
Don Carlos

The offers he was directed to make to this Prince in the
name of his Government, consisted of a pension of thirty
thousand pounds sterling, in return for which the Infant was to
undertake similar engagements to those subscribed to by Dom
Miguel   Further, the Spanish claimant was not to live at Rome,
as it was feared that his presence there just now might exercise
a baneful influence on the Papal Government, already so badly
disposed towards Spain

M de Miraflores started on his mission the day before
yesterday, and Lord Palmerston on his part sent Mr Backhouse,
one of the under secretaries at the Foreign Office, to Portsmouth ,
the latter is directed to offer Don Carlos any assistance that it is
in the power of the English Government to give him, always
excepting a monetary loan, as to which this Government
is perfectly immovable   He was at the same time to sound the
Infant as to his views respecting M de Miraflores' proposals
It was thought that the refusal of a monetary loan was the best
support the English Cabinet could give the Spanish negotiator,
for it was supposed that the Infant and his suite, composed of
about sixty persons, would be utterly without resources

This was not so however, and Mr Backhouse has just

Asturias, and was elected to the Cortes at Cadiz   proscribed   in 1814, he took refuge
in France   returned to Spain a few years later, was elected Deputy in 1820, but had
again to expatriate himself in 1823   He was made Minister of Finance in 1833, and
Minister of Foreign Affairs and President of the Council in 1835   but retired at the
end of a month   He died in Paris in 1843

informed Lord Palmerston that Don Carlos did not intend to continue his journey just now , that, on the contrary, he wished to disembark at once and remain in England for some time He does not desire to hear anything of M de Miraflores' proposals , according to what he says, he does not mean to give up anything and will never cease to prosecute his rights , he will not consent to receive a penny on condition of submitting to any restrictive engagement whatever

Lord Palmerston attributes the Infant's resistance to the counsels of the Princess de Beira and the Bishop of Leon, both of whom are on board the *Donegal* , and without concealing from ourselves the bad effect this will have on the insurgents in the north of Spain, there is not much importance to be attached to it

After Don Carlos' reply to Mr Backhouse, the Marquis de Miraflores gave up the idea of seeing the Prince, to whom he wrote a letter, enclosing the draft of the compromise —copies of which I forward herewith—and returned to London

Don Carlos has sent for M de Sampayo, who acted as Dom Miguel's consul general, and requested him to take a house for him at Portsmouth for a fortnight, and then to look out for a country seat for him near London   But the most remarkable thing, and which seems a positive fact, is, that the Infant has a credit of one million francs (which has been sent by M de Blacas,) in the hands of M de Saraiva, Dom Miguel's minister in London   One must conclude from this, that everything was prepared in case of accidents, and that Don Carlos intends to live in England for some time   Of course it is quite understood that the English Government will make no objection to this , it even looks upon this decision with some favour, in the belief that it will be easier to keep an eye on his movements, and the intrigues of his partisans

The news of the republican revolution in Lisbon, so pompously announced in some of the papers, was nothing but a stock-jobbing fraud, arising out of some shouting in the theatre, when Dom Pedro was present, against his Government, for having allowed Dom Miguel to escape   I do not know whether such a violent spirit of animosity on the part of the Portuguese people justifies the decree, in consequence of which all the convents in Portugal and in the Portuguese possessions are abolished   This decree, however useful it may be in itself, seems to me to have been issued too hastily, and may be the cause of fresh troubles in the country , the Government, barely established, has at any rate committed an imprudence in provoking the whole of the clergy, now united in their hatred against it, and it is impossible not to recognise in this fresh act of Dom Pedro, the bad feeling which has influenced him for the last two years

The immediate arrival in England of the Duc de Palmella has been announced , he is coming from Lisbon with Admiral Parker, who retires from the command of the Tagus station, where he will be succeeded by Sir William Gage [1]

Some people say that the Duc de Palmella's journey is only on private affairs, but it is difficult to believe that political reasons do not occasion it

LORD PALMERSTON TO THE PRINCE DE TALLEYRAND

STANHOPE STREET, *June 16th*, 1834

MON CHER PRINCE,

Backhouse informs me that Don Carlos does not wish to continue his journey just now, and that, on the contrary, he wants to disembark at once with the intention of remaining here " some time " As for Miraflores' proposals, he will not hear them mentioned , he renounces nothing, he will never cease to prosecute his rights, and he will not accept a single penny on the condition of remaining quiescent It seems that his courage has risen wonderfully, since he finds the Bay of Biscay between himself and Rodil

All this is natural enough, and of no great importance The only result will be, that Spain will save thirty thousand pounds a year, and that her interior tranquillity will not be disturbed in the least Ever yours

PALMERSTON

THE COMTE DE RIGNY TO THE PRINCE DE TALLEYRAND

PARIS, *June 18th*, 1834

MON PRINCE,

Rouen [2] writes to me on the 28th May, that the English squadron was at Nauplia, and that it had *fifteen hundred troops* on board and six field pieces The admiral spoke of going towards the Dardanelles, but was still waiting for a few days for orders from Malta

This half measure appears singular to me, but is quite in accordance with the language held by Lord Ponsonby at Constantinople up to the 30th of May I am inclined to think that

---

[1] See William Hall Gage, born in 1777, entered the Navy at 29, and had a most brilliant career He was made Lord of the Admiralty in 1841, was promoted to the rank of admiral in 1862, and died in 1865

[2] Baron Rouen was at that time French minister in Greece

he has since modified this language, and that he has even advised the admiral not to assemble his fleet on the coast of Asia. In any case, however, Russia will use this as a pretext to remain under arms, and we shall be perpetually thwarted

A Russian, named Mayenvorth, who is in business here, tells every one that he has received the assurance from Medem, that if another English vessel enters the Mediterranean, the Russians will go to the Bosphorus. We know that their maritime position in the Black Sea is only guaranteed by the castles in the Bosphorus, for Sebastopol is not properly fortified on the sea-front

THE COMTE DE RIGNY TO THE PRINCE DE TALLEYRAND.

PARIS, *June* 23*rd*, 1834

MON PRINCE,

Sainte-Aulaire informs me that there has been a great stir in Vienna on account of the appearance of the English squadron in the Archipelago. Pozzo was greatly excited about it, and I am quite exhausted with my endeavours to get him to see the matter in its true light—a naval cruise which a new admiral thought it his duty to make, without any political object. At least, I suppose this is so

Swiss matters are getting complicated. Rumigny[1] is not always wise. The Sardinian minister told me yesterday, that, his Cabinet having declared themselves satisfied with the language of the deputation, everything was going on smoothly, when a fresh Note arrived which revived the whole question[2]

We have written to Egypt, telling them that they must fulfil the engagements entered into with the Porte, and so remove all pretexts. All this stir will end in giving the Russians an excuse for remaining under arms in the Black Sea, and so checkmate us in that quarter. Our elections are going on satisfactorily, of the three hundred nominations already known, the opposition have lost twenty-four, all well filled. We shall have two legitimists at Marseilles[3]

---

[1] The Comte de Rumigny was at that time French minister in Switzerland

[2] A Swiss deputation waited upon the King of Sardinia, during a journey which that prince was making in Savoy, in order to express the regrets of the Swiss Government for the unfortunate skirmish of February last (see page 259). The King received them very graciously, which however did not prevent the Swiss Cabinet from addressing a Note to the Directory on the 20th of June, to complain of the insufficient measures taken by the police

[3] The general elections of June 22nd, resulted in a greatly reduced republican opposition. On the other hand, the legitimists, who had not been at all represented in the preceding Chamber, gained twenty seats

THE PRINCE DE TALLEYRAND TO THE COMTE DE RIGNY.

LONDON, *June 26th*, 1834

MONSIEUR LE COMTE,

I went to see Lord Palmerston this morning and have just had a long talk with him . . on the various points touched on in your despatch

He admitted that Sir Robert Morier,[1] while sharing the views which guided our embassy in Switzerland, was nevertheless not quite in accord with M de Rumigny in the course he had just adopted Sir Robert Morier thinks that it will need great prudence and skill to maintain the Helvetian Diet in the position which it has taken up, with regard to the neighbouring Powers

Lord Palmerston, while making the most of Sir R Morier's narrative, nevertheless told me that he quite saw how important it was, that England and France, under present circumstances, should show they were of one mind on all questions He wishes you to be convinced that as regards this, he fully appreciates the reasons detailed in your despatch

He also gave me the assurance, that he would not only write to Switzerland, but also to the English ministers at Turin, Stuttgard, and Munich, directing them to make such representations as we desire to the Governments to which they are accredited

As he thought that, according to Lord Minto's reports, M Ancillon especially, had adopted quite erroneous ideas respecting Swiss affairs, he suggested also, sending such observations to Berlin as he hoped would produce a good effect I believe that the instructions I have just referred to, which Lord Palmerston is sending to the various ministers, will be sent off by courier to-morrow

He (Lord Palmerston) showed me Lord Ponsonby's last despatches, which are almost identical with those from our own ambassador I could not fail to see that the news contained in these despatches much engrossed the English Government

. . I obtained Lord Palmerston's promise that he would send instructions to Alexandria, directing that Mehemet Ali should be given to understand that he must put an end to his unreasonable demands upon the Porte It will not be easy to make the Viceroy listen to reason on the question of the arrears claimed by the Sultan, as it appears that nothing was put in

---

[1] Sir Robert Morier, an English writer and diplomat, born in 1790, was at that time minister in Switzerland.

writing on this subject in the Convention of Kutaya, and everything relating to the arrears was arranged verbally, but Colonel Campbell will be instructed to insist on this point, as well as with regard to the districts of which Ibrahim demands the surrender.

I asked Lord Palmerston to give me some fresh information respecting the movements of the English fleet in the Archipelago, and he gave me the same reply I had the honour to transmit to you a short time ago England, he said, considers it necessary for her safety in the present state of the east to keep a fleet in the Archipelago

This fleet, which winters at Malta, goes through a course of naval manœuvres every summer, and no change has been made this year in the usual custom Moreover, the English Government would be very pleased to see itself freed from the heavy expense entailed by maintaining this fleet, which would no longer be required, if an end were put to the intrigues which disturb the east

The last despatches received from Lisbon, dated the 9th, affirm that the errors in the Portuguese ratifications of the treaty of 22nd April, were not caused by bad faith, and that we shall immediately receive fresh ones, as full and complete as we have a right to demand

LONDON, *July 6th*, 1834

I had the honour to inform you in my last despatch, that I should make use of the observations you had made to me, as to the effect produced among several of the Cabinets by the movements of the English fleet in the Mediterranean

I saw Lord Palmerston for some time yesterday, and after acquainting him with your views and the particulars contained in Admiral Roussin's despatch, I thought I ought again to attack him openly on the Eastern question, which, with good reason, occupies the attention of all the Cabinets just now After going through all the various phases of this question with him, I succeeded in proving that, in my opinion, France and England could now only take one of the two following courses they must either adopt the measures recommended by Admiral Roussin, and attack the Russian maritime establishments in the Black Sea, and this meant war, or they must continue to do all in their power to maintain the general peace, and in that case, they ought as much as possible to avoid all half measures, all causes for disquietude to the other Powers, and adhere to a firm but moderate and conciliatory line of conduct.

I put on one side the first proposition, which it was not necessary to discuss just now, and which moreover would first have to be preceded by an offensive treaty of alliance between England and France

I therefore confined myself to discussing the second proposition, and reiterated the considerations which I had already entered into in my previous conversations, respecting the movements of the English fleet in the Mediterranean   I said that these movements could not fail to have a very dubious effect on the St Petersburg Cabinet, that in reality they were only a demonstration, the issue of which was perfectly plain, and that in all these sort of things a half measure without any results did more harm than good

Finally, looking at the question from a purely French point of view, I gave Lord Palmerston to understand that the King's Government, having constantly to reply to the questions of the Austrian, Prussian, and Russian representatives in Paris, with respect to the matter we were then discussing, could not help feeling some uneasiness about any enterprise in the Black Sea, which France would have to answer for on the Rhine, that we considered that a purely defensive treaty between ourselves and England, would serve much more effectually to intimidate Russia than naval cruises, that we had been compelled to abandon that measure because just now the English Cabinet objected to it, but that that Cabinet must not in its turn be surprised if we acted with caution and reserve in an affair, the results of which were so important to us, that if, for instance, we should not think it necessary to send our fleet to the Archipelago this year (and with regard to this I knew nothing of the views of our Government), the English Government would have to accept in explanation, the efforts we were already making in keeping up a large land army

Lord Palmerston began by expressing his regrets at the difficulties which had hitherto stood in the way of, and were still opposed to, concluding the treaty of which I had so often spoken to him

From the way in which he explained matters, I was enabled to see, as I have already had the honour to write to you, that these difficulties did not come from him, but that they arose in the Cabinet   I should not even be greatly surprised if the English Government were, before very long, to come round and consent to form a treaty, the advantages of which are so self-evident

Then referring to my observations on the uselessness of the movements of the English fleet, Lord Palmerston brought forward the considerations I mentioned in my last despatch, which tended to prove that the anxiety manifested by Russia and Austria, sufficiently testified to the importance attached by those Powers to the naval demonstrations of England , he is still fully convinced of the efficacy of these demonstrations, and I doubt the English fleet being recalled before the end of the utumn

Lord Palmerston however admitted that the account I had just given him of the peculiar position occupied by France, was quite correct, and that we might have reasons for not acting in the same way as England under such circumstances, and reciprocally. I thought the essential point for us would be to preserve our liberty of action in this affair , for this reason, I asked him plainly whether his Government desired that our fleet should also go to the Archipelago this year

He replied, that however satisfactory such a movement on our part might be for the sake of general effect, his Government did not actually ask for it   The discussion ended with this question, Monsieur le Comte, and the result of my conversation shows me that England is determined just now to keep her men-of-war in the Mediterranean, but that we are in no way obliged to follow her example

I will insist on this latter point, as I believe that as a matter of fact our fleet in the Mediterranean could not without some inconvenience, come out during this present season

The English Cabinet will have no cause to complain, as it did not formally ask us to send our vessels to sea, and moreover, we are keeping up a very large army which would be a heavy weight in the scale, if, later on, an open rupture in the East should supervene   It would at any rate be an equivalent to the English fleet, for there is no doubt that then there would be war on the Rhine as well as in the Black Sea

This reason, which quite justifies us as far as England is concerned, ought not, I think, to be less powerful with the Chambers and public opinion in France

We may also hope, that the northern Cabinets will feel themselves somewhat indebted to us for having avoided a course which is superfluous to demonstrate the union of England and France, now so fully proved to the eyes of all Europe

LONDON, *July 7th*, 1834

I have learnt with great satisfaction that Swiss affairs have taken a turn for the better ; it is to be hoped that the intrigues of the Austrian Cabinet will cease before the positive decisions of the Helvetian Diet   These will no doubt be conceived in sufficiently conciliatory terms to enable the Governments of Austria, Sardinia, Wurtemberg, and Baden to withdraw decently the extraordinary claims they have put forward

You will see that Lord Palmerston has expressed himself to the Austrian *Chargé d'Affaires*, in such a manner as to convince him that England has not separated herself from us in this question   Lord Palmerston quite realizes, as you so well remarked, M le Comte, that this is a question involving the principles on which the alliance between France and Great Britain rests   Austria wished to try how far our two Cabinets would put up with her demands, it was well that she found us very firm in this first attempt

I informed Lord Palmerston of the Note which you instructed M Alleye¹ to transmit to the Germanic Diet, in reply to that of June 12th   He thanked me for having shown it him, and considers it so thoroughly suitable, that he proposes to make Mr Cartwright² reply in almost similar terms

Your view of the contest between Comte d'Armansperg,³ and the other members of the Regency is fully shared by the English Cabinet, which will continue to support the efforts of Comte d'Armansperg in every way⁴   I am inclined to think that the King of Bavaria will himself retain the count at the head of the Regency, seeing that he, as well as M de Gise, his Minister for Foreign Affairs, is anxious to keep M d'Armansperg as long as possible out of Bavaria

I have just been informed by the Portuguese minister in London, that the fresh Portuguese ratifications of the treaty of 22nd April, were transmitted to M le Baron Mortier on the 21st June   As soon as you have received them, M le Comte,

---

· Baron Alleye de Ciprey, at that time French minister to the Germanic Confederation

· The English minister at the Germanic Confederation   He was previously commissioner of the London Conference at Brussels

³ Joseph Louis, Comte d'Armansperg (1789-1853) a Bavarian statesman   He was the Bavarian plenipotentiary at the Congress of Vienna, in 1814 and was made President of the Council of the Greek Regency in 1832

· A Council of Regency had been nominated in Greece, by the King of Bavaria, during the minority of King Otto   It was composed of Comte d'Armansperg, President, Councillor de Maurer, and General Heydeck   Discord very soon broke out in their midst   Comte d'Armansperg was accused of keeping all the power in his own hands, of unduly favouring English interests, and of alienating public opinion by filling all posts with Bavarians   On the 2nd of May, General Heydeck and M de Maurer attempted a sort of *coup d'état*, and immediately after, passed a series of resolutions, which deprived the president of the direction, and of the administration of the Finances of Foreign Affairs   But the King of Bavaria supported M d'Armansperg and recalled M de Maurer, who was replaced by M de Kobell, a Bavarian statesman   General Heydeck was forced to give in, and M d'Armansperg resumed the Presidency of the Council, together with all the powers he had arrogated to himself

will you kindly send the old ones to M le Chevalier de Lima, who is instructed to return them to Portugal I am very glad that this matter has been so happily arranged by the measures we adopted, for it caused us serious embarrassment at the time of the exchanges

The Infant Don Carlos has established his whole family in his new house near London. He has been visited there by the minister of the Two Sicilies,[2] and a great number of the Tory party Most of those who have seen him are greatly amazed at his ignorance of his rightful position and interests He is addressed as King, and his eldest son as Prince of the Asturias, by all those who come to see him

I have just received your letter informing me that the King has had the goodness to grant me leave of absence, of which however I shall probably not avail myself until after the closing of Parliament

THE PRINCE DE TALLEYRAND TO THE COMTE DE RIGNY

Telegraphic Despatch   LONDON, *July* 9*th,* 1834

Lord Grey and Lord Althorp [3] have tendered their resignations to the King, who has accepted them The King has summoned Lord Melbourne, who it appears will form the new Cabinet

THE PRINCE DE TALLEYRAND TO THE COMTE DE RIGNY

LONDON, *July* 14*th,* 1834

MONSIEUR LE COMTE,
For the last few days a report has been spread in London that Don Carlos has left for Spain, but particulars as to this piece of intelligence were so very vague and contradictory, that it was difficult to place any trust in them Even now that the actual fact is beyond a doubt, there is a variety of opinion as

---

[1] Louis Antoine d'Abreu e Lima, Vicomte de Carreira, a Portuguese diplomat, born in 1785, one of the plenipotentiaries at the Congress of Vienna, Secretary to the Legation, and *Chargé d'Affaires* at St Petersburg, then minister at the Hague from 1824 to 1830 He was accredited to Paris in 1833

[2] The Comte de Ludolf

[3] The English Cabinet had been much disturbed ever since the late changes When therefore in the month of July, violent debates took place in the House of Commons respecting the coercive Bill for Ireland, Lord Althorp, the Chancellor of the Exchequer, seeing that he no longer possessed the necessary weight to carry the Government measure in the House of Commons, sent in his resignation without even waiting to put this to the test Lord Grey, who for some months had wished to resign, took advantage of this circumstance to retire from office

to how it has taken place Some people maintain that the
Infant embarked on board an English vessel, *The United
Kingdom*, for a port in the north of Spain   This is the report
made by the English police , but on the other hand, the Spanish
minister thinks he has proof that the Infant left London the very
same day on which the English papers stated he had been
present at the Italian Opera with all his family, that he went to
Paris, accompanied by General Moreno and a Frenchman [1] who
had organized the whole enterprise, and that from thence the
Prince and his two companions had continued their journey
towards the Spanish frontier, where the measures taken by
M Colomarde [2] would assure them a free entry into Spain

I give you the facts communicated to me by Lord Palmerston
and the Marquis de Miraflores, without being able to say which
are the true ones, for in affairs of this nature, which rest almost
entirely with the police, it is very difficult at first to ascertain the
truth

The formation of the new English Cabinet is not yet
definitely concluded, although it is pretty nearly decided   The
King first sent for Lord Melbourne with the view of forming a
coalition ministry. This attempt having fallen through, his
Majesty made a second appeal to Lord Grey in the hope of
inducing him to return to office, but the repeated requests of the
King proving ineffectual to overcome Lord Grey's firm resolution
to retire, Lord Melbourne has been chosen to replace him as First
Lord of the Treasury   It appears that the other members of the
Cabinet will continue in their present posts, and at a meeting of
the ministers to be held this evening, Lord Melbourne's successor
at the Home Office will be decided on   It is also possible that a
successor will have to be found for the Marquis of Lansdowne,
who, it is said, still intends to resign   Lord Grey has succeeded
in persuading Lord Althorp to come in again as Chancellor of the
Exchequer, and thus resume his place as leader of the House of
Commons

LONDON, July 15th, 1834

.   The ministers assembled this evening, for the purpose
of completing the arrangements necessitated by the King's choice

---

[1] M Auguste de Saint-Sylvain
[2] François Thadée Colomarde, a Spanish statesman, born in 1775   Was first
Secretary to the Council of Castile, then Minister of Justice in 1824   He retained
his portfolio until 1832, was an earnest partizan of absolute power, and actively persecuted the constitutional party   On the death of King Ferdinand, he sided with
Don Carlos, and was obliged to retire from office   He took refuge in France, where
he for some time served the Pretender's cause , but he soon withdrew altogether from
public life, and retired to Toulouse, where he died in 1842

of Lord Melbourne to replace Lord Grey as First Lord of the Treasury   I have just been informed that they have decided to ask Lord Duncannon to replace Lord Melbourne at the Home Office   Lord Duncannon,[1] who was Commissioner of Woods and Forests, without a seat in the Cabinet, will be succeeded by Sir John Hobhouse,[2] who will receive a seat in the Cabinet

Lord Melbourne left for Windsor this morning, for the purpose of submitting these propositions to the King, but no doubt is expressed as to their being accepted by his Majesty

There will probably be some other less important changes, in consequence of the retirement of Lord Howick,[3] Earl Grey's son, who filled the post of under secretary at the Home Office[4]   The Cabinet may therefore be considered to be reconstituted, and one can now form an opinion as to what it will be

I must begin by telling you, M le Comte, that the changes which have just taken place will in no way affect the present relations between France and England   Lord Duncannon and Sir John Hobhouse have always professed views which ought completely to reassure the King's Government on that point

Looking at the present position of the English Ministry as regards its foreign relations, one cannot conceal from oneself that it has sustained an irreparable loss in Lord Grey, whose noble character and well known loyalty inspired both his friends and enemies with confidence   It is difficult to believe that the more advanced and reformatory opinions of the two new members of the Cabinet, can compensate in the eyes of the country and of all Europe for Lord Grey's withdrawal from the high position he occupied

I am told by persons, as impartial as it is possible to meet with in the midst of the violence of party spirit, that the successive retirement, during the last few weeks, of Mr Stanley, Sir James Graham, the Duke of Richmond, the Earl of Ripon, and finally of Earl Grey, has so enfeebled the Ministry that there is but little guarantee for its future duration   One must be more fully

---

[1] John William, Baron Duncannon of Bessborough, 1781-1847

[2] John Cam Hobhouse, born in 1785, became a member of Parliament in 1820   In 1821, he was Secretary of the War Department, then Secretary of State for Ireland   Commissioner of Woods and Forests in 1834, and President of the India Board in 1846   He was created a Peer in 1851 with the title of Lord Broughton, and died in 1869

[3] Henry George Howick, Earl Grey, born in 1802, member of the House of Commons in 1826, Under-Secretary of State for the Colonies in 1830, then transferred to the Home Office, War Minister and Privy Councillor in 1835   He retired in 1839, but was again Colonial Secretary from 1846 to 1852   He succeeded his father in the House of Lords in 1845, with the title of Earl Grey

[4] A few days later, the Earl of Carlisle, Lord Privy Seal, also sent in his resignation, and was replaced by Lord Mulgrave   The Cabinet, thus reconstructed, lasted until the month of November, at which period the Tories came into power

cognisant, than I can be, of the slight divisions which will always exist in the Cabinet, to be in a position to judge how far this opinion is justly founded What however appears to be beyond any doubt, is, that the necessity they are under of passing the Irish Church Bill in the House of Lords before the end of the session, almost renders a collision between the two Houses (which has for so long been dreaded by the Government) inevitable Will a fresh batch of peers be made ? This question, answered affirmatively, might possibly decide some other members of the Cabinet to retire, answered negatively, it is not easy to see how the Government can go on between the contrary desires of the two Houses

I need not remind you, M. le Comte, that my observations on this matter are of a strictly confidential nature, and that it is to the advantage of the King's Government that nothing should be indiscreetly revealed

I repeat again, that the English Cabinet, as it has now been reconstructed, will remain well disposed towards France , this is the main point for us, and must guide our policy until other circumstances, which it would be imprudent to prejudge, place us in a position to alter it

P.S —I have just been informed that the Infant Don Carlos, who was said to have left London on the 2nd of this month, disembarked at a port in Biscay on the 9th, where he was very favourably received It is said he was only accompanied by one Frenchman I send you this bit of news, without however guaranteeing it, for it is impossible in the face of the diverse accounts which succeed each other so rapidly, to gauge the exact truth This last piece of news has however reached the English Government, which attaches some confidence to it This morning M. de Miraflores assured me that he had received positive proof that Don Carlos had traversed France to go to Navarre

THE COMTE DE RIGNY TO THE PRINCE DE TALLEYRAND

PARIS, *July* 17th, 1834

MON PRINCE,

The observations contained in your letter, accord perfectly with the ideas we have formed here as to the composition of the English Cabinet What chiefly concerns us is, to be assured that the friendly relations between the two countries will be continued This is very important in the present circumstances

We hear from Genoa that, although Dom Miguel did not wish to break the engagement to which he had subscribed, he will soon be so badgered and excited, that he will meditate a return to the

Peninsula if the death or the illness of his brother gives him a favourable opening.[1] There is no doubt that Don Carlos has sent for him, and is quite ready to extend to him the same hospitality in Navarre, that he himself received from him in Portugal

I read an article in *The Globe* of the 15th, which makes some allusions to the results which might arise from the treaty of April 22nd

I have little doubt that Spain will make an appeal to us, and I think, mon Prince, it would be well if you could sound the English Cabinet on this point beforehand

Marshal Soult has this morning sent in his resignation,[2] that he means it, is certain, and the King is just now trying to persuade Gérard, who still hesitates, dreading the Tribune and the responsibility I believe he also thinks of the awkwardness of coming in alone ; he spoke of Jacob's feebleness I do not know whether he has gone any further in his confidential talks with Thiers. I, for my part, am quite ready to facilitate matters, all the more so, that I am alone in my opinion, (which is contrary to the prevailing one) that to make a long opening speech and thereby raise a discussion on the address, will be quite useless, and will only serve to create a disturbance and render foreign questions more difficult to deal with .

Madame de Dino will be more skilful than Champollion if she deciphers this, but my hand is shaking terribly, as I am slightly feverish to-day

THE PRINCE DE TALLEYRAND TO THE COMTE DE RIGNY

LONDON, *July 17th,* 1834

MONSIEUR LE COMTE,

I have the honour to transmit to you herewith the copy of a letter which I have just received from the Spanish minister, and which was accompanied by a Note, copy of which is also here enclosed, addressed by that minister to Lord Palmerston This Note, which is a perfect illustration of the thoughtlessness of a step, taken, I think, somewhat hastily, will necessarily

---

[1] Dom Pedro had been ill for some time He got rapidly worse towards the end of August, and died on the 24th September, at the age of thirty-six

[2] There was downright hostility in the Cabinet between Marshal Soult and several of his colleagues, especially M Guizot and M Thiers A sort of conspiracy was organized, to get the Marshal to send in his resignation He was known to favour military rule in Algeria M Guizot and M Thiers talked of substituting a civil administration Marshal Soult opposed it, and threatened to retire He was taken at his word, and his resignation accepted As for substituting the civil administration, which had served as a pretext in this incident, there was no question of it at this time

place the English Government in the position of having to come to an understanding with us, as to the course the London and Paris Cabinets will have to take under the new circumstances in which Spain will be placed. I beg you, Monsieur le Comte, to kindly let me know the intentions of the King's Government with regard to this, and to give me the instructions which it is absolutely necessary I should have in so important a question, one too which is so intimately connected with the interests of France.

I have simply acknowledged the receipt of this Note to M de Miraflores, and as it is plain that it is his own work, and that he has not had time to receive orders from his Court, you will no doubt consider that we should wait, before taking any decisive line, until the Spanish Government has enunciated its views directly on this matter.

I have the honour to send you a copy of the Bill brought into Parliament last session, respecting the execution of the conventions concluded between France and Great Britain for the suppression of the slave trade.

THE COMTE DE RIGNY TO THE PRINCE DE TALLEYRAND

PARIS, *July 18th*, 1834

MON PRINCE,

I am writing from the Council itself: the order, naming Marshal Gérard as successor to Marshal Soult, has just been signed and will appear in the *Moniteur* to-morrow, together with proper explanations respecting Marshal Soult, whose retirement is, after all, voluntary.

We have no fresh news from the frontier, except that the troops on both sides are being concentrated, and there is every prospect of a speedy engagement.

THE COMTE DE RIGNY TO THE PRINCE DE TALLEYRAND.

PARIS, *July 21st*, 1834

MON PRINCE,

I need hardly tell you how greatly Don Carlos' arrival in Spain embarrasses us.

The Queen has rather brought discredit on herself, and her party presents itself between her and her sister—at the head of an army.

On the other hand, Toreno's financial scheme announces a reduction in the interest on the Spanish *rentes*. This affects

a number of the lower classes in Paris, who are beginning
to make a great outcry

Under all these different influences, we are on the eve of
a public discussion, in which the treaty of April 22nd will play
a great part, both owing to what it has promised, what it has
already done, and also what it has not been able to prevent

Either it exists, or it no longer exists

If it does not exist, then we fall back on our former position
as regards the Queen's Government, formal recognition and
promises of support and aid , and there is no doubt that we shall
be appealed to in that sense with all the more force and even
reason, because Don Carlos has traversed the whole of our
territory

If the treaty exists, there will probably be an appeal to
Articles 3 and 4,[1] and the step taken by M de Miraflores is a
forerunner of that which the Madrid Cabinet will put in execution

It is the principle therefore which we must first decide , the
consequences we can arrange for afterwards

You will perceive, mon Prince, how very difficult it will be to
draw up first the speech, and then the address   In the discussion, we shall not fail to be told that England having arranged
her affairs with Portugal, Dom Miguel having gone after signing
his renunciation, we have been utilized to pull their chestnuts
out of the fire, and have then been left in the lurch, &c

And in addition, think of all these Carlist movements on our
southern frontier, of a Carlist restoration in Spain, just when
Berryer is made a deputy at Toulouse and Marseilles   I already
perceive an ill-natured feeling on this subject among the ministerial
deputies who have arrived ; and here we shall find both parties
in the Chamber leagued together to accuse us of weakness,
while at the same time they will prevent our taking any more
active steps in the north of the Peninsula, and we shall have to
adopt a medium course, changeable and idiotic, and lay ourselves
open to all the false ideas of a national dignity, which will blame
us for our inaction

The King I know, fears the northern Powers ; he dreads a
war, he is afraid to enter Spain even for a few steps   I also
dread this, but there is quite as much to fear on the other hand
After all, we have not yet received a request from Spain, but
before it arrives, I should wish us to be all agreed, so that no
fresh divisions may arise in the Cabinet, and I foresee that there
will be some on this important subject before very long

[1] These were the articles in the treaty which provided for the eventual intervention of France and England   The Spanish Cabinet did not make an official appeal
till the following year (May 17th, 1835)

THE PRINCE DE TALLEYRAND TO THE COMTE DE RIGNY.

LONDON, *July* 21*st*, 1834

MONSIEUR LE COMTE,

I had a long talk with Lord Palmerston yesterday relative to Spanish affairs and the fresh complication created by Don Carlos' presence in the revolted provinces He agreed with me, *that the object of the treaty of April 22nd had not been attained,* and was very much struck by the remark contained in your despatch No 63, that the consequences of this treaty should ultimately have turned to the benefit of the Infant, as he now finds himself transported into the midst of his partisans, whereas, before the treaty, all access to the Basque provinces was virtually closed to him

I pointed out to Lord Palmerston that if he once admitted, as we did, that the object of the treaty had not been fulfilled, it must also seem necessary to him that some measures should be taken to complete the work which both our Courts had in view when they arranged it

" On that point," he said to me, " we are not disinclined to think that *something* must be done to aid the cause of the Queen of Spain, but in order to determine that *something,* we must first know the nature of the demands which Madrid will make to London and Paris We shall send some lightly armed vessels to the northern coast of Spain, to watch the movements of the insurgents , the presence of our flag in those parts may be of use to the Spanish Government, but that is the only measure we can take, until the Madrid Cabinet asks for more direct assistance "

Lord Palmerston having once admitted that the treaty of April 22nd, though executed in the letter, was not so in principle, and that *something* would have to be done to complete its execution, I did not insist further, and should even have waited for a positive request to come from Madrid, before speaking again to him about it, when a few hours ago, I received your despatch No 66

After having read it, I thought that its contents were too serious, not to ask Lord Palmerston to confirm what he had told me yesterday, and which was so complete an answer to the questions you put to me The despatch of vessels by the King's Government to St Sebastian, Bilboa, Santander, etc , which is quite in accord with the step taken by the English Government, gave me besides the opportunity of reverting to our conversation of yesterday

Lord Palmerston did not hesitate to repeat to me what he had said before, namely, *that he did not consider that the object of the treaty of April 22nd had been attained*, and that both his Government and ours would have to do something to insure the execution of this treaty I repeat these same words, as they were those used by Lord Palmerston, both yesterday and to-day

He informed me besides, that he had just received a second Note from M de Miraflores, in which the latter renews the requests contained in the first, and draws up some of the stipulations which should be inserted in the new treaty or supplementary convention, which will have to be concluded

The Marquis de Miraflores desires, among other things, that an auxiliary Portuguese corps should be sent into Spain, in the same manner as a Spanish corps had pursued the two Pretenders into Portugal

Lord Palmerston said that he would send the same reply to this Note that he had done to the former one, declining to take any action in the matter of its contents, until the intentions of the Madrid Cabinet were known, and I suggested quietly, that it was especially important with regard to the entry of Portuguese troops into Spain to know the wishes of the Madrid Cabinet I think you may now sound M le Chevalier de Lima on this very delicate point The measure determined on by the English Government, to send some vessels to the northern coast of Spain, cannot fail to produce a good effect , for, when carried out, together with that of a similar nature which you mentioned to me, it will show that, from the very commencement we have agreed to support the Queen's cause

These, Monsieur le Comte, are the only particulars I am in a position to furnish you with, in reply to your last despatches

I will only add one remark, namely, that it is my opinion, the English Government would be much displeased to see any armed intervention on our part in Spain, yet on the other hand, the measures it would agree to adopt to assist the Queen's cause, would probably not suffice , but all this is of course only hypothetical

THE COMTE DE RIGNY TO THE PRINCE DE TALLEYRAND

PARIS, *July 25th,* 1834

MON PRINCE,

The despatches from Madrid are not very reassuring and do not encourage one to interfere

It is as well that you should know that the foreign ministers here, who can easily perceive the King's personal views, take advantage of them to inform and encourage Don Carlos ; we have *actual proof* of this In all their private conversations they constantly assert that if we support the Queen by an armed intervention, there will be a general war ; they induce their Courts to send precise Notes on this subject, and declare that they will stop us very quickly. I should therefore like it to be decided either one way or the other, before such language is addressed to us

What would suit us best would be that Spain should not ask us for anything, and I have not given any encouragement on this subject to Rayneval

The English vessels have quitted Smyrna , this is as well, for their stay there was a source of perpetual irritation to Constantinople, and nearly the whole of its dragomanate almost entirely to no purpose

MADAME ADELAIDE TO THE PRINCE DE TALLEYRAND

NEUILLY, *July 25th*, 1834

OUR beloved King, to whom I read your letter, of which he thoroughly approves, wishes me to give you his views as to the Spanish matter He will give all the moral support he can to the young Queen's crown, and thus give strength and solidity to her Government He believes that such moral support will be more efficacious than an armed intervention, he will therefore make every effort to avoid such intervention but at the same time he knows the vicissitudes of human life too well to pledge himself that it shall never take place , on the contrary, he wishes it to be known, that he will always be ready, no matter what it may cost him, to take such bold measures as it may seem to him the interests of France, which are the sole motive of his conduct and his thoughts, demand

The King desires me also to tell you, that he is quite aware that there are people who consider, that with a body of ten, twelve, or fifteen thousand French troops at the outside, we might carry off Don Carlos, bring him into France, and then withdraw these troops again at once into French territory The King does not believe in the success of such an attempt, even if it were made It would be exceedingly difficult to cut off Don Carlos in the mountains or to pursue and take him prisoner But the King also thinks, that even if it were possible, the name of Don Carlos *carried off by the French*, would be more formidable than his presence, which will become a source of continual embarrassment to his partisans, and especially those who have to guard him He says that such an abduction would be compared in Spain to that of Ferdinand VII by Napoleon, and would be even more advantageous than hurtful to his cause Whereas if Don Carlos' influence is lessened by the action of Spain, and he finds that he has to retire into French territory because Spain will have nothing to do with him, his cause will be lost, and we shall then be able, without any inconvenience, to take such preventive measures against him as will preserve Spain from the dangers to which his return might later on expose her. This, mon cher Prince, is one of the views the King wishes to confide to your discretion, he knows you will only make a good use of it, and he regrets exceedingly not being able to discuss personally with you all his opinions on this very serious and complicated question

He begs you will always, at all hazards, keep in view, that as any intervention by France in Spain must necessarily weaken the former on the Rhine and along the Alps ; it would be *desired* and not *dreaded* by the northern Powers, and that consequently as it might cause them to make war, France would never think of embarking in such an undertaking, unless England bound herself by an alliance to make common cause with her

All this, mon Prince, is under the seal of the most profound secrecy

THE PRINCE DE TALLEYRAND TO THE COMTE DE RIGNY

LONDON, *July* 25*th*, 1834

MONSIEUR LE COMTE,

I saw Lord Palmerston yesterday, and after a long conversation together on the present situation of Spain, I made him see all the difficulties in which this question would involve the King's Government, just at the time when the assembling of the Chambers would oblige him to explain the policy he intended to pursue in the affairs of the Peninsula I also told him that it was absolutely necessary for us to know the opinion of the English Cabinet, with respect to the value it attached to the treaty of April 22nd, and further, whether after what he, Lord Palmerston, had said to me two days ago, the French Government would be authorized to declare officially, that France and England both recognized that the object of the treaty not having been attained, some fresh measures would have to be adopted to provide for its execution In conclusion I added, that in the event of the English Government recognizing with us the non-execution of the treaty of April 22nd, it might perhaps be possible to inform me at once, and even before we have been asked to give any assistance, what measures England would think of proposing in order to aid the cause of the Queen of Spain

Lord Palmerston, to whom I had shown all the reasons which made me anxious to have categorical replies, if not on all points, at least on that relative to the value and importance to be attached to the treaty of April 22nd, promised to submit my observations to the other members of the Cabinet to-day, and I now hasten to transmit to you the result of this conference with his colleagues which he has just communicated to me

The English Government thinks that a phrase, somewhat like the following, might be introduced in the speech at the opening of the Chambers

" England agrees with us, that the object of the treaty of 22nd April has not been attained, and the four Powers signatory thereto are now occupied in deciding the measures which will have to be taken under the present circumstances "

This, Monsieur le Comte, is the phrase which I drew up with Lord Palmerston and which has his complete approval   The King's Government nevertheless is not obliged to adhere to the actual wording of this phrase, but it could not deviate from the spirit of it without running the risk of going beyond what the English Government would approve

As regards the measures to be adopted, Lord Palmerston said that it was impossible to arrange anything until a request had come from Madrid, and that it would be useless just now to discuss the question of an armed intervention on our part in Spain, before the development of events in the Peninsula rendered such an important step imperative

I did not wish to insist further, as it seemed to me that for the present the phrase which I have just had the honour to communicate to you, was a sufficient answer to the exigencies experienced by the King's Government   In fact, if a discussion is raised in the Chamber of Deputies as to the results of the treaty of April 22nd, it will be sufficient to state that the signatory Powers have recognized that as the object of the treaty has not been attained, they must consider what further steps should be taken, but that these steps are a matter of negotiation, the details of which could not yet be made public

I think, M   le Comte, that you will agree with me regarding this, and I shall impatiently await your reply to this despatch

I must add, that Lord Palmerston, both in his own name and that of his colleagues, expressed the earnest desire that some phrase in our opening speech should allude to the union of France and Great Britain   It would not, I think, be difficult to include it in that relative to the events in the Peninsula

M Tricoupis, the Greek minister in London, has informed me of some propositions which had been made to him a few days ago by the new Russian *Charge d'Affaires*, in the name of his Government   One of these propositions was to induce the Greek Government to ask the three allied Courts for a declaration recognizing the neutrality of the Greek kingdom   M Tricoupis, while undertaking to transmit this overture to his Government, told me that he had informed the Comte de Medem, that a declaration such as he proposed would undoubtedly oblige his Government, in case of war, to close her ports against French and English vessels

The second proposition related to King Otto, whom the Russian Government was anxious to see embrace the Greek religion, or at any rate declare his firm intention to bring up his children in that religion   M Tricoupis replied that King Otto not having as yet attained his majority, was not obliged to express himself on this point , that in any case it was a matter of conscience which could not be settled by a treaty, and that as far as the religion of the young King's children was concerned, there was no necessity to trouble about that since he had none, and was not even married

I have just seen Lord Palmerston, who informed me of an alteration made at the Cabinet Council, relative to the phrase which [I had the honour to communicate to you, as expressing the opinion of the French and English Governments on the treaty of 22nd April   He told me, that having only consulted a few of his colleagues when he saw me, he had afterwards considered the matter of too serious a nature not to be dealt with by a Cabinet Council and that it was by the general advice of the Council that the new phrase had been modified and sent to Lord Granville to be submitted to you

Lord Palmerston read this phrase to me, which appeared to contain, although in a less distinct form, the substance of that I have sent to you   I expressed this view to Lord Palmerston, adding that it was just possible that the King's speech would have already received the sanction of the Ministerial Council, before Lord Granville made his communication to you, and that consequently it would be too late to make any alteration

I think I may say that in my opinion there would be no difficulty in keeping to the first draft which I sent you, if you prefer that one

THE COMTE DE RIGNY TO THE PRINCE DE TALLEYRAND

PARIS, *August* 3*rd*, 1834

MON PRINCE,

I thoroughly understand what has occurred, Palmerston has taken advantage of your absence to do what he would have found very difficult had you been in London

However, all this is now finished Here opinions are greatly divided some declare we have not said enough, others think we have said too much

Dupin is against all armed intervention, the *Journal des Débats* for any sort of armed intervention, I can only influence it thus far, but cannot keep it silent

It is impossible for us to know what Don Carlos and Rodil are doing in their mountain fastnesses I am rather uneasy as to the designs, not of Rodil himself, but of his surroundings The massacre of the monks at Madrid [1] has revived the insurrection, and the conspiracies that have been traced and brought to light at Madrid, show that there are divisions in the Queen's party

The accounts from Catalonia are better I should much like you to send me by special courier, Lord Londonderry's speech in the House of Lords [2]

It has occurred just in time for our debates here, which will commence the end of this week

[1] Some murderous scenes had stained Madrid with blood The cholera had broken out in the capital As in Paris, the populace refused to believe in the malady, and attributed the epidemic to the effect of poison, which they declared had been distributed by the priests On the 17th of July armed bands attacked the convents in the towns, and massacred most of the priests they found

[2] Lord Londonderry had given notice that he would bring forward a motion on the affairs of the Peninsula On the 4th of August, he violently attacked the policy of the Cabinet in the House of Lords This is what he said of France

"As regards the alliance with France, I do not think it is fair to give that country a preference over all the others, and I cannot join in the eulogies so often lavished on the three days of July

"Louis-Philippe governs on the principle of force he has filled the provinces and the capital with his troops, his proclamations and his conduct in general are as arbitrary as those of Charles X, only Louis Philippe has acted with greater frankness and skill As far as the quadruple treaty is concerned, I can conceive nothing really more base, more atrocious, than the course that has been adopted as regards Portugal in negotiating this treaty We had pledged ourselves to a positive neutrality, but under the mask of such neutrality the Government prepared an armed intervention in concert with a powerful ally I really think that for a great nation such conduct is atrocious'

Lord Londonderry added, that England had gained nothing by this policy, and wound up by demanding "that a humble address should be presented to his Majesty praying him to order that copies of the whole correspondence and of the information which had led to the negotiation and the conclusion of the treaty of April 22nd, might be laid on the table" This motion was rejected by a large majority

4th August

Harispe[1] writes us that Rodil has gained a decided advantage over Zumalacarreguy Don Carlos has retreated to our frontier, and Harispe has no doubt that he will ere long be forced to recross it

Here are the demands from Madrid, duplicates of which have been sent to Lord Palmerston by Villiers and M de Miraflores

An armed intervention finds but little support in the Chamber. The King does not care about a declaration at all, and we could, in fact, consider the phrase in the speech as an equivalent

On the other hand, Toreno, with his loan in London and the bankruptcy he has brought on our small landowners, gives us no means of assisting him, it is said he is reducing the interest to two-fifths We have written very strongly about this, but Spain wants a bankruptcy, and I fancy she cannot do anything else This will make Toreno as popular in Madrid as he is the reverse here

THE COMTE DE RIGNY TO THE PRINCE DE TALLEYRAND

August 4th, 1834, 9 o'clock in the Evening

MON PRINCE,

We have just received the following despatch from Bayonne, dated up to to-day

" The insurgents have been beaten at all points since the 1st Rodil attacks with great energy " [2]

I shall receive the details this evening

THE PRINCE DE TALLEYRAND TO THE COMTE DE RIGNY

LONDON, *August 5th*, 1834

MONSIEUR LE COMTE,

I have the honour to transmit to you herewith, the copy of a document of which you are already aware, namely, the Note by which Lord Palmerston replied on the 28th of last month, to the renewed proposals of the Spanish Minister I send at the

---

[1] Jean Isidore, Comte Harispe, born in 1761, served as a volunteer in 1792, became Brigadier-General in 1807, and served specially in Spain Placed on the un-attached list under the Restoration for having rallied round the Emperor during the Hundred Days, he re entered the service in 1830 and was created a peer of France He commanded a division in 1834 on the Pyrenean frontier He was made a Marshal of France in 1851, and died in 1855

[2] General Rodil had just been placed at the head of a formidable force On reaching Logrono on the Ebro, he heard of Don Carlos' arrival in the revolted provinces He determined to do his utmost to secure his person, he covered the country with fortified outposts and won signal successes, but the claimant always succeeded in eluding him in the midst of the greatest dangers

same time a literal translation of the fresh Note which the Marquis de Miraflores has just addressed to Lord Palmerston, and in which he dwells on the different points, which the Spanish Government is desirous should be inserted in the additional articles of the treaty of April 22nd

A similar communication will no doubt have been made to you by M. le Duc de Frias, and as it will have engaged your full attention, I shall be greatly obliged, if you will make known to me the intentions of the King's Government, respecting the five new propositions of the Madrid Cabinet

The first expresses a desire which has been forestalled by the French Cabinet, and which cannot, consequently, cause any difficulty   I believe that this is equally so with the second,[1] and as regards the third, which relates to the entry of a body of Portuguese troops, it does not seem possible that under the given circumstances, we should make any objection

But respecting the fourth proposition, I particularly wish to have positive, precise, and fully detailed data   I am not in a position to judge as to the nature, the quantity, or the value of the material assistance with which the King's Government would propose to furnish Spain, and I must therefore ask you, M. le Comte, to send me a fully drawn up and complete article to which I shall have nothing more to add, but to ask for the signature of the other plenipotentiaries

I must also beg you to acquaint me with the form you wish given to the species of guarantee and moral support, which is the subject of the fifth proposition of the Spanish Government.

You can understand, M. le Comte, that these two last points contain questions which I am not in a position to solve, for it requires much more knowledge than I possess, of the resources which the King's Government means to employ in favour of Spain and the extent to which it would pledge itself to take part in the affairs of the Peninsula

As it is very probable that my opinion will soon be asked respecting the additional articles that are to be added to the treaty of 22nd April, I venture to beg you will hasten as much as possible, the despatch of the instructions and orders I await from you

LONDON, *August 7th*, 1834.

I have just had an interview with Lord Palmerston, on the subject of the demands recently made by the Madrid Cabinet to

[1] The first proposition was relative to the measures to be adopted by the French Cabinet on the Pyrenean frontier ; the second to the assistance which England was to furnish to Queen Isabella's Government

the French and English Governments He acquainted me with
the views suggested to him by a close examination of these demands, which led him to doubt the possibility of adding any
articles to the treaty of April 22nd, or even of making a fresh
treaty In fact, he said, the demands of the Madrid Cabinet
touch on points which cannot possibly form the subject of
stipulations in a treaty, but are matters of police regulation,
which every Government is always free to adopt Thus the
French Government has a right to forbid the introduction into
Spain, by her land frontier, of any species of assistance in favour
of the Spanish insurgents It can, in conceit with the English
Government, cause the Spanish coasts to be watched, and prevent
the delivery of contraband munitions of war within the limits laid
down by the law of nations But it is not necessary that such
measures should be stipulated for in a treaty, it would even be impossible to do so, without admitting the rights of neutrals, and
consequently, without invalidating in advance all pursuit that
would be made of foreign vessels, which might attempt to land
arms, ammunition, &c, in Spain, for the insurgents Without
a formal declaration of war by France and England against
Don Carlos, which could not reasonably be asked for, it would be
very difficult for those two Powers to obtain the recognition by the
other Governments of a blockade of the Spanish coasts It would
therefore be much better, that the Spanish Government should
declare her ports blockaded, and that the French and English
vessels should lend their aid in maintaining this blockade, always
acting within the limits assigned them by the rights of neutrals

As for the demand for material aid made by the Madrid
Cabinet, no treaty is required to satisfy this, every Government
is at liberty in this respect to do what it thinks best, and the
aid will be none the less real, that it is given without a
treaty

Lastly, as regards the official declaration, which the
Spanish Government is desirous should be given by the Governments signatory to the treaty of 22nd April, the English Cabinet
does not in any way oppose it, but it thinks that such a declaration might merely form the subject of a diplomatic Note, which
could be made public in Madrid if necessary

There can be no question of the entry of Portuguese troops
into Spain, since the Cabinet of Madrid has made no mention of
this project in the demands it has addressed to the English
Government, and has, on the contrary, insisted that the cordon of
Portuguese troops, which will assemble on the frontiers of
Portugal, shall not be allowed to enter Spain.

Having gone over these different considerations with Lord

Palmerston, we arranged to meet the Spanish and Portuguese plenipotentiaries, and invite them to send us a Note containing such demands as may reasonably enter into such a document, we shall at the same time inform them of our intention to reply to this Note by a counter-note, expressing the opinion of both our Governments on the present situation of the Peninsula, and containing the assurances of our support when circumstances will permit   This counter-note might then be made public in Madrid, and would thus, no doubt, render that moral support to the Spanish Government which it asks of us

This, M le Comte, is the scheme which we have drawn up , it can be modified but in any case, it will exempt us from concluding a convention or making additional articles to the treaty of April 22nd

I shall be particularly obliged, if you will let me hear whether this scheme has met with your approval and that of the King's Government.

London, *August 9th*, 1834

After several conferences between Lord Palmerston, the Spanish and Portuguese Ministers, and myself, in which M de Miraflores and M de Sarmento vehemently insisted that the additional articles should be added to the treaty of April 22nd, we have agreed to the draft of an additional convention, which I have the honour to transmit to you   It has received the approval of the English Cabinet

I, nevertheless, did not deem it advisable to say that I was ready to sign these additional articles, and stated that I must refer the matter to my Government

A careful examination of the project which I send you, M le Comte, will no doubt convince you, as it did me, that it does not offer any real objection to the King's Government, since it contains no fresh engagements, except that of not allowing any supplies for Don Carlos' army to pass our frontier, and we have provided for this point by the stipulations in the first article

One consideration alone makes me pause, though in reality it does not appear to me of very great importance

By Article II , the English Government undertakes to furnish assistance in arms and munition of war, the value of which is to be repaid later on by Spain   Might not this last stipulation give rise to wrong interpretations by the Chamber of Deputies and the newspapers ?   May not the King's Government be accused of having deprived French trade of the sale of those articles which will be delivered to the Spanish Government by England ?

Such an accusation would be without foundation, for it is perfectly evident that, as always happens in such cases, England will not recover ultimately any of the disbursements she may be called on to make, and that it is a positive gain for us to avoid such expenditure But I am ignorant whether the French Ministry is able to take advantage of this opinion, and I have therefore decided to suspend my assent to the article

To sum up, the additional draft of convention is sufficiently insignificant, to offer no danger whatever to our accepting it Its very insignificance would almost be objectionable, if we could not always affirm, that it contains all the demands made by the Madrid Cabinet Only one point in the project is of value, namely, the recognition by France and England, that the aim of the 22nd of April has not been attained

I still persist in thinking that this fact would be proved just as effectually if it were mentioned in the speech of the King of the French at the opening of the Chambers, and also in that which the King of England will make at the end of next week, when Parliament is prorogued If need be, even an exchange of diplomatic Notes between France and England on the one part, and Spain on the other, would suffice to replace the somewhat pompous preamble of a convention which stipulates for such unimportant obligations

We were however finally obliged to give in to the reiterated solicitations of M de Miraflores and M de Sarmento the former of these gentlemen especially, pointed out to us several passages in M Martinez de la Rosa's despatches, which, he said, imposed upon him the necessity of trying to obtain the additional articles of the treaty of April 22nd

LONDON, August 12th, 1834

It seems to me, that the draft of the additional articles which was inclosed in my despatch, is quite in accord with the intentions which you have expressed in the name of the King's Government

The declaration mentioned in the preamble of the articles, is conceived in terms sufficiently vague, not to give me cause for any serious objection

I should have preferred, as I informed you in my despatch yesterday, that the phrase in the King's speech should be adhered to , but it was impossible to make additional articles to the treaty of April 22nd without assigning some reason for them, and I think the words used for this purpose say as little as it was possible to do

The stipulations in the first article having received your

approval, there only remains the unimportant objection I pointed out to you in Article II

I do not think you wish that the proposition of the King's Government to the Madrid Cabinet, with respect to the transport of the Foreign Legion of Algiers to the coast of Spain, should form a fresh additional article   I shall only bring it forward if you send me instructions to do so

Just as I was finishing this despatch, I saw Lord Palmerston, who informed me, that at the request of M de Miraflores, and in accordance with the unanimous opinion of the Council, he would propose to me to add the following article to those which I had the honour to send you yesterday   " In the event of fresh circumstances arising, which would require fresh measures, the high contracting parties pledge themselves to such action in this matter as may be mutually agreed on "

I did not conceal from Lord Palmerston, that I neither approved of the spirit nor the form of this article, which was offensive to the Spanish Government, for it suggested a doubt as to its strength, and the publication of such a doubt on the part of the three Courts might produce a very bad effect in Madrid   I concluded by saying, that in communicating this article to you, I should express the objection I had to it   If you refuse to adopt it, I think it would be as well for you to send me a despatch to that effect so expressed, that I can show it

LONDON, *August 15th*, 1834

I have the honour to transmit herewith, the speech just made by the King of England on adjourning Parliament until the 25th of next September   When reading the speech, the King gave a special intonation to the sentences relating to the foreign policy of France, which appeared to cause quite a sensation in the diplomatic gallery

LONDON, *August 19th*, 1834

I hasten to send you the additional articles which we have just signed   I think the King's Government cannot fail to be satisfied with their contents[1]   You will perceive that we have

[1] The following is the text of the additional convention to the treaty of the quadruple alliance, as drawn up and signed on the 18th August, 1834
[2] His Majesty the King of the French Her Majesty the Queen of Spain, His Majesty the King of Great Britain and Ireland, His Imperial Majesty the Duke of Braganza, Regent of the kingdom of Portugal and of the Algarves, the high contracting parties to the treaty of April 22nd 1834, having given their serious attention to the recent events which have taken place in the Peninsula, and being fully convinced

made some alterations, as I informed you yesterday, in the original draft of these articles, the most important is that at the end of Article II   By this article, England pledges herself to the Queen Regent by a much more decided line of policy, whilst the first article remains the same, and pledges France to no further obligations than she has already been anxious to fulfil

I am very well satisfied that this additional convention to the treaty of April 22nd has, by the suppression of the last part of Article II, taken an entirely political character [1]   You will no doubt perceive, M le Comte, that by this it connects itself more intimately with the treaty of April 22nd, and with the views of the Courts when they entered into it

M de Talleyrand had arrived at the end of his task   A few days after he had signed the additional articles to the treaty of the quadruple alliance, he took advantage of the leave granted him, and returned to France   Three months later he determined to resign his post as ambassador, and wrote the following letters to the King, to Madame Adelaide, and to the Ministers for Foreign Affairs —

that in this fresh state of affairs, fresh measures have become necessary to fully attain the end of the said treaty ,

"The undersigned" (here follow the names of the plenipotentiaries) "being furnished with authority from their respective Governments, have agreed to the following additional articles to the treaty of April 22nd, 1834

"'I   His Majesty the King of the French pledges himself to take such measures in those portions of his states which border on Spain, as will be best calculated to prevent every description of assistance in men, arms, or munition of war, being conveyed from French territory to the insurgents in Spain

"'II   His Majesty the King of Great Britain and Ireland pledges himself to furnish Her Catholic Majesty with such arms and munition of war as Her Catholic Majesty may require, and further to assist her with naval forces, if such should be needed

"'III   His Imperial Majesty the Duke of Braganza, Regent of the kingdom of Portugal and of the Algarves   . fully sharing the sentiments of his august allies, and wishing to acknowledge by a fair return the engagements contracted by the Queen Regent of Spain in the second article of the treaty of April 22nd, 1834, under takes to give assistance, should occasion require, to Her Catholic Majesty, by every means in his power, in such form and manner as shall afterwards be agreed on between their said Majesties

"'IV.   The above articles will have equal force and equal value,' &c , &c .   .

              "TALLEYRAND,   PALMERSTON,
              "MIRAFLORES,   C P DE MORALS SARMENTO"

[1] See page 255, for the tenor of the original draft of this treaty   The alterations which had been effected, were thus expatiated upon by M. de Talleyrand in a despatch dated August 17th

              "We have agreed to confine ourselves to the signature of the three articles while however altering some expressions in Article II, which by their commercial tone take away from the strength and dignity of the measures stipulated for by this article "

THE PRINCE DE TALLEYRAND TO MADAME ADELAIDE

VALENÇAY, *November 12th*, 1834

Mademoiselle will have noticed that I have abstained for some time from writing to her about myself and distracting her attention for a single moment from the painful crisis[1] which must have greatly fatigued the King But now that the crisis is over, I claim a fresh proof of Mademoiselle's kindness, with all the confidence of a tried servant I beg her to prevail upon the King to give a favourable hearing to a letter I am sending to the Foreign Office It contains my resignation I am induced to believe that the King will be disposed to accept it, Monseigneur the Duc d'Orléans having expressed to me that, in his opinion, I could no longer be of any use in London He is right, for I am old, I am infirm, and I grow sad at the rapidity with which I see my own generation dying out A man of times gone by, I feel myself a stranger to the present

I must also repeat to Mademoiselle what the Prince Royal feels so strongly, namely, that we have obtained from England during the last four years all that could possibly be of *use* to us May she never transmit to us anything hurtful' England has altered greatly, and I do not think she can pause in the new course she is pursuing I do not feel myself called on to follow her therein Here also, in addition to the difference of policy, a personal question has arisen Lord Palmerston and I no longer agree, nor do we satisfy one another It is not right that the King's business should suffer by this misunderstanding These are my reasons I believe they are founded on common sense and expediency, and I feel convinced that the King's admirable sagacity will consider them worthy of my devotion to his interests I will not therefore further urge my attachment to his person, but will once more revert to the need I feel of having complete rest before I die I also think I owe it to the place I may fill in history, not to compromise the remembrance of those services which I was fortunate enough to be able to render to France, amidst the countless vicissitudes through which she has passed during the last fifty years

In remaining in office, henceforth without an object, I should be of no use to my country, and could only injure my own dignity

I will make no excuses to Mademoiselle for having written at

[1] The ministerial crisis of November 1834 After the three days Ministry presided over by the Duc de Bassano, the Cabinet of the 11th October returned into power under the presidency of Marshal Maison

such length on one subject , her noble friendship will, I know, be only further strengthened by my unreserved confidence So high a mind, so tender a heart, will preserve to me my most cherished consolations—*her remembrance and her kindness*

TALLEYRAND

THE PRINCE DE TALLEYRAND TO THE MINISTER FOR FOREIGN AFFAIRS [1]

VALENÇAY, *November 13th*, 1834

MONSIEUR LE MINISTRE,

When the King appointed me to the Embassy in London four years ago, the very difficulty of the mission made me accept it I believe I have fulfilled the duties, both to the advantage of France and that of the King—two interests ever present to my mind and closely connected in my thoughts

During these four years, the general peace which has been maintained has permitted all our relations to be much simplified our policy, isolated as it then was, has now become blended with that of other nations , it has been accepted appreciated, and honoured, by upright men and intelligent minds in all countries. The co-operation of England, which we have succeeded in obtaining, has cost us nothing, it has not affected our independence or our national susceptibilities , and such has been our respect for the rights of others, such has been the candour of our actions, that so far from inspiring distrust, our guarantee is now sought against certain influences which are disturbing ancient Europe

It is certainly to the King's undoubted wisdom and to his great ability, that these very satisfactory results must be attributed I claim no other merit for myself than that of having divined before any one else the King's inmost thoughts, and told them to those who, later on, were convinced of the truth of my words

But now that Europe knows and admires the King, the most serious difficulties have for that very reason been surmounted , now that our mutual alliance is probably as important to England as to ourselves, and that from the course she seems inclined to pursue, she must prefer a mind less given to ancient traditions than mine , now that I think I can, without any want of devotion to the King or to France, respectfully entreat his Majesty to accept my resignation, I pray of you, Monsieur, to present it to him

---

[1] In consequence of the dissolution of the Ministry, two or three intermediary ones having been successively nominated, M de Talleyrand was obliged to address this letter to the Minister for Foreign Affairs simply, without designating any one (Note by Madame la Comtesse de Mirabeau)

My great age, the infirmities which are its natural consequence, the rest it counsels, and the thoughts it suggests, render this step of mine a very simple one, which is fully justified, and is indeed only a duty I trust to the King's inestimable goodness to look upon it in this light

Accept

THE PRINCE DE TALLEYRAND TO KING LOUIS PHILIPPE

VALENÇAY, *November 23rd,* 1834

SIRE,

Your Majesty will forgive my delay in thanking you for your fresh kindness, your confidence, and, I venture to say, your friendship I would I could reply to them more satisfactorily, but I cannot refuse to listen to the serious warnings inculcated by the sad ceremony at which I have just had to assist [1]

From it I have gained courage to persevere in a determination, the most painful part of which is the thought of displeasing the King He will pardon me if he will deign to recognise the devotion with which, in spite of my great age, I have served him for the last four years, and he will perhaps still think kindly of me now, when the death of my old friends and the weight of years no longer permit my actions to equal my zeal

It would be very unjust to seek to find any other motives than those indicated in the last lines of my letter to the Minister for Foreign Affairs It would be a great mistake to attribute my resignation to a matter of either English or French personality Thanks to you, Sire, I have won for the Revolution of July the right of citizenship in Europe My task is accomplished, and I must now persist in retiring because I have the right, and it is necessary that I should do so

Were I to set aside this true and simple desire, and to search for still further reasons, I should tell the King, that no one honours the Duke of Wellington more than I do, that I feel assured that to him alone will belong the honour, if such a thing is still possible, of arresting the decadence of England [2] But however much I respect his character, his strength, and his prudence, I could not, if only from the simple fact of his having

The burial of the Comtesse Tietzkewitz, born Princess Poniatowski   (Note by M. lame la Comtesse de Mirabeau)

[2] Lord Melbourne's Cabinet had just resigned (November 14th) The Duke of Wellington had been provisionally appointed, while awaiting the arrival of Sir Robert Peel, who was travelling, and whom the King wished to appoint as his new minister For nearly a month the Duke of Wellington alone represented the entire English Government He became Minister for Foreign Affairs in Sir Robert Peel's Cabinet

taken office, recall my resignation, founded on such serious grounds and already publicly known for some days, without at once becoming a party man in both countries, and on that account less fitted to render the King faithful service

I have never been a party man ; I have never wished to be one, and in this has lain my strength   When I started four years ago for England, I was in the eyes of France (so exacting in her national susceptibilities) what I have always desired to be— the man of France ! now I should be in her eyes the man of the Duke of Wellington !

The King in his indulgent goodness too often forgets my great age , he forgets that it is not permitted to an octogenarian to set aside prudence, for that which renders the faults of old age so sad, is, that they are irreparable

I believe it will not be difficult for the King to make a suitable choice for London   M de Saint-Aulaire would, as he has done at Rome and Vienna, know how to make his Government respected and himself esteemed   M de Rayneval, full of experience, skilful and prudent, would perhaps, under the present circumstances, be even a still better choice, for he knows better than any one else, the interests and the difficulties of the Peninsula, the fate of which will no doubt be one of the first things with which the new English Government will have to deal

Nevertheless, I see so many divers interests to be attended to, or at any rate to be discussed, that I am more and more convinced another Conference is imminent   If it should suit your Majesty to send me to it, I would willingly make a final trial of my strength in so short a mission   In this alone, taking everything into consideration, I might perhaps still be able to serve the King   He would not blame me for the infirmities of my age and the exhaustion of my life

I am, Sire,

THE PRINCE DE TALLEYRAND

KING LOUIS PHILIPPI TO THE PRINCE DE TALLEYRAND.

PARIS, *November* 25*th*, 1834

MON CHER PRINCE,

I have never seen anything more perfect, more noble, more honourable or better expressed, than the letter I have just received from you   I am most deeply touched by it   There is no doubt that it costs me a good deal to admit the justice of the greater portion of your reasons for not returning to London, but I am too sincere, and too much the friend of my friends, not to recognise that you are right   Nevertheless, to be thoroughly

frank with you, I fear that the weight of the sorrow that has
overwhelmed you, has led you to overrate that of your years, and
what you are inclined to look upon as warnings   Believe me,
the more fully I appreciate the great services which you have
rendered to me, and likewise to France, the more I feel that
you alone could bestow them again, and you surely cannot
conceal from yourself how much your resolution, well founded
as it is, will increase my difficulties   It is impossible to settle
anything until the English Ministry is reconstituted, but I quite
enter into your views ; we must prepare for the future, and it is
for this reason, mon cher Prince, I so earnestly desire that
you should return to Paris as speedily as possible   I am very
anxious to hear your views and tell you mine   I feel that I need
the help of your experience, and above all the advice of that
enlightened friendship which is so precious to me   I like to
repeat to you how fully you can count on mine, and on all those
feelings which I have for so long entertained for you

LOUIS PHILIPPE

END OF PART XII

APPENDIX.

No 1—THE DUC DE BROGLIE TO M BRESSON [1]

8th October, 1832

WE continue to hope that the naval measures will exercise sufficient weight on King William s mind, to destroy his last illusions

If this hope is realised, all difficulties will disappear

But it is not at all impossible that this Prince, strengthened in his obstinacy by the signs of discord which have so unfortunately arisen in the Conference, may persist in rejecting the only arrangement which is now admissible, and that, at the risk of calling upon his country for fresh sacrifices, he will still wait for more favourable chances in the future than those for which he has vainly hoped during the last two years

In this hypothesis, the measures taken for the blockade might be insufficient   I may as well tell you, monsieur, that until this insufficiency has been proved in the most incontestable manner, we shall not come to the determination of regarding it as the basis of our calculations and previsions

But, the fact once recognised, more efficacious measures will certainly have to be taken   Then, and only then, should France and England unite their forces to oblige Holland to evacuate Antwerp, and it seems to us impossible that, under such circumstances, our allies would not give their full assent

There is moreover, monsieur, a method of humouring Russia's susceptibility, and of giving to the proceeding of the allied Courts all the appearance of that complete improbability, which, in reality, has never ceased to exist   As the Dutch occupy Antwerp, which must some day be restored to Belgium, so the Belgians occupy Venloo and those portions of Luxemburg and Limburg which have been assigned to Holland by the treaty of the 15th November.   It might be arranged, that simultaneous with our taking possession of Antwerp, the Prussians should receive over Venloo and the territories in question from the Belgians, take charge of them provisionally, and hand them over to King William when he finally decides to accept the treaty of the 15th November   .

No 2—M BRESSON TO THE DUC DE BROGLIE [2]

BERLIN, *October 24th*, 1832

IF we show any weakness, if we make any further concessions, advantage will be taken of it, as has just been done, to retard by a few days, even by a few hours, the decision which has become indispensable to us   It is not

[1] See page 13   [2] See page 13

from my ill will, but from a foolish dread of imaginary evils For this
reason, on first looking at it I much regretted the proposal relative to
Venloo Since then, I feel assured that it has produced a good effect,
that it is much appreciated, and is felt to be reassuring But, notwithstanding all this, it has been insufficient to stimulate the Prussian Cabinet
You have nothing to fear from that quarter. I will, if you desire it, stake my
existence on this You may go straight ahead, carry out your expedition
well, no one will interfere with you, and if Russia tries to take advantage of
this circumstance to rouse prejudice or irritation against us, it will only be
waste of time They are quite reconciled to it here, and although they do
not wish to acquiesce, they quite feel that we are doing right, and we shall be
thanked for it later on

Do not therefore lose a moment, M. le Duc Strengthen the good cause
and sound doctrines by preparing a success for them They are, alas ' too
much compromised everywhere You will gain great glory by doing so much
good Believe me, I have carefully weighed every word I say I know well
that peace or war depends upon the disposition shown by Prussia, and that
if I am mistaken, I shall be left to blush for shame and eternally to regret
all the evils I have provoked But I am not mistaken, I know the ground
on which I stand

No 3--THE PRINCE DE TALLEYRAND TO THE DUC DE BROGLIE[1]
(*Private*)

October 27th, 1832

MON CHER DUC,

Our ratifications have been exchanged I am very glad that you
are satisfied, the more so as I have served a Ministry I like and of which
you form the chief interest I was obliged to send off the communications at
once, and I hope I have written as prudently as the circumstances required
The Gordian knot will be cut when Venloo is placed in the hands of the
Prussians

There will be no inconvenience in this, and it will release us from all the
demands of the Northern Powers, who, if Prussia is satisfied, dare not
express any doubts as to our good faith It is, besides, a mark of respect to
the King of Prussia, whose good will it is most essential to retain , for it acts
as a barrier, which we must endeavour to make insurmountable I beg you
to urge M. de Werther to write in this sense to his Court I on my side will
stir up M. de Bulow You will see therefore that it must be quite understood,
that even if the King of Holland refuses, the King of the Belgians must
evacuate the territories which do not belong to him This will place the
King of Holland still further in the wrong, without in any way endangering us,
since we must stipulate that the King of Prussia shall evacuate Venloo as
soon as the King of the Netherlands shall have acceded to the treaty of the
15th November

Adieu, a thousand kind remembrances,   TALLEYRAND

No 4 KING LOUIS PHILIPPE TO THE DUC DE BROGLIE[2]

VALENCIENNES, 11 *o'clock in the evening,*
Wednesday, January 9th, 1833

MON CHER DUC,

I hasten to send you, as you wish, the extracts from the despatches
of 7th and 8th January, which you sent me Thank you much for the trouble
you have taken to make them so clear and exact

1 See page 15   2 See page 13

In thinking over all the circumstances, I believe that our expedition to Antwerp produces, both at home and abroad, a much greater sensation than we could possibly have hoped for The refusal of the Hague is with the view of not seeming to give in to us, and of seeing whether our desire to avoid a war will not make us give in to the earnest wishes of Prussia, I think for that very reason, now that we have made propositions which have been rejected, we must abstain from making any more, and wait till the King of Holland condescends to make some to us I do not think that we shall have long to wait, I see even still less reason for making any advance, as he dare not close the Scheldt and the feeling in his country is opposed to his policy of resistance I think, therefore, that it is now our turn to stand aloof

The Governments in France and England are both firmly seated, our union has been drawn closer by our victory and the loyalty of our return therefore, in soldiers' language, let us *stand at ease* and see what will happen

L P

No 5—THE DUC DE BROGLIE TO THE PRINCE DE TALLEYRAND [1]

PARIS, *January* 16th, 1834

MON PRINCE,

I acquainted you in my last despatch of the impression I formed after reading the Dutch Note and the counter-project which accompanied it The King is absent The President of the Council has followed him to the army. I have not yet been able to get the rest of my colleagues together and discuss matters thoroughly I am consequently unable to transmit to you just now the views of the Cabinet The ideas which I shall embody in this letter are therefore personal, and I submit them to you simply to receive the benefit of your advice

The reply of the King of the Netherlands is just what I expected He eludes our propositions and only seeks to gain time ; the tone is conciliatory, and the aim evasive Were we to defer to him, the result would be to place Holland precisely in the same position in which we wish, and have every reason to wish, to place Belgium Such a result would be to establish a most favourable *statu quo* for Holland, in which King William would remain indefinitely, without recognising the independence of Belgium, negotiating without ceasing, and awaiting some favourable chance for a general war

Possessed of the whole of the territory assigned to him by the treaty of November 15th, collecting tolls both on the Scheldt and the Meuse, confirmed in his new claim of a right of transit *via* Sittard and Maestricht, relieved from the interest of the Belgian debt, and freed from our coercive measures, he would set us at naught, reserving his question of the intermediary waters, the syndicate, the pilotage and the beacons, as pretexts for quibbling and never settling anything

The difficulty therefore does not seem to me whether we shall or shall not accept these propositions, but what course of action we should adopt after having appreciated their full importance

It appears to me that our first care must be to fully assure our present position and not allow it to be injured in any way

According to the terms of the Convention of the 22nd October, we are acting as the signatories and the guarantors of the treaty of November 25th. We have undertaken to execute this treaty by means of joint action, provided that the negotiations respecting two or three articles of the treaty, which

[1] See page 61

it had been agreed to should be reopened, were not merely for the purpose of adjourning the matter indefinitely, and ending by cancelling it We have taken this course, because we were fully convinced of the King of the Netherland's bad faith After the taking of Antwerp, we were willing once more to put his desire of bringing matters to an end to the proof We only asked for a very simple matter, that he should recognise and carry out all those portions of the treaty which he did not object to We promised on that condition to give up our coercive measures That proposition was not accepted , our coercive measures must therefore be continued It is a question of our dignity , all chances of success are involved therein If we desist before three-fourths or four-fifths of the treaty are carried out, we shall have done nothing, we shall have gained nothing , the Antwerp expedition will have been utterly useless we shall indeed be in a much worse position than we were before for we shall have exhibited the climax of our strength and our resolution If we were then to attempt any threats we should only be laughed at

A second, though no less important point, was the intervention of the three Powers

The King of the Netherlands seemed averse to treating only with England and France He wanted the concurrence of the whole Conference We have no reason to object to this But Prussia, Austria, and Russia have withdrawn on the ground that the employment of coercive measures seemed to them unfair and inopportune , as our opinion has not changed and our conduct remains the same, it is for those Powers to approach us if they wish to do so , it is not for us, whom they have in a way denounced to Europe, to seek them and throw ourselves into their arms If the King of the Netherlands desires their intervention, let him bring them to us, let him reconcile them to those coercive measures which we shall not abandon, or else let him of his own accord render those coercive measures unnecessary, by accepting our propositions and carrying out forthwith all that portion of the treaty which he does not contest

As for the root of the question, this is my view the object of our propositions was to simplify the difficulty of separating that part of the treaty which was contested, from that which was not, and thus show plainly, the very slight importance of the points in dispute , to invite both parties in the name of common sense not to rush into expenses a hundred times greater than the objects claimed, but to disarm, and to threaten the peace of Europe no more

The King of the Netherlands accepts the idea of a preliminary Convention, but he expects that two or three of the disputed points will be introduced into it Of what use then is a preliminary Convention ? If negotiations have to be entered into both with him and the Belgians, why not negotiate the whole matter at once from the beginning to the end ?

I think we ought to say to him You do not want a preliminary Convention, that is to say, a Convention which is all arranged beforehand, which can either be accepted or *not*, since it only consists of such preliminary points as have been agreed to by both sides Very well ' What you want is to negotiate By all means then let us negotiate But let us negotiate to some purpose , let whatever is arranged be definitely so, and then bring forward all your claims at once, and let us regulate everything by one and the same arrangement Do not keep anything back, and then pull it out of your pocket just when everything is on the point of being settled, and thus adjourn everything afresh

The three following proposals occur to me

We are quite ready to negotiate, but on condition that the coercive measures are not discontinued

We are quite willing to negotiate with Austria, Prussia, and Russia, but on condition that those three Powers come forward of their own accord and do not ask us to give up coercive measures beforehand

We are quite willing, I repeat, to negotiate, but it must be simultaneously, on all the disputed points, and so as to have done with them once and for all If you desire the cessation of the coercive measures, carry out that portion of the treaty which you do not dispute If you desire a partial Convention, then let it be a Convention which bears solely on those points which have already been agreed to by both sides, and which are not subject to negotiation

I repeat, it appears to me that these ideas, expressed in language moderate and conciliatory, though at the same time firm and resolute, would deprive the King of the Netherlands, and likewise his friends, of all hopes of trifling with us any more, and we should not have to wait long for the end , whereas if, on the contrary, we fall into the trap, and if we allow ourselves first to be induced to give up the coercive measures, and then to be drawn into a series of negotiations, we shall inevitably entangle ourselves in a hopeless difficulty

There is however one point which, in my opinion, should be kept quite distinct from all the rest

I refer to the closing of the Scheldt This is a fresh departure, as to which it is necessary above all to be very explicit

The free navigation of the Scheldt is not a Dutch or a Belgian question , it is a European one All the nations of Europe, France and England especially, have a direct and personal *interest* in this question All the nations of Europe have further, a direct and personal *right* to maintain the free navigation of the Scheldt, in terms of the article of the Congress of Vienna

The five Powers signatory to the treaty of 15th November have a special right in this They notified by a protocol *ad hoc* in 1830, that they would look upon any attempt to close the Scheldt as an act of hostility on the part of the King of the Netherlands, and the King of the Netherlands solemnly declared, that he intended to leave the Scheldt open, and would remain a simple spectator of what might take place there, until the conclusion of Hollando-Belgian affairs

The Powers therefore have a positive right, not only to the freedom of the Scheldt, but to the provisional maintenance of the *statu quo* and the provisional absence of all tolls

I think that England and France must refuse to entertain any negotiations until the Scheldt is open I even believe it would be well to add, that in case of refusal on this point, they will consider what steps they must take, and make it plain that in reprisal, and considering the closing of the Scheldt as an act of hostility, they will commence by confiscating the vessels that have been seized, in order to utilise the amount realised thereby to indemnify Belgium, which is more especially affected by the closing of the Scheldt

If we are not careful to settle this question before all the others, we may be sure that the freedom of the Scheldt will be sold to us as the price of some fresh concession It seems to me a matter that must be dealt with at once, and with a very high hand

Such, mon Prince, are the views which have occurred to me ; I will wait until I hear from you what value I may attach to them, before drawing up anything definite All I can learn concerning Prussia and Austria, leads me to think that if we only stand firm, they will come round to our views , but we have reached a very critical and decisive point, where it will depend upon our action, whether we shall lay down the law or have to submit to it Accept, mon Prince, the testimony of my utmost devotion

V BROGLIE.

No 6 —THE DUC DE BROGLIE TO THE PRINCE DE TALLEYRAND [1]

PARIS, *January* 21*st*, 1833.

PRINCE,

We have just received some very important news from Constantinople On the 24th of last month, Ibrahim Pasha has completely routed, near Konieh

To save the Porte and prevent the intervention of Russia, is plainly the double aim assigned at this moment to the policy of France and England The active and immediate joint action of both Governments is necessary to reassure the Porte, and I will proceed to indicate to you, mon Prince, the measures by which we think this joint action should be carried out

It is necessary, first of all, that Lord Ponsonby should at once start for Constantinople, where his prompt arrival will show the firm determination of the London Cabinet not to remain inactive in the midst of the crisis that has befallen the Ottoman Empire Jointly with Admiral Roussin, he should declare to the Porte, that France and England take upon themselves to guarantee the preservation of the Sultan's throne, but on the express understanding that the Ottoman Government, whose independence they are thus protecting, will not itself sacrifice this independence by admitting foreign armies into its territories and allowing them the free passage of the Bosphorus and the Dardanelles, the real key of the Empire

At the same time, both Courts should formally ask Mehemet-Ali to stay the march of his troops , they should besides offer their mediation to obtain fair concessions for him, but also give him to understand, that in the event of his abusing the advantage he has gained, by endeavouring to dethrone the Sultan, or imposing inadmissible demands, they will feel themselves reduced to the necessity of interposing, in order to prevent catastrophes irreconcilable with their interests

Such demonstrations would probably suffice to decide Mehemet-Ali to confine his ambition within the limits which we desire Nevertheless, provision must be made in the event of their not being successful It is quite evident that in this state of affairs, our interest being dominant, the principle which must direct our action is to prevent Russia from bringing forward any plausible pretext for occupying, (on the plea of being an auxiliary of the Porte,) either Constantinople, the two straits, or the provinces in Asia Minor It might be advisable, Prince, that henceforth the French and English Cabinets, in the event of action becoming necessary either on the coast of Syria or on that of Egypt, should combine in such a manner, that the Divan of Constantinople, reassured of its existence by so powerful a diversion, would no longer be tempted to abandon itself to the armed protection of Russia

Pray, mon Prince, lose not a moment in conferring with Lord Palmerston on this important question You will quite understand the impatience with which we shall await the decisions of the London Cabinet on a matter in which the slightest delay may cause the most serious consequences

You will have to consider whether it will be necessary to make the resolutions we may come to, the subject of a communication to the St Petersburg Cabinet Among the considerations which will aid you in forming an opinion on this matter, will no doubt be the great danger of still further increasing the gravity of the complications which may supervene in Eastern affairs by showing ourselves at first too engrossed by them

[1] See page 77

We learn from Constantinople, that the Prussian and Austrian Missions have supported General Mouravieff's offers   It is difficult to believe this support to be sincere on the part of Austria   M de Metternich, as might have been foreseen, exhibits much perturbation at the possibility of Russian intervention in the affairs of Turkey, and although in the present position of Europe one cannot expect to see him side with France and England in order to prevent it, it is not improbable, that if we were once pledged to do so, so far from thwarting our efforts, he would in some way assist them, even while probably finding fault with them in public   This minister is not the man to sacrifice to temporary combinations a real and vital interest, such as the removal of the Russians from Constantinople would be for Austria   .

No 7 —THE DUC DE BROGLIE TO THE PRINCE DE TALLEYRAND [1]

PARIS, *February 8th*, 1833

MON PRINCE,

In my despatch of yesterday, I mentioned a conversation I had had the evening before with M le Comte d'Appony   I now send you the details, as I think their perusal will not be without interest to you.

You will no doubt remember that about six weeks ago, M de Metternich proposed to the English Government to bring the Belgian affair to an end, by assembling a kind of Congress, at which all the questions relative to this affair were to be discussed afresh   The proposition was equivocal and hesitating , it was insinuated that the Congress might be held elsewhere than in London, and it was even reported in Germany, that this Congress was to be held either at Aix-la-Chapelle or Frankfort

Be that as it may, Lord Palmerston, in answer to this rather embarrassing and non-conclusive overture, made a very vigorous reply   This reply, which formed a lengthy despatch taking about twenty minutes to read, was shown me by Lord Granville   In it, the Belgian matter was reviewed subsequent to the twenty-four articles , it was proved by very forcible logic, that all the questions relative to Belgian affairs had been definitely decided by the treaty of November 15th ; that France and England had made Belgium accept this solution , that the three other Powers, so far from acting in the same way with the King of Holland, had, on the contrary, encouraged him in his resistance by the delays attendant on their ratifications , that if some points had again come under discussion at the request of the three Powers, it was on the understanding that no alterations should be made, except with the free assent of the two parties interested , that such assent not having been obtained after six months of fresh negotiations, no other course remained open but to constrain Holland by forcible measures, and thus bring about the same result as had been obtained from Belgium by persuasion , that France and England had adopted this course on the refusal of the other three Powers, and that nothing remained but to persist in it, unless the King of Holland, brought back to more reasonable ideas by experience or the advice of his allies, made us such fresh proposals as might suit Belgium   Lord Palmerston concluded, by rejecting all propositions for a fresh Congress to arrange what had been already settled and only now required to be put into execution

This was the despatch which occasioned my interview with the Comte d'Appony

He gave me a despatch to read, in which M. de Metternich com-plans bitterly at not hearing anything further as to the position of the Belgian affair, or the intentions of France and England ; he complains that a *dénouement* is no longer possible, and seems disposed to abandon everything ; he complains especially of England and of Lord Palmerston, his obstinacy and his daring ; he also accuses Lord Palmerston of having misrepresented his proposition Its object was not to assemble a new Congress, but only to resume the Conference, by admitting to it the Dutch and Belgian plenipotentiaries ; he never intended that the territorial portion of the treaty of November 15th should be again discussed, but only the points contested by the King of Holland ; it never entered his head that the Congress should assemble elsewhere than in London, &c   After a series of lengthy lamentations, M de Metternich addresses himself to me as a man of greater moderation and more conciliating than Lord Palmerston (and here follows a shower of compliments and flatteries), in order to know what I really thought of the Belgian question, what were the intentions of England, and whether, in her dealings with us, she behaves in the same way as she does towards Austria, answering questions that were never asked, misrepresenting the views presented to her, and evading all the points in discussion

The reading of this document was followed by that of a private letter, in which the same subject is treated in a jocose manner, and in which Lord Palmerston is accused of answering white when one says black, and good morning when one wishes him good-night

I listened to all this very quietly and without interrupting M d'Appony When he had finished, I began by pointing out to him, that the proposal referred to in this despatch had not been communicated to us by the Austrian Government   At this remark M d'Appony coloured up to the whites of his eyes   I continued saying, that not knowing the terms in which the proposition was couched, it was impossible for me to decide whether Lord Palmerston had or had not understood it properly ; that not being able to judge of the merits of the demand, I could still less judge of the merits of the reply, and that therefore I must decline all intervention in a controversy to which my Government was a stranger

'However,' I continued, "if you desire to know the views of the French Government on the position of the Belgian affair and its future, I have no hesitation in making them known to you, and I will endeavour to explain matters to you sufficiently clearly not to deserve the reproach addressed by M de Metternich to Lord Palmerston"

I then went over the whole subject of Lord Palmerston's despatch (without however making any remarks thereon), following the various arguments step by step, and wound up by telling M d'Appony that such were the views of the French Government, and that on this point there never had been the slightest difference of opinion or the least misunderstanding between it and the English Government

I paused every now and then to ask M d'Appony whether I had made myself thoroughly understood, whether he wished any further explanations, or whether there was anything in my language which was not perfectly clear

M d'Appony, to whom no doubt Lord Palmerston's despatch had been communicated, and who saw me produce it under the name of the French Government, quite recognised that his attempt to separate the two Governments and bring about a division between them had no chance of success, and took this for granted

Then changing his tactics, he said he would not speak to me in the name of his Government, having no orders to that effect, but only in his own name and in ordinary conversation

"As long as you persevere with coercive measures," he continued, "we cannot join you, we are too deeply pledged against the employment of such measures, but if you would abandon them, the Conference would reassemble as a matter of course, and with the addition, as M de Metternich proposes, of the Dutch and Belgian plenipotentiaries, everything would be speedily terminated"

"What guarantee," I then asked him, "can you offer us, that the King of Holland would now show himself more disposed to end matters than he has done in the past? If we renounce coercive measures, we are giving in to him, it is as much as telling him he may resist as long as he likes, and no harm will befall him By admitting his plenipotentiary to the Conference, equally with that of Belgium, we give him an advantage he did not possess before, it would be leading him to believe that everything was to be again discussed, it would furnish him with the means of objecting to everything and throwing obstacles in the way at every moment How could we hope that matters, under these circumstances, would progress either quicker or better?"

"Oh!" replied M d'Appony, "but if France and England gave Europe such a great proof of their desire to terminate the Belgian business, and there wish for peace, the three Powers would then be with them, heart and soul, we should second you with all our efforts, nothing would be neglected by us, to induce the King of Holland to give in"

"Ah!" I exclaimed, "then were you not entirely with us last summer? Did you not then second us with all your efforts? Did you then neglect anything that would have caused the King of Holland to give in? Can you do more in the future than you were able to do in the past?"

M d'Appony coloured up a second time and made no reply

After a few minutes' silence, seeing that the conversation had come to an end, I said to him, "I in my turn will now speak to you, not as the mouth-piece of the French Government, but merely as a friend, and we will discuss some simple hypotheses We will suppose that England and France accept the *invitation* of the three Powers (I laid stress on the word invitation), we will suppose that they consent to *allow the Conference to reassemble*, by abandoning the coercive measures, and that the trial having been made, the King of Holland shows himself just as obstinate as he has done in the past. would you then approve of the employment of coercive measures, would you join us in putting them in force?"

"But," replied M d'Appony with some embarrassment, "we were not opposed to *pecuniary* coercive measures" "Yes, indeed," I answered, "and it was just on account of your refusal that the Conference separated Look at Protocol No 70 You have, it is true, consented since then, but only individually, and in order to prevent the siege of Antwerp Besides, what if the pecuniary coercive measures did not suffice?"

"We have morally consented to *maritime* coercive measures"

"Yes, but there again, only when you saw we were determined to take Antwerp, and in order to prevent the siege Moreover, Russia has never consented"

"I think we can arrive at that"

"If you should ever have any proposals to make to me on the part of your Government on this subject," I concluded, "I will have had time to think over it Just now we have neither of us anything official to communicate to one another"

And thus ended this conversation

M de Werther called yesterday He read me a despatch very much in the same style as M de Metternich's, tending towards the same end, but much shorter and making no mention of the proposal submitted to England. He then entered into a short conversation in which he introduced the same officious insinuations, the despatch also contained similar praises and personal flatteries, to the detriment of Lord Palmerston and the English Government Finally, these two gentlemen, knowing how intimate I am with Saint-Aulaire, who has just arrived here, made him their confidant, asked him to repeat to me their conversations with him on the same subject, and even went so far as to let him read the despatches they had communicated to me

If we take these advances, in connection with the tone of the St Petersburg despatch relative to Marshal Maison, which Pozzo showed you—a despatch which replies to a purely official communication by protestations of *friendship*, and this just when I had purposely told M d'Appony (about six weeks before) that it seemed Russia wished to keep in *peaceful* but not *friendly* relations with us—the conclusion I draw therefrom is as follows

The three Powers are much afraid that this Belgian affair will be terminated without their intervention Spring is approaching The cruisers will soon show signs of activity Public opinion is getting excited in Holland They therefore wish above all things to recommence negotiations They would even go so far as to approve the use of coercive measures in the future, but as for *present* coercive measures, their *amour-propre* is affected, their disapprobation has been too plainly manifested for them to draw back now, they must find some expedient to save this point of honour

On the other hand, the King of Holland, who is perfectly aware of the situation, makes capital out of it, by refusing to treat *definitely*, without the concurrence of the five Powers

It might be worth considering whether, without losing our present position or placing ourselves at the discretion of the three Powers, we could offer them some means of joining us without the humiliation of having to contradict themselves, which would withdraw them from the King of Holland, and place them on our side

This is my view of the matter

The Conference, it is true, exists no longer, but the elements of the Conference are still in London, the plenipotentiaries of the five Powers are still there, and see each other daily

What is there to prevent M de Bulow, M de Wessenberg, M de Lieven and M Van de Weyer being sounded all at the same time in private converse, as to the most reasonable solution of the three or four questions still in dispute ?

When all are agreed, or at any rate pretty nearly so, Lord Palmerston might do what he did last August, namely, draw up a scheme and some articles which might be *officially* communicated to the persons who had already been sounded

If the scheme was secretly agreed on, France and England would draw up a so-called preliminary Convention, in which however all the difficulties would be solved, and in which a special article would simply state, that the said preliminary Convention having been agreed to by Holland and Belgium, and by France and England, would by the signature of the Russian, Austrian, and Prussian plenipotentiaries be converted into a definite treaty, and substituted for the treaty of November 15th

It would be necessary in drawing up the articles, to approach as near as possible to the Prussian scheme, so as to gain M de Bulow's interest

The Convention once drawn up, would be sent officially to Brussels and to the Hague, and would at the same time be officially communicated to the plenipotentiaries of the three Powers, in the same manner as the Convention of October 22nd

The three Powers would support the Anglo-French proposition at the Hague, by their ministers, they would declare themselves ready to convert it into a definite treaty, and would inform the King of Holland that if he persisted in rejecting such reasonable proposals, they would unite with France and England, and reassemble the Conference to concert measures to force him to submit

In this way, the three Powers would re-enter into the negotiation without contradicting themselves too evidently, their present good will could be utilised without suspending our coercive measures, and the King of Holland would be caught in his own snare

I submit these ideas to you, mon Prince, without attaching any other importance to them, than that of being enlightened thereon by your clear and experienced views. You are on the spot, and must therefore know a hundred times more about the matter than I can possibly do I hand the whole conduct of this affair over to your discretion, and pray you to pardon this lengthy gossip Please accept the testimony of my greatest devotion

V. Broglie.

No 8—Madame Adelaide to the Prince de Talleyrand [1]

Tuileries, February 13th, 1833

. . . . I have communicated to our beloved King, the information you have sent me relative to Portugal and Queen Dona Maria I must tell you quite frankly, that we have never desired such a very delicate situation either for Nemours or any of our children I am fully persuaded that they will be much happier remaining in France as they are In this respect therefore, our views could never give umbrage to the English Government This *always* troubles me, not for the matter itself, but as showing the feeling of prejudice, estrangement and mistrust, which, in spite of all, still exists, against us, and which I look upon as very unfortunate in the interests of both countries But, as regards this Portuguese business, I say again, we neither think of it nor desire it, for any of our children At the same time it seems to me, that it would not be to our interest to have an Archduke, and by such arrangement give Austria the same influence in Spain as she already possesses in too great a degree in Italy I submit this idea to you, while asking you to think of some other choice, and to write and tell me which Prince you think it would be most desirable to see there and that we should do well to support I should have thought some Neapolitan Prince. For my own part, I must confess, I should much prefer him to an Austrian, whom we must above all avoid

No 9—Lord Palmerston to the Prince de Talleyrand.[2]

Stanhope Street, April 16th, 1833

Mon cher Prince,

Here is the Note M Dedel has just given me It is, as I told him, a very slight affair, after such an amount of consideration

As to the new draft for the armistice, it has the merit of being perfectly incomprehensible, or rather it can be read in two ways, for we have always held, that before last November there was a continuous suspension of arms, whilst the King of the Netherlands, on the other hand, always declared that he was free to recommence hostilities whenever he pleased As regards

this, the Note does not help us in the least No mention is made of the
neutrality, and there is this to be noticed, that an armistice is bilateral, and
that if the Dutch provoked the Belgians to any slight aggression on the
frontier, or if they alleged some infraction on the part of the Belgians, they
might declare the armistice to be broken But an undertaking on the part
of Holland to respect the neutrality of Belgium, would be a tie from which
Holland could not so easily escape

No mention either is made in this note as to the opening of commercial
communications via the town of Maestricht, but I fancy that when the
river is opened, the roads will no longer be closed

Of course you are aware that Prince Metternich proposes an arrangement which would be excellent, if Holland would adopt it, namely, a Convention between us both and Holland, by which the embargo would be
removed, the indefinite armistice concluded, the Scheldt placed on the
footing of November last, and the Meuse opened ; a treaty would at the
same time be signed between the five Powers and Holland, by which the
latter finally accepts the twenty-one articles, regarding which there are no
reservations ; the other three articles would form the subject of immediate
negotiations

For my part, I can see nothing but good in these proposals

But we must wait and see whether they come back to us from Berlin
just as they left Vienna

No 10 — MADAME ADELAIDE TO THE PRINCE DE TALLEYRAND

NEUILLY, *July 20th*, 1833

I hasten to thank you for so promptly sending us news of the
Conference, which interests us so much I must tell you that our beloved
King greatly regrets, especially as England is supporting him, that you
did not insist more strongly that the adoption and ratification of the twenty-
one articles by the five Powers should not again be brought under discussion He thought that the Conference would at once have declared this
to the Dutch plenipotentiaries, and that it would only have dealt with the
three reserved articles He sees with astonishment that instead of this, only
those of the twenty-one articles which are in accord with the Dutch scheme
are to be initialled, and that the others are to be again discussed, which appears to be in direct contradiction to the engagements entered into with
Belgium by the five Powers and formally ratified by a treaty , so much so,
that for his part, he does not see how he could ratify an act sullied by such a
contradiction I hasten to let you know this, as I feel sure these reflections of
our beloved King cannot fail to strike you, and that your talent and your
zeal will enable you to find some means of remedying this first false step,
which disturbs us greatly.

No 11 — No 85 THE DUC DE BROGLIE TO THE PRINCE DE TALLEYRAND

PARIS, *August 1st*, 1833

PRINCE,

I have received the despatches Nos 146 and 147, which you did
me the honour to write The information they give as to the progress and
the tenor of the negotiation has much interested me

A courier from Admiral Roussin informs us that the Russian troops
have departed ; this happy piece of news would have given us still more

complete satisfaction, if it had not been accompanied by the almost positive confirmation of another fact, which up to now we felt inclined to doubt, namely, the conclusion of a defensive alliance between the Porte and Russia I send you the text of this treaty, such as our ambassador's dragoman was enabled to write it out in haste, from the dictation of Reiss Effendi

We are still ignorant as to whether or not this alliance is to be made public. It would, I think, be very little use to decide upon what measures we may have to take in order to prevent the consequences arising from this matter, before knowing all the circumstances pertaining thereto, but I think that France and England can hardly refrain from demanding explanations from the Porte, as to the reason and aim of so unexpected and serious an act, which cannot be explained by the necessity for protection against foreign enemies, for all the Powers have agreed to protect her, and it therefore seems only for the purpose of paving the way for the intervention of a foreign government in the home disturbances of the Ottoman Empire, an act, in fact, which may be looked upon as changing the principles admitted up to now with regard to the navigation of the Bosphorus, and as creating in this respect a privilege in favour of Russia, which the other Courts could never consent to recognise A demand for explanations thus expressed would be an actual protest, the advantages of which I need hardly point out to you.

Pray speak to Lord Palmerston about it . .

No 12 — THE DUC DE BROGLIE TO M BRESSON

PARIS, *August* 13*th*, 1833

MONSIEUR,

When you receive this despatch, you will already have learnt the events which have just occurred in Switzerland Everything seemed to tend towards more friendly relations between the parties which for the last three years have divided the Helvetian Confederation That which so ardently desired a revision of the Federal compact, and which decreed the emancipation of the country of Basle and the outlying districts of Schwytz, had already made numerous concessions, and seemed quite disposed to make further ones Extreme opinions had lost all credit in the Diet of Zurich, which was under the exclusive influence of moderate and conciliatory men The assembly of Sarnen appeared latterly for its part to be animated by a wise and peaceful spirit, and conferences were to be held to decide some disputed points [1]

Unfortunately these satisfactory feelings were only sincere on one side Facts speedily proved that the attitude lately assumed by the Cantons, whose delegates were assembled at Sarnen, was only, at least in the opinion of some of their leaders, assumed to hoodwink their too confiding adversaries, and the attacks so unexpectedly made at Kussnacht and the country round

---

[1] A civil war broke out in 1831, between the town of Basle and the country surrounding it, brought about by the refusal of the town grand council to allow the inhabitants of the country to return to the old franchise The Diet intervened, and authoritatively divided the territory of Basle into two parts Basle city and Basle country A similar division had taken place in Schwytz between the original Canton and the districts which had been added to it La Marche Finsiedeln, Kussnacht, and Pfaffikon Basle city and Schwytz united with the five Cantons of Uri, Unterwalden Neufchâtel, and the Valais, and tried to form a separate league for the defence of their interests The six seceding Cantons sent delegates, who first met at Sarnen, then at Schwytz, and declared themselves independent of the Federal Diet of Zurich War broke out between the Confederation and the dissentients The latter began by taking possession of Kussnacht, but they were speedily vanquished On the 4th of August, the Federal troops gained possession of Schwytz, and on the 10th of Basle

Basle, revealed schemes which loyal men and friends of their country were very far from anticipating

Under these circumstances, the Diet has acted with as much energy as prudence   By crushing at its initiation this attempt at a civil war, it has given itself time to concert and provide complete measures for the removal of the dangers which this unforeseen outbreak signalised   The task which it has still to accomplish is no doubt a difficult one , for in order not to fail in its duty, it must combine prudent circumspection with wise vigour While endeavouring to make the aggressions of a blind party impossible in future, it must hold in check the passions of the opposite party, whose apparently cooled ardour these late events have roused afresh   It must restrain the disorganisers—the systematic innovators only recently so discouraged, and to whom what has just occurred has given fresh chances , such a task, I repeat, is very ticklish   Nevertheless, the examples of the past give us the firm hope, that supported by the good sense of the Swiss, the Diet will be able to triumph over these obstacles

But one would have to look upon them as almost insurmountable, if the dread of foreign intervention were to agitate men's minds, wound national susceptibilities, inspire irritation and exaggeration (which always follow fatal disturbances) in some, and animate others with hopes as dangerous as they are ill founded   No doubt such an intervention is now no longer possible To be convinced of this, one need only look at the present position of Europe Nevertheless, as the most unreasonable propositions are often the best received when party spirit is rife—for they find only too ready an echo in turbulent spirits, who utilise them to stir up the masses—the King's Government has thought that the most efficacious way to contribute to the tranquillity of the Helvetian Confederation, was to declare both by its language and its attitude, the principle from which it is resolved never to depart as regards that country, namely, that to the Swiss alone belongs the right to settle the differences in which they alone are interested, and which foreign interference, no matter of what kind, would render almost insolvable, by making them unnecessarily a European question

The Vienna and Berlin Cabinets are too enlightened not to share our views fully as to the impossibility of an intervention , but I think they do not sufficiently realise the necessity of dispelling the hopes and the fears which may be raised in Switzerland on this subject , I even fancy, that deceived by inexact reports, they fondly trust to the possibility of moderating and restraining the innovators, by adopting a vaguely threatening and ambiguous tone towards them , at least it is only in this way that I can explain the proposals, the proceedings, and the perpetual agitation of the Prussian and Austrian envoys   This would be a very dangerous error , it would be an almost certain means of taking away all credit from the supporters of moderate measures, who would be accused of yielding to foreign dictation, and who to avoid this imputation would be forced to fall in with the extreme opinions which hitherto they have been able to control

Do not neglect anything, monsieur, to make the views I have just expressed to you plain to M Ancillon   Urge him to send instructions in conformity with the spirit of prudence and wisdom which the circumstances demand, both to the Prussian envoy and to the authorities at Neufchâtel   I am writing in the same sense to M de Rumigny, and we would fain believe that in future all the representatives of the Great Powers will adopt this course with the Helvetian Confederation

It was with some surprise we learnt that M de Bombelles[1] had noised

---

[1] Louis, Comte de Bombelles, Privy Councillor to the Emperor of Austria and Austrian Minister Plenipotentiary in Switzerland

abroad the account of an interview, in which I was said to have expressed to the Austrian Ambassador or *Chargé d'Affaires*, an opinion absolutely in conformity with that of his Government as to the danger of introducing the slightest modification into the Federal compact of 1815 This assertion is quite unfounded, and might have too serious consequences for me not to request M. de Rumigny to rectify it ; but I could have wished, in the interest of all, that we had not been constrained to exhibit the dissent which exists between the Great Powers on so important a question

No 13 —M. Bresson to the Duc de Broglie[1]

BERLIN, *December 17th*, 1833

MONSIEUR LE DUC,

I thank you for making me the mouthpiece of a policy so clear, so loyal, and so national   M Ancillon will no longer be deceived by the miserable manœuvres employed to delude him   He, I am sure, regrets his previous insinuations   I did not wish to force his last entrenchments, and accepted his explanations so as to put an end to a painful discussion   I read him the private letter you did me the honour to write   He did not dare openly to blame M de Metternich, but it was with difficulty he restrained his indignation   If he is himself wanting in frankness, and if he goes back from his words and his promises, it is not from duplicity, but from weakness   He is incapable of premeditated falsehood   I don't know which is most to be admired, M de Metternich's perfidy or his want of skill   It would be impossible for any one to fall more completely into his own trap   I shall take care that all this is not ignored or lost sight of in Berlin

M Ancillon said, that in order not to increase the awkwardness of the proceeding to which he had so imprudently committed his Government, it must appear as coming from himself and he must not disavow it   This *rôle* has probably been hinted to him from Vienna and St Petersburg   But the people who surround the King, and whom your energy has intimidated, are profuse in explanations and excuses, which are equivalent to a dis-avowal   Good Prince Wittgenstein is especially amusing ; it is so easy to disquiet him, that I now do all I can to reassure him   He said to Lord Minto. "But how could we possibly dream of a war ?   The King would have to place himself at the head of the army, and just see how completely that would upset all his habits !"   The whole of his *entourage* is composed of very excellent persons, truly pacifically inclined, who only ask to be allowed to end their days in peace   Nothing but the most flagrant provo-cations could rouse them to action   After the King dies, matters will be different, and no one can speak with any certainty as to the Prince Royal's views   But, thank God, we are a long way from that !   The father may easily outlive the son   No one would grieve at this in Prussia

Accept . .

No 14 —The Duc de Broglie to the Prince de Talleyrand[2]

PARIS, *January 2nd*, 1834

PRINCE,

A short time ago, M de Bacourt informed me that some attempts were being made to bring about more intimate relations between Austria and England respecting Eastern affairs, to which I drew M de Sainte-

[1] See page 184   [2] See page 202

Aulaire's attention. This Ambassador, on his side, thought he had noticed more frequent and intimate communications than usual between M. de Metternich and Sir Frederick Lamb, especially after the arrival of a courier for the latter on the 20th of December. The Austrian Chancellor, without entering into any full explanations with M. de Sainte-Aulaire, expressed the most lively satisfaction at the news brought by this courier. He said, that thanks to the efforts of the French Government to calm England, the London Cabinet now took the same view of the Eastern question as did those of Vienna and Paris. Sir Frederick Lamb appears to have held somewhat similar language to M. de Sainte-Aulaire. All this is very mysterious and though I believe that the aim of M. de Metternich's policy is to throw uncertainty into our arrangements, by allowing us to suppose that he has some private understanding with the English Government, I should be glad if you could give us some information as to whether there is any reality in these apparent intimate relations. I need hardly tell you, that so far from being annoyed at a combination which would associate Austria with a policy of guarantee against the ambitious schemes of the Russian Government, we could in the present circumstances only find in it cause for satisfaction.

No. 15—THE DUC DE BROGLIE TO THE PRINCE DE TALLEYRAND [1]

PARIS, *March 27th*, 1834

PRINCE:

I made known to you the resolution come to by the Spanish Government, to send an army into Portugal for the sole purpose of dispersing the partisans of Don Carlos. Mr Villiers, seconded in this matter by M. de Rayneval, whose support he requested, has in vain endeavoured to induce M. Martinez de la Rosa to give a more general aim to this expedition, by directing it both against Dom Miguel and Don Carlos. The Spanish Minister however refused, not wishing, as he said, to create fresh obstacles (unless absolutely necessary) to the small body of troops which was about to cross the frontier of the two kingdoms. We have reason to think, and this is also Mr Villiers's opinion, that the dread of displeasing the Northern Powers has greatly influenced M. Martinez's determination.

It is besides easy to foresee, that the Spanish troops, once on Portuguese ground, may through the force of circumstances find themselves drawn into making common cause with the Pedrists. This consideration has not escaped the Spanish Cabinet. Thus, while M. Martinez de la Rosa, in order to maintain the ground which he thinks he ought to take, has rejected the overtures of M. Sarmento Dom Pedro's envoy, his colleague the War Minister, has discussed with this latter a scheme of combined emigration, without its appearing as such, which, while facilitating the movements of the Spaniards, would place Dom Miguel, as regards his brother's troops, in a dangerous and difficult position.

If the Spaniards have determined on an enterprise, the consequences of which they have seemingly dreaded for some time, it is because they despair of overcoming England's repugnance to a material intervention in Portugal. Nevertheless, the news we have received from Lisbon might induce us to believe that this repugnance is no longer so absolute.

Lord Howard, after receiving much more extended powers from London than those with which Lord W. Russell was entrusted, has drawn up a scheme of Convention intended for the pacification of Portugal, which he has sent to Lord Palmerston, after having communicated it to M Mortier as well as to Dom Pedro's minister, who appeared very well satisfied with it The following are the principal clauses

The Queen's Government will accord a full amnesty to all those of her adversaries who, within a given time, take the oath of allegiance to her Those who refuse to do so will be permitted to sell their effects and quit Portugal

The rank of the Miguelite officers will be assured to them with half-pay.

Dom Miguel will retain his personal fortune and his appanage, or receive an equivalent Portuguese, French, and English vessels will be placed at his disposal to take him out of the country

All disputes which may arise as to the meaning of the stipulations of this treaty, shall be decided by a commission composed of the French and English Ministers and the Swedish *Chargé d'Affaires*

Lastly, if Dom Miguel should refuse these conditions, the English Government will place troops and war-vessels at Dona Maria's disposal, in order to put an end to the hostilities

I ought to remark, that in Lord Howard's communication to the Lisbon Cabinet, there never was a question respecting this last clause, and it was probably only through inadvertence, that the English envoy made it known to M Mortier You will no doubt deem it advisable, mon Prince, to avoid any mention of it in your interviews with Lord Palmerston

What we do not know, and what it is most important that we should know, is, up to what point the views enunciated by Lord Howard are his own, or are connected with the instructions he may have received I should much like you, if possible, to furnish us with some explanations on this point The interests of France and those of England are identical, in the double struggle which at this time is devastating the Peninsula A sound policy therefore prescribes to both Governments joint action there, and as far as we are concerned, we are quite ready to second by every means in our power, the scheme of the London Cabinet for the pacification of Portugal, as soon as that Cabinet makes it known to us

M. LE DUC DE CHOISEUL.

Begun at Bourbon-l'Archambaud in 1811, and finished at the residence
of Madame la Duchesse de Courlande, Châteauneuf, near St Germain,
in 1816

M LE DUC DE CHOISEUL.

M LE DUC DE CHOISEUL, though wanting in culture, possessed natural talent and ample assurance, and this, together with an illustrious name and a slightly foreign polish, placed him on a footing of equality with the *grands seigneurs* both of France and Germany The branch of the House of Choiseul to which he belonged, was attached to the service of the Dukes of Lorraine His father, the Comte de Stainville, was grand chamberlain to Francis, the last Duke of Lorraine, who became Grand Duke of Tuscany, and subsequently Emperor of Germany, by his marriage with Maria Theresa [1]

By a curious coincidence, in 1757, M le Comte de Stainville, the father, Chevalier of the *Toison d'Or*, was Austrian minister in Paris, while the Comte de Stainville, his son, Chevalier of the Order *du Saint Esprit*, was French ambassador at the Court of Vienna   At the same time, also, another son was *abbé commandateur* and prior of Reuil, while the third son was major of a Croat regiment in the heart of Hungary

The treaty of 1736[2] having incorporated Lorraine with

---

[1] The Emperor Francis (1708-1765) belonged to the House of Lorraine   He succeeded his father, Duke Leopold, in 1729, under the name of Francis III   In June, 1738, he received Tuscany, which the death of the Grand Duke Gaston, the last of the Medicis, had left without a master (1737)   In 1736, Francis married the Archduchess Maria Theresa, daughter of Charles VI   On the death of her father (1740), the Archduchess claimed the entire succession of the House of Austria, in right of the Imperial Edict, entitled the *Pragmatic Sanction*, her claim being contested by France, gave rise to the war known as the Austrian war of succession   The Imperial dignity, therefore, departed from the House of Austria, and was conferred on the Elector of Bavaria, who took the name of Charles VII   Francis of Lorraine did not become emperor until after the death of the former (1745)   He reigned until 1765

[2] The treaty of Vienna, which put an end to the war of succession in Poland   It recognised the rights of the Elector of Saxony, who was crowned under the title of Augustus III   As for Stanislas Leczinski, whose interests France had supported, he received Lorraine in compensation, under the condition that at his death that duchy should revert to France   Stanislas having died in 1766, Lorraine at that period became a French province

France, the House of Choiseul had to return to the birthplace of its ancestors The young Comte de Stainville began his career as a sub-lieutenant in the *Régiment du Roi*, and soon after commanded the *Régiment de Navarre* He distinguished himself in the field as a colonel, but he played a still more brilliant part in society His first successes created a great sensation M de Stainville was the lover of Madame de Gontaut,[1] whose affection for him amounted to distraction She was the eldest daughter of M Crozat du Châtel,[2] lieutenant-general and *Cordon Rouge*, under whom the Comte had served in the war of 1740 Madame du Châtel, *née* Gouffier, was in the habit of assembling every evening at her house persons distinguished for their wit and ability, such as Madame du Deffant,[3] Pont-de-Veyle,[4] and the Chevalier de Curten [5] M de Stainville, also, although somewhat inattentive owing to the number of infidelities of which he was guilty towards Madame de Gontaut, never failed to drop in for a few minutes Correctness in little attentions was one of his principles M de Gontaut, one of the favourites of Louis XV, gay and easy-going without much intelligence, qualities most in request in Madame de Pompadour's society, had taken a great fancy to him, but had not yet been able to introduce him into this innermost circle, where a rather unfavourable opinion had been formed of his character It was currently reported in Madame de Pompadour's circle that Gresset [6] had taken M de

[1] Antoinette Crozat du Châtel (1728-1747), daughter of the lieutenant-general of that name and of Maria Theresa Gouffier de Heilly, married the Duc Charles de Gontaut, younger brother of Marshal de Biron, in 1744 The issue of this marriage was the Duc de Lauzun

[2] Louis François Crozat, Marquis du Châtel, belonged to a rich family of financiers, one of its members had recently ennobled himself by buying the Marquisate of Du Châtel in Brittany

[3] Marie de Vichy Chamrond, born in 1667, member of one of the oldest families in Burgundy, married, when quite young, the Marquis du Deffant, from whom she was shortly after separated Her *salon* was for forty years the centre of a witty and distinguished society She died in 1780

[4] Antoine de Ferriol, Comte de Pont-de-Veyle, born in 1697 His father was President of the Parliament of Metz He was himself Commissary-General of the Naval Galleys He wrote some comedies and a number of short poems He died in 1774, having been Madame du Deffant's friend for over fifty years

[5] Maurice de Curten, of Swiss origin, passed into the French service Born in 1692, he entered the army in 1706, became a major general in 1743, lieutenant-general in 1748, and Grand Cross of the Order of St Louis in 1757 He died in 1766

[6] Gresset, a comic poet, born in 1709 at Amiens, died in 1777 *Le Méchant,* which is the best of his comedies, was written in 1747.

Stainville as one of the principal characters in his comedy of *Le Méchant* This, a few *bons mots*, and a sufficiently pronounced ambition, made him pass for a dangerous man, and probably his brilliant career would have been retarded, if a circumstance, which ought to have increased the disquietude that his appearance caused, had not on the contrary served to put an end to it The King had shown some preference for a very beautiful woman whom the Comte de Choiseul-Beaupré,[1] *menin* to the Dauphin, had just married, Madame de Pompadour became very jealous of her A kind of party had already been formed at Versailles which favoured this intrigue ; and M de Stainville, who had been badly treated by Madame de Pompadour, and was a relative of Madame de Choiseul, naturally found himself ranged on the side of the new favourite It is supposed, that later, having himself paid her court, and finding that she did not possess sufficient *esprit* and ability for the *rôle* he wished her to play, he sacrificed her, and conveyed to Madame de Pompadour, through M de Gontaut's agency, to be shown to the King, some letters, which in the first moments of her passion she had written to himself And as Madame de Choiseul died most unexpectedly very shortly after, it was also said, that he was not a stranger to her death This is not the only suspicion of this kind which was entertained against M de Stainville Though fully persuaded that none of them had any foundation, I feel some embarrassment in not being able to attribute my motives for this conviction to the morality of his life, being obliged rather to seek for them in the fickleness of his character Madame de Pompadour, calmed down, looked around her for fresh tools, and passed immediately, rather too quickly perhaps for M de Stainville's reputation, from the most marked coldness towards him to a degree of interest of which she lost no time in giving him proofs During these circumstances Madame de Gontaut fell seriously ill, and on her death-bed, she earnestly entreated her young sister, who was then only fourteen years old, to marry M de Stainville, wishing to carry away with her in death the satisfaction of having assured the fortune of her

---

[1] François, Comte de Choiseul-Beaupré, was a lieutenant general and *menin* to the Dauphin (the term *menin* was of Spanish origin, it was a designation given to the six gentlemen who were specially attached to the person of the Dauphin) In 1751, he married Mademoiselle de Romanet, a niece of Madame de Pompadour

lover, and likewise, as the excited state of her mind induced her to believe, the happiness of her sister

The species of fascination which M de Stainville exercised over the whole of this family, quickly decided the mother as well as the daughter, and having thus become master of an income of a hundred and twenty thousand francs, he had only to consider what steps he should take to enter a career for which his birth, his talents, his energy, and the mediocrity of those who filled the chief places, gave him special advantages His views inclined to an embassy in Rome A few flatteries, judiciously addressed to M Rouillé,[1] Minister for Foreign Affairs, the support of his brother-in-law, M de Gontaut, his return to favour with Madame de Pompadour and the degree of dislike that the King still felt for him, all combined to obtain for him this brilliant removal, and he went to replace M de Nivernais The magnificence of his first arrival in Rome effaced that of all the ambassadors who had preceded him, the lavish luxury of his surroundings, the splendour of his house, the choice of his intimate associates, soon created him the arbiter of all the ecclesiastical nominations, he succeeded in gaining the friendship of Benoit XIV,[2] who always spoke of him as *his dear son*, and who, in the frequent and intimate converse he had with him, could never refuse him anything It was at this time that M de Stainville conceived those first impressions which have since resulted in the destruction of the order of the Jesuits The favour which he enjoyed with the Holy Father placed him on an intimate footing with the heads of that order, and one of the General's recorders had imprudently allowed him to see the secret register, in which *the Society* inscribed all the names of its pupils, with remarks as to their character and sentiments from their childhood upwards, there, under his own column, he read, that if any important places became vacant, he must be

[1] Antoine Rouillé, Comte de Jouy, born in 1689, of an old legal family, Councillor to the Parliament in 1711, Naval Secretary of State in 1749, and Secretary of Foreign Affairs in 1754 He tendered his resignation in 1757, and was made Chief Superintendent of Mails He retired in 1758, and died in 1761
[2] Benoit XIV (Prosper Lambertini) was born at Rome in 1675 He entered holy orders, and was made Bishop of Ancona, then Archbishop of Bologna He had been Cardinal since 1726 In 1740, he was elected Pope in succession to Clement XII He died in 1758

looked upon as a man who did not and never would like *the Society* [1]

The more friendly relations of M de Stainville with Madame de Pompadour, were not of such a nature but that another and an older man should be equally favoured with himself The Abbé de Bernis,[2] an older and more intimate favourite, as ambassador at Venice was likewise somewhat irksomely paving his way to future elevation

M de Stainville did not fail to profit by the relations between their respective posts, and also some disputes which the Republic of Venice had at that period with the Holy Father, to establish a correspondence, which speedily brought about an intimacy , so much so, that when the Abbé de Bernis returned to France as the ostensible plenipotentiary of the famous treaty of 1756, and immediately after entered the Cabinet as a minister, while awaiting the retirement of M Rouillé, he quite looked upon M de Stainville as one of his future colleagues in the grand and sudden change about to take place in the political balance of Europe

On his part, M de Stainville, who had had enough by this time of ecclesiastical negotiations, and was devoured by the wish to take part in the great events that were brewing, kept up a very regular correspondence with Madame de Pompadour, carefully executed the commissions for curiosities and other things which Italy might present to him, for the favourite, and obtained through her, leave of absence towards the end of 1756, which enabled him to return to Versailles

During the winter, great changes occurred in the Ministry ; [3]

---

[1] The Jesuits were in fact expelled from France under the Ministry of Choiseul (1762-1764)

[2] François Joachim de Pierres, Comte de Bernis, was born at the Château de Saint-Marcel en Vivarais (1715), and belonged to one of the oldest families in France He was early destined for an ecclesiastical career, nevertheless, although he bore the title of abbé from his youth upwards, he did not take the vows till he was forty years of age He owed his nomination as ambassador to Venice (1752) to the protection of Madame de Pompadour On his return to Paris in 1755, he negotiated, though without holding any official title, the treaty of 1756 with the Imperial ambassador He was almost immediately made Secretary of State for Foreign Affairs and then Cardinal Disgraced and exiled in 1757, he came out of his retirement in 1764, was made Archbishop of Alby, then ambassador to Rome in 1769 He was dismissed from this office in February, 1791, for having refused to take the oath to the Civil Constitution, and died in 1794

[3] This is an allusion to the revolution in the Cabinet, which marked the King's

it is outside my subject to enter into this , but I cannot, in passing,
refrain from saying that M d'Argenson's dismissal,[1] and that of
M de Machault,[2] had a very fatal influence on the war which
broke out in 1757   The Abbé de Bernis was then appointed
ambassador to Vienna, a favour which was the natural consequence of the treaty he had signed with M de Stahremberg ,[3]
but as the Empress Maria Theresa urgently pressed for the
arrival of the French ambassador, and good M Rouillé still held
on to office, the Abbé de Bernis, rather than lose the ground
or sacrifice his career, got himself nominated ambassador to
Madrid, where no very urgent affairs had to be dealt with , and M
de Stainville was appointed to proceed immediately to Vienna, in
his stead   His preparations were speedily made ; all the pomp
of his surroundings passed on directly from Rome, and he himself
arrived at Vienna in the beginning of August   He found the
Imperial Court, hitherto so forlorn, now filled with confidence
after the victory of Kollin,[4] gained by Marshal Daun,[5] the
effect of which had been to raise the siege of Prague ,
Marshal d'Estrées[6] also had just gained that of Hastenbeck [7]

return to health   During his illness (following Damiens' outrage), Machault and
d'Argenson had taken it upon themselves to send Madame de Pompadour away   On
her return, she insisted on their dismissal   Machault resigned in favour of Peirenc de
Moras, and d'Argenson in favour of his nephew, the Marquis de Paulmy, February,
1757

[1] Marc-Pierre de Voyer, Comte d'Argenson, born in 1696, belonged to an old
family of Touraine, which shed a brilliant lustre on the seventeenth and eighteenth
centuries   Seven of its members filled high positions in the State   He himself was
Lieut General of Police (1720), Minister of State (1742), Secretary for War (1743-
1757)   He died shortly after his dismissal in 1764

[2] M de Machault was at that time Minister of Marine

[3] George Adam, Prince de Stahremberg born in London in 1724, was of an old
Austrian family   Ambassador at Paris in 1755, he was recalled to Vienna in 1766,
and became a State Minister, and later on Governor of the Low Countries (1780)
He died in 1807

[4] Kollin, a town in Bohemia of 6,000 inhabitants, situated on the Elbe.   The
Austrians gained a victory here on the 18th of June, 1757

[5] Leopold, Comte de Daun, born at Vienna in 1705, became field-marshal in
1748   He was Commander-in-Chief of the Imperial forces during the seven years'
war   Conqueror at Kollin and Hochkirchen, he was beaten at Leuthen and at
Torgau   He died in 1766

[6] Louis le Tellier, Marquis de Courtenvaux and Duc d'Estrées, born in 1697, was
the grandson of the celebrated Louvois   His mother was the sister of Comte Victor
d'Estrées, Marshal of France.   He having died without children in 1737, his nephew
inherited his name and his title   The Comte, later on Duc d'Estrées, was lieut-
general in 1744, and marshal in 1757   He lost his command in Germany owing to
court intrigues, and died in 1771

[7] Hastenbeck, a village in the Electorate of Hanover   The French victory took
place on the 20th July, 1757

over the Duke of Cumberland [1] Two months later, M de Stainville would have found in the Vienna Cabinet evidences of the greatest deference , but at this period, that Cabinet had assumed a very haughty attitude The French ambassador was however very well treated by the Empress, and especially well received by the kind Emperor Francis I , who welcomed him as a Lorrainer and the son of his present minister at the French Court

But Comte de Kaunitz [2] received him with the utmost coldness The *hauteur* he maintained during the first interviews, showed M de Stainville, that he should certainly not find in him the State Secretary of the Papal Court   The insignificant results of the battle of Hastenbeck, compared with the successes which followed the affair of Kollin, and the raising of the siege of Prague, which liberated the forty thousand men who were shut up in that town with Prince Charles,[3] caused the Austrian Minister to adopt a tone and manner very displeasing to the French ambassador

But in the month of November, all this haughtiness and pride vanished in consequence of the two battles gained within five days of each other by the King of Prussia in person , that of Rosbach [4] against the French, and the victory over the Austrians under the walls of Breslau [5] The French and Austrian armies were so completely defeated, that it was impossible to say which of the two had been most humiliated Thereupon reproaches of unfitness were freely scattered on both sides M de Stainville, a born satirist, fell with pitiless severity on Marshal Daun, and M de Kaunitz did not in any way spare

---

[1] William Augustus, Duke of Cumberland, born in 1727, was the third son of George II Placed at the head of the English army on the Continent, he was perpetually beaten He was more fortunate in Scotland, where he defeated Prince Charles Edward He died in 1765

[2] Wenceslas-Antoine, Comte, then Prince de Kaunitz Rietberg, born in 1711, Aulic Councillor in 1735, Imperial Commissioner to the Diet of Ratisbon under Charles VI , ambassador at Rome, then at Turin under Maria Theresa, Minister of State 1749, and ambassador at Paris On his return he was made State Chancellor He died in 1794

[3] Charles, Prince of Lorraine, born in 1712, was the brother of the Emperor Francis Field marshal and commander-in-chief of the Imperial and Hungarian troops, he took part in the wars of the Austrian succession and in the Seven Years' war.

[4] Rosbach, a village in the Saxon Electorate near Merseburg The French were commanded by Soubise

[5] The battle took place within seven kilos of Breslau, close to the village of Leuthen or Lissa.

the French generals   The Chevalier de Curten, an old lieut-
general, was then in Vienna, having come thither at the same
time as M de Stainville, he had a military commission, the
object of which was the retaking of the Saxon Electorate, which
was to be effected by Soubise's army, jointly with the imperial
troops under the command of the Prince de Hildburghausen [1]

The Chevalier Curten was considered an excellent officer, and
was certainly one of the most amiable and most *piquant* men of
his time   His mission, being but a minor affair, was brought to
an end by the great events of the war which had just occurred,
but he did not trouble much about it   He was constantly asking
what had become of the imperial army, to which he received
in reply a similar question as to Marshal Soubise's army   So
that, notwithstanding all these mishaps, which would inevitably
end by some modification of German influence, or by the cession
of some provinces, but not as yet by the abdication of any
crowned head, or the destruction of a kingdom or an empire,[2] it
was quite possible to pass a winter in Vienna pleasantly enough
When the complaints of M de Kaunitz became somewhat
stronger, M de Stainville sent the Comte de Montalet to him,
and he, under pretence of the greatest zeal, inquired most
minutely into the particulars of the great Austrian army, expressing a strong desire to join it, being, he said, destined to
have the honour of serving with it

Fresh levies were being raised everywhere for this army, and
M de Kaunitz, even while criticising poor Marshal Daun, whom
the Empress supported on account of her favourite, Madame
de Daun, was secretly advancing towards fortune, a quiet, modest
man, whom he had met by chance, and who, a few months later,
by raising the siege of Olmutz,[3] became the saviour of the
Austrian power

M de Laudon [4] became the most distinguished man among

---

[1] Joseph de Saxe Hildburghausen, a German sovereign prince, born in 1702, was
made field marshal in the Austrian service in 1735   He commanded an unfortunate
expedition against the Turks in 1739   He also took part, without much success, in
the Seven Years' war, and died in 1787

[2] In allusion to the treaties imposed later on by Napoleon

[3] Olmutz an Austrian town in Moravia   The King of Prussia had besieged it,
but being unable to take it had to beat a retreat

[4] Laurest Baron de Laudon, born at Tootzen, in Livonia, was originally of a Scotch
family, which had emigrated at the beginning of the fourteenth century   He was for

all those whom Austria employed during the course of the famous Seven Years' war For M de Lascy,[1] whose name has been perpetuated by the beautiful letter written to him by Joseph II when dying, had more talent for organisation than for execution, and showed himself much better fitted to be an able War Minister than a great general

The numerous forces which were being assembled, the formation of a large military organisation, and the high hopes which were the result of these efforts and changes, soon permitted M de Kaunitz to resume that air of careless indifference, which so cruelly wounded M de Stainville's *amour-propre* Sometimes at the theatre, where their boxes were actually side by side, M de Kaunitz would come in, take his seat with his back to the ambassador's box, and pretend not to perceive until about the fifth act that M de Stainville was beside him At another time, when invited to a formal dinner at the French ambassador's, instead of arriving at two o'clock, he would pitilessly keep about thirty people, who by their rank and birth certainly seemed to merit some consideration, waiting until six o'clock, then in the middle of dinner he would suddenly shove aside his plate, smooth the table-cloth in front of him, and drawing a small inkstand or pencil from his pocket, commence writing, leaning half across the table, or else produce a small toilet-case and begin to clean his teeth   .

It was customary to assemble every evening at this minister's house, where his sister, Madame la Comtesse de Questemberg, did the honours of his *salon* fairly well None of the ministers ever failed to attend, because M de Kaunitz generally came in about eleven o'clock, which was always a favourable time

eight years in the Russian service (1731-1739), and then offered his services to Frederick II , who refused them , he then went to Austria, became a general in 1757, and field-marshal in 1758, he played a glorious part in the Seven Years' war Called on to undertake a campaign against the Turks in 1788, he died in the midst of his successes on the 7th July, 1790

[1] Joseph, Comte de Lascy, born in 1725 at St Petersburg, came originally from a noble Irish family His father was a general in the Russian army He himself entered the Austrian service, and became field-marshal in 1760, after numerous brilliant successes during the seven years' war After the peace he entered the Aulic Council, and worked with the Emperor Joseph II for many years Entrusted with the command of the troops against the Turks in 1788, he was beaten, and requested to be replaced by Laudon, notwithstanding that he was his personal enemy He died in 1801

either to speak to him on business, or hear from him the
last accounts which came in daily from the army ; he was
always privately informed whether the French ambassador had
arrived, and if, owing to circumstances, it was important for the
latter to see him, he would keep him waiting until an hour after
midnight, and at last send a message by his valet to say that he
would not appear, without even taking the trouble to invent
an excuse   Then M de Stainville, greatly annoyed, would
return home, saying to whoever was present that it was impossible to do business with such a man   The Empress, who
was informed through private sources of M de Stainville's
vexation, lost no opportunity of telling him of M de Kaunitz's
innumerable slights towards herself   But she believed and
said, that this minister was so indispensable, that she forgave him
all his vagaries   The Empress's kindness was so frequently put to
the proof, that for some time it was thought that M de Kaunitz's
relations with this Princess were more intimate than mere official ones would be   It needed all the *éclat* of an incident with
an opera dancer to prevent this idea from becoming thoroughly
established   There was a very beautiful Italian at the theatre,
called La Taghatzi   M de Kaunitz was publicly known as her
admirer   Some rigid moralists of the Court, and Doctor Wasa-
Sivieten, out of devotion and possibly also from a secret wish to
please, so stirred up the Empress's conscience about this scandal,
that she caused even a greater one, by having the dancer carried
off one morning and taken across the frontier into Italy, with the
strict injunction not to appear again at Vienna   M de Kaunitz,
considering himself outraged, went to the Empress with his
resignation in his hand, caused her to change her decision, and
La Taghatzi returned with all the honours of the adventure , and
in order that no one should doubt his triumph, M de Kaunitz,
the next day, drove her in his *calèche* along all the public
promenades of Vienna   No credence must be given either, to
the sentiment which the Empress was supposed to entertain for
General O'Donnell ,[1] she loved the Emperor, who was a very

[1] General Comte Charles O'Donnell, born in 1715 in Ireland, entered the
Austrian service in 1736   Became a lieut.-field-marshal in 1757, Governor-General
of the Low Countries after the peace, and later Inspector-General of Cavalry   He
died in 1775

handsome man, and even forgave his little infidelity with the Princess d'Auersperg [1] for the sake of the children

But I am wandering from my subject   The mutual ill-will between these ministers resulted in the two Courts being anything but satisfied with the success of their grand alliance At Vienna, where men were even scarcer than money, they no longer wished to continue the system of a combined army ; the allies agreed to act separately, and Austria, in consequence, claimed the choice of the alternative in the execution of the treaty, which fixed the respective assistance at eighty thousand men or eighty thousand millions   The Empress, who had never for a moment ceased to use all her arts of fascination with M de Stainville, flattered herself that she would procure the subsidy She even on this occasion obtained assistance from the Emperor, who always treated M de Stainville with the familiarity of a compatriot and fancied he had great influence over him   The Empress wrote to Madame de Pompadour.   M de Stahremberg had almost obtained the point through the friendliness of the Abbé de Bernis, but M de Stainville's opinion on the matter retarded the decision   Eighty millions, at this period, was a very large subsidy   England, who since then has thrown away enormous sums, only gave Frederick II fifty thousand pounds sterling,[2] and one might say that he earned his money well, and that if France had preserved him as an ally at that price, Austrian influence would not have lasted so long in Germany Moreover, as it was not desired, either on one side or the other, that these slight differences should prove detrimental to the alliance, the design of a closer and more intimate union was at this time formed, by the proposal of a marriage between the infant Archduchess, Marie Antoinette, who was still in her cradle, and the future heir to the crown of France

M de Stainville on this occasion received a marked proof of favour , he was created an hereditary duke (and took the title of Duc de Choiseul) , at the same time his brother-in-law, the Comte de Gontaut, was made duke by brevet, a sufficient honour for this

---

[1] The Princess Josepha d'Auersperg was the daughter of Jean, Prince de Trautson. Born in 1734, she had married in 1744 Charles d'Auersperg, sovereign Prince of Germany

[2] 1,250,000 francs

latter, since his son, or rather M de Stainville's son, since known under the ever brilliant name of Duc de Lauzun, was naturally called to inherit the peerage of Marshal de Biron,[1] his uncle This double favour accorded simultaneously to the two friends was the work of Madame de Pompadour, and as much the fruit of M de Gontaut's assiduity, as of the regularity of the correspondence of M de Stainville, who never allowed a courier to depart without sending a private letter to the favourite containing a brief summary of his despatches Madame de Pompadour would not have felt quite so flattered had she known how extensive and confidential was M de Choiseul's private correspondence All the couriers took the letters first to Madame de Robecq,[2] then to Madame de Luxembourg,[3] to the Abbé de Bernis, whose influence M de Choiseul tried to weaken in his correspondence with the favourite, to M de Gontaut, to M de Soubise, to M de Praslin,[4] to the Comte de Castellane,[5] to M du Châtelet,[6] and to the Chevalier de Beauteville ,[7] and in return M de Choiseul received replies from them which kept him fully advised of all that was taking place in the double intrigues of Versailles and Paris

Just then M de Choiseul had an idea of obtaining a high place at Court But M de Gontaut convinced him that those places were burdened with reversions , he on his part reflected that he would probably not have any children by Madame de Choiseul, whose health was very delicate This fragile little woman, whose romantic temperament was ten times more ardent

[1] Louis Antoine de Gontaut, Duc de Biron, son of the Marshal Duc de Biron, born in 1701, entered the army, and took part in the Bohemian campaign as major-general , became a lieut -general in 1743, Marshal of France in 1757, and Governor of Languedoc in 1775 He died 1788
[2] The Princess Anne de Robecq was the daughter of Marshal Duc de Montmorency-Luxembourg She married Anne de Montmorency, Prince de Robecq, a lieut -general and grandee of Spain She died in 1760 aged 32
[3] Madeline Angélique de Neufville Villeroi, Duchesse de Luxembourg (1707-1787)
[4] César Comte de Choiseul, created a duke and peer in 1762, and known thenceforth under the name of Duc de Praslin, born 1712 He became lieut -general, ambassador at Vienna in 1758, Secretary for Foreign Affairs in 1760, and Minister of Marine in 1766 He was exiled in 1770, and died in 1785
[5] Michel, Comte de Castellane, Governor of Niort, ambassador at the Porte, and major-general in 1762
[6] Louis Florent, Duc de Châtelet Lomont, born at Semur in 1727 He was a son of the celebrated Madame du Châtelet, so well known, thanks to Voltaire He was made major-general, and went to Vienna as ambassador
[7] P de Buisson, Chevalier de Beauteville, quartermaster-general to the army of Flanders (1745), major-general (1758), minister to Switzerland (1762)

than her body had strength, was very *exigeante*, and very jealous of any woman to whom her husband made himself agreeable M de Choiseul therefore failed pretty nearly in anything approaching to an intrigue which he attempted during his sojourn in Vienna

Having received information from M de Gontaut that Madame de Pompadour was beginning to tire of the Abbé de Bernis (who, about to become a cardinal, took upon himself to make demands for which his qualifications gave no guarantee), M de Choiseul altered the tone of his private letters, giving them that special direction which fresh circumstance required He endeavoured to induce Madame de Pompadour to look upon him as a rival and successor to the Abbé de Bernis, as one upon whom she could always count, and sought to prevail upon the abbé to accept him as a faithful fellow-labourer, whose services he might command should he succeed in accomplishing the great step it was his secret ambition to attempt The Abbé de Bernis, sure of a cardinal's hat, began to speak of his ill-health, nevertheless insinuating, whenever he was entreated to remain, that he would be ready to prove his gratitude and his devotion if the supreme control of the Council was given him For this they had been waiting Arrangements were made for M. de Choiseul's return, and measures were then devised for investing him with the position which the future cardinal disdained to occupy M de Bernis, on his side, proceeded to draw up a long memorandum, in which he tried to prove to the King the necessity of having a Prime Minister who would control the entire work of all the departments with a firm hand The critical position of affairs was probably favourable to this view But the King's repugnance to this kind of tutorship was well known to Madame de Pompadour, who, moreover, having now nothing but this *rôle* to play, without any of the inconveniences of the title, had no wish whatever to be deprived of it Two months sufficed for all these manœuvres, and in the beginning of November, when the *biretta* arrived from Rome, M de Choiseul came from Vienna to take up the post which the cardinal was about to quit M de Choiseul's sudden arrival and the certain amount of discord that prevailed among the views of the parties interested, could not fail to produce very startling contradictions Thus M de Choiseul, who in the official announcement in the gazette had only been named as an assistant, chosen by the cardinal, to conduct the Foreign Office Department under his direction, and who was not over favourably received by the King, was in the same week created a peer at the opening of the Council, because of the claim raised by Marshal d'Estrées, that the Marshals of France took precedence of those dukes who were not peers The cardinal also quitted the minister's official residence, and installed himself in the finest apartments of the Château de Versailles, where on the first Tuesday, the day for the ambassadors' audience, he received them with great solemnity in concurrence with the new minister, to whom they then only seemed to go as to the Chief Secretary, thus M de Choiseul, Minister for Foreign Affairs, duke and peer of France, in the midst of all these honours, appeared only to occupy a secondary post

The cardinal had delivered his memorandum to the King himself, and took possession by main force of the high place of which he thought himself secure

The King said nothing, allowed matters to slide, and would no doubt have given in, if Madame de Pompadour, to whom the King had shown the memorandum, and who was greatly offended at it, had not united with M de Soubise, M de Gontaut and M de Belle-Isle,[1] in representing the author of it as a very ambitious man, who wished to possess himself of a place, which the personal feelings of the King, his well-known views on this subject, and the last advice of Cardinal Fleury,[2] ought to prevent ever being re-established This method of recalling to him his

[1] Louis Fouquet, Duc de Belle-Isle, was the grandson of the celebrated Super-intendent Fouquet Born at Villafranca de Rouergue in 1684, he entered the army early, and took part in the Spanish campaign as colonel A major-general in 1719, he was implicated in the trial of Leblanc, Secretary of State for War, accused of peculation, and imprisoned in the Bastile Made a lieut -general in 1732, he received the governorship of Metz and the three bishoprics in 1736, which he retained till his death Created a Marshal of France in 1741, he very ably conducted some delicate negotiations at Frankfort, where he paved the way for the election of the Emperor Charles VII Soon after, he distinguished himself in the Bohemian campaign, and at the retreat of Prague (1743) The following year he was made a prisoner in Hanover, and imprisoned for one year in England In 1757, he was made War Secretary, and died in 1761

[2] André Hercule, Cardinal de Fleury, belonged to the old *noblesse* of Languedoc He was born at Lodève on June 22nd, 1653. Almoner to the Queen, he was made Bishop of Fréjus in 1698 On the death of Louis XIV, he was made preceptor to the new King, over whom he soon gained an immense influence In 1726, Cardinal Fleury became a State Minister and Postmaster General, and was soon after created a cardinal He continued his official duties until his death in 1743

own principles, afforded the King evidence of the most sincere attachment to himself and his dignity, and did not fail in its effect Cardinal de Bernis was sent into exile [1]

Thus this gentle and amiable man, far more fitted for the delights of society than for the deep intrigues of a Ministry, was removed from the chief direction of affairs His life later on regained some *éclat* by means of his ecclesiastical position, his large fortune, and the good use he made of it He finished his career very happily, his last moments being devoted to the care, it might almost be said to the support, of the virtuous daughters of his benefactor History will say but little about him

M de Choiseul remained in sole charge of foreign affairs It will not perhaps be uninteresting to learn what use he made of his power, and the position in which he placed France as regards the other Courts of Europe

One of the principal acts of his government was the treaty of January, 1759, with Austria By this treaty, France reduced the subsidy of eighty millions, agreed upon by the treaty of 1756, to forty millions But through unjustifiable carelessness, a large force, sufficient in fact for a matter of the greatest national interest, was placed at the disposition of Austria

It was not till 1761 that M de Choiseul, alarmed at the evils of every kind experienced by France, tried to shorten their duration by a special peace with England, hoping thereby to bring about one with Germany also The first mention of these relations had been brought over to London by M le Bailli de Solar,[2] the Sardinian ambassador

M de Bussy[3] was thereupon accredited to Mr Pitt,[4] and Mr Stanley went to France

---

[1] November, 1758

[2] Ignace Solar de Breille, known under the name of Bailiff of Solar, born in 1715, a grand cross of Malta Sardinian Ambassador in France (1758-1765) After the peace of 1763, he received the Abbey of St Jean des Vignes de Soissons

[3] François de Bussy, born in 1699, entered the Foreign Office in 1725 as *Chargé d'Affaires* at Vienna, then at London in 1737 Minister Plenipotentiary in London 1740, Chief Secretary at the Foreign Office 1749 He died in 1780

[4] William Pitt, Earl of Chatham, one of the greatest of English statesmen, born in 1708, entered Parliament when he was 21 He was leader of the Opposition until 1746, became Vice Treasurer of Ireland and Privy Councillor under the Newcastle Government (1755-1761) In 1766, Pitt was created Earl of Chatham, and entered the House of Lords He then again took part in public affairs for a short period, and died in 1775

Notwithstanding the concessions made by M de Choiseul in his negotiations with England, it was impossible even to establish the preliminary basis, Lord Chatham still saw too many happy chances in the war to wish seriously to make peace He began the negotiations to make himself popular, and he concluded nothing, because he was a statesman After various attempts of every kind it became necessary to abandon the idea The only political success gained by M de Choiseul at this period, and which gives him, as it were, a place in history, was the family compact with Spain,[1] by which it may be said that France—without weakening her continental position, in fact rather by strengthening it, and without undertaking any onerous burdens—was assured, either in peace or war, of the permanent co-operation of a Power which, at that time, possessed the greatest maritime resources, and the rich treasures of America and India If this friendly arrangement with Spain had been made at the same time as the treaty of Versailles with the Court of Vienna, it is quite possible that England would never have gained the victories which led to the disastrous peace of 1763

This period of our history will no doubt induce political writers, if any such should still exist a few years hence, to ascertain whether, as a general theory, treaties of permanent alliance are of use to the parties which contract them These sort of transactions are generally supposed to lead to very happy results Nevertheless, experience has proved, that whenever a Power tries to weigh down the scale in her favour, she introduces into such an agreement a spirit of caution and egotism injurious to the common cause As soon as the stipulations for friendly relations, assistance, and definite aid have been settled, all efforts are directed towards interpreting the clauses, and eluding the demands, in fact to evading the consequences of the engagements just contracted, and when the *casus foederis* becomes so self-evident that it can-

[1] This family compact consisted of a Convention signed at Paris on the 15th August, 1761, between the representatives of France (Choiseul) and of Spain (Grimaldi), by which the Sovereigns of the House of Bourbon, Louis XV, Charles III, King of Spain Ferdinand, King of the Two Sicilies (son of Charles III), and Philippe, Duke of Parma (his brother), contracted an offensive and defensive alliance for the mutual guarantee of their States This alliance lasted as long as the French monarchy

not be misinterpreted, a thousand circumstances are used as pretexts, to retard the preparation and complicate the execution of the very plainest articles The ally who is attacked, has had time to lose several provinces before receiving either a single man or a single coin from the other, who ought to have come to his assistance with aid of every kind Would the four coalitions which have been successively formed since the French Revolution, have so speedily fallen through, if each of the contracting parties had faithfully and in good time used every effort in the interest of the common cause ?

But even taking for granted the loyalty of the ally whose intervention has became necessary, would not natural obstacles, distance, the delay in raising levies, and the state of the roads at some seasons of the year suffice to render useless such aid, which, if only the half had arrived in time, might have given another direction and different results to most important events ?

For example, Prussia would certainly have made a more vigorous resistance if, before the battle of Jena, the Emperor Alexander's headquarters had been at Custrin [1]

Among the reasons for the dilatoriness of allies, must also be counted the dislike to seeing their troops, guns, and war material badly employed and their regiments placed at the most dangerous posts , also to losing their men and money, often without obtaining any other advantage from their co-operation than that of assisting at the taking possession of conquests made by their allies

A great portion of the inconvenience attached to treaties of alliance between continental Powers might be removed by an understanding between the maritime Powers, and it was on this account that the treaty of 1761 with Spain, although made too late, is still the most able act of M de Choiseul's Ministry In fact, it is easy to understand that assistance, even if of no great value, becomes of importance at once, when, transported by sea, as it can threaten various points of the common enemy's territory almost at the same time, and subsequently,

[1] At the time of the battle of Jena, the Russian army had not yet passed the German frontier Napoleon had to go in search of it in the heart of Poland, and only reached it in January—that is, three months after the battle of Jena

when it becomes a question of arranging the conditions of peace and sharing the fruits of a lucky war, it is possible to take the part of one of the Powers without too greatly injuring the interests of the other

However, these few remarks on a question of such vast interest, and one which ought to be treated with the utmost care and consideration, are only applicable, as has been seen, in a case where war, following closely on the completion of the treaty, obliges the contracting parties to carry out its clauses For everyone must look upon an alliance, contracted with deep deliberation and wisdom between Powers of the first rank, with the noble idea of securing a permanent peace, and removing the possibilities of war, as one of the grandest achievements of diplomacy, the only object of which would be to compel by a just and imposing mediation all restless, ambitious, and obstructive Powers seeking to disturb the general equilibrium, to adopt ways of quietness and moderation, and to encourage the free and easy interchange of the products of different countries

Nevertheless, it is necessary to exercise great care in a compact of this nature, for it must be drawn up in the interest of Europe at large, indeed of everyone It is indispensable therefore that this interest should be carefully established and very evident, and it will not be sufficiently so if those, that is the nations whom it affects, are not convinced that the arrangement is for their own special advantage For, were they to entertain any distrust, all political alliance would become deceptive and even dangerous In the state of civilization to which Europe has now attained, the tendency of all nations is to stand on a common level, and if they thought they were being diverted from this path, they would speedily blame their Governments, and work against them with irresistible force

Henri IV's[1] schemes of a Christian alliance, the perpetual

---

[1] Talleyrand here recalls the grand scheme of European reorganization so long dreamt of by Henri IV He wished first to bring about a lasting state of equilibrium in Europe, by obliging each nation to keep within its natural frontier Europe, thus divided into a certain number of States, about equal in size and strength, would then have become a great Christian Republic A supreme council of deputies from all the States was to be charged with the prevention of wars by settling disputes This scheme of the federation of all Christian nations was Henri IV's favourite topic of conversation with Sully, but he had not the time, nor probably the intention, of carrying it out in reality

peace of l'Abbé de Saint-Pierre,[1] were planned during a period
when the Governments possessed the entire confidence of their
people   These left it to their Sovereigns to provide for and
direct their destinies   The Sovereigns on their side, possessed
all the power requisite to conduct such great interests   The
great State bodies were but the auxiliaries of this power, and if
sometimes they tried to diminish its action, they never went so
far as to expose it to the discretion of the people   The conception of sovereignty was very complete in men's minds, presenting
itself everywhere as a tutelary power, against which no resistance was legitimate

During such a period it was possible to create political
systems, and that which the great soul of Henri IV had conceived might have been carried into execution

But the progress of civilization, by raising the middle
classes, diminished the distance which divided them from the
Government   They began to examine its structure and its acts ,
ere long, criticism arose and brought on distrust, the result of
which was, that more sincerity and ability were needed in
governing the people than were formerly necessary   Under
such circumstances, therefore, it would require great skill and
foresight to form one of those alliances, whose only object would
be to guarantee universal peace

I pause here, surprised that I should have been unable to
resist the attraction of generous views, which have caused me to
go outside the circumscribed matter within which I ought to have
remained

M de Choiseul's inherent pride, his almost unlimited and
uncontrolled power, and the carelessness of his habits, made him
despise those countries too much where civilization had only
just dawned   He disdained to notice the changes that were
then taking place in the north, and could not be induced to
consider Russia in any way   That Power, meanwhile, began, by
a sort of instinct, to follow the policy which led her towards
the centre of Europe, the tendency of which (without having

[1] Charles Castel, Abbé de Saint-Pierre (1658 1743), celebrated for his plan of a
perpetual peace   He had taken up Henri IV 's ideas, and spent his life in submitting
various schemes of reform to the different ministers

as yet a decided object) was to arrive at a point where she would one day exercise a preponderant and dangerous influence on the affairs of the Continent   He did not realize how far the advantageous relations which England was beginning to open up with that Power might extend, and as a result of this blindness, he tried to foster a misunderstanding between Sweden and Denmark, whereas he ought to have endeavoured to bring these two small Powers together, as they, with the assistance of France, were alone capable of closing at will the commercial communication which, from force of circumstances, must closely unite Russia with Great Britain   He at the same time showed his contempt for the Court of St Petersburg in the most offensive manner   He recalled the old Marquis de l'Hôpital,[1] who enjoyed great consideration and even some favour at the hands of the Empress Elizabeth[2]   He replaced him by the Baron de Breteuil, a simple minister plenipotentiary, to whom he gave such stringent orders, as rendered it impossible for him to profit by the advantages that might be expected from the fall of the Comte de Bestucheff,[3] a declared partizan and probably a pensioner of England   Nevertheless, all attempts to incense the Empress Elizabeth proved futile   She, of her own accord, gave explanations respecting the want of consideration shown towards herself

But her unexpected death gave the throne to Peter III.,[4] whose inclinations were totally opposed to those of his aunt   He was secretly attached to the military service of the King of Prussia, and had received direct, without their passing through

---

[1] Paul de Galuccio, Marquis de l'Hôpital, descended from a noble family of Neapolitan origin, born in 1697, entered the army, and became a lieutenant-general in 1745   Ambassador at Naples in 1739 he went on to St Petersburg   He died in 1776

[2] Elizabeth, daughter of Peter the Great, born in 1709, succeeded the Empress Anne in 1741, and died in 1761

Alexis Bestoujet-Rumine or Bestucheff, descended, it was said, from an English family who had migrated to Russia in the fifteenth century, was born at Moscow in 1693   He first took service with the Elector of Hanover, who when he became King of England sent him as Ambassador to St Petersburg   He then entered the Russian service, was sent as Minister to Copenhagen, then Minister of State under the Empress Anne, and Grand Chancellor under the Empress Elizabeth   Exiled in 1757, he was recalled by Catherine in 1762, and died in 1766

[4] Peter III., son of the Empress Anne and nephew of Elizabeth, married, in 1746, Sophie d'Anhalt-Zerbst known later as Catherine the Great   He succeeded to the throne on 5th January, 1762 was deposed a few months later, arrested, and strangled in his prison (July, 1762)

any intermediary hands, and with certain mysterious formulas, the successive ranks of captain and colonel. That of general, to which he was promoted on his succession, and the uniform of which he at once wore, seemed to him the very height of glory. He at once sent orders to the general of his army, which was fighting against the King of Prussia, to range himself on his side and to continue the war, under his direction, against the Austrians [1]

This extraordinary policy was, unfortunately for the Prince, associated with one still more dangerous, namely, his manifest intention to repudiate his wife, the famous Catherine II, who did not long allow him to give himself up to all the eccentricities to which the disordered state of his mind inclined him.

M de Choiseul's indifference to all that was passing in Russia was so great, that at the time of Peter III's violent death, the only Frenchman accredited to St Petersburg was the Abbé Duprat, Baron de Breteuil's secretary, whom he had left there as *Chargé d'Affaires.* It was this Abbé who collected all the details which M de Rulhière, then at Warsaw with the Baron de Breteuil, transmitted to us as if he had been the actual eye-witness of a piece of work, or rather a piece of news, written with great elegance, but in which exactitude played but a secondary part.

A fresh reign, a new minister and a very enterprising Sovereign, however, compelled France to have a real diplomatic agent at St Petersburg, and M de Choiseul found himself obliged to order the Baron de Breteuil, who had come home on leave, to return to his post. But faithful to the policy he had adopted of humiliating the Sovereign, though doing nothing to check the policy of the country, he gave M de Breteuil no other instruction than to ask the new Empress to send him the *Reversale,* by which the Empress Elizabeth, on receiving from France the title of Empress, had consented not to claim any other rank, as regards France, than that accorded to the Czars of Muscovy [2]

---

[1] The treaty of peace between Prussia and Russia is dated May 5th, 1762

[2] Until the reign of Elizabeth, the Russian Sovereigns were only recognized officially under the title of Czars of Muscovy. In 1745, Elizabeth determined to obtain her recognition as Empress by the Courts. For this purpose she signed an Act, called the *Reversale,* in 1745 with France, by which Louis XV, " out of friendship, and as a special favour to her, condescended to recognize the Imperial title." In return, the Empress

As what I am now writing is more the sketch of an epoch, taken as a whole, than an historical picture of facts, all I must guard against is not to mix up, in the impressions I wish to give, the period when M de Choiseul's power was not unlimited, with that in which he was absolute master of France

Peace had become a general necessity in Europe, and as treaties were then faithfully kept, it was easy to establish friendly relations between States who had hitherto been belligerents   The occupation of a conquered country was not prolonged after peace was declared, as has been witnessed in later days; the independence of each country was completely restored, and the ruinous consequences of war ceased with it

The death of George II,[1] King of England, permitted the question of peace to be seriously entertained   His successor, George III,[2] accustomed to be on the most intimate terms with the Earl of Bute,[3] who was his governor during the time he was Prince of Wales, accorded him such complete and full confidence on his accession to the throne, that he at once sent for him in place of Lord Chatham   The Earl of Bute, having been made Prime Minister, hoped, through his personal interest, to secure to England, by a peace of which he would gain the credit, all the immense advantages which had accrued to her from the war   He therefore spoke of the possibility of coming to an understanding, and at the instigation of the Bailli de Solar, of whom mention has already been made, he placed full confidence in the overtures made to him, and added some *éclat* to a fresh

did not claim, as regards France, any other rank of precedence than that of Czarina of Muscovy   On the 3rd December, 1762, Catherine declared that the Imperial title had always belonged to the Czars, and that she would refuse to enter into relations with those States who did not recognize her as Empress   Breteuil received orders to confirm the *Rétroacte* of 1745, reminding her of the definite condition which Catherine seemed disposed to forget   Spain followed his example   (See a series of memorandums on this subject in Martens *Recueil de Traités*)

[1] George II, King of England, son of George I, born in Hanover in 1683, ascended the throne in 1727, and died in 1760

[2] George III, King of England, grandson of George II, born in 1738, succeeded his grandfather   He became insane in 1810, and died in 1820

[3] John Stuart, Earl of Bute, born in Scotland in 1713, was elected a Scotch representative peer in 1737   Gentleman of the Bedchamber to the future King George III, he was intrusted with his education (1751)   On his pupil's accession, he was called to the Council as Secretary of State and Lord of the Treasury (1761)   He signed the treaty of 1763, and seemed to be at the zenith of his power when he suddenly resigned   He died in 1792

negotiation by sending the Duke of Bedford [1] to France The
compliment was returned by sending the Duc de Nivernais to
London The former had Mr Hume [2] as secretary of legation, and
the latter was accompanied by the Chevalier d'Eon [3] in the same
capacity Notwithstanding these little incongruities, which always
bring M de Choiseul's carelessness to the front, the treaty advanced
with such speed, that it was ready for signature in the beginning
of September 1763 It would indeed have been signed, if the
Spanish plenipotentiary, M de Grimaldi, [4] had not opposed it,
under the belief that the English were about to receive a severe
check in Havannah The check did not occur, the English took
Havannah, and it was necessary, ere getting it back, to give them
Florida, for which M de Choiseul indemnified Spain by ceding
Louisiana to her All was agreed to, and peace was signed at
Fontainebleau on November 2nd, 1763 [5]

It is almost impossible in these days to believe in the intervention in so important a negotiation, of the Bailli de Solar, the
representative of a Government which, in our time, without the

---

[1] John Russell, fourth Duke of Bedford (1710 1771), was First Lord of the
Admiralty in 1744 He retired in 1751, and was made Lord Lieutenant of Ireland,
and Lord Privy Seal in 1761 On his return from Versailles, where he had gone to
negotiate the treaty of Paris, he entered the Grenville Cabinet, where he remained
until his death

[2] David Hume, English historian and philosopher, born at Edinburgh in 1711
He was Secretary to the Embassy at Vienna and at Turin He went to Paris in
1763, as Secretary to the Marquis of Hertford, the English Ambassador, and not in
1761 with the Duke of Bedford, as stated above He died in 1776

[3] Charles d'Eon de Beaumont, called the Chevalier d'Eon, was born at Tonnerre in
1728 A singular celebrity has attached itself to his name, his sex was for a long
time a matter of doubt, and if it is now affirmed that he really was a man, public
opinion, on the faith of lying confessions, considered him, for a lengthened period, to
be a woman The Chevalier d'Eon was one of the most stirring agents of the secret
diplomacy of Louis XV After a mission to Russia and a short sojourn with the
army (1758), he was sent to London in 1762 as Minister *ad interim* He was very
unwilling to give place to the Comte de Guerchy, the new Ambassador This was the
commencement of a series of endless adventures and complications Possessed as he
was of the King's secrets, he for several years trifled with the King and his Ministers,
lived in the most magnificent style while in London, and obliged the King in the end
to give in Louis XVI permitted him to return to France He soon after went back
to England, where he died in 1810

[4] Don Geronimo, Duc de Grimaldi, grandee of Spain, born at Genoa in 1720
He entered the diplomatic service, and was Ambassador to Paris in 1761, Minister
of Foreign Affairs in 1764 He tendered his resignation in 1776, and died in Italy
in 1786

[5] By this disastrous peace, France ceded nearly all her colonies to England
Canada, all the islands and coast of the Gulf of St Lawrence, the whole of India
she again raised the fortifications of Dunkirk, and evacuated Hanover, Hesse, and
Brunswick

opposition of a single European Cabinet, has been excluded from among the number of the Great Powers

The peace concluded with the King of Prussia, followed in the course of a few weeks by that with England, ere long brought about one between Prussia and the Court of Vienna[1] Thus ended the famous Seven Years' war, which our forefathers found so full of important issues, but which has paled sensibly before the present generation, in face of the great struggles it has been called upon to witness

The following year Madame de Pompadour died, and no apparent change was visible either at home or abroad   The death of this woman, who for so many years had played the part of Prime Minister—who in revenge for some proposal or some verses written against her by Frederick II, had been the real author of the alliance between the Houses of France and Austria, the consequence of which might have been to annihilate the weak counterpoise that Prussia was beginning to bring into the affairs of Europe—who by a breath had overthrown the Cardinal de Bernis, for the crime of having for one moment contemplated occupying the position which the Bishop of Fréjus[2] had held at the beginning of that reign—the death of this woman, I repeat, was scarcely news for France, and did not even cause any disturbance in the King's household

Fallen completely for the last five years under the influence of the Duc de Choiseul, blasé, tired of all her pleasures, sometimes opposed by the very man whom she had raised so high, and who had betrayed one of her friends, Madame d'Amblimont,[3] and driven away the other, Madame d'Esparbès,[4] by publicly insulting her ; still further humiliated by the kind of superiority which Madame de Gramont[5] and Madame de Beauvau[6] had assumed in the King's private circle, at which she had now

[1] The treaty of peace between Prussia and Austria was signed at the Château de Hubertsburg, near Leipzig, February 15th, 1763
[2] Cardinal de Fleury
[3] Probably Marie-Anne de Chaumont Quitry, married in 1754 to Claude de Fuchsamberg Comte d'Amblimont
[4] Mademoiselle Louard de Jouy, married to the Comte d'Esparbes de Lussan, Major general and governor of Montauban   She died at a very advanced age
[5] Beatrix de Choiseul Stainville, Duchesse de Gramont, sister to the Duc de Choiseul
[6] Marie Sylvie de Rohan Chabot, Marechale and Princesse de Beauvau Craon

only the sad privilege of doing the honours; overcome by infirmities which for a long time had driven Louis XV from her couch, and likewise him who had sought her favour, Madame de Pompadour quitted this life without regret

The King continued indifferent; he even seemed to be rather relieved than grieved at this change in his mode of life, and the loss of a tie which among crowned heads generally replaces natural likings. He only retired during two evenings for decency's sake. On the third day, when he returned from hunting at Rambouillet, after receiving his courtiers at his *débotté* as usual, he went up to Madame de Pompadour's apartment, the room was exactly the same, the bed alone had been removed. There he found Madame de Gramont, Madame de Beauvau, M. de Choiseul, M. de Gontaut, M. de Chauvelin,[1] and other persons belonging to his private circle. The name of the woman who had occupied this apartment for eighteen years, and who had introduced therein all that had made the home life of the King, was no longer mentioned.

Dating from that period, everything succumbed to the rule of M. de Choiseul, whose audacity and will met with neither check nor opposition. His career had reached its zenith; he changed ministers, recalled ambassadors, disquieted all the Cabinets of Europe, braved the heir to the throne, set aside parliamentary decrees, and restored decrees of council, issued proclamations, gave *lettres de cachet*, won for himself every species of favour, and handed France over to his friends. It was not until 1768, that a slight cloud on the horizon began to menace him from afar.

An almost obscure individual was working, certainly quite unintentionally, to put an end to this career, which seemed so firmly established

M. du Barry,[2] a small proprietor of Toulouse, was living a

---

[1] The Chevalier Bernard de Chauvelin was a brigadier in 1774, lieutenant-general in 1749, commandant of Corsica, then Minister at Genoa, Ambassador at Turin in 1753, and Master of the King's Household in 1765. He died in 1773

[2] Comte Jean du Barry Cères, born at Levignac, near Toulouse, belonged to an obscure family. Having come to Paris and being unable to enter the diplomatic service, he contrived to realize a large fortune by the sale of supplies and provisions. His brother was Comte Guillaume du Barry, husband of Madame du Barry. On the death of Louis XV he hastened to quit France, but soon returned and lived at Toulouse. He fell a victim to the guillotine there in 1794

somewhat disreputable life in Paris   Intimately associated with
all the shady intrigues of the times, he sought by their means to
lead an existence of daily dissipation, on a scale of luxury
scarcely to be conceived

He had constituted himself a giver of suppers to women of
ill fame, of whom he always supported one or two, passing them
on to other men when he thought he could by so doing gain
some advantage   At first his connections of this nature did not
extend beyond the offices of the ministers, for in that society he
found slight favours were readily accorded, or promises made, still
more readily fulfilled, by the dupes from the country who always
abound in the capital

He introduced himself as a general provider to Maréchal de
Richelieu [1] and the Duc de Duras [2] He had even enticed them to
some of his more select suppers at which were assembled M de
Thiard, the Chevalier de Durfort, [4] the Comte de Bissy, [5] the
Abbé de Mastin, M de la Tour du Pin, [6] and several witty men
of letters, such as Moncrif, [7] the Abbé Arnaud, Cailhava, [8] his

---

[1] Armand Duplessis, Duc de Richelieu, was the grand-nephew of the great
Cardinal   Born in 1696 he was a mousquetaire at Denain in 1712   Ambassador at
Vienna 1724   Lieutenant-general in 1744, he distinguished himself at Fontenoy and
at Raucoux   Ambassador at Dresden, Marshal of France (1748), Governor Guienne
(1755)   Commanded the expedition to Minorca in 1756, and the army of Hanover in
1757   He died in 1788

[2] Emmanuel de Durfort, Duc de Duras, born in 1715, belonged to an old family of
Guienne   His father was a marshal of France. He himself became a lieutenant-
general in 1748, Ambassador to Spain 1751 first gentleman of the bedchamber 1757,
became a marshal in 1775, and died in 1789

[3] Henry Comte de Thiard nephew of Cardinal de Bissy, born in 1726 Brigadier-
General 1760, lieutenant-general, and chief equerry to the Duc d'Orléans 1762 He ,
had a command in Provence 1782, then in Brittany 1787, was arrested in 1798, and
guillotined on the 9th Thermidor, year II

[4] The Chevalier Joseph de Durfort-Boissière, born in 1745, was a captain in the
Regiment of Chartres

[5] Claude de Thiard, known under the name of Comte de Bissy, was brother of
the Comte de Thiard   Born in 1721, he became lieutenant general in 1670, and
commandant in Languedoc   He was member of the Academy   He died in 1818

[6] The family of La Tour du Pin belonged to the old noblesse of Dauphiné   The
Marquis Philippe, born in 1723, became a lieutenant general in 1788   Obliged to
give evidence at the Queen's trial, his testimony caused him to be suspected and
arrested , he was guillotined soon after (1794)   His brother Comte Louis, born in
1725, was major general and chamberlain to the Duc d'Orléans   He emigrated, and
did not return to France until the Restoration

[7] François Paradis de Moncrif, so called after his mother (Moncrieff), who was an
Englishwoman   He was secretary to Comte d'Argenson, then to the Comte de
Clermont, reader to Queen Marie Leczinska, and secretary to the Duc d'Orléans
He wrote several novels, comedies, and operas, entered the Academy in 1733, and
died in 1770

[8] Jean Cailhava, born at Estandous near Toulouse (1731), wrote all his life for

compatriot Robbé,[1] who told amusing stories, also actors of
dramatic proverbs , Goy, better known under the name of My
Lord Goy ; in fact, every one who could in any way assist in
making these evenings amusing   His assiduity in discover-
ing *débutantes* in gallantry had brought him in contact with the
celebrated Lebel, the King's head valet and provider in ordinary
for the so-called *parc aux cerfs*   These two poachers had often
met on the same paths, and M du Barry felt no scruples at
placing himself under the orders of the head contractor

In the winter of 1767–68, after a very dejected conversation on
the difficulties of the times as regarded their business, especially
in doing it well, M du Barry mentioned to Lebel a young
person who had been with him for four years, but who he undertook should in a few days regain that innocent deportment which
the King's age required

Lebel, either carried away or at his wit's end, accompanied him
and saw Mademoiselle L'Ange,[2] the name under which she was
then known   After paying her several visits privately one after
the other, he speedily made up his mind   Du Barry, an apt
assistant in these sort of enterprises, lost no time in constructing
a scheme in which Lebel could co-operate

L'Ange had a young cousin, not very pretty, but possessing
a good figure, and very agreeable, who was her companion
both at home and abroad   The Marquis d'Arcambal, commandant of Corsica, was in love with her   Through M
d'Arcambal and some clerks in the War Department, M
du Barry had procured the contract for the supplies in
Corsica for a man named Nalet, a very good thing, by which
he, Du Barry, had covered his expenses for the last two
years   He told L'Ange to humour Lebel's wishes, and promise
him a successful issue if he could introduce her to the King's
favour, and procure a place as farmer-general for Nalet, who would

[1] Pierre Robbé de Beauveset, born at Vendôme 1712   He wrote several frivolous
poems, but more particularly known for his profane and licentious tales , he died
in 1792

[2] Marie Jeanne Gomart de Vaubernier, Comtesse du Barry, born at Vaucouleurs
in 1746.   On the death of Louis XV., she was exiled to the Abbaye de Pont aux
Dames, near Meaux.   She quitted this soon after and retired to her country house at
Luciennes   She was guillotined in 1793

marry her, that then everything could be arranged   Lebel, who did not wish a husband mixed up in the affair, said it would be quite sufficient to call him a cousin, but as M du Barry insisted on the marriage, and as Nalet was in Corsica, it was decided to present her to the King as a married woman, but one who had only gone through the religious ceremony, and had not lived with her husband   Lebel thereupon invited her, together with her cousin, to sup with him at Versailles   The King, through a glass door at no great distance from the table, was able both to see and hear her, doubtless an ordinary practice of his at such preliminaries   The first impression was very favourable   Their behaviour and conversation had been all planned by a master's hand and each one played their part to perfection   A fancy towards a woman married but yet a virgin induced the King to order Lebel to invite her a second time   At this point M du Barry confided this adventure to Marshal de Richelieu, who advised him, instead of making L'Ange Madame Nalet, to marry her to his own brother, M Guillaume du Barry, and to carry out a little romance, rather clumsy in the main, but which he thought capable of the development it afterwards assumed   It was no longer therefore an aspirant for the *parc aux cerfs* who was presented to the King, but a lady of position, it was even deemed advisable that she should not appear to be badly off M du Barry exhausted the chest of the Corsican supplies in order to provide an elegant wardrobe, a grand equipage and rich liveries for her whose future *rôle* was not as yet well assured She nevertheless made her first appearance at Compiègne with this imprudent *éclat* She lodged in the town, kept very much at home during the day, and did not go out till about midnight, when she drove to the château, where she slept, returning each morning in the same carriage followed by two servants   It is probable that the police reports, which might have revealed the whole plot to the King, were diverted by Lebel, or possibly the information only reached him after his fancy had become a confirmed passion

M de Choiseul, fully aware of all that was passing, was somewhat disquieted, but he only exhibited disdain, expressing himself in very contemptuous terms, all of which were carefully repeated to the King by Madame du Barry herself. Her behaviour and the course she adopted only served to increase the King's infatuation, and incense him still further against the obstacles which his weakness foresaw. The death of Lebel still further increased the ascendency of the favourite. As she had had the skill to let the King see that she was quite independent of that confidant, and had shown herself superior to the subordinate part for which she was originally intended, all that Lebel had said in her praise, up to the last moment, was regarded by the King as a kind of dying testament, dictated by the conscience of a most faithful subject. The cousin who had remained with M. du Barry, therefore, was believed by the King to be that Mademoiselle L'Ange who had been talked of, in fact, a regular state of confusion was created in this unfortunate Prince's mind, which blinded him completely, and made him reject as absurdities or calumnies all attempts made to enlighten him as to the real state of affairs.

Her stay at Compiègne having ended, the Countess Guillaume du Barry returned to Paris and went back to Comte Jean, now her brother-in-law, without having received a single proof of her royal lover's generosity, not even the smallest present, so much so, that the disinterested and impassioned air she knew how to assume had succeeded in convincing the King that with her he had found the supreme happiness of being loved for himself alone. At the end of a few weeks the resources of the Corsican commissariat chest began to run low. By the advice of her brother-in-law, Madame du Barry had the audacity to ask M. de Choiseul in Paris for an advance of money for her *protégé* Nalet. She accompanied her request by some friendly overtures. M. de Choiseul, true to his pride and his licentiousness, committed the double blunder of rejecting her advances, saying that he knew nothing of what occurred outside his department, and at the same time granting her more than she asked for. All however would have been lost without this slight help.

Marshal de Richelieu, who had been kept *au courant* by M. du Barry, judging that a considerable change was then about to take place at Court, thought there was no longer any danger either to his position or his purse in coming to the front, and he undertook to carry through the request for Madame du Barry's presentation, by telling the King that he was acquainted with the Du Barrys, that they were of good family, and that in his province they were respected as equal to the first families in the country

By means of a small monetary bribe and extensive promises, Madame la Comtesse de Béarn,[1] a woman of position, was induced to present at Court the new favourite, who however did not appear in public except on that one day at Versailles, but occupied herself in private, by quietly preparing for the demon-stration in her favour on the occasion of the journey to Fontainebleau The King, on his side, carried away by his inclination and gaining confidence by the unexpected success of the presentation, thought that by changing the scene, a fresh departure could be introduced When making his arrangements with M de la Suze, the Grand Chamberlain, as to the distribution of apartments at Fontainebleau, he reserved for himself, without any explanation, those formerly occupied by Madame de Pompadour, had the doors of communication with his own apartments, which had been walled up, reopened, and the day after his arrival at this new abode, some servants and the women of Madame du Barry arrived there without any fuss Two days later she herself was established there

Madame de Gramont and Madame de Beauvau, who were invited to a private supper the same evening, made some excuses to avoid going This had been fully expected, as the scornful remarks showered on the new favourite by these ladies, who had been so indulgent to Madame de Pompadour, were well known, and care had been taken to secure some other ladies, better satisfied with themselves and not holding their heads quite so high, among the first Madame de Béarn, the *Maréchale* de Mirepoix,[2] and the old Princesse de Talmont,[3] who was a cousin of the late Queen Courtiers did not fail to appear, and thus it

---

[1] The Comtesse de Béarn was the widow of a gentleman of Perigord, an officer of the *Gardes du Corps*

[2] Anne de Beauvau-Craon, born in 1707, married first to Jacques de Lorraine, Prince de Lixing, and secondly, in 1739, to Pierre de Lévis, Duc de Mirepoix, Marshal of France

[3] Marie Louise, Princesse Jablonowska, born in 1700, married in 1730 Anne de La Tremoaille, Prince de Talmont, she died in 1773 Her father was cousin german to King Stanislaus

came about that this new mistress, that L'Ange, destined at one
time for the *parc aux cerfs*, for a moment Madame Nalet, and
made Comtesse du Barry the same day, found herself occupying
the place of Madame de Pompadour Lebel's death had dispersed
the *parc aux cerfs*, Madame du Barry remained in peaceable
possession of the King's heart, without any rivals, and the King
believed he had found a new and more pleasant existence
When the Court moved from Fontainebleau, it seemed quite
natural to continue the same arrangement, almost all M de
Choiseul's friends took up the plausible and easy position of
going every evening to Madame du Barry's to keep him well informed as to the affairs of the King's household   M. de Choiseul,
for his part, surrounded himself with the women of Madame de
Pompadour's former circle, and persuaded himself that matters
would continue in this way, and that while Madame du Barry
remained mistress of the pleasures and amusements, he would
remain master of business matters

This situation, so fine in theory, but unlikely to last.
nevertheless continued for some time   Intrigues however
supervened   M le Maréchal de Richelieu brought forward M
d'Aiguillon,[1] and criticisms on M de Choiseul's administration
began to make themselves heard   The ministers, jealous of the
absolute power he wielded, commenced to attend the little court
of the favourite   M de la Vrillière[2] and M Bertin[3] were the
first to come, the cloak of the Abbé du Terray[4] and the
robe of the Chancellor de Maupeou,[5] offered a gay contrast to

[1] Armand Vigneiod Duplessis-Richelieu, Duc d'Aiguillon, was a member of the
cardinal's family, born in 1720, he became governor of Alsace, then of Brittany,
where he had to sustain a long struggle with the Parliament of Rennes   Very hostile
to Choiseul, he replaced him in the Foreign Office in 1770   It was during his
ministry that the division of Poland took place   Exiled on the accession of Louis
XVI , he died in 1782

[2] Louis Phélippeaux, Comte de Saint-Florentin, Duc de la Vrillière, born in 1705,
succeeded his father as Secretary of State of the King's household (1725), Minister of
State 1751, and created a duke in 1770   He quitted the Ministry in 1775, and died
two years after

[3] Henri Bertin, born in 1719, member of an old legal family, Parliamentary coun-
sel 1741 , President of the Grand Council 1750 , Intendant of Roussillon, then of
Lyons , Lieut -General of Police 1757 , Comptroller-General 1759-1763   Obliged
to give up this post owing to the hostility of Parliament, he nevertheless remained
Minister of State   In 1774 he was for a very brief period Secretary of Foreign Affairs
He died in 1792

[4] At that time Comptroller-General

[5] René de Maupeou, born in 1714 , Parliamentary counsel , President à mortier
1743 , Chief President, 1763   Made Chancellor in 1768, he undertook to free the

her toilet powder Ere long an underhand war was commenced against M de Choiseul, in which Madame du Barry as yet took no part She was flattered, even amused, at the visits of these gentlemen , she had sufficient judgment to find some disloyalty in them She neither had, nor cared to have, a taste for business , her aim was attained, her position was secured, and she only wished to enjoy it, though sometimes she permitted herself to use, and even encouraged sarcasms against the women of the former circle, to prevent the King from feeling any regrets at having lost them, but she had never yet ventured anything against M de Choiseul The *éclat* which surrounded him awed her, and any slight attentions from him would have secured the maintenance of that neutrality which she was quite ready to continue A ten minutes' visit during one of the King's hunting excursions, would at this period have flattered and charmed her , and the King, to whom on his return she would not have failed to mention it, would have been very pleased Polite relations would thus have been established between them, and this would have sufficed to stifle the intrigues at their very birth

M de Choiseul seemed inclined to adopt this course, but the haughty spirit of the women by whom he was surrounded decided otherwise No relations of any kind could be tolerated The separation of the two parties became marked, and Madame du Barry, who would have liked only to occupy herself with dress, pleasures, and gaiety, found herself obliged to interfere in business matters, and to learn, much against her will, lessons in politics which she then tried to repeat with as little *gaucherie* as she could manage

Nearly two years passed thus without M de Choiseul's enemies gaining ground Each day the favourite was accused of having badly learnt, and still worse repeated, the lessons so perpetually instilled into her Matters had reached this point when, in the middle of the year 1770, a great quarrel arose, which became the battle-field on which all these Court interests were destined to meet

royal authority from the continued parliamentary hostility He got rid of the old Parliament and replaced it by another, consisting of all sorts of persons, which is known in history as the Maupeou Parliament (January, 1771) Maupeou was exiled on the accession of Louis XVI , and died in 1792

A French navigator had taken possession of the Falkland Isles, which had for some time been abandoned [1] Spain claimed them, repaid the cost of the establishment he had founded, and made good her right to proprietorship by sending a small garrison there, which certainly would not have influenced the commerce of any one But England, ever disquieted about anything of this kind, and taking advantage of a very vague article in the Peace of Utrecht, intervened, maintaining that those islands ought to belong to her, and that she alone had the right to occupy them She threatened Spain and commenced warlike preparations, the first cost of which was ten times the value of the contested possession, but which betrayed her secret desire to prevent the restoration of the navies of Spain and France The French navy, especially, had begun to awake from the lethargy into which the Seven Years' war, ending with the unfortunate treaty of 1763, had thrown it

M de Choiseul did not hesitate to pronounce himself strongly in favour of carrying out the family compact which had been his own work, and his cousin, the Duc de Praslin, who for the last five years had toiled unceasingly and successfully to re-establish the navy, supported him in the Council in bringing about most violent measures, no better suited to the condition of Spanish finances than they were to those of France. Nevertheless, the Court of Madrid listened submissively, for ever since the treaty of 1761, it had entirely given itself up to the directions of the Versailles Cabinet

M de Choiseul, believing that in a resumption of hostilities and a costly war, he saw a sure way of remaining in office and overthrowing the Abbé de Terray, upheld the Spanish cause even more hotly than the Court of Madrid itself, and inspired the Spanish Ministry with claims and demands from which he then declared it was impossible to withdraw The Comptroller-General, who owing to operations tarnished by bad faith had exhausted

---

[1] The Falkland Isles, or Malouines, are situated in the Southern Atlantic Ocean, near the coast of Patagonia , discovered in the sixteenth century, they remained a long time without a recognized master Bougainville led a French colony thither in 1763, but these were dispossessed two years after by the Spaniards Then the English intervened In 1771, Spain definitely ceded these islands to them, and they now belong to England without dispute

the source of obtaining loans, found himself at his wits' end, and did not know how to satisfy the demands for money with which the Minister of Marine overwhelmed him   The King's Council had become a sort of arena, in which the two influential ministers daily defeated their adversaries

Madame du Barry, at the close of the council (from which the King always returned in favour of M de Choiseul's views), generally inquired as to the result of these discussions   Already there were murmured hints respecting the dismissal of the Abbé Terray, and by a sure but unseen channel, the favourite became secretly disposed to abandon him, and to approve of M de Choiseul's proposition to replace him by State Councillor Foulon, Director of War and Naval Finances, a man who thoroughly understood the art of transferring the funds of these two great departments, and who, by the adoption of somewhat mysterious language, gained credit for possessing both ideas and resources   In consequence of the contracts for supplies for both these departments having been influenced by M du Barry, M Foulon had formed an intimacy with him, and was thus assured of some little interest

As the reiterated attacks against M de Choiseul produced no effect, some disquietude arose round Madame du Barry   Her cousin Chon, who occupied a sort of semi-subordinate position in her establishment, fully instructed in all that was taking place, and alarmed at the power which a war and a new Comptroller-General might give to M de Choiseul, came to Paris to consult M du Barry, who by the life of perpetual expedients that he led, had gained a certain business aptitude   M du Barry, much elated that his relations should come back to him for advice, went privately to see the Abbé de la Ville,[1] one of the chief Secretaries in the Foreign Office   This latter was an ex-Jesuit, very ambitious, whom some bishops of the Jesuit party had often inspired with the hope of some day becoming a minister himself   The small part he played was however totally eclipsed by the brilliancy of M de Choiseul's party, to whom he showed an almost monastic submission, though

---

[1] L'Abbé Jean Ignace de la Ville, born in 1690   French Minister at the Hague (1743), chief clerk in the Foreign Office (1755), bishop *in partibus* of Triconia and Director of Foreign Affairs (1774), died in 1774   He had entered the Academy in 1746

it did not entirely deceive M le Duc de Choiseul M du Barry, who lived in an atmosphere of both intrigue and power, scarcely required to display the hopes of becoming a Minister before the Abbé de la Ville's eyes He found him quite *au fait* with the matter of the Falkland Isles, and inclined to make the most of the embarrassment to France of a fresh and certainly costly war

" The cause is a very slight one," said the Abbé, " and the real object can only be the ministerial interest of M de Choiseul's party At the point which matters have now reached," he added, " there is only one way of preventing it the King must take upon himself to write a confidential letter to His Catholic Majesty His reply will assuredly prove that he is disposed to avoid a war, by giving up the Falkland Isles, the object of all this stir "

Nothing could have suited Du Barry better He at once hastened to his sister-in-law, and instructed her fully how to bring the matter before the King, by stating it as her own idea, and then, in order to give him confidence as to her clear-headedness, she was to wind up by saying · " I am certain that if you only have courage to send for the Abbé de la Ville, and command him to tell you candidly what he thinks as to the success of this direct step with the King of Spain, he cannot fail to approve it, and in this way you will be able to see the extent of the great fidelity with which you believe M de Choiseul serves you "

The King, more and more struck by the intelligence of Madame du Barry, replied " But under what pretext can I send for this Abbé ? The Duc de Choiseul will hear of it "

" How good and simple you are," she exclaimed, " I do not know him, I have never even seen him, but I will undertake that you shall find him here , and to put you completely at your ease I will get him to come here about dusk, dressed in secular clothes, with a bag to his wig and a sword by his side "

The King, charmed with the idea of a comic element thus mingled with the most serious affairs, gave his assent , and the Abbé having been immediately informed, at once attended this honourable and mysterious *rendezvous* dressed in grey

Shortly after his arrival, the King came in, and after a little pleasantry about the costume, began to speak to him as his

master, but withal a trusting one   He told the Abbé that he
had thought of writing to the King of Spain, and that as a faithful servant, he desired to hear from him frankly what his ideas
were as to the real feelings of His Catholic Majesty, and also
with regard to such a letter

The Abbé de la Ville did not fail to reply, that if Sovereigns
would always thus take their matters in hand, they would very
speedily be arranged, and the work of their ministers and ambassadors greatly diminished

The King, well pleased, then made some reflections on M de
Choiseul's administration

The Abbé, with a certain amount of reserve which permitted it to be seen that he shared the same views, abstained
from speaking against his minister out of respect to his master,
but said he could not possibly defend him

The interview did not last long

The King dismissed the Abbé with marks of the greatest kindness, and the latter departed, his head filled with all kinds of
chimeras

The King was now quite determined to write to the King of
Spain   As his *amour-propre* had prevented his asking the Abbé
de la Ville to draft a minute of the letter, he began to consider
how he should word it   The beginning was no easy matter

" You will do it all wrong," said Madame du Barry, " leave
me to draft it for you "

He consented, laughingly   A courier was immediately dis-
patched by Madamoiselle Chon, to fetch M du Barry, known as
the *roué* from Luciennes, to draw up this important composition
that same night

Du Barry started at midnight, but as the night was very dark
and the waters had overflowed, he was upset and almost thought
he was drowned, in the horse-pond at Marly   But he arrived at
last, dried himself, and forthwith proceeded to carry out his little
bit of work as well as he could   The contents of the letter
were somewhat as follows

" That having had already too many wars to carry through
during his reign, and having arrived at a time of life when he had
nothing to wish for but to finish his career in peace, and to

employ the end by restoring order in his home administration and especially in his finances, he confided this wish in a friendly spirit to his cousin, assuring him nevertheless, that if he considered that the interests of the Spanish monarchy or of his personal honour required that he should go beyond this great consideration, he would not hesitate to subscribe thereto, on receiving a reply by the private courier who was taking this letter "

Madame du Barry copied this draft letter with her own hand ; the next morning she got the King to transcribe it at her table, and her hair-dresser was entrusted with this great mission, which only took him eighteen days to accomplish

Charles III's[1] reply, drawn up by O'Reilly,[2] who was the person specially in his confidence, was just what was wished. Charles gave the King his cousin the greatest possible praise for the humanitarian sentiments which guided him, protested that his personal wishes were in entire conformity with them, and submitted himself completely to the King's decision

Nothing now appeared more evident to the King than the intrigues of M de Choiseul's party The parliamentary quarrels which were rife at this epoch, and which were directed against the Chancellor, represented him and his adherents as men who were ready to sacrifice both home and foreign affairs to their own ambition The proposals at their private councils were reported, exaggerated, and envenomed in every possible way

During the interval of the courier's journey, the King had begun to treat M de Choiseul and his friends coldly, this coldness turned into positive dislike on his return, and during the three or four days preceding their disgrace, they could obtain neither word nor letter from him So much so, that M le Duc de Choiseul who had in his portfolio the account of the expenses of both his depart-

---

[1] Charles III, King of Spain, son of Philip V and Elizabeth Farnese, born in 1716 He reigned first of all over Parma, which he had inherited from his mother (1731), then the kingdom of the two Sicilies (1734) In 1759, he was called to the throne of Spain by the death of his brother Ferdinand VI He died in 1788

[2] Alexander, Comte O'Reilly, born in Ireland about 1730, first entered the Spanish army, then passed into that of Austria, where he served under the command of his compatriot Lacey (1757), afterwards entered the French service, and finally returned to Spain, where he obtained the rank of colonel He became successively Governor of Madrid, Inspector-General of Infantry and Captain General of Andalusia On the death of Charles III he fell into disgrace (1788) He was about to part to take command of the army against France when he died (1794)

ments for the year 1770, could not get it approved or signed by
the King, and thus lost nearly fifteen hundred thousand francs
of unexpended funds, which the King, according to his custom,
always gave him as a gratuity at the end of each year's service

At last, on the 23rd December, 1770, the King having
summoned up courage, just as he was going out hunting,
sent M de la Vrillière with a very curt letter to M de
Choiseul banishing him to Chanteloup, and another, a little less
severe, to M de Praslin, directing him to retire at once to Praslin.
During the whole of this day the King was so lost in thought,
and kept looking at his watch so often, that it was easy to see
something extraordinary was taking place. He did not seem
at his ease until he heard, on his return to Versailles, that his
orders had been carried out before mid-day, and that he had three
offices to give away

Then it was that Madame du Barry really began to play the
great part of favourite Through the Prince de Condé's influence,
she got M de Monteynard [1] an old lieutenant-general, a very
mediocre officer and still more mediocre minister, appointed to
the War Department The navy, through Chancellor de
Maupeou's interest, was confided to M de Boynes,[2] a State
Councillor, who had submitted the scheme of replacing Parliament
by the Grand Council, and the Foreign Department, which she
could not at once give to the Duc d'Aiguillon, was provisionally
placed in the feeble hands of M de la Vrillière The Abbé de la
Ville, who from his seat in the office saw all these changes and
departures, did not yet give up all hope But two months later,
when Madame du Barry succeeded in overcoming the King's
dislike to M d'Aiguillon, he was very thankful to receive as a
reward the bishopric *in partibus* of Triconium, together with an
abbey The King did not wish him to quit the office where he
thought he was necessary

---

[1] Louis François, Marquis de Monteynard, born in 1716 at the Château de la
Pierre, in Dauphiné, of an old noble family of that province Major-General in
1748, Inspector-General of Infantry and Lieut General in 1759, Secretary of State
for War (1771–1774)

[2] Étienne François Bourgeois de Boynes, master of requests, Attorney-General
attached to the royal household 1753, Intendant of Franche-Comte, first President of
the Besançon Parliament 1757, State Councillor 1761, Minister of Marine 1771 He
retired in 1774, and died in 1783

Thus ended this Ministry, which may be called a reign of eleven years, and which has left some individual names, but few actual facts for history A short *résumé* of it and the characteristic traits of those persons who had some influence or took some part in the affairs of that time, will assist in deciding the importance which should be assigned to this period in our annals

The treaty of 1756, which occupies a very prominent part, had been effected with inconceivable rapidity, and exhibits throughout the impulse given by the tenor of the treaty signed in the preceding January between England and Prussia Want of thought shows itself in every one of the Articles Truly, if the treaty of 1756 had been more carefully planned, if it had been drawn up by cooler heads, if the danger that France ran, by uniting herself at that period with a Power that had so many subjects for quarrels on the Continent, had been more fully recognized, the principal condition of the treaty, namely that the war which was just then breaking out between France and England, was to be excepted from the *casus foederis*, would never have been agreed to France would never have been duped by that appearance of reciprocity, which the mutual guarantee established, when that very guarantee, only extending to the possessions which the contracting parties owned in Europe, assured to Austria all her territory, and yet permitted France, exhausted by the continental war, and without having committed any act of violation, to lose all her finest colonies But it is only fair to state, that M de Choiseul was not consulted, and that he did not assist at any of the conferences at which the conditions of this famous treaty were drawn up He was at Rome, busy with the affairs of the Rota, or the quarrels of the Jesuits, when M. l'Abbé de Bernis and M de Stahremberg negotiated it at Versailles M de Choiseul did not come back from Rome until the end of that same year, 1756 It is necessary therefore to absolve his memory from signature of the treaty, while leaving it to bear the weight of a great number of its results and fatal consequences

Carried away, as he was, by the whirlwind of the affections and the interests of Madame de Pompadour, he identified himself with the new policy, flattering himself that he would be

able to avert all danger by a constant supervision, of which the
carelessness of his nature rendered him quite incapable He
would have required the constant attendance of M Pfeffel [1]
to draw his attention incessantly to the almost imperceptible
encroachments by which the Court of Vienna, skilled in such
matters, daily increased its influence, by causing the recognition
of her claims in all questions touching the Germanic Constitution, whilst the guarantor of this great charter, the protector
of the treaty of Westphalia, in a word, the King of France,
without even perceiving it himself, became the instrument of the
enterprises and successes of this growing ambition

It would, however, be a mistake to think that what I most
object to in the treaty of 1756, is the new scheme of alliance
which it established, and the new direction it gave to
French policy The French, so long accustomed to regard
Austria as a rival power and natural enemy, whom France
must always have cause to fear, would look upon an alliance with
her as something monstrous, something absolutely unnatural
Prejudice greatly influences the manner in which a thing of
this kind is looked at, one would probably have to search for its
origin in the personal rivalry of the sovereigns who fought over
the dominion of Italy, rather than in the rivalry of two Powers
founded on the same basis, but even in our day, this prejudice
is so strong and so widely spread, that I feel the necessity
of fully explaining my views on this subject

All alliances whose object is conquest are injurious, first
to those against whom they are directed, and finally to those
who have made them But whatever the result, they could
never be durable for a thousand reasons, some of these I have
already mentioned Such alliances therefore can in no case form
a political system, and it is useless even to speak of them

But alliances can be formed whose object is not to make

[1] Christian Frederick Pfeffel, son of Jean Conrad Pfeffel, a German lawyer and
diplomatist Born at Colmer in 1727, he was First Secretary at the Embassy in Saxony
1754 In 1758 he was called to Paris by Cardinal de Bernis, who nominated him
Councillor to the Legation at Ratisbon, and subsequently *Chargé d'Affaires ad
interim* at the Diet In 1761, he entered the service of the Duc de Deux Ponts, who
nominated him Resident in Bavaria Again recalled to Versailles in 1768, he was
attached to the Foreign Office as King's Counsel He retained this place until the
Revolution, dismissed in 1792 he re entered the service of the Duc de Deux Ponts,
and died in 1807

war, but to re-establish and maintain peace, not to acquire fresh provinces, but rather to assure to each contracting party the preservation of its own possessions—not to imperil the safety and tranquillity of other States, but to prevent each State from threatening the security of another No one can deny that alliances, the conditions of which are calculated to attain this end, present incalculable advantages But very few Powers can contract such alliances The Great Powers, or rather Powers of the first rank, can alone do so

Then also it is necessary that their geographical position should be no obstacle to the development of their means of influence Thus Spain could not with any benefit enter into such an alliance, for, unless the alliance applied specially to maritime relations and interests, she could only bring a much lesser influence to bear than her actual strength would seem to promise

This influence would in fact be almost null

Prussia is geographically a Power so badly constituted, that she cannot help being animated with a spirit of conquest and cannot fail to be dependent upon it With a very extended frontier, powerless to create a navy, seeing that her limited revenue barely suffices to keep up her land forces, she must always in this respect be at the mercy of England, who could at any moment ruin her whole trade Obliged to keep her troops dispersed over a long and narrow frontier, she must always be dependent on Russia, who could invade the Duchy of Posen or Silesia before a Prussian army could be got together

Yet, notwithstanding a frontier, which would seem to demand peace, or preclude the possibility of departing from it unless compelled by foreign aggression, the feeling of self-preservation, makes it almost a necessity for Prussia to be continually bent on making conquests A State whose configuration is such, that the result of a single battle may so dismember it as to intercept all communication between its several parts, is in too dangerous and precarious a position, not to seek constantly to alter it, and it seems certain that, either the Prussian Power must speedily come to an end, or she must unite under her rule a considerable portion of Germany

It is very true, that at the period of which we are now speaking and before the division of Poland,[1] she was not exposed to the same dangers, because she did not occupy the same rank ; but if she owes more *éclat* to the ambition of the famous prince who conquered for her the position she now occupies, she owes him nothing for rendering her permanent existence more solidly assured

Russia until she took a place in the political system of Europe, never had any continuous relations with France, neither had she had any intimate ones unless it be recently, when all the natural relations of the different States were upset, and when these two Powers, being the only ones remaining intact on the Continent, formed an alliance together, the one in order the more easily to make further conquests, the other in the hopes of participating in them [2] Such views could not fail to bring these two allies speedily into collision In the struggle that took place, Russia ran but a very slight risk We still feel the results of the dangers to which France was then exposed She even now bears the penalties of that ambition which brought her nearer to Russia The same motive could alone unite these two countries again in the future The old relations between the different European States, have either been re-established or have been replaced by fresh ones But France and Russia have still no joint interests whatever, those that divided them formerly, must continue to do so, if possible, still more in the future, and if, against all the warnings of prudence, a day should arrive, when France will a second time seek this alliance, the inevitable and immediate effect would be to produce close and intimate relations between Austria and Prussia, who, having risen again to the rank from which they had fallen, are now in a position to look after their own preservation, and are no longer reduced to waiting patiently for uncertain chance combinations to afford them protection However little security an alliance with Prussia might present, Austria, having no longer a choice, would fain

[1] Poland has been divided three times, in 1772—1773, in 1793, and in 1795 In 1773 Prussia obtained the country of Warmia, and the Palatinates of Pomerania and of Kulm In 1793, Dantzig, Thorn, Czenstochau, and the best part of Great Poland. In 1795 that portion of the Palatinates of Podlachia and Masovia, situated on the right bank of the Bug, on the north extended as far as the Niemen
[2] Treaty of Tilsit

have to content herself therewith France would then be placed
in so false a position, that the most to be feared for her
would be that Austria and Prussia should not succumb For
were this to happen, the same causes, which have already changed
into enemies, allies so little suited to one another, would very soon
separate them again, and the success of the fresh struggle that
would take place between them, would be less doubtful than
the former which France began, whilst compelling the troops
of nearly the whole of Europe to fight beneath her flag The
establishment of friendly relations between the three Northern
Powers, at the expense of France, could not fail to be brought
about, and we should soon see a repetition of the events of 1813
and 1814, probably with even far more serious results

Everything considered, I do not see that France and Austria
could form an alliance, except with the object I have just pointed
out Their size, their power, and their riches are such, that they
have no reason to envy anyone, and they have nothing to wish
for but to keep possession of what they have They have the
necessary strength to maintain peace all round them by their
concord As the strongest Powers of Central Europe, they would
also be the strongest in the whole of Europe, if, during the last
century, another Power had not risen in the North, whose terrible
and rapid progress must make one dread that the numerous
encroachments by which she has already signalised herself, are
but the prelude of still further conquests, which will end in
swallowing up everything The common danger with which this
Power threatens both Austria and France, must be a further tie
between these countries and ought indeed to be the strongest of
those which must unite them One of them is more exposed
to it, but from the moment that she falls, the other must necessarily
follow, and with her all the rest of Europe

By this it will be seen how much harm, especially for the
future, has been done by the man, who by forcing Austria to
throw herself into the arms of Russia, has probably advanced
by several centuries the sway which this latter Power will
exercise God grant that the Cabinets of Europe may be sufficiently enlightened not to bring it about sooner [1]

Too little attention was paid in the last century to the giant

strides of Russia, as soon as she once began to come to the front
Because, for several centuries, her name was almost, as it were,
unknown, no one imagined there was anything to fear from her
Russia was only looked upon as a country which, from its enormous size, and vast steppes and the rigour of its climate, which
rendered it secure from all invasion, had great advantages over
other countries, no one realised that having nothing to do for its
defence, it might unite all its efforts for attack   The almost
savage people who inhabit it, combining a fierce courage and a
coarse physique which doubled its strength, trained to absolute
submission and passive obedience, having but few wants, and
those never going beyond the barest necessaries, were an instrument in the hands of the Government, as easy to handle as it
was formidable   Although all this was palpable, no one thought
anything of it, the small vanity of some philosophers having
been flattered, nothing more was needed to make them sing the
praises of Catherine II, her Government, her people, and even her
conquests   These were taken for granted without further
question, and it soon became the fashion to admire what one
knew nothing about, and what ought only to have inspired fear
And yet, what after all was and still is this nation, this people,
this Government, which the philosophers of the eighteenth century
so thoughtlessly set to work to laud !   It is certainly rather
curious to notice, that at the very time these latter became the
accusers of all the Governments of civilised Europe, which they
represented as absolute and oppressive, and as having usurped the
rights of the people, they should have reserved all their praise for
a Government, despotic by nature, that they should have grown
eloquent with regard to the pretended slavery of a civilised
people, already freed some time back from the old tie of servi-
tude, whilst they had nothing to say as to the fate of a whole
nation of serfs   For in Russia there is no middle class, only a
small number of masters and a multitude of slaves [1]   This fact
alone will suffice to prove the great distance there is between
that country and others

It will be seen that nothing which constitutes the real glory

---

[1] The enfranchisement of the serfs in Russia only dates from 1861.   It was the
work of the Emperor Alexander II

of a nation can be found there , that where almost the whole of
the subjects are the property of a few, there can be neither
generosity or noble feeling And as a fact, high-toned feelings
are not remarkable in this people, either among the masters or
the serfs Some people talk a little about the goodness of the
former, of their kindness to their peasants, and the happiness which
the latter enjoy But it needs all this kindness and this happiness
to prevent the serf from being constrained by too much misery to
think of the possibility of changing his mode of existence This
therefore is but a very slight matter for praise But be that as it
may, whatever opinion one may have as to the inherent virtues and
vices of such a social organization, what must be quite apparent
to everyone, is, that the influence on the rest of Europe, of a still
completely barbarous nation, no matter what form or what tone
its Government takes, would be a great calamity. What then
would be the result of its dominion ?[1]

As will be seen, it is not the alliance with Austria in itself, for
which I blame the treaty of 1756, for such an alliance, in my
opinion, is the sole means of averting or least retarding the period
of this calamity. It is the small motives which brought about
the making of this treaty, the narrow ideas that prevailed, the
little results that were counted on, the puny passions by which
all were led away ; for everything was small in this matter

Neither is it for having allowed this treaty, of which he was
not the author, to subsist so long, that I blame M de Choiseul .
it is because he did not once, during the whole time of his
long and all-powerful administration, dream of giving a really
useful direction to this new policy of alliance,—because he
adopted this policy and never even attempted to see how he
might turn it to advantage One of the most serious reproaches

[1] When this portion was written in 1816, Austria did in truth appear to be the
natural barrier to oppose to a threatening savagery But since that period, amid
the numerous startling events which took place on all sides, and amid the fresh combinations which freed the minds of men as well as countries, Austria remained
stationary , she remained antiquated and isolated in the midst of Europe, whilst
the North made real progress and freedom was at last introduced into all branches
of administration and political relations Prussia, from being protected, became pro-
tectress France gave herself a form of government which consecrates all that liberty
against which Austria makes a stand Henceforth, national alliances will never be the
same, for what will in future form the basis of all durable treaties, will be that which
creates, extends, and consecrates the benefits of civilization (1829) (Note by Prince
de Talleyrand)

M de Choiseul has deserved, is assuredly that he never noticed what was passing in the North , that he never foresaw what was gradually preparing, and that consequently he made no provision for anything   This alone would justify what I have said, as to his carelessness, his want of forethought, and the shallowness of his views

Nevertheless, it cannot be denied that careless people who are clever, sometimes originate or adopt useful ideas, provided they are not given thereby too much work in details   M de Choiseul, foreseeing the judgment that history would pronounce upon him, was desirous to mark his Ministry by a political act which would have some *éclat* and which seemed to *balance the Austrian alliance.* He therefore conceived the project of the *family compact* with the King of Spain and the other sovereigns of the House of Bourbon   We willingly recognize that this compact, signed 15th, August 1761, was a conception truly worthy of a statesman It offered immense advantages to those Powers whom this important act united   By assuring to France the complete security of her Pyrenean frontier, it gave her greater freedom of action on her other frontiers , it also gave her the support of the Spanish Navy, which in its turn received that of the French Navy, and both found resources in the ports of Naples and Sicily   Lastly, this union of the three branches of the House of Bourbon, gave them the almost exclusive dominion of the Mediterranean

But in order that this family compact should really benefit the three associated Powers, it ought to have been formed at the beginning of the Seven Years' war, and not at a period when France, already exhausted by the disasters of that war, must inevitably drag Spain down with her, and thus hasten the decadence of this latter Power   Besides, as we have already said, the most evident result to France from her close alliance with Spain at this time, was having to give Louisiana up to her, in order to indemnify her for the loss of Florida

If we investigate the other acts of M de Choiseul's Ministry, which history has collected, we find first the occupation of the county of Avignon, a proceeding possessing neither utility nor glory   A mere fad made them take it, and the fear of the devil

made them give it up No pretence whatever was made to justify
either its invasion or restoration [1]

The conquest of Corsica,[2] which dates from the same period,
must be considered important, if we shut our eyes to the number of men it cost us to take, and the amount of money to
keep The advantages hoped for for the navy have so far been
almost nil, but it forms a French province in the Mediterranean,
of which the English, until they got possession of Malta, were very
envious There is a possibility that this possession may yet be
of use to us in the future

A matter of home discipline, and one which cannot fail to mark
M. de Choiseul's Ministry, was the destruction of the Order of
the Jesuits [3] He fancied that he had often encountered their
influence in ecclesiastical matters as well as in parliamentary
quarrels ; and although with a clergy so enlightened and
mingling so much with the great world as that of France, the
work of the Jesuits would prove less objectionable, than it would
with a narrower minded and less consistent clergy, he was perhaps
right in seeking to circumscribe the power of the Order, or even
to crush it But I will not go into that question, it would
lead me too far afield from my subject Nevertheless, it is but
right to say, that a monarchical government such as that of
France at that date, might have found more help than danger in
allowing the guidance of family education, and up to a certain

---

[1] Avignon was occupied by French troops in 1768 M de Choiseul was at that
time at issue with the *Court of Rome* about the Jesuits Pope Clement XIII had
condemned, as attempts "against the liberty of the Church, the cause of God, and the
rights of the Holy See," the edicts by which the Jesuits had been expelled from the
Catholic States All the Powers resisted, making common cause one with another
Naples took possession of Benevento and Ponte-Corvo—France occupied Avignon
Clement XIV , Clement XIII's successor, having signed the pastoral letter of sup
pression, Avignon was immediately after evacuated (1773)

[2] The Genoese ceded Corsica to France with full sovereignty, for the sum of two
millions Treaty of Versailles, May 15th, 1762

[3] Towards the end of the eighteenth century, the Jesuits found themselves
attacked by all the Catholic Powers Portugal gave the signal (1759) , France
followed suit (1762-64), then Spain (1766), Naples, Parma (1767), Venice, Modena,
and Bavaria Lastly, Maria Theresa herself joined the general movement Soon
after (July 20th, 1773), Pope Clement XIV ordered the suppression of the Order
In France, the struggle, begun on the occasion of a casual incident, was energetically
supported by Choiseul and the Parliaments, the King allowing himself to be led by
them In 1762, the Parliaments of Paris, Rouen, Bordeaux, Rennes, Metz, Pau,
Perpignan, Aix, and Toulouse, burnt all the statutes of the Society, and ordered its
members to quit the territory under their jurisdiction Finally, in November
1764, a royal proclamation entirely suppressed the Society.

point of public opinion, to remain in the hands of the Jesuits
In support of this opinion, I may remark, that in 1789, not a
single member of the young nobility had been brought up by the
Jesuits   But M de Choiseul, supremely careless, and an enemy
to all power which did not emanate from himself, destroyed the
Jesuits solely because he thought he had not complete influence
over them   It was in reality a State question, but he made it a
question of intrigue

M. le Duc de Vauguyon [1] and M   le Dauphin [2] supported
them ; M de Choiseul intrigued to attack them   Later on he
made war against the philosophers (in the comedy he got Palisot [3]
to write) because they took from him some portion of that
empire over which he wished to reign supreme during his day
No motives of a high order determined his course ; he saw men
who were capable of forming many opinions, and it was to the
interest of his self-love to get rid of them all

M de Choiseul's hatred to the Jesuits was also the chief
cause of the disastrous expedition to Cayenne at the beginning
of 1764   He arranged all the details in accordance with the
memorandums given him by M de Préfontaine [4] This latter, a
man of some ability and intrigue, by means of a few philan-
thropic phrases, and some insinuations against the Jesuits, whom

[1] Antoine-Paul-Jacques de Quélen, Duc de la Vauguyon, born January 17th, 1706
Became a colonel in 1733, and a brigadier in 1743, for his gallant behaviour during the
retreat from Prague Major-general after Fontenoy (1745), lieutenant-general in 1748
He had been nominated *menin* to the Dauphin in 1745   In 1758 he was made
Governor to the Duc de Bourgogne's eldest son, and successively Governor to his other
three sons   The Dauphin died in his arms in 1765   He himself died in 1772

[2] Louis, Dauphin, son of Louis XV., born in 1729, died in 1755   He was twice
married   in 1745 to Maria Theresa of Spain, who died the following year without
issue, and in 1747 to Marie-Josephe of Saxony, by whom he had four sons ; the Duc
de Bourgogne died young, and the other three sons were Louis XVI , Louis XVIII ,
and Charles X

[3] Charles Pallisot de Montenoy, a French poet, born at Nancy (1750)   He was
the son of a Councillor of the Duc de Lorraine   He wrote several comedies and
various poems   He died in 1814   The author alludes here to the campaign which
Pallisot waged against the philosophers ; he never ceased attacking them, both on the
stage and in his poems, notably in *the Cercle*, a comedy in which he made an attack
on Rousseau (1755), *Les Philosophes* (1760), *Les Petites Lettres sur de grands
Philosophes* (1757), directed against Diderot ; and *La Dunciade , ou, Guerre des Sots*,
a satirical poem (1764), &c

[4] M Bruletout de Préfontaine had lived in Guiana for twenty years, when he came
to Paris in 1762, and laid before the Duc de Choiseul a scheme for an agricultural
colonization of that country   The Minister accepted it, and sent him back to
Cayenne with the brevet of lieutenant-colonel   His scheme failed, and he died
in 1786

M. de Choiseul wished to deprive of all their large and rich possessions in the Colonies, succeeded in getting his scheme accepted

By the treaty of 1763, France had ceded Canada and Acadia,[1] in perpetuity to the English The inhabitants of these Colonies, especially Acadia, exhibited a great attachment to France. On the other hand, the fate of the negroes was beginning to arouse some interest M de Choiseul got the King's Council to decide, that in the midst of the negro colonies, settlements should be formed, in the cultivation of which only white people were to be employed. With this view, about three thousand Acadians were shipped to St Domingo, two thousand to Martinique, eight thousand to Guadaloupe , the whole expedition started for Cayenne. Two hundred and thirteen vessels of every tonnage left France, carrying about ten thousand five hundred persons Acadia furnished eight thousand, and two other vessels arrived at the same time from other Colonies M de Chauvalon[2] was made Superintendent , M de Béhague[3] Military Commander, and the Chevalier Turgot[4] who had been consulted, was appointed Governor-General Never was improvidence and carelessness pushed to a greater extent Twenty thousand people were landed on a shore, where they found neither houses, shops, doctors, nor hospitals, not even shelter from the intense heat of the sun, which at $4°55'$ is fatal to persons not acclimatized, if the necessary precautions taught by experience are neglected

As a result, in the course of a fortnight, half those who had landed died, and at the end of five months, only three hundred

---

[1] Acadia belonged to the English since the treaty of Utrecht (1713)

[2] Jean Baptiste-Thibauld de Chauvalon, born in Martinique in 1725, was a pupil of Réaumur and of Jussieu In 1757 he was sent to Guiana as superintendent-general Arrested on his return to France, he was condemned to perpetual imprisonment for embezzlement (1767) , he succeeded in getting a fresh trial, and was acquitted in 1776 Made commissary-general of the colonies, he died in 1783

[3] Antoine, Comte de Béhague belonged to a noble Dutch family A lieutenant colonel in 1761, he was made military commandant at Guiana (1763), major-general in 1771, lieutenant general in 1791, and Governor of Martinique, where he re-established order after the insurrection Obliged to quit the island in 1793, he went to England, whence the Comte d'Artois sent him to Brittany to head the insurrection He died in England in 1802

[4] The Chevalier Etienne Turgot, Marquis de Cousmont, brother of the celebrated statesman, belonged to an old Norman family His father had been Provost of Merchants at Paris He was first a Knight of Malta and commanded a galley Brigadier in 1764, he was made Governor of Guiana It was through him that the Superintendent Chauvalon was recalled to France , arrested himself on his return to France, he was speedily released , after this he lived in retirement, and died in 1789

remained out of the whole expedition. But all this happened far away, and the magic circle that surrounded M. de Choiseul prevented all access to the truth

In his administration of the War Department, M. de Choiseul caused endless worry to the army. Fresh changes were introduced every year. New kinds of instruction, new manoeuvres, new tactics, new uniforms, all these delighted the young French *noblesse*, who ever active and brave, admired the Minister who abandoned old-fashioned notions, and, it was said, perfected those tactics by which it was thought that the Prussians had covered themselves with glory. As if the good or evil success of military achievements does not always depend upon the talents of the general. The art of war varies in Europe every ten years. Sometimes one Power has a finer infantry, sometimes the cavalry decides the fate of a battle, or else the artillery proves more efficient. No fixed rules can be laid down as to this ; everything depends upon the genius of him who commands.

M. de Choiseul's influence extended also in a very disastrous manner over the finances, owing to the unfitness of those whom he induced the King to appoint. He named M. de Silhouette[1] in order to please the Duc d'Orléans. This Minister began by having the silver plate of all private persons, even that of the King, brought to the Mint ; whereas the Court of Vienna, for whom France had ruined herself, had a gold set made and gloried in displaying it at the gorgeous marriage of the Archduke Joseph with one of the Princesses of Parma.[2]

M. de Silhouette, having shown symptoms of insanity whilst

---

[1] Etienne Silhouette, born at Limoges on the 5th July, 1709, died 1769. Councillor of the Parliament of Metz, Master of Requests, *Secrétaire des Commandments*, then Chancellor to the Duc d'Orléans, Royal Commissioner of the Indian Company and Comptroller-General in 1759. He provoked a great outcry against himself by suspending the State debts for a whole year, and was forced to retire after being in office for eight months. It is perhaps not generally known that this Minister gave his name to those drawings which represent a profile traced round the shadow of a face. It is indeed asserted that one of his chief amusements was tracing such portraits on the walls of his château, which were soon covered with them. Society did not fail to turn this little diversion into ridicule, and called the drawings by the name of their author, a name which they have always retained.

[2] The Archduke Joseph, son of the Empress Maria Theresa, afterwards Emperor Joseph II., married on the 6th October, 1760, the Princess Isabella of Parma, daughter of the Duke of Parma, and niece of King Charles III. of Spain. He died without issue in 1763.

at the King's Council, was replaced by M de Lavordy,[1] a simple Councillor of Parliament, only distinguished as being one of those who most strongly opposed the registration of pecuniary edicts which everyone disliked   He was supposed to have weight with his party.   So he had when he was opposed to the Court but he had none when he wanted to support it   M. de Lavordy proving useless, he was dismissed, and M de Choiseul appointed M. d'Invault[2] in his place, and with his usual carelessness, gave as a reason for this choice, that he had always liked him and been at school with him

It may be asserted that of all the selections due to M de Choiseul's influence, there was only one good one, namely that of the Duc de Praslin.   His lucky star aided him on that occasion   It has often been thought that in making this choice, he had only sought for an assistant who would submit to his caprices   Instead of which, M. de Praslin proved to be a man possessed of great strength of mind ; he had a decided and noble character with healthy views, which he expressed even with some brusqueness   But his naturally fine abilities were often rendered useless by the wretched state of his health ; there was not a quarter of an hour in the day, in which he could devote himself entirely to his work   Whenever he felt well, he never hesitated to oppose his cousin, and often blamed him severely   He was both esteemed and feared by his family   Madame de Gramont knew how to conceal her character before him , and as, notwithstanding his heavy brows and plain severe countenance, he possessed a vast fund of affection, he had allowed himself to grow so fond of the Duc de Choiseul, that after he had pointed out his errors to him, he felt really grateful if the latter corrected them, and even when M de Choiseul persisted in them, M. de Praslin was disposed to excuse and defend them

The portrait I have just drawn of M. de Praslin, leads me naturally to speak of M de Choiseul's appearance   Nature had

---

[1] Clement de L'Avordy or Lavordy, born in 1723, Councillor of Parliament, and Comptroller-General in 1763   He only remained in office a few months, and then lived in retirement , he died on the scaffold in November 1793

[2] Etienne Maynou, Seigneur d'Invault, born in 1721 , Councillor of Parliament, 1741, Comptroller-General and Minister of State 1768   He was only a short time in office.

also been very chary in her gifts to him, he was plain and his hair was red, though, thanks to the arts of the toilet, he had succeeded in changing it to blonde; the outlines of his face and head were very ordinary His eyes were bright and intelligent, he was well built, and he derived a great advantage from the beauty of his hands, which were small, slender, white, and finished off with exquisite nails His haughty carriage, his full face and high forehead, formed a complete contrast to the overhanging hair, pallid complexion and retiring air of M de Praslin—never were two men more entirely dissimilar, both morally and physically

Madame de Pompadour had very little mind; her blue eyes, possessing neither brilliancy nor vivacity, betrayed the emptiness of her head Although she had been brought up and had lived in the financial society of Paris, which at that time was rather distinguished, her style was bad, and her language was vulgar, faults which she was not able to correct even at Versailles She differed in every way from Madame du Barry, who though less well educated, had succeeded in acquiring a sufficiently pure style in conversation Madame du Barry's eyes were not so large, but they were intelligent, her face was well formed and her hair was extremely beautiful; she liked conversation,[1] and had caught the art of telling a story brightly, they both possessed the art of lying, to perfection

Madame de Giamont, despite the family likeness, had in her youth possessed what is known as *la beauté du diable.* She was plump, with a pink and white complexion, her character was exalted, and her mind was open and strong She would have been eloquent, if the disagreeable tone of her voice had permitted it She wrote well There was something specially attractive in her manner, notwithstanding its decision In her *salon,* only one opinion was allowed to prevail, all those who liked M de Choiseul were gladly welcomed there; any others gained no admittance She perfectly worshipped her brother, and was devoted to his friends Love affairs only claimed her attention for a brief period in her youth The day she entered

---

[1] And her writing Some pages of recollections written by her, and entrusted to Morande, author of the *Gazettier Cuirassé*, notwithstanding their brief length, are not wanting in grace and interest. (*Note by the Prince de Talleyrand*)

into society, she took the highest position and this she retained
to the day of her death

Among the men who played a notable part under M de
Choiseul's Ministry, the Chancellor Maupeou seems to deserve
separate mention He was a man full of invention, and intelligence, and at the same time, malicious, and fawning *ad nauseam*
Vulgar men and men of bad style, delighted in him, but in all
good society he was disliked This however did not trouble him
He followed the course he had traced out for himself, and never
once deviated from it Had he lived in Louis the XI's time,
he would have been his Prime Minister and most intimate
servant

M. d'Aiguillon, like M de Choiseul, began his career as a
favourite of fortune He had been very successful, having entered
the world with far greater advantages ; he was born a rich man,
had inherited high honours, and possessed a very handsome person
But he had neither nobleness nor elevation of character To
politics he was an utter stranger ; he had read little, he had never
travelled, and only knew Europe from what he heard of it in
Paris The quarrels of countries, states, and parliaments together
with a few military studies, had been the whole work of his life
The great political fault for which he has been blamed was having
ignored the first partition of Poland, before it was completed, but
this error dated further back than him , it resulted from the
mysterious manœuvres of the Court of Vienna not having been
understood by the Ministry of his predecessor, and it was
one of M de Choiseul's lucky strokes of fortune, that he
did not remain six months longer in office ; for it is more
than doubtful whether he would have gained any advantage
therefrom

M de Choiseul's downfall differed in many very notable ways
from the other Ministerial disgraces which occurred during the
reign of Louis the XV Prior to him, none of the Ministers
exiled by that monarch, received either tokens of sympathy or
marks of affection and gratitude from anyone but their own
families, and even then permission to visit them was asked for
with much precaution and only in cases of illness The Cardinal
de Bernis at Soissons, M. d'Argenson at Les Ormes, M de
Machault at Arnonville, M de Maurepas at Bourges, and to go

still higher, even M. le Duc [1] himself at Chantilly, had remained completely isolated   No one dared to mention their name in the presence of the King, who flattered himself by thinking that he saw in this complete silence around him universal approbation of the decision he had taken.   This, however, was not the case as regards M de Choiseul.   The tone in good society during his long Ministry, was rather to be the courtier of the Minister than the courtier of the King

It was the fashion for people to identify themselves with M de Choiseul's interests during the struggle which took place between his influence and that of the favourite   Madame du Barry's circle had never risen to so high a level as that of Madame de Pompadour, her charms, the women, the men, and the Ministers who surrounded her, shone but feebly compared with the numerous and powerful supporters of M de Choiseul

The habit that had sprung up of speaking of the King with a want of respect ; the contempt which it was customary to express with impunity respecting the friends of Madame du Barry, had established in men's minds a sort of independence which the age and the weakness of the King had licensed   Some of M de Choiseul's friends, young men on whom he had bestowed early favours, ventured to ask permission to visit him at Chanteloup· Those surrounding the favourite made a mistake, when they counselled her to treat these first requests with contempt , their number increased, and soon it was no longer possible to refuse them   Several ladies set the example of going to Chanteloup without permission   Many men, who were not attached to the Court by ties of service, ventured to follow their example.   Ere long there assembled at Chanteloup, a crowd, a kind of Court, which almost seemed to rival that of Versailles

The mediocrity of the new Ministers, the want of consideration for those who remained,[2] the utter indifference displayed by the King in the most important matters, deprived the decisions of the Council of all character of durability   Hence arose a kind of insubordination which destroyed the *prestige* of constituted

---

[1] Louis Henri, Duc de Bourbon, grandson of the great Condé, Chief of the Council of Regency during the minority of Louis XV , and Prime Minister after the death of the Regent (1723)   He was exiled to Chantilly in 1726 by the young King.
[2] Those Ministers who continued in office were La Villiere, Terray, and Maupeou   The new Ministers were M d Aiguillon, M de Montevnard, and M de Boynes

authority This may be looked upon as the commencement of that
spirit of opposition, which manifested itself so startlingly during
the subsequent reign   They went so far as to erect a pyramid
in the gardens of Chanteloup, on which vanity inscribed the names
of all those who came to pay fashionable homage to the illustrious exile ; and when one sees that these same names are found
again twenty years later, on the famous list of *émigrés*, one is
perhaps better able to judge of the inconsistency and the thoughtlessness of the actions of the French nobility at this period, and also
of the injustice of its judgments.   Moreover, that mocking, gay,
heedless, and ever wild spirit in the French nobility, reappears constantly in our history.   It is met with at Madame de Longueville's,
and also at Coblentz   But there is also another spirit which
although it belongs to another class of society, is no less French ,
it needed a Henry IV. to subdue the old leaguers and burgesses
of Paris ; in 1791, they showed that they could become masters

M de Choiseul's personal affairs soon began to feel the
enormous expense to which this sort of celebrity subjected him ;
the reckless magnificence in which he had lived at Versailles,
was kept up in his brilliant retreat, and as the salaries of War
Minister, Minister of Foreign Affairs, Colonel-General of the Swiss
Guards, and Postmaster-General, as well as the private gifts which
were annually made to him, could no longer be counted among his
receipts, he was obliged to supplement these by living on his
small patrimony and the fortune of Madame de Choiseul , her
devotion was rewarded by the pleasure she felt in offering the
whole of it to his memory, by paying his debts after his death

It had been fully expected, and everything led to the belief,
that on the death of Louis XV , public opinion would oblige the
new King, to recall to the head of affairs a minister whose
downfall had apparently been so generally disapproved of   But
five years of absence from the Court, had much diminished
popular favour True, the spirit of criticism and even opposition to
the Government, after the happy trial it had made of its strength
on the occasion of M de Choiseul's exile, had gained much
greater confidence, and increased in strength more and more, but
its direction was changed.   Less decided and more vague in its
object, the opposition looked farther ahead and aimed higher.
The interest in M. de Choiseul had died out   Notwithstanding,

therefore, the weakness of Louis the XVI, and the influence and support which the Queen gave to the hopes and ambitions of M. de Choiseul, her entreaties only succeeded in cancelling his exile. The prejudices of the young King, fostered by *Mesdames* his aunts [1] gained the day   The feelings and interests of the Court were no longer the same as at the close of Louis XV's reign. New Ministers, new hopes, and growing ambitions presented themselves on all sides ; the old courtiers withdrew or died out.   The Queen was not consulted in the choice of the Prime Minister. This choice once made, it was no longer possible to go back from it, and recall M de Choiseul to the only office which he could well accept   Thus died out the *éclat* of this brilliant career, more remarkable for its social successes, than famed in history for characteristic traits of real merit and actual glory. M de Choiseul ended his life with the discredit which always attaches to a man who is persecuted by his creditors, and whose time is solely occupied in staving off their attacks   Grief, aggravating a slight malady, caused his death   He died without regrets and without much notice   To history, M de Choiseul will only be a man who governed France for eleven years with the despotism which was the fashion of the day   No victories gained, no grand treaties, or useful measures were ever associated with his name, he paved the way for great evils, felt even down to our day, by the arbitrary proceedings he introduced into the different administrative departments, and by the spirit of criticism and want of consideration for Royal Authority, which he encouraged to the last day of his life

M de Choiseul did not realise that this spirit of criticism under an arbitrary government, and without legal redress, becomes at once a most serious decomposing element   The Revolution, so long prepared for by everything that could and ought to have prevented it, is a terrible proof of this   Henri IV was the last of our Kings who knew when to give in and when to resist

---

[1] Louis XV had eight daughters
Louise Elizabeth (1727-1759), married to the Duc de Parma , Anne (1727-1752) , Marie (1728 1733), Adelaide (1732-1800) , Victoire (1733-1799) , Sophie (1734-1782) , Thérèse (1736-1744) , Louise (1737-1787)   Madame Louise became a Carmelite nun —*Mesdames* Adelaide, Victoire, and Sophie did not marry, and spent their life at the Court of their nephew, Louis XVI   It is to them that the above allusion is made

INDEX

A

THE END.

RICHARD CLAY AND SONS, LIMITED, LONDON AND BUNGAY.

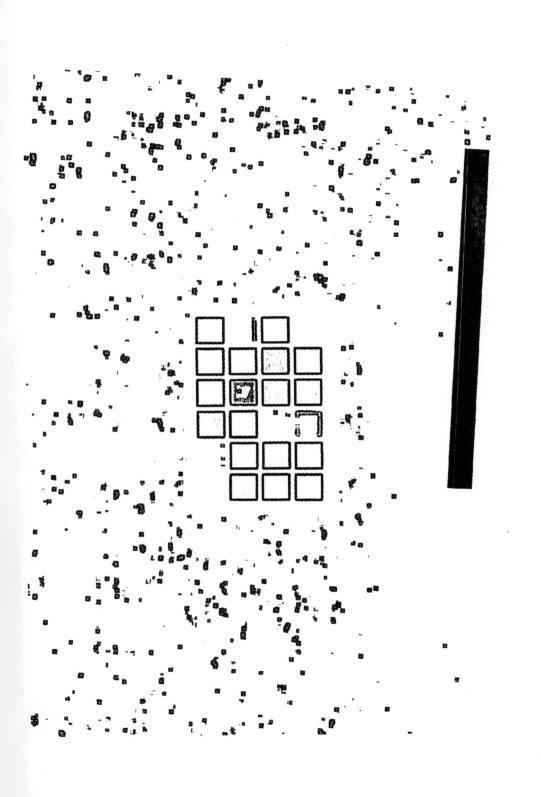

CPSIA information can be obtained
at www.ICGtesting.com
Printed in the USA
LVHW080204161219
640627LV00009B/154/P

9 781372 338069